Teaching Young Children
An Introduction

 Michael L. Henniger

Western Washington University

Merrill,
an imprint of Prentice Hall
Upper Saddle River, New Jersey   Columbus, Ohio

Library of Congress Cataloging-in-Publication Data

Henniger, Michael L.
    Teaching young children : an introduction / Michael L. Henniger.
        p.   cm.
    Includes bibliographical references and index.
    ISBN 0-13-606583-X
    1. Early childhood education.   I. Title.
LB1139.23.H45   1999
372.21—dc21

98-37062
CIP

Cover photo: © David Young-Wolff, PhotoEdit
Editor: Ann Davis
Developmental Editor: Gianna Marsella
Production Editor: Julie Peters
Photo Editor: Nancy Ritz
Design Coordinator: Diane C. Lorenzo
Text Designer: Anne D. Flanagan
Cover Designer: Ceri Fitzgerald
Production Manager: Laura Messerly
Illustrations: Carlisle Communications, Inc.
Director of Marketing: Kevin Flanagan
Marketing Manager: Suzanne Stanton
Marketing Coordinator: Krista Groshong

This book was set in New Baskerville by Carlisle Communications, Inc., and was printed and bound by R. R. Donnelley & Sons Company. The cover was printed by Phoenix Color Corp.

© 1999 by Prentice-Hall, Inc.
Simon & Schuster/A Viacom Company
Upper Saddle River, New Jersey 07458

Photo credits: American Montessori Society, 37; Bill Aron/Photo Edit, 2: Robert Brenner/Photo Edit, 347, 387; Corbis/Bettmann, 34; Scott Cunningham/Merrill, 13, 152, 197; Mary Kate Denny/Photo Edit, 435; Jay Dorin/Omni Photo Communications, Inc., 251; Dan Floss/Merrill, 186, 266, 335; Gordon Gainer/The Stock Market, 254; Ken Karp/PH College, 206; Lloyd Lemmerman/Merrill, 337; Library of Congress, 41; Anthony Magnacca/Merrill, 24, 54 (both), 56, 60, 94, 99, 117, 130, 141, 150, 174, 178, 236, 260, 274, 280, 282, 291, 302, 310, 328, 370, 375, 393, 399, 420, 430, 440, 449; Ted Mahieu/The Stock Market, 9; Lawrence Migdale/Photo Researchers, Inc., 72; Margaret Miller/Photo Researchers, Inc., 404; Michael Newman/Photo Edit, 122; Jonathan Nourok/Photo Edit, 17; Photo Disc, Inc., 162, 320; Barbara Schwartz, 97, 157, 359; James Shaffer/Photo Edit, 169; A. Tilley/FPG International, 193; Anne Vega/Merrill, 30, 50, 67, 78, 126, 134, 183, 218, 225, 229, 244, 294, 341, 350, 363, 380; Tom Watson/Merrill, 101; Todd Yarrington/Merrill, 110, 191, 212, 315, 410; David Young-Wolf/Photo Edit, 306, 414, 424, 444.

Printed in the United States of America

10 9 8 7 6 5 4 3 2 1

ISBN: 0-13-606583-X

Prentice-Hall International (UK) Limited, *London*
Prentice-Hall of Australia Pty. Limited, *Sydney*
Prentice-Hall of Canada, Inc., *Toronto*
Prentice-Hall Hispanoamericana, S. A., *Mexico*
Prentice-Hall of India Private Limited, *New Delhi*
Prentice-Hall of Japan, Inc., *Tokyo*
Simon & Schuster Asia Pte. Ltd., *Singapore*
Editora Prentice-Hall do Brasil, Ltda., *Rio de Janeiro*

[Handwritten notes:] 800 – 526-0485 / www. prenhall.com / prenticehall.com / $ 60 (1st) / $ 46.50 / Instructors Teachers / Test Bank / Windows / 7–10 days

Preface

Educators involved in teacher preparation occasionally hear students make statements such as *"I wasn't successful teaching fourth grade, but I know I can do better with younger children. They're great fun to be around and so easy to teach."* Although it is true that young children are exciting and enjoyable, teaching them is far from easy. Students new to the field of early childhood education need to develop an awareness of both the challenges and joys involved in working with young children. This book presents both perspectives, providing a comprehensive, balanced overview of early childhood education.

Conceptual Framework of the Text

This textbook provides an introduction to the field of early childhood education. It provides a framework for understanding how to teach children from birth through age eight by clearly identifying and discussing **five foundations of early childhood education.** Each element is a critical component of quality programs for young children:

1. **An understanding of children and their development.** Educational experiences for young children need to be based on children's developmental abilities and interests. An understanding of child growth and development is a necessary starting point for early childhood education.

2. **Opportunities to play.** Young children from birth through age eight need times during their school day to engage in quality play experiences, both indoors and on the playground. Play is one of the most important ways for young children to learn about the world around them.

3. **Guiding young children.** Assisting with the social and emotional development of young children is another key element of early education. Guiding development in these areas requires a strong knowledge of child development and sensitive interactions between adults and children.

4. **Working with parents, families, and communities.** The development of mutually supportive relationships with parents, families, and the community is another essential element of teaching at this level. Strong relationships help ensure maximum opportunities for growth and development in young children.

5. **Diversity issues and young children.** An understanding of, and respect for, diversity is the final essential element of early education. Differences due to culture, gender, and physical and/or mental capabilities influence each of the other four foundational elements and must be studied, understood, and discussed in the early childhood classroom.

Each of these five foundational elements is discussed in an individual chapter dedicated to the topic (see Part II). To emphasize the importance of these themes, however, child development, play, guidance, family and community partnerships, and diversity are also integrated into each chapter of the book.

Organization of the Text

The text is organized into four major parts. **Part I is an overview and introduction to the field of early education.** Chapter 1 describes the different program options for young children, discusses how these options are funded, outlines the roles and responsibilities of teachers, and describes teacher preparation programs. Chapter 2 discusses historical figures and events that have had a major influence on early education today. Chapter 3 describes four early childhood program models: Montessori education, the High/Scope curriculum, the Bank Street model, and the Reggio Emilia program.

Part II specifically focuses on the five foundational elements of early childhood education. Chapter 4 addresses child development and learning and provides an overview of this important topic. Chapter 5 looks at play as an essential element of early education and presents a strong rationale for including play in the classroom. Chapter 6 deals with guiding young children and addresses issues related to helping children successfully manage their emotions and strengthen their social interactions. Chapter 7 overviews home, school, and community relationships. The chapter emphasizes building strong two-way relationships through quality communications. Chapter 8 discusses diversity issues in the early childhood classroom and also describes strategies for integrating diversity into the core of the curriculum.

Part III addresses planning and assessment issues in early childhood education. Chapter 9 describes the planning and preparation needed for the indoor classroom and discusses a centers-based approach to classroom organization. Chapter 10 provides details for preparing an outdoor play area for young children. Unique to this text, this chapter identifies the elements needed for quality outdoor play experiences. Chapter 11 addresses activity planning and assessment issues in the early childhood classroom. The chapter includes discussion of an integrated curriculum and the project approach.

Part IV provides specific information on the major elements of the early childhood curriculum. Chapter 12 addresses physical development and the teacher's role in facilitating motor learning. Chapter 13 discusses specific ways in which teachers can assist with social and emotional development in young children. Chapter 14 emphasizes the mathematics, science, and social studies curriculum. Chapter 15 addresses language and literacy learning in the early childhood classroom. Chapter 16 describes art and music experiences that are appropriate for young children and presents a rationale for including them in the curriculum. Chapter 17 discusses television viewing, video games, and computer use by young children. The chapter also describes the developmentally appropriate use of computers in the early childhood classroom.

Special Features of the Text

This text was designed to be reader-friendly and uses a clear, well-organized, informative, and personal writing style. Throughout the text, the reader encounters thorough overviews of important topics and current references for further study. Vignettes of children and teachers and questions presented throughout the chapter encourage the reader to think, reflect, and discuss with others the topics presented.

Teaching Young Children: An Introduction is **unique** in several ways:

- First, the **five foundations of early education** are clearly identified. These elements are discussed in individual chapters and then integrated into the content of later sections of the book.

- A second unique element is the separate **chapter on outdoor play.** Although several other texts present information on planning outdoor play environments, this text provides a complete chapter identifying the outdoor play area as a significant component of early education.

- Finally, the concluding **chapter on technology** is unique in its description of play-oriented, developmentally appropriate computer experiences.

Several **special features** were built into the text to assist the reader's understanding of important concepts and to add interest.

- Each chapter opens with a short **vignette** designed to give the reader a mental image of early childhood classrooms and issues related to the content of the chapter. These real-world images help the content come to life and stimulate interest in the chapter discussion.

- To emphasize the importance of play and diversity issues, each chapter also includes either a special feature called **"Celebrating Play"** or another called **"Celebrating Diversity."** Each provides useful information about play or diversity related to the chapter content.

- The **"Focus On . . . "** boxes in each chapter extend the discussion of important issues. Each "Focus On . . . " feature box concludes with questions and action tasks designed to stimulate the reader's thinking and understanding of the topic.

- The **"Into Practice"** feature boxes describe practical classroom applications of the chapter content, helping readers to make the transition from theory to practice, and providing them with successful classroom-tested strategies.
- Four full-color **video case studies**—designed to be used with the accompanying ABC News/Prentice Hall video *Current Issues in Early Childhood Education, Volume 2*—make connections between the video segments and chapter content by asking students to *see* the corresponding ABC video segment, *think* about the chapter content as highlighted in the case studies, and *act* upon the information provided. These video case studies promote reflective classroom discussions and direct students in authentic tasks that provide opportunities to apply what they have learned. One video case study is found in each of the four major sections of the text.

Ancillaries and Supplements

Several additional materials are available for instructor and student use to support learning and instruction:

- An **instructor's manual** includes suggestions for teaching, additional instructional resources, and test items for each chapter.
- **Test items** are available to instructors in the instructor's manual, or in electronic format in the Prentice Hall Custom Test package, which allows instructors to create customized exams on the personal computer.
- A **companion video series** titled *Current Issues in Early Childhood Education, Volume 2* features four thought-provoking video segments of varying length and is available on adoption of this text to all instructors. These video segments, chosen from award-winning news programs on ABC, are integrated into the text through the four video case study color inserts.
- The **companion web site,** located at **http://www.prenhall.com/henniger,** is an Internet resource that includes a syllabus builder tool and a media library for use by the instructor. Students can use this site as an electronic study guide, checking their understanding of concepts with chapter summaries and quizzes with hints, discussing current and important issues with fellow students using a message board or chat room, and expanding their knowledge base by exploring related web sites.

Acknowledgments

No book of this complexity can be completed without the assistance of a great many competent and supportive people. Grateful thanks are given to the following staff at Merrill/Prentice Hall: Ann Davis, senior editor; Gianna Marsella, development editor; Luanne Dreyer Elliott, freelance copyeditor; Julie Peters, production editor; and Nancy Ritz, photo coordinator. Their support and assistance throughout this process have been invaluable.

I also thank the reviewers of this text for their thoughtful commentary and helpful suggestions. They are Beverly B. Dupre, Southern University of New Orleans; Elizabeth Engley, Jacksonville State University; Richard Fiene, Pennsylvania State University; Carol S. Huntsinger, College of Lake County, Illinois; and Elizabeth Walker-Knauer, Cuyahoga Community College.

Many thanks go to my wife, Lisa, as well. She has been an encouragement to me throughout this experience and supportive of the long hours I had to spend in my office over numerous evenings and weekends. Thank you, Lisa, for your flexibility, for your encouraging words, and for the understanding you displayed throughout the process.

Michael L. Henniger

Contents

I Introduction to the Field   **1**

1 Overview of the Profession   **2**

Foundations of Early Childhood Education   5

An Understanding of Children and Their Development 5 / Opportunities to Play 5 / *Celebrating Play . . . In the Primary Grades* 6 / Guiding Young Children 7 / Working with Parents, Families, and the Community 7 / Diversity Issues and Young Children 8

The Scope of Early Childhood Education   8

Infant/Toddler Programs 9 / *Focus on . . . The Issue of Quality* 10 / Preschool Programs 10 / Day Care Programs 11 / Programs for Children with Special Needs 11 / *Focus on . . . Multiage Classrooms* 12 / Kindergartens 12 / Primary Education 13

Funding: Who Pays for Early Education?   14

Programs Run for Profit 14 / Cooperative Programs 14 / Federally Funded Programs 15 / State and Locally Funded Programs 15 / *Focus on . . . Head Start* 16 / Corporate Day Care 16 / *Focus on . . . The Power of Teaching* 18 / College-and University-Supported Programs 18

Teaching Young Children   18

Roles of the Early Childhood Educator 19 / Responsibilities of the Early Childhood Educator 19 / *Focus on . . . Advocacy* 20 / Skills Needed to Teach Young Children 21 / Should I Teach? 22

Professional Preparation of Early Childhood Caregivers   23

The CDA Credential 24 / Two-Year, or Associate Degree, Programs 25 / Four-Year Programs 25 / Coordinating Efforts 25

Resources for Professional Development   26

Professional Organizations 26 / Journals 27 / Reference Materials 27

Summary   28

∿ **2** *Historical Contexts*   *30*

Historical Figures Influencing Early Childhood Education   32

European Contributors 33 / *Celebrating Play . . . Vygotsky's Thoughts on Play* 39 / *Focus on . . . The Contructivist Perspective on Learning* 40 / American Influences 40

Historical Events Influencing Early Education   43

Child Study Movement 43 / The Great Depression 44 / *Focus on . . . Improving Teacher Salaries* 45 / World War II 46 / The Launching of Sputnik 46 / *Video Case Study: Early Head Start* / The War on Poverty 47

Summary   48

∿ **3** *Types of Programs*   *50*

The Montessori Program   53

Montessori's Work Experiences 53 / *Focus on . . . Montessori's Work Experiences* 54 / Play Times 55 / Characteristics of the Montessori Classroom 55 / *Focus on . . . Montessori Options* 58

The High/Scope Curriculum   58

Focus on . . . Constructivist Early Childhood Education Programs 59 / Theoretical Basis 59 / The Plan–Do–Review Sequence 60 / The Curriculum 61 / *Focus on . . . Research of the High/Scope Model* 62 / Structure of the Class Day 62 / The Teacher's Role 63 / *Focus on . . . High/Scope's Child Observation Record* 64

The Bank Street Model   64

Theoretical Underpinnings 65 / Program Goals 65 / *Focus on . . . The Behaviorist Perspective* 66 / Governing Principles 66 / *Celebrating Diversity . . . Programs for Children Who Are Gifted and Talented* 68 / Curriculum and Materials 68

The Reggio Emilia Program   69

Focus on . . . The Project Approach 70 / The Environment 70 / Children, Parents, and Teachers 71 / Cooperation, Collaboration, and Organization 71 / The Atelierista 72 / The Importance of Documentation 72 / Projects 73

Summary   74

II *Foundations*   *77*

∿ **4** *Understanding How a Child Develops and Learns*   *78*

The Developmentally Appropriate Classroom   80

Key Perspectives on Learning and Development   81

John Bowlby (1907–) 82 / Abraham Maslow (1908–1970) 83 / Howard Gardner (1943–) 85 / Arnold Gesell (1880–1961) 85 / Maria Montessori (1870–1952) 86 / Lev Vygotsky (1896–1934) 87 / Erik Erikson (1902–1994) 88 / Jean Piaget (1896–1980) 89 / *Focus on . . . Piaget's Conservation Experiments* 90

Children: Developmental Similarities and Differences   91

Into Practice . . . What Children Can't Do . . . Yet 92 / Infants and Toddlers 93 / Children Age Three to Five: The Preschool Years 95 / Children Age Six through Eight: The

Primary School Years 98 / Children with Special Needs 100 / *Celebrating Diversity . . . Attention-Deficit/Hyperactivity Disorder* 102 / *Focus on . . . The Well-Being of Children* 104 / *Into Practice . . . Signs of Giftedness in Preschoolers* 105

Learning About Children   106

Studying Development and Learning 106 / Observation: Tool for Understanding 106 / Communicating with Parents 106

Summary   107

 5   *Play in Childhood   110*

Defining Play   113

Characteristics of Childhood Play 113 / *Into Practice . . . Games from Other Cultures* 114 / Definitions of Play 114

Why Children Play: Theories   116

Classical Theories 116 / Contemporary Theories 117 / *Into Practice . . . A Pretend Grocery Store* 119

Cognitive Play Types   119

Celebrating Play . . . Children's Invented Games 120

Social Play Types   121

Benefits of Play   122

Intellectual Growth through Play 123 / Building Social Skills 124 / *Focus on . . . Making a Case for Play* 125 / Language and Literacy Development 125 / Physical Development 127 / Emotional Development 127 / *Focus on . . . Play Deprivation* 128 / Play and Creativity 129

Facilitation Childhood Play   129

Preparing the Play Environment 129 / Creating a Climate for Play 120 / Adult Involvement in Play 131

Summary   133

 6   *Guiding Young Children*   *134*

What Is Guidance   136

Building Self-Esteem 137 / Dealing with Social/Emotional Issues 137 / Growing toward Independence and Self-Control 138 / *Into Practice . . . Rules for the Classroom* 139

Principles of Guidance   139

Initial Considerations 139 / Indirect Guidance 140 / Building Relationships 141 / Physically Guiding Children 142 / *Video Case Study: Building Brains* / Verbal Guidance Strategies 143 / *Celebrating Play . . . Noise and Messiness: Part of the Play?* 144 / Discipline Strategies 145 / *Focus on . . . Using Problem Solving* 148

Guiding Routines   148

Arrival and Departure 149 / Transitions 149 / Snack/Meal Time 149 / Toileting 150 / Rest Times 151

Dealing with Feelings and Emotions   151

Accept Feelings as Valid 151 / Be Calm and Direct 152 / Help Child Verbalize Emotions 152 / *Focus on . . . Responding to Feelings* 153 / Suggest Alternatives 154

Guiding Social Interactions 154

Be a Careful Observer 154 / Can Children Solve Their Own Problems? 155 / Define the Limits of Acceptable Behavior 155

Group Guidance 156

Consider the Physical Setting 156 / Careful Planning and Organization 157 / *Into Practice . . . Circle Time* 158 / Mixing Active and Quiet Times 158

Guidance for Children with Special Needs 159

Summary 159

❧ 7 *Working with Parents, Families, and Communities* 162

Family Life Today 165

The Missing Extended Family 165 / Divorce and Single-Parent Families 165 / Celebrating Diversity . . . Families Today 166 / Blended Families 166 / *Focus on . . . Kids Count: Ranking the States* 167 / Two-Career Families 167 / Older and Younger Parents 168 / Ethnic/Cultural Diversity 168 / Family Mobility 169

Is Involvement Worth the Effort? 170

Benefits to Teachers 170 / *Into Practice . . . Involving Parents in the Classroom* 171 / Benefits to Parents and Families 171 / Benefits to Children 171 / *Into Practice . . . Involving Parents at Home* 172

Building Strong Two-Way Relationships 172

Providing Mutual Support 172 / *Into Practice . . . Elements of Good Communication* 173 / Communication: The Key 173

Effective Communication Methods 175

Telephone Calls 175 / Written Communications 176 / Visual Communication Tools 177 / Home Visits 177 / Parent Meetings 179 / Parent-Teacher Conferences 179

Factors Influencing Quality Involvement 180

Into Practice . . . Checklist for Parent-Teacher Conferences 181

Families Having Children with Special Needs 181

Connecting with the Community 182

Involving the Community in the School 183 / Involving the School in the Community 184

Summary 184

❧ 8 *Diversity Issues and Young Children* 186

Diversity as a Foundation 188

Attitudes about Diversity 189

Racial/Cultural Attitudes 189 / Attitudes about Gender 190 / People with Special Needs 190

Encouraging an Acceptance of Diversity 192

Begin with Self-Analysis 192 / Talk about Differences 193 / Expose Children to Diversity 194

Inappropriate Responses to Diversity Issues   194

Ignore Diversity 194 / The Tourist Approach 194 / *Into Practice . . . Resources for Diversity Materials* 195

Integrating Diversity throughout the Curriculum   196

The Antibias Curriculum 196 / Using Toys that Promote Diversity 196 / Diversity through Games 198 / *Focus on . . . Anatomically Correct Dolls* 199 / Quality Children's Literature 199 / *Into Practice . . . Diversity through Pictures* 200 / The Visual-Aesthetic Environment 200 / *Celebrating Diversity . . . Holidays* 201 / Meaningful Diversity Experiences 201

Individuals with Special Needs   202

Developing Inclusive Environments 202 / Social Interactions in the Classroom 202 / Collaborating with Other Professionals 203 / *Focus on . . . Reverse Gender Bias in Early Childhood Education* 204

Issues of Gender Equity   204

Language 205 / Accessibility Issues 205 / Attitudes 206

Working with Parents and the Community   207

Parent Involvement in Diversity Issues 207 / Changing Attitudes 207

Summary   208

 III   *Organizing for Instruction*   *211*

9   *Planning the Physical Environment: Indoors*   *212*

Planning Guidelines   214

Basic Considerations 215 / Active and Quiet Centers 215 / Dry and Wet Centers 216 / Spaces for Varying Group Sizes 216 / Personal Spaces 217 / Assessing the Physical Space 218

The Centers-Based Classroom   219

Art Center 219 / *Into Practice . . . The Art Center* 220 / Manipulative Center 220 / *Into Practice . . . A Classroom Library* 221 / Book/Quiet Center 221 / Block Center 221 / *Into Practice . . . Unit Blocks* 222 / Housekeeping Center 223 / Dramatic Play Center 223 / *Into Practice . . . Dramatic Play Prop Boxes* 224 / The Music Center 224 / Discovery Center 225 / Other Creative Center Options 226

Age-Related Considerations   227

Infant/Toddler Classrooms 227 / Children Three through Five 229 / *Celebrating Play . . . Infant/Toddler Toys* 230 / Primary Children 232

Selecting Equipment and Materials   232

Criteria for Selection 234 / Commercial Materials 234 / Teacher-Made Equipment 235 / *Focus on . . . Teacher-Made Materials* 237

Children with Special Needs   237

Changing the Physical Environment   238

Balancing Consistency and Change 238 / Rotating Materials through Centers 239 / Observe and Listen to Children 239

Health and Safety Issues   239

Into Practice . . . Hand Washing Procedures 240 / Planning a Healthy Environment 240 / Safety Concerns 240

A Place for Parents?   241

Summary   241

∞ 10   *Planning the Physical Environment: Outdoors*   *244*

Importance of Outdoor Play   246

Planning Guidelines   247

Basic Guidelines 248 / Fixed Equipment 248 / Movable Equipment 249 / *Into Practice . . . Playing in the Gutters* 250 / Variety of Play Options 251

Play Areas Outdoors   252

Transition Area 252 / Manipulative/Construction Area 252 / *Celebrating Play . . . Play and Risk Taking* 253 / Dramatic Play Area 253 / Physical Area 253 / Sand/Water Play Area 254 / Natural Areas 255

Developmental Considerations   255

Infant/Toddler Play Spaces 256 / Children Three through Five 256 / *Focus on . . . Guidance Issues Outdoors* 259 / Primary Children 259 / The Child with Special Needs 260 / *Celebrating Diversity . . . Outdoor Play for Children with Special Needs* 262

Selecting Equipment and Materials   263

Commercial Equipment 263 / Donated Materials 263 / Adult-Made Equipment 263

Planning for Regular Change in the Outdoor Environment   265

Outdoor Prop Boxes 265 / Teacher-Movable Equipment 266 / Child-Movable Equipment 267

Health and Safety on the Playground   267

Playground Injuries 267 / Safety Guidelines 268 / Health Considerations 269 / The Teacher's Role 269

Parent and Community Involvement   267

Into Practice . . . Cleaning Sand 270 / *Video Case Study: Playgrounds*

Committing to the Outdoor Environment   271

Summary   272

∞ 11   *Activity Planning and Assessment*   *274*

Creating a Developmentally Appropriate Curriculum   276

Guidelines for the Developmentally Appropriate Curriculum 277 / Developmental Considerations 277 / *Into Practice . . . Making National News Developmentally Appropriate* 278 / Observation as a Curriculum Tool 279 / Curriculum Goals 280 / Planning Activities and Lessons 281

The Integrated Curriculum   284

Why Implement an Integrated Curriculum? 284 / Planning and Preparation 286 / *Celebrating Play . . . Reinventing Mathematics* 287 / *Focus on . . . A Curriculum Web* 290

The Project Approach   290

Scheduling Issues 292

Assessment 293

The Role of Observation in Assessment 293 / The Portfolio and Its Use 295 / *Focus on . . . Making Good Observations* 296

Involving Parents 297

Into Practice . . . Organizing Portfolios 298

Summary 298

IV *The Curriculum* **301**

∾ **12** *Enhancing Physical Development* **302**

The Importance of Motor Skills 304

Social Skills and Physical Development 305 / Motor Activities and Emotions 305 / Connections to Cognitive Development 305

Foundation for Physical Fitness 306

The Components of Physical Development 307

Physical Growth 307 / Gross Motor Development 308 / *Focus on . . . Physical Attractiveness* 309 / Fine Motor Skills 310 / Phases of Motor Development 311 / Perceptual-Motor Development 312

Teaching Physical Development 312

Basic Considerations 312 / *Into Practice . . . Instructional Strategies for Physical Education* 313 / Physical Development and Play 313 / Organized Physical Activities 314 / *Into Practice . . . Who Should Participate in Movement Activities?* 316

Enhancing Physical Development Indoors 316

Organized Games and Activities: Indoors 316

Enhancing Physical Development Outdoors 318

Rough-and-Tumble Play 318 / Organized Games and Activities: Outdoors 318 / *Celebrating Diversity . . . Including Children with Special Needs* 322

Teaching Children to Care for Their Bodies 322

Health Education 322 / Safety Issues 324

Working with Parents and Families 324

Understanding Physical Growth 324 / Importance of Active Play 325 / Nutrition Information 325 / Competitive Sports 325

Summary 326

∾ **13** *Supporting Social and Emotional Development* **328**

Toward Social Competence 330

Building a Sense of Self 331 / *Into Practice . . . Enhancing Self-Concept* 332 / *Into Practice . . . Building Teacher–Student Relationships* 333 / Teacher–Student Relationships 333 / Peer Interactions 334 / *Video Case Study: Wild About Learning* / *Celebrating Play . . . Socialization on the Playground* 336

The Social Development Curriculum   336

The Environment and Materials 337 / Activities and Themes 338 / *Celebrating Play . . . Games and Socialization* 339

Helping Children with Emotional Development   340

What Are Emotions? 340 / Dealing with Feelings 341

Materials and Activities for Emotional Development   342

Focus on . . . Playing Out Feelings 343

Stress as a Factor in Social and Emotional Development   344

Stress Factors 344 / *Focus on . . . Symptoms of Abuse* 345 / Helping Children Cope 346

Connecting with Parents and Families   347

Summary   348

∾ *14*   *Mathematics, Science, and Social Studies Learning*   *350*

Goals of the Cognitive Curriculum   352

Focus on . . . Brain Research—Blessing or Curse? 353 / Learning Facts 353 / Critical Thinking 354 / Problem Solving 354 / Lifelong Learning 355

The Constructivist Approach   355

Mathematics and Young Children   357

Classification 357 / Seriation 357 / Patterning 358 / Number Concepts 358 / *Focus on . . . The Language of Mathematics* 360 / Measurement 360 / Geometry 361 / Problem Solving 361 / *Focus on . . . Logo and Problem Solving* 362

Science Learning   362

Scientific Content 363 / *Into Practice . . . Gardening with Young Children* 365 / The Scientific Process 365 / Developing Scientific Attitudes 366 / *Celebrating Diversity . . . Helping All Children Learn Math and Science* 367

Young Children and the Social Studies   367

Understanding Self 368 / Understanding Others 371 / *Into Practice . . . Constructivist Social Studies* 372

Integrating Cognitive Learnings throughout the Curriculum   372

Infant/Toddler Materials and Activities 372 / Children Three through Five 373 / The Primary Grades 374

Parental Roles in Cognitive Development   375

Supporting the Importance of Cognitive Development 376

Assisting with Classroom Learning   376

Home Learning Tasks   376

Summary   377

∾ *15*   *Language and Literacy Learning*   *380*

Language Learning   383

Theoretical Perspectives 383 / Language Development 383 / Linguistic Systems 384 / *Focus on . . . Chomsky on Language Development* 385 / Facilitating Language Learning 386 /

Celebrating Play . . . Language Skills Can Blossom with Physical Activity 388 / Language Learning Materials 389 / *Into Practice . . . A Trip to the Post Office* 390

Literacy Learning   390

Literacy Development 391 / Learning to Read and Write 391 / *Focus on . . . Reading to Infants and Toddlers* 392 / Children's Books 395 / *Into Practice . . . Children's Literature on the Web* 396 / Writing Tools 397 / *Focus on . . . Children's Choice Awards* 398

Encouraging Parent Involvement   399

Into Practice . . . Getting Children to Write 400 / Taking Advantage of Daily Living 400 / Simple Home Learning Tasks 401

Summary   402

❧ 16   *Using the Creative Arts to Support Development and Learning*   404

What Is Creativity?   407

Defining Creativity 407 / Characteristics of Creative Individuals 408 / Assisting with the Creative Process 408 / *Focus on . . . Mozart on Creativity* 409 / Creativity and Play 410

The Young Artist   411

Why Include Art? 411 / Developmental Trends in Art 412 / *Focus on . . . Misconceptions about Art* 413 / The Early Childhood Art Curriculum 414 / The Adult Role in Art Experiences 415 / *Focus on . . . The Art of Reggio Emilia* 416

Music and the Young Child   418

The Importance of Music in Early Childhood 418 / Musical Development 419 / The Music Curriculum for Young Children 419 / *Into Practice . . . Music for the Nonmusician* 421 / Facilitating Musical Experiences 421

Activities in Art and Music   422

Activities for Infant/Toddlers 422 / *Into Practice . . . Singing Songs with Young Children* 423 / Art and Music for Preschoolers 424 / The Primary Years 425 / *Celebrating Diversity . . . Multicultural Musical Instruments* 426

Summary   427

❧ 17   *Using Technology to Support Development and Learning*   430

Television and Young Children   433

Time Spent Viewing 433 / Sex, Violence, and Advertising 433 / *Focus on . . . Sex and Violence on TV* 434 / Redeeming Aspects? 435 / Guidelines for Parents 435

The Video Game Dilemma   436

The Debate Over Value 436 / Parental Roles 437

Can Computer Use Be Developmentally Appropriate?   437

Computers and Play 438 / Social Interactions 439 / Developmental Abilities 440 / The Child with Special Needs 441

Selecting Computers and Software   441

Celebrating Diversity . . . Assistive Technology 442 / Hardware Options 442 / Selecting Computer Software 443 / *Into Practice . . . Drill and Practice Software* 445 /

Focus on . . . Software Reviews 446 / Helping Parents to Select Software 446 / *Into Practice . . . Classroom Homepage Connections* 447

Computers in the Classroom   447

Focus on . . . Surfing The Net 448

Interacting with Children Using Computers   448

Summary   449

References   *451*

Index   *465*

I

Introduction to the Field

❧ *1*

Overview of the Profession

❧ *2*

Historical Contexts

❧ *3*

Types of Programs

1 *Overview of the Profession*

In this chapter you will

- Develop an understanding of the foundations for early childhood education.

- Learn about the many different types of programs for young children.

- Identify the sources of funding for early childhood programs.

- Determine the roles, responsibilities, and skills needed for teachers of young children.

- Investigate the current training typical of teachers in early childhood education.

- Become familiar with the resources for professional development available to early childhood educators.

Adrienne has just been offered the job she interviewed for last week. After spending several years at home caring for her children, it's time to reenter the work force.

One of the first challenges she faces, however, is finding quality child care for her daughter and son: four-year-old Alyssa and two-year-old Mark. During the past few months, Adrienne and her husband have been exploring the many different early childhood programs available in their community.

Adrienne knows how important it is to her children's growth and development that they continue to be stimulated and well cared for when she is not with them. Therefore, she and her husband have been visiting preschool and day care centers in her area, meeting with teachers, talking with other parents, touring classrooms, and observing the children enrolled in these different programs. They have also been collecting information on teacher-to-student ratios, staff qualifications and turnover rates, and the approach to early childhood education in each program.

Finding affordable, high-quality programs where Alyssa and Mark will have lots of personal attention and many opportunities to learn and play will take careful planning, but with so many possibilities, the right option is sure to present itself. ✷

P erhaps, like Adrienne, you have had some exposure to early childhood education. Or, this may be your first introduction to working with children from birth to age eight. In either case, this book will help you begin to explore a most interesting and challenging profession. Because this is an introductory text, however, a great many issues are described only briefly here. You will need much more study and practice before you have the knowledge and skills necessary to teach at this level. As you read through the chapters of this book, discuss what you are learning with others, and observe children and teachers in the classroom, you will develop a deeper understanding of the field of early childhood education.

This first chapter introduces you to the many different types of programs associated with early childhood education and introduces you to the professional aspects of becoming an early childhood educator. Before discussing these issues, however, the chapter begins with an overview of the five key elements of early childhood education described in more detail in Chapters 4 through 8.

The five key components described next form the foundation for quality early childhood programs. Each is essential in classrooms designed for young children.

An Understanding of Children and Their Development

The first of these essential elements is an understanding of child development and learning. Early childhood educators believe that educational experiences are based first on children's needs and interests. To know these needs and interests, adults must understand children, both individually and collectively. By studying child development, teachers of young children know the normal patterns of behavior for children at specific ages. They also realize that individual differences exist between children, and they are able to identify those variations. All of this knowledge helps early childhood teachers plan for materials and activities in the classroom.

> ᭪ *Kate Appleton is preparing for the coming week in her kindergarten classroom. Kate remembers overhearing Noell and Jaleen talking excitedly about the recent class field trip to the zoo. The monkeys were particularly intriguing to these two and others in the class. Planning some activities centering on this interest seems appropriate and fun. Kate uses her general knowledge of child development and individual differences to select books, computer software, and discussion topics for the coming week.*

This approach is very different from the typical procedures used in many primary classrooms. Content experts carefully organize and structure the content to be taught in most elementary schools, which is presented in a specific sequence. In science, for example, the textbook may call for the study of insects first, followed by birds, and later still, the investigation of primates. Rather than looking at children and their developmental needs and interests first, teachers who use this more structured approach with their primary grade students allow the teaching materials to dictate the sequence and appropriateness of learning activities.

Opportunities to Play

A second essential component of early childhood education is providing children with times during the day to engage in play with peers and exciting materials. Play is one of the major ways in which young children learn about the world around them. Rather than having adults *tell* children what they need to know (an efficient strategy for many adult situations), children need the chance to manipulate real materials and learn for themselves important information about their environment.

> ᭪ *Lattice and Malcolm are in the block area in their preschool classroom. They are working together building a road, schoolhouse, and a parking garage. Lattice is*

5

While most preschool teachers include many opportunities for children to play, most primary classrooms are organized around tasks that exclude play as an option for learning (Stone, 1995). With the heavy emphasis on teacher-directed learning found at this level, little time is left for this valuable activity. Yet play can provide many opportunities for primary children to be creative, problem solve, and learn about the world around them.

Wassermann (1990) is one of many advocates of play in the primary grades. She gives the following example of a second-grade classroom in which play is very effectively used:

> As I walk through the door, the sight dazzles me. Five groups of children are working in investigative play groups with dry cells, buzzers, low-wattage light bulbs, and switches. They are carrying out inquiries with these materials. Bob (the teacher) has used the following activity card to guide them:
> Use the materials in this center to find out what you can about electricity and how it works.

- What can you observe about the dry cells? The buzzers? The light bulb?
- Talk together about your observations and make some notes about what you did. (p. 21)

Wassermann describes the intensity and enthusiasm of the children involved in this playful activity. Everyone is busy exploring the materials provided. Many choose to continue the science activity rather than go outside for recess. There are no discipline problems to deal with. This playful task has created an ideal situation for creatively learning about science.

1. Spend some time in a primary classroom looking for the kind of experience described here. Discuss your observations with other classmates.

2. Why isn't this mode of teaching/learning used more often? Discuss your thoughts with others.

struggling to find just the right block for her portion of the roadway. Malcolm suggests she try the "long, long one like mine," and Lattice discovers that his idea solves her problem nicely. As these children continue their play together, they solve additional problems, practice the important skill of cooperation, and indirectly learn about the mathematical properties of their play materials.

When children have large blocks of time to choose their own materials and playmates, the learning that takes place can be quite amazing.

While most parents and teachers recognize play as an enjoyable experience for children, many fail to see the learning potential of this important activity. Consequently, play is often viewed as frivolous and is excluded from the more meaningful work experiences in the classroom. Early childhood educators, however, believe that play is a very important way in which children learn about language, develop intellectual concepts, build social relationships and understandings, strengthen physical skills, and deal with stress. In short, play enhances every aspect of child development and is an essential ingredient in early education.

Guiding Young Children

The third key element of early childhood education emphasizes the importance of guiding the young child's social/emotional development. Although educating the mind is critical during the early years, teachers of young children find it equally essential to help children develop a strong sense of self, learn to relate in positive ways with adults and peers, and work through the many positive and negative emotions they experience. Guiding young children in these areas requires a solid background in child development and a sensitive, insightful adult.

> *Carly is a quiet but capable second-grade child in Maggie Harris's classroom. Lately, however, her behavior has been less than desirable. Carly seems distracted and sits staring out the window much of the day. Maggie has noticed that Simone, Carly's best friend, has been playing with other children more often during recess and decides to discuss this with Carly. During free choice time, she takes Carly aside and brings up the issue of Simone's friendship. Maggie's concern and interest have the desired effect, and Carly opens up about her sadness at having to share her best friend. They discuss several ideas that could help Carly feel better about her situation. With follow-up, Maggie feels that she has made important progress in understanding and helping Carly.*

Some adults may downplay this activity as tangential to the main mission of education, yet Maggie and other early childhood teachers recognize it as an important part of their teaching role. The development of effective social skills and the promotion of emotional health are valuable components of the early childhood curriculum. While this makes the teacher's role more complex, the overall benefits to children are immense.

Working with Parents, Families, and the Community

The fourth essential element of early childhood education is the development of mutually supportive relationships with parents, families, and the community. Although this concept has just recently gained support among educators in general, teachers of young children have had a long tradition of working closely with families and community members. Effective two-way communication, a climate of caring, and the involvement of parents and others in the educational process all provide early childhood teachers, parents, and their children with many benefits.

> *Larry Marshall is in his second year of teaching third-grade children. He tried to communicate with parents and get them involved last year, and he has worked extra hard this term to build stronger relationships with families and*

community members. The results have been truly surprising. Larry expected to see greater student progress and satisfaction and is pleased to find these results. Unanticipated results are the benefits that parents reported in informal conversations. One parent confided, for example, that she was learning some very helpful discipline tips from watching Larry in action. She was using similar techniques at home with good success and feeling much better about this aspect of her parenting. Larry also finds that he is personally benefitting from his work with parents. When they share their special talents in the classroom, for example, Larry, along with the children, is challenged and invigorated by the experiences.

When educators work with parents and community members, everyone benefits.

Diversity Issues and Young Children

The final foundational element of early education is an understanding of, and respect for, the many elements of diversity that have an impact on the lives of young children. Cultural backgrounds, variances due to gender, and physical and/or mental differences among children all influence development and learning. Furthermore, each of the other four foundations of early childhood mentioned earlier is impacted by diversity. The following examples help highlight the importance of diversity and its interrelatedness with these other foundational areas:

• Two-year-old Sabrina has just been diagnosed as having a hearing loss. After being fitted for a hearing aid, next month she will start attending an early learning program designed to help her catch up with her peers in oral language development.

• Three-year-old Andy is walking with his teacher and several other children as they explore the science exhibit at the local children's museum when he notices a woman ahead of him and says: "Teacher, why is that lady's skin so much darker than mine?"

• After school, seven-year-old Audrey likes to get out her paint set and create imaginative pictures using a variety of vibrant colors. Her twin brother, Darian, prefers racing around the cul-de-sac on his bicycle, weaving around a self-constructed obstacle course.

• At the open house, five-year-old Franklin has just introduced you to his two parents. Corinne and Angela mention their interest in helping out in the classroom occasionally.

The Scope of Early Childhood Education

Although quality early childhood programs have in common the five elements just described, they also have many differences, because of the children these programs are designed to serve. In this section, we will identify and discuss the many options that exist today.

The major challenge for caregivers in infant and toddler programs is to consistently meet their physical and emotional needs.

Infant/Toddler Programs

The fastest growing segment of early childhood programming is the infant/toddler component (birth to two years of age). Until fairly recently, most very young children were cared for by family members in the home. Recent research in the United States, however, has found that 23 percent of babies in their first year of life and 33 percent of one-year-olds are cared for outside their homes (Lally, 1995). Statistics on the family suggest this trend will likely continue. Hernandez (1995) cites research indicating that the percentage of women between the ages of twenty-five and fifty-four in the work force will increase from 75 to 83 percent by 2005.

Although most current infant/toddler programs operate in a home environment with small groups of children, the number of center-based programs caring for larger groups of very young children is increasing. In either setting, the major challenge for teachers is to form a close relationship with each child in his care (Raikes, 1996). Consistently and lovingly meeting the physical and emotional needs of very young children is an extremely important and challenging task.

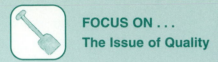

FOCUS ON . . .
The Issue of Quality

Quality day care programs for young children are essential. In reality, however, the positive characteristics found in many early childhood classrooms vary considerably. While some are truly excellent, others range from adequate to poor. Katz (1994) suggests five perspectives that can help adults determine the quality of an early childhood program:

1. *Top-down perspective.* The adult-to-child ratio, staff qualifications, turnover rates for staff, quality of materials and equipment, and provisions for health and safety are all components of this perspective.

2. *Bottom-up perspective.* Perhaps the most important indicator of quality is the child's subjective experiences in it. Do children in the program learn and grow from interactions with materials, equipment, and people there? If so, quality is high.

3. *Outside-inside perspective.* Since parents and their children are the consumers of early education, parental perspectives on program quality are important.

4. *Inside perspective.* Staff members can provide many insights on program quality by assessing relationships between colleagues, parent–teacher relationships, and the general climate of the school.

5. *The ultimate perspective.* The community and society at large also assess quality through policies, laws, and regulations governing early childhood programs.

1. *What is your sense of the quality of early childhood programs in your community? Discuss your thoughts with classmates.*

2. *Can you identify factors that might lead to lower or higher quality programs for young children? Make a list of possibilities, and discuss with others.*

Preschool Programs

Traditionally, preschool programs were designed for children between the ages of three and five as a way to enhance social and emotional development. These nursery school options became popular in the 1920s and continue to be highly valued by middle-class families. More recently, prekindergarten programs have been promoted as a way to help children who have been identified as at-risk of failing in the K–12 system develop the skills they will need to be successful in later years. Many preschool programs today have also expanded their age range downward to include two-year-olds.

Rather than being full-day programs, most preschool classrooms operate half-time or less. A common model is to enroll children for three to five half-day sessions per week. With the increasing numbers of single parents and dual-career families, however, these partial-day sessions are often combined with the chance to participate in day care as well. This blending of preschool and day care options often makes it difficult to separate the two programs.

Day Care Programs

Day care programs, as the name implies, are designed to provide children with quality care and education for full days. As the numbers of single parents and dual-career families have increased, the need for day care options for young children has also grown. Typically, day care programs provide care for children from the beginning to the end of the parents' work day. It is not uncommon for some children to be in a day care setting from seven o'clock in the morning until six o'clock at night. As indicated earlier, other children may attend a day care center part-days to participate in preschool.

A variety of day care options are available. The most common type is called the **family home day care.** These programs operate out of the caretaker's home and enroll only a small number of children. **Day care centers** are programs located in buildings either designed for, or remodeled to be used with, young children. More children are typically enrolled in these programs, with several teachers hired to work with groups of children. **School-based day care** is becoming a more popular option in many locations. Public schools are setting aside space in their elementary schools for day care programs under their direction. **Corporate day care** is also growing in popularity. An increasing number of businesses are offering on-site child care as a convenience and service to their employees. **Before- and after-school care** is a final option available in many settings. These programs may be provided at the elementary school, or children may travel to other sites to receive this care.

Programs for Children with Special Needs

Early childhood programs designed for children with special needs are also available in most communities. Federal legislation over the past two decades has mandated these important options. Public Law (PL) 94-142, enacted in the mid-1970s, requires that all children with special needs beginning at age three years be provided a free and appropriate public education. The availability of these programs was extended to birth by PL 99-457. The intent of both these laws has been to educate children with special needs in classrooms with their normally developing peers. This integration effort has led to early childhood special education programs that are blended with other options for young children.

While many educational efforts for children with special needs are integrated with other early childhood programs, **early intervention programs** for children with special needs are also available (Spodek & Saracho, 1994). These programs are designed to help identify children's disabilities and assist children and families in growth and development. Options for infants and toddlers are most common and

FOCUS ON . . .
Multiage Classrooms

A relatively recent approach to structuring early childhood classrooms is referred to as the *multiage approach.* As the name implies, rather than having, for example, separate groups of five-, six-, and seven-year-old children, students are mixed together in the same room. Multiage classrooms can be traced back to the one-room schoolhouses that existed in America until the early part of the twentieth century; renewed interest has surfaced since the 1980s. When children are allowed to remain with the same teacher over a period of several years (referred to as *looping*), many benefits can occur (Viadero, 1996):

- *Younger children learn from older classmates.* As younger children observe and interact with their older classmates, the opportunities for learning are greater.

- *Older students reinforce their own understandings.* As older students assist in the teaching process, they are able to consolidate and strengthen their knowledge of the information they are sharing.

- *Stronger teacher–student relationships.* Having the same students for more than one year means the teacher doesn't have to start over each year in learning about each child's abilities and building new relationships.

- *Fewer children are retained in grade.* In multiage classrooms, students who stay with the same teacher avoid the potential stigma associated with retention. Studies indicate that students who are held back more often drop out of school later on.

1. Find an article on multiage classrooms (also called *nongraded* or *ungraded classrooms*), and read more about this interesting option. What do you see as the strengths and limitations of this approach?

2. Spend some time observing in a multiage classroom. What did you see that you liked or disliked?

often combine limited small-group experiences with home visits where the parent and home visitor work together to assist with the infant/toddler's development.

Kindergartens

It may surprise you to know that publicly funded programs for five-year-old children are a relatively new option in many states. Many public schools either didn't provide kindergarten or offered it only for parents who were able to pay for the service. As of early 1997, New Hampshire was one state that still did not fully fund kindergarten programs (Jacobson, 1997).

Traditional kindergartens in the United States were half-day programs designed to help children develop social and emotional skills through a play-oriented experience. Despite the many benefits of this focus, many programs today are more academic and present a curriculum that looks much like that of the

These second graders learn many valuable concepts with math manipulatives.

first-grade classroom. In addition, many kindergarten classrooms are now full-day programs that typically meet three days a week. Research on this option suggests that the longer school day is beneficial when teachers provide a curriculum that allows children time to playfully learn about their world (Rothenberg, 1995).

Primary Education

Grades 1 through 3 in elementary schools are referred to as *primary education* and have been a part of American schooling from its very beginnings. For most of this period, the methods and materials for teaching at this level have mirrored those used with older elementary students. Instruction was teacher-directed and included mostly small- and large-group teaching combined with independent work for students.

Beginning in the 1960s and 1970s, the popularity of theorists such as Piaget (Flavell, 1963) led to new teaching strategies for this level. Educators began to view primary-aged students as more like preschool and kindergarten children in their thinking than older elementary students. More opportunities to learn through hands-on manipulation of objects and interacting with peers was implemented.

Although instruction at the primary level remains teacher-directed in a majority of classrooms, many primary teachers are engaging in a variety of interesting teaching and learning strategies. The **multiage classroom,** in which two or three grades are grouped together for instruction, is one option being tried. In some instances, the teacher remains with the same students for several years. Using an **integrated curriculum,** in which mathematics, reading, science, and social studies are all learned simultaneously through the teaching of specific themes, is another example of this effort. Creating **classroom centers** where children can independently explore materials and activities of their own choosing is yet another strategy being used.

Funding: Who Pays for Early Education?

Another way to conceptualize programs for young children is to look at who pays for the services. In general, it is either the public (through local, state, or federal funds), the families involved in the early childhood program, or some combination of these two. In this section, we will look at this issue in more detail.

Programs Run for Profit

Approximately 60 percent of all child care programs are run as businesses to generate profits for their owners (Wash & Brand, 1990). The revenue generated from parent fees is the major source of income for these programs. This money must be used to pay for teacher salaries, space/housing costs, and the expenses for toys and equipment used in the program. Locally owned day care centers and family day care homes are the most common for-profit options. National corporations also are making money in the child care business. Kindercare is the largest of these options, with over one thousand franchised centers nationwide. In addition to child care, some preschool programs are operated for profit as well.

The remaining programs discussed in this section are operated basically as not-for-profit operations. Any money left over after all bills are paid is used to buy new materials or otherwise improve the quality of the program itself.

Cooperative Programs

An important option that began in the 1920s is often referred to as the **parent cooperative.** Parents in these programs pay their children's educational costs. These expenses are kept low by involving parents as assistant teachers in the classroom. Each family unit is expected to spend a specified number of hours each month helping out in the classroom. This allows the program to operate with fewer paid adults and makes the overall costs to parents lower. Many community colleges and universities operate cooperative programs for their students. High school child care programs for teen parents also follow this cooperative model and require parent participation to reduce overall program costs.

In addition to keeping the educational expenses low, early childhood cooperatives are excellent parent education experiences. By participating in a school environment with specially trained adults, parents have many opportunities to learn about children and gain experience in positively interacting with them. Discussing common problems with other parents whose struggles are similar is also helpful to many parents.

Federally Funded Programs

The federal government spends a relatively small amount of its budget on programs for children in their early years. But the support it does provide meets some important needs. The most well-known early childhood program funded by federal money is the **Head Start** program. Begun in 1964 as an attempt to help low-income four-year-olds catch up academically with their more advantaged peers, Head Start has stood the test of time as an important program for young children. Educating children who are usually age three to five, the Head Start program is considered comprehensive because of its emphasis on all aspects of the child's development. In addition to focusing on social, emotional, intellectual, language, and physical development, Head Start emphasizes good health and provides resources and assistance with medical, dental, nutritional, and mental health needs. Similar programs, like **Early Head Start,** which focuses on children younger than three, have grown out of Head Start's success. The primary criterion for admission into a Head Start class is the income level of parents. Unfortunately, many more families meet the income eligibility than Head Start serves.

A second group of programs receiving federal money is designed for **children with disabilities.** Options integrating children into regular classrooms and those providing separate services are funded in part by government dollars. Generally, the level of federal support is less than what it actually costs to educate children with special needs. State or local assistance is used to make up the difference.

Elementary schools benefit from additional federal support known as **Chapter I.** Originally called Title I, this program provides substantial funds to help elementary schools improve the academic achievement of disadvantaged children and those identified as at-risk for future failure in school. Realizing the importance of the early years, many elementary schools spend most of these federal dollars on programs for kindergarten and primary-aged children.

The federal legislation that reauthorized Chapter I funding also created an early childhood program option called **Even Start.** With goals similar to the Head Start program, Even Start provides money for educational experiences to young low-income children. In addition, however, the program promotes the development of literacy skills in parents. As they improve their own abilities, parents are better able to assist and encourage their children in school-related tasks.

State and Locally Funded Programs

In recent years, the federal government has cut back support to children and families. As a result, state and local governments have had to increase their financial

FOCUS ON . . .
Head Start

Head Start was designed to serve the needs of young children from low-income families. It provides a comprehensive program to meet their emotional, social, educational, health, nutritional, and psychological needs. Although not all children who are eligible are served, because of underfunding, approximately 450,000 participate nationwide. In addition, approximately 140 Early Head Start programs are in operation across the nation.

Head Start has four major components (U.S. Department of Health and Human Services, 1990):

- *Education.* In addition to providing learning experiences to stimulate intellectual development, the Head Start program emphasizes social and emotional growth as well. Children participate in indoor and outdoor play experiences and engage in more structured learning.
- *Health.* Head Start places a strong emphasis on early identification of health problems, because many children served have never

seen a doctor or dentist. This comprehensive health care includes medical, dental, mental health, and nutritional services.
- *Parent involvement.* Parents are viewed as the single most important influence on the child's development. It is therefore essential for parents to be involved in parent education, in the classroom, in program planning, and in operating activities.
- *Social services.* This component of Head Start is an organized method of assisting families in assessing their needs and then guiding them to resources to help meet those needs.

1. *Read more about the Head Start and Early Head Start programs. Share what you learned with your classmates.*
2. *Visit a local Head Start or Early Head Start program, and observe how the program operates. Talk to a teacher, and find out more about this important program.*

contributions to maintain programs for children and families. In addition to providing for public K–12 education, state and local agencies help fund a variety of other options. Some states, for example, supplement the federal money designated for Head Start so that more low-income children can be served. Washington state's Early Childhood Education and Assistance Program (ECEAP) is one such example. State and local support for the inclusion of children with special needs is also common. Local governments and philanthropic organizations (like United Way) also give money to nonprofit programs for children and families.

Corporate Day Care

A small but growing number of businesses are providing on-site day care for their employees (Shellenbarger, 1994). These programs are usually jointly funded, with

A small but growing number of businesses are offering on-site child care for their employees.

corporations partially subsidizing the costs and parents paying the balance. Businesses that have implemented day care programs cite many important benefits (Seefeldt, 1990):

• Lower employee absences, tardiness, and turnover
• Improved productivity, morale, and health
• Enhanced community and public relations

Although these are powerful benefits, many corporations still find it difficult to invest in this option for its employees. One problem is that it takes approximately one thousand employees to generate the necessary numbers of children to make a child care center financially viable (Seefeldt, 1990). Some businesses are also finding that employees who don't have young children may resist adding this benefit unless they receive other compensation. Despite these and other issues, corporate day care should continue to grow in the years ahead.

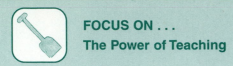

Most of us can remember one or more teachers who have had a powerful impact on our lives. Perhaps it was an act of kindness, a belief in you as a person, or the excitement this person brought to the classroom. Unfortunately, others may remember teachers who callously or carelessly hurt the students around them through their words or actions. Teachers have great power to do either much good or considerable harm.

Haim Ginott (1972) had the following to say on this important topic:

I have come to a frightening conclusion. It is my personal approach that creates the climate. It is my daily mood that makes the weather. As a teacher, I possess tremendous power to make a child's life miserable or joyous. I can be a tool of torture or an instrument of inspiration. I can humiliate or humor, hurt or heal. In all situations it is my response that decides whether a crisis will be escalated or de-escalated, a child humanized or de-humanized. (p. 13)

The power of teaching is real at all levels but perhaps more so when adults work with young children. Fortunately, most teachers use this influence to assist positively in the growth and development of children.

1. Remember a favorite teacher you had as a younger student. What did that person do or say that made him or her stand out in your memory? Discuss your thoughts with others.

2. Do you see yourself as a person capable of using the power of the teaching role to do good for young children? Why or why not?

College- and University-Supported Programs

Many colleges and universities have child care programs for students and employees and find similar benefits to those stated above for corporations. Generally, the expenses for these day care options are shared. Some support is provided by the college or university, with parents who use the service paying the balance.

In addition to the obvious child care benefits, college and university programs are often designed to serve as research and training sites as well. Faculty who want to study child development or examine the effectiveness of a specific teaching strategy are able to use the child care facility for this purpose. In addition, early childhood teacher preparation programs often use campus child care centers as sites for their students who need direct experiences with young children.

Teaching Young Children

Now that you have had some initial exposure to the field of early childhood education, take a slightly more personal look at what teaching young children is like. This will help you to understand the training and skills needed to work in the field. Look at your own personal characteristics and motivation and see how they compare with the descriptions being presented. Is there a good match? If so, your interest in early childhood education could lead to a productive career choice. If not, you may need to think carefully before committing to this profession.

Roles of the Early Childhood Educator

Teachers of young children serve in many roles as they assist those youngsters in development. The most obvious role is that of **facilitator of learning.** Helping students know more about the world around them has been a time-honored expectation for teachers. Because young children are naturally curious about nearly everything, it is also an exciting one.

Teachers also serve as **counselor** to the children in their care. Obviously, early childhood personnel don't have specific training as counselors, but they use many of the same skills as they guide children in their social and emotional development. For example, helping Alanna recognize she is mad at Derrick for taking her toy truck is an important form of early counseling.

More routine tasks also are expected of teachers who work at the prekindergarten level especially. The role of **janitor,** for example, may be shared among preschool teachers. While larger programs may hire a specialist, many teachers of young children also serve as a **cook** for their children as they prepare nutritious snacks and possibly meals. Although it is very important to get children involved in the basic chores of the school, it is often necessary for the teacher to go beyond the basics in providing these services.

Early childhood teachers also serve as **educational specialists.** Because of the integrated nature of the early childhood curriculum, it is necessary for teachers at this level to be comfortable with, and to lead children in learning experiences in, music, art, and physical education. These specialists may be available at the elementary level; however, the best early childhood teachers add to the limited opportunities these specialists can provide.

Perhaps summarizing many of these roles, teachers of young children also become a **parent substitute** for their students. Most parents fulfill their responsibilities well while children are in the home. But young children continue to need parenting in the school environment even when their own parents are not around. Love, guidance, encouragement, assistance, and modeling are all needed by young children and are essential components of the early childhood teacher's role.

Responsibilities of the Early Childhood Educator

In addition to their specific roles, early childhood teachers also assume important responsibilities. Overall, the early childhood educator's foremost responsibility is to be an **advocate** for children and their families (NAEYC, 1996a). *Advocacy* simply means promoting the causes of children and families. Taking leadership in helping meet the needs of children and families is an important responsibility early childhood educators must assume.

FOCUS ON . . .
Advocacy

Following are several important reasons explaining why early childhood educators should make advocacy for children and families a high priority:

• *Importance of the early years.* It is critical that young children and their families receive the best possible education and care in the early years. Decision makers at all levels need to hear this message repeatedly.

• *Powerless children and families.* It is virtually impossible for children to speak for themselves about their educational, emotional, and physical needs. Many families also need the support of articulate, dedicated professionals advocating on their behalf.

• *Low priority of early education and care.* The lack of program support for young children and families is painfully obvious. Early educators and others must work hard to raise the priority of young children and families in the eyes of others.

The National Association for the Education of Young Children (1996a) suggests five specific steps you can take to help children and families:

1. *Speak out on behalf of children and families at every opportunity.* Educate parents, public officials, community members, and others about the importance of early education and family support.

2. *Find ways to positively influence the life of one child or family.* As one individual, you can't make things better for all children and families.

But you can tutor a child, become a big brother or sister, or help a family find the resources they need to resolve a current problem.

3. *Hold public officials accountable for making the well-being of children and families a high priority in both word and deed.* Find out where public officials at all levels of government stand on issues related to children and families, and then remind these people regularly of their stated commitments.

4. *Suggest ways that organizations to which you belong can meet the needs of children and families.* Employers, clubs, religious organizations, and neighborhood groups can all be encouraged to adopt a school, class, or a specific group of families and work to meet their specific needs.

5. *Urge others to champion the causes of children and families.* Your efforts can make a difference in the lives of others. But, by encouraging co-workers, friends, neighbors, and parents to do the same, you multiply exponentially the potential benefits to children and families.

1. *Can you list two or three relatively simple tasks that you could do right now to assist children and families?*

2. *Talk to an early childhood teacher, and find out what he or she does or would like to do as an advocate for young children and their families.*

An additional responsibility of early childhood educators is **continuing education.** Research by scholars in the discipline as well as innovations by educators in the classroom contribute to our understandings of how best to educate young children. The closing sections of this chapter focus on opportunities for continuing education and professional development.

Section I: Ethical Responsibilities to Children.   Our paramount responsibility is to provide safe, healthy, nurturing, and responsive settings for children. We are committed to supporting children's development by cherishing individual differences, by helping them learn to live and work cooperatively, and by promoting their self-esteem.

Section II: Ethical Responsibilities to Families.   Families are of primary importance in children's development. Because the family and the early childhood educator have a common interest in the child's welfare, we acknowledge a primary responsibility to bring about collaboration between the home and school in ways that enhance the child's development.

Section III: Ethical Responsibilities to Colleagues.   In a caring, cooperative workplace, human dignity is respected, professional satisfaction is promoted, and positive relationships are modeled. Our primary responsibility in this arena is to establish and maintain settings and relationships that support productive work and meet professional needs.

Section IV: Ethical Responsibilities to Community and Society.   Our responsibilities to the community are to provide programs that meet its needs and to cooperate with agencies and professions that share responsibility for children. Because the larger society has a measure of responsibility for the welfare and protection of children, and because of our specialized expertise in child development, we acknowledge an obligation to serve as a voice for children everywhere.

Note. Adapted from "NAEYC's Code of Ethical Conduct: Guidelines for Responsible Behavior in Early Childhood Education" by the National Association for the Education of Young Children, 1996, *Young Children, 51* (3), pp. 57–60.

Last, early childhood professionals must follow a shared code of **ethical conduct,** based on a set of core values with deep historical roots in the field of early childhood education. The code of ethical behavior developed by the National Association for the Education of Young Children (NAEYC, 1996d) provides guidelines for responsible behavior in relation to students, families, colleagues, and society. Members of the NAEYC agree to engage in behaviors that demonstrate high standards and commit to monitoring the conduct of others. Excerpted quotes from this code appear in Figure 1–1.

Skills Needed to Teach Young Children

The responsibilities and challenges of teaching make it one of the most difficult of occupations. The best teachers are successful in taking advantage of their personal strengths and in building their teaching ability through many interactions with children and others. Good teaching requires skill in three main areas: interacting with children, preparing the environment, and working with other adults.

Interacting with Children. The early childhood teacher spends much of her day engaged in informal interactions with children. "Kelly, please put the puzzle back on the shelf before you get out another toy." "Adrian, that must have really hurt. Tell Mark how that makes you feel." "I'm not sure what ants eat, Ariel, but we can probably find some information on the computer." Times like these provide many opportunities to assist child growth and development. Sensitive teachers learn the right times to step in and communicate with individual children and times when it is best to simply stop and observe what is taking place.

Teaching also requires skills in working with both small and large groups of children. Getting their attention, maintaining their interests in a project or topic, making smooth transitions from one part of the activity to the next, and presenting information in an exciting way are just some of the skills a teacher must use to be successful in working with a group of young children. Often, teachers must use several skills almost simultaneously to make sure everything moves along effectively.

Preparing the Environment. Early educational experiences are best when children actively manipulate materials. This process of learning by doing allows the young child to build stronger understandings of the world around her. This requires that the teacher carefully plan and prepare the materials in the learning environment. Knowing about student interests and needs, the early childhood teacher must organize and plan for materials that can stimulate the young child's understanding. By regularly rotating new materials in and out of the classroom and playground, children can be continually challenged to grow and learn from their surroundings.

Although this may sound relatively easy, in reality it requires plenty of hard work. The teacher must rely on her own insights, knowledge of children, and organizational skills to make sure the classroom is an exciting place for children.

Working with Other Adults. Most people enter teaching to work with children, but teachers also must often interact with other adults. Communicating effectively with the other teachers, aides, and administrators will make the many tasks associated with teaching more manageable. In addition, strong relationships with parents and community members are essential for good teaching in an early childhood classroom.

Many teachers are surprised to learn about the importance of these adult relationships. Furthermore, making interactions with other adults work isn't easy for many teachers. They require the use of different strategies and a new mind-set to be successful.

Should I Teach?

Take a careful look at the roles, responsibilities, and skills described here. Can you envision yourself taking them on if you were working with young children? The challenges of teaching are very real. The rewards are also clearly identified. Only one question remains: Is teaching in the early childhood environment a career you should pursue? While *you* must make this decision, others can assist you in this process. Consider doing any or all of the following as you reflect on teaching as a possible career:

- *Observe early childhood teachers at work.* If possible, observe several teachers so that you see a variety of teaching styles. Try to critically analyze all that the teachers are doing while interacting with children. Can you see yourself doing the same sorts of things?
- *Spend time working with children.* The more time you can spend interacting with children, the better your chances of determining if you fit. Try seeing yourself as a teacher and putting on all of the roles discussed earlier.
- *Ask for feedback from others.* Teachers who can observe you working with young children are probably the best source of information about your teaching ability. Ask them to be honest with you. Everybody has both strengths and weaknesses. Find out about both.
- *Self-analysis.* Although self-analysis may be a struggle, it is often helpful to critique your own skills. Identify your personal strengths and weaknesses. How do they match the roles and skills of teachers?

As you investigate early childhood education as a career option, you will realize that you will be stronger in some roles or more skilled in certain areas than others. Which aspects of the job might be more difficult for you? What could you do to make the difficult roles more workable for you? Fortunately, quality educational programs can help guide and train you in these areas.

Professional Preparation of Early Childhood Caregivers

Teacher education programs are clearly defined for those preparing for K–3 classrooms; not so for prekindergarten education. In many cases, a high school diploma is the only requirement for beginning work in these settings, despite the many complex roles and responsibilities that skilled early childhood educators must take on. Increasingly, a two-year college preparation program or a four-year degree is required for teaching prekindergarten children. Teaching within the early childhood classroom occurs at a variety of levels. Assistant teachers, associate teachers, head teachers, and supervisors all play important roles (NAEYC, 1984). Saracho and Spodek (1993) describe these four roles and the levels of teacher preparation and educational requirements for each:

Level 1. Early Childhood Teacher Assistant. This entry-level position allows people to assist in the implementation of activities under the supervision of a more experienced provider. The suggested educational requirement for this level is the high school diploma or its equivalent.

Level 2. Early Childhood Associate Teacher. The associate teacher is expected to implement program activities independently and may have responsibilities for a group of children. Training for this level is demonstrated competency in the six basic areas of the Child Development Associate (CDA) program (discussed later).

Level 3. Early Childhood Teacher. Teachers at this level coordinate the efforts of teacher assistants and associate teachers and assume more direct responsibilities for groups of children. Expected educational background is completion of a bachelor's degree in early childhood education or child development.

Level 4. Early Childhood Specialist. At this level, educators take responsibility for supervising and training staff, designing curriculum, and administering programs. In addition to a minimum of a bachelor's degree, the specialist should have at least three years of full-time teaching at the early childhood level.

Because of these different levels, the training required for teaching varies. Most teachers of young children follow three main routes in becoming a teacher: the CDA credential, two-year programs, and four-year programs.

The CDA Credential

The CDA credential is a national program designed to improve the qualifications of those who teach in prekindergarten classrooms. The CDA credential is a

Practical, hands-on experiences with young children are an important component of both two-year and four-year programs.

nondegree option that is based on demonstrated competencies in six areas: (1) maintaining a safe and healthy learning environment, (2) advancing physical and intellectual competence, (3) supporting social and emotional development, (4) establishing positive relationships with families, (5) ensuring a well-run program meeting individual needs, and (6) maintaining a commitment to professionalism (Phillips, 1990).

Two-Year, or Associate Degree, Programs

Many community colleges offer two-year programs to prepare interested students to teach in prekindergarten programs and serve as administrators at this level. Providing a combination of child development course work, early childhood instructional methods, and practical experiences with young children, these programs provide excellent preparation for teaching in infant/toddler and preschool classrooms. The following content summary is an example of a two-year program in early childhood education (semester system):

Introduction to early childhood education	3 credits
Practicum experiences	10 credits
Curriculum development	3 credits
Creativity and play	3 credits
Working with parents	3 credits
Special needs children	3 credits
Child development	5 credits
Language and literacy	3 credits
Cognitive development	3 credits
Social and emotional development	3 credits
Infant and toddler care	3 credits

Four-Year Programs

To teach at the elementary level, prospective teachers must complete a four-year degree in elementary education from an accredited college or university. Traditionally, these programs have emphasized the preparation of elementary and secondary teachers. This is in part due to the fact that in most states there is no required teacher certification before kindergarten; however, more states are developing teaching certificates that either specialize in preparation at the primary (K–3) level or that also include the prekindergarten level (birth through grade 3).

Coordinating Efforts

Unfortunately, for many years, little effort has been made to have two-year colleges and four-year institutions working together to articulate student course work and to help students move to the next step in the educational sequence.

Students seeking training in early childhood education have often been blocked from making smooth transitions by colleges and universities who battle over issues of quality and comparability of course work.

These roadblocks are slowly beginning to erode, and national professional organizations are working to ensure that students can move through a continuum of educational experiences leading to increasingly advanced early childhood training (Association of Teacher Educators & National Association for the Education of Young Children, 1991).

Resources for Professional Development

Although professional development begins with initial teacher training, this process continues throughout your career. As you gain experience in the classroom, make careful observations of children, have conversations with other educators, and attend professional conferences, your growth as a teacher continues. By actively participating in professional organizations, subscribing to professional journals, and being aware of other sources of information on early childhood education, caregivers can grow in their abilities to meet the needs of children and families.

Professional Organizations

Two professional organizations emphasize early childhood education. By far the largest and most influential is the **National Association for the Education of Young Children (NAEYC).** With a membership of over 95,000 in 1996 (Bredekamp & Glowacki, 1996), NAEYC promotes quality education and care for children and their families from birth to age eight. Members receive the journal *Young Children,* which provides teachers and others with many practical ideas for the early childhood classroom. More recently, NAEYC began publishing the *Early Childhood Research Quarterly* for those interested in studies of children, families, and curriculum. In addition to publishing a strong list of books for early educators, NAEYC holds an annual national conference that attracts over 25,000 participants. State and local affiliates of NAEYC provide additional opportunities for workshops and professional growth for early childhood educators.

The second professional organization for early educators is the **Association for Childhood Education International (ACEI).** Although the focus of this organization is broader, with an emphasis on children from birth through adolescence, the early years have been a major interest of many participants. Smaller in size than NAEYC, ACEI has nonetheless had a significant influence on the directions in early childhood education. Members receive the journal *Childhood Education* and have the opportunity to participate in national and regional conferences. Books and other publications are also available through the national headquarters. Finally, ACEI offers a research publication titled the *Journal of Research in Childhood Education.*

Other professional organizations are also available that have special interest groups or that focus on aspects of early childhood education. Some examples of these groups include

- American Montessori Society
- Council for Exceptional Children
- International Reading Association
- National Council of Teachers of Mathematics
- World Organization for Early Education

Journals

In addition to the journals from NAEYC and ACEI mentioned earlier, many professional publications are helpful to those involved in early childhood education. These can be divided into two broad groups: (1) research publications emphasizing child development and family issues and (2) journals that focus primarily on ideas useful to the practitioner.

Some examples of the journals on child development research are

- *Child Development*
- *Developmental Psychology*
- *Early Child Development and Care*
- *Merrill Palmer Quarterly*
- *Monographs of the Society for Research in Child Development*

Journals published for practitioners include

- *The Arithmetic Teacher*
- *Child Care Information Exchange*
- *Day Care and Early Education*
- *Dimensions of Early Childhood*
- *Early Childhood Education Today*
- *The Reading Teacher*

Reference Materials

One set of tools that is very useful to early educators as they work to increase their knowledge of children and teaching is a rich collection of reference materials. In addition to journals, many books provide insights on issues relating to early childhood education. For example, numerous texts are available that describe in more detail the importance of play in child development. These resources provide a more in-depth understanding of issues of interest to caregivers.

The **Educational Resources Information Center (ERIC)** is another very important reference system that can provide quick and detailed assistance in locating information on children and families. This computer-based information retrieval system is funded by the U.S. Office of Education and can help educators locate articles, books, and microfiche on topics of interest. The ERIC system also includes sixteen clearinghouses, which focus on interest areas within education. The ERIC Clearinghouse for Elementary and Early Childhood Education specializes in information and resources relating to young children.

A third reference option that is growing rapidly with the expansion of materials on the Internet is the availability of **Web sites** with information on children and families. The following are samples of this ever-expanding option:

- Ask ERIC Home Page: http://ericir.syr.edu/
- Children, Youth and Family Consortium: http://www.fsci.umn.edu/cyfc
- ERIC Document Reproduction Service: http://edrs.com/
- Family Network: http://family.com
- National Child Care Information Center Home Page: http://ericps.ed.uiuc.edu/nccic/nccichome.htm

Summary

This chapter has provided you with a broad introduction to the field of early childhood education. The essential foundations are understanding child development, play, guidance, working with parents and families, and the importance of diversity in child growth and development. The different types of early childhood programs include infant/toddler programs, preschool education, day care, programs for children with special needs, kindergartens, and primary education. The issue of who should pay for early education is significant; the various options include programs for profit, federally funded programs, state and locally funded programs, corporate day care, and college/university-supported programs.

This chapter also addressed teaching in the early childhood classroom. An understanding of the teacher's roles and responsibilities and of the skills needed for teaching at this level will help you to decide whether teaching is a good career choice for you.

Different educational paths are available to those wanting to enter the field, and resources are available to assist early educators in continued professional development.

For Discussion and Action

1. Talk to an early childhood teacher about the five foundations of early education presented in this chapter. Does the teacher feel they are all essential elements to good teaching at this level? Are there others that he or she would add? Discuss this with your classmates.

2. See if you can find examples of the different types of early childhood programs within your community. Are there infant/toddler options? Preschools? Family day care homes? Day care centers?

3. Discuss with your classmates the issue of who should pay for early childhood education. Is it the parents' responsibility or the government's? What role should corporations play?

4. Spend some time thoughtfully creating two separate lists, one identifying your personal strengths and the second listing your weaknesses. Compare those lists with the roles of early childhood teachers and the skills needed to be successful. What do you think? Is there a good match? Why or why not?

5. What are the requirements for early childhood teachers in your state? Compare and contrast programs available at the community college and university levels.

Building Your Personal Library

Goffin, S., & Lombardi, J. (1988). *Speaking out: Early childhood advocacy*. Washington, DC: National Association for the Education of Young Children. This text begins with a definition of advocacy and then describes the process needed to implement advocacy efforts. It includes an excellent appendix listing national organizations assisting with the needs of children and families.

Jalongo, M., & Isenberg, J. (1994). *Teachers' stories: From personal narrative to professional insight*. San Francisco: Jossey-Bass. Using stories from early childhood teachers, this book discusses issues relating to advocacy and professionalism. The teacher narratives describe how others have dealt with these important issues.

Paciorek, K., & Munro, J. (1998). *Annual editions: Early childhood education*. Sluice Dock, CT: Duskin/McGraw-Hill. This book is an edited collection of interesting articles on early childhood education. It is a good overview of many of the issues in the field. The book is updated each year with new articles.

2   *Historical Contexts*

In this chapter you will

■ Learn about the early European influences on early childhood education.

■ Study the beginnings of early education in the United States.

■ Review historical events that have impacted directions in early education.

It is a beautiful spring day, and Ms. Gregory's kindergarten class is excitedly exploring the outdoors. Marta and Gina are digging contentedly in the garden in preparation for some later planting. Erik and Daniel have discovered an ant hill and are down on their hands and knees carefully observing the scurrying workers. Nateesha and Elizabeth have taken two tires and are building their own pretend bird's nest by collecting twigs and grass for the base of the nest. Several children are playing a loosely organized game of tag and are running gleefully around on the grassy field. Still others are playing on the climbing structure in the middle of the playground, while three children swing and chat on the swing set nearby.

While everyone is so actively engaged, Ms. Gregory has taken the opportunity to carefully observe her children's actions. She is particularly interested in their social interactions and is focusing on the friendship patterns and general communication strategies children use as they interact with their peers. Ms. Gregory is very pleased with the skills she is seeing her students use. ❧

Although the preceding scene is typical of many early childhood classrooms, it may surprise you to know that these options haven't always been available to children. For most of recorded history, for example, boys were the only ones to receive formal education. Playing outdoors and learning from nature weren't promoted until the eighteenth century. Toys and equipment designed specifically for young children appeared around the middle of the nineteenth century, and formal playground equipment became available near the beginning of the twentieth century.

This chapter examines the historical roots of current practice in early childhood education. By examining the people and events from the past that have shaped early childhood education, you can develop a deeper understanding of this exciting field.

Historical Figures Influencing Early Childhood Education

Having introduced the scope of early education today in Chapter 1, we will now identify and discuss key people from the past who have had a major impact on directions in early childhood education. Understanding the contributions of these individuals provides insight into the theory and practice of programs for young children.

Some of the people discussed next are **theorists.** Although they identified important issues related to children and teaching, they didn't actually put these ideas into practice working with children. Others were **practitioners** who, in addition to presenting new and interesting ideas about child development and learning, also worked in the classroom, teaching young children.

European Contributors

For the past several centuries, Europe in particular has been the leader in promoting innovative educational theory and practice. The beginnings of many key elements in early education today can be traced to these European theorists and practitioners.

Martin Luther (1483–1546). Martin Luther is best known for his efforts in religious reformation, yet he had a significant impact on educational thinking as well. Because of his conviction that the Bible was the key to Christian reform, Luther began to promote improved education, particularly the ability to read, as an essential in German society. To establish a personal relationship with God, he felt, everyone needed to be able to read the Bible.

As an early educational theorist, Martin Luther suggested many revolutionary ideas for his time (Braun & Edwards, 1972):

- *All towns and villages should have schools.* This was not common in Luther's time but leaders of the day began to take the idea seriously.
- *Both girls and boys should be educated.* Up until this time, education was almost exclusively for boys. Luther's emphasis on everyone reading the Bible, however, required that both sexes be taught.
- *Schools should foster intellectual, religious, physical, emotional, and social development.* This concept of educating the whole child is an essential element of early childhood education today.

John Amos Comenius (1592–1670). Comenius was another early educational theorist who presented many new and important ideas about children and learning. Although his interests were broader than early childhood education, one of his books in particular addressed issues in working with young children. Titled *School of Infancy* (Comenius, 1896), this text describes many ideas that are very much a part of early education today. He suggested, for example, that the first years of life are crucial to overall development and that adults must take advantage of this time to assist the child's growth. Comenius also believed that **movement and activity** were sure signs of healthy learning experiences. Young children, he stated, learn best from **natural, real-world experiences.**

In other writings, Comenius also made clear his views on the teacher's role in learning and identified who he felt should be educated. He said this about the goal of education: "To seek and find a method by which the teachers teach less

Jean Jacques Rousseau

and the learners learn more, by which the schools have less noise, obstinancy, and frustrated endeavor, but more leisure, pleasantness" (Braun & Edwards, 1972, p. 31). Comenius advocated for enjoyable educational experiences and for learners who take charge of their own learning. He also was one of the first to promote the idea that all children should be educated. Rather than teaching just the sons from wealthy families, Comenius wanted boys and girls, bright and dull, and rich and poor children to receive an education.

Jean Jacques Rousseau (1712–1778).   Although Rousseau lived a tumultuous and undisciplined life, which included the abandonment of all five of his children, his educational writings have had a significant influence on the direction of early childhood theory and practice. Rousseau's most well-known book, titled *Emile,* describes the ideal early education of an imaginary child (Rousseau, 1762/1979). From his writings, it is clear that Rousseau was advocating educational experiences that were very different from what children of his day were receiving. He proposed:

• *Negative education.* By this, Rousseau meant that formal educational experiences should be postponed until children are twelve years old.

- *Learning from nature.* Young children could learn all they needed to know from the natural world around them. Books should be forbidden during this period.
- *Education should focus on sensory experiences.* Touching, tasting, and experiencing new sights and sounds were Rousseau's building blocks for early learning.
- *Children need to choose their learning experiences.* Rousseau believed that when left to their own devices, children would select the best tasks for developmental progress.
- *Childhood is a stage in development.* One of the first to make this claim, Rousseau recognized that children can be distinguished from adults in more ways than just size. They think differently, reason differently, and require different ways of learning.

Rousseau's educational theory, although idealistic and naive as presented in *Emile,* has significantly impacted the thinking of many theorists and practitioners. Often referred to as a **naturalist,** his belief in the innate goodness of children and allowing development to simply happen is deeply imbedded in current thought about early childhood education. Much like a flower grows with water and good soil, young children prosper when adults prepare a quality environment for learning, step back, and watch for the results.

Johann Pestalozzi (1746–1827).   Pestalozzi, an early childhood practitioner, was inspired by the writings of Rousseau and was determined to apply Rousseau's principles in raising his own children. While he quickly learned that the unlimited freedom proposed by Rousseau needed to be tempered with adult guidance and limits, Pestalozzi continued to believe in Rousseau's basic ideas and worked to refine their implementation.

In 1799, Napoleon invaded Switzerland and left the town of Stanz with a great many homeless and destitute children. Pestalozzi took charge of an orphanage there, and his educational career took root. Working with children who others had written off as incapable of learning, Pestalozzi was able to demonstrate remarkable progress within a few short months. Gradually, other educators learned of his programs and spent time studying his methods.

Pestalozzi's most well-known publications were actually novels written for the general public of his day. Although the characters in these books portrayed many of his educational thoughts through their actions, most of what we know about Pestalozzi's methods and theories come from the writings of others (e.g., Guimps, 1890). Pestalozzi has been described as a great teacher who made every effort to love and care for his students in addition to educating them. He modeled much of what we currently do in early childhood education:

- *Careful observation of children.* Pestalozzi was a perceptive observer of children and used what he saw to plan learning experiences for them.
- *Recognizing the potential in each child.* He saw every child as having the ability to learn, given the right circumstances. He believed in their potential, when others had given up on them.

- *Importance of teacher–student relationships.* Pestalozzi felt that before children could learn they needed a strong relationship with their teacher. Once the confidence and affection of each child had been won, learning was a much simpler process.

- *Strengthening peer relations.* He encouraged older children to tutor younger students and in general promoted good relations among his students.

- *Sensory learning.* Pestalozzi recognized the importance of learning experiences that took advantage of young children's natural interest in using their senses.

Friedrich Froebel (1782–1852).   After discovering he had an interest and aptitude in teaching, Froebel spent time studying the techniques of Pestalozzi. Although he liked much of what he saw, Froebel eventually developed his own approach to teaching. His educational interests were broad: Froebel wanted to remake all of education. Needing to begin somewhere, however, he focused initially on working with five-year-old children. Froebel named his program the **kindergarten** (meaning "children's garden" in German), and this approach gradually spread throughout Germany and later to the United States.

Froebel wrote two books that outline his approach to teaching young children. In *Education of Man* (Froebel, 1886), he describes his teaching materials and techniques. *Mother-Play and Nursery Songs* (Froebel, 1906) emphasizes the role of mothers in the young child's development.

Froebel's contributions to early childhood education were many. One important idea was his emphasis on the **benefits of childhood play.** Froebel extolled the virtues of play throughout his writings:

> It gives, therefore, joy, freedom, contentment, inner and outer rest, peace with the world. It holds the sources of all that is good. A child that plays thoroughly, with self-active determination, perseveringly until physical fatigue forbids, will surely be a thorough, determined man, capable of self-sacrifice for the promotion of the welfare of himself and others. (Braun & Edwards, 1972, p. 67)

Froebel also emphasized the **value of singing** at home and in school as a pleasant way to learn. He encouraged mothers to spend time singing with their children and also incorporated songs and musical experiences into his kindergarten classroom. Froebel felt that music helped build teacher–student and parent–child relationships, was an excellent tool for teaching young children concepts, and was also fun for both children and adults.

During observations of young children engaged in play, Froebel was intrigued by the number of times they joined hands and made a circle. He incorporated this natural tendency into his teaching, and what we now call **circle time** was born. Froebel recognized that the circle brought children together in a setting that was easy to manage while creating a more personal atmosphere that helped improve interactions.

Maria Montessori (1870–1952).   The courage and determination of Maria Montessori are exemplified by her initial choice of careers. Despite the many obvious

Maria Montessori

and more subtle challenges, she became the first female physician in Italy near the end of the nineteenth century.

Montessori's first professional interest was in mental retardation. She felt that institutionalized children were eager for learning experiences and could, if given appropriate instruction, grow more normally. Like Pestalozzi before her, Montessori took up the cause of young children who the rest of society had rejected. After careful observations of children classified as retarded and the study of earlier educators such as Itard (1962), Seguin (1907), and Froebel, Montessori was ready to begin her educational career.

In 1898, Montessori assumed the directorship of a school for children termed "defective." Her reputation spread when she prepared these "idiot" children to successfully pass examinations for primary certificates. At the time, these examinations were typically the highest educational accomplishment of most Italians.

Montessori's most well-known educational program was opened in 1907 and called **Casa dei Bambini** (Children's House). Located in the slums of Rome, Casa dei Bambini was where Montessori further developed her theories about children and refined her teaching techniques. Montessori detailed her fascinating ideas in several books (e.g., Montessori, 1949/1967), and other writers also have summarized her work (e.g., Lillard, 1972, 1996). A more detailed discussion of her practice and theory can be found in Chapters 3 and 4.

Margaret McMillan (1860–1931).   Margaret McMillan and her sister Rachel had a significant impact on early education in England at about the same time Montessori was gaining popularity in Italy. These early activists were concerned about the health problems of children growing up in low-income areas in London. To help correct the health issues they identified, the McMillan sisters founded the **Open-Air Nursery.** After Rachel's untimely death, Margaret continued to refine their program for young children.

The Open-Air Nursery was designed for children from one to six years of age, and as the name implies, emphasized outdoor play. The McMillans felt that the health benefits of outdoor activities were just what their children needed. The McMillans provided opportunities for gardening, playing in a sandbox, and building with scraps of materials in the "junk heap." Baths, clean clothes, healthy meals, medical and dental care, and learning experiences were additional components of the program.

Margaret McMillan emphasized several important concepts in her program that are considered important in early education today:

- *Facilitating emotional development.* McMillan recognized that young children need more than physical health and intellectual stimulation to develop normally. Emotional well-being was equally important and needed to be addressed by teachers.

- *Parent involvement.* Monthly parent meetings, home visits, strong parent–teacher relations, and support for families during crises were all emphasized in the Open-Air Nursery.

- *Children's art.* McMillan considered children's spontaneous drawings and artwork important to their overall development and made sure they were encouraged.

Lev Vygotsky (1896–1934).   Vygotsky was a Russian scholar who began his study of developmental psychology and education in the 1920s. Unfortunately, his death from tuberculosis at age thirty-seven prematurely ended a brilliant career. Nonetheless, Vygotsky's contributions have been substantial (Charlesworth, 1996). Three important concepts from Vygotsky's work have significantly influenced early childhood education. First is the **zone of proximal development,** the most well-known of his ideas (Vygotsky, 1978). The zone of proximal development is the gap between the child's independent performance of a task and that which he can perform with the help of a more skilled peer or adult. Children who are functioning in their zone are being challenged and growing with the assistance of others at a maximum rate. Second, Vygotsky's thinking about the **relationships between language and thought** in childhood have also influenced teaching and language learning in the early years. Third is the **value of play** in the development of symbolic thinking and the overall growth of children. These ideas are discussed in more detail in Chapter 4.

Jean Piaget (1896–1980).   Piaget is another theorist who has had a major impact on early education. A true scientist from an early age, Piaget published his

CELEBRATING PLAY . . .
Vygotsky's Thoughts on Play

Although Vygotsky's ideas on play don't really qualify as a theory, his writings about play have become very influential in our thinking about its importance (Berk, 1994). In particular, he felt that make-believe (dramatic) play was a major contributor to the child's social, language, and cognitive development. Vygotsky's high regard for play can be seen in the following quote:

Play creates a zone of proximal development in the child. In play, the child always behaves beyond his average age, above his daily behavior; in play it is as though he were a head taller than himself. As in the focus of a magnifying glass, play contains all developmental tendencies in a condensed form and is itself a major source of development. (Vygotsky, 1978, p. 102)

Vygotsky felt that imaginary play has two critical features that help make it so influential in the child's development:

The first characteristic is that play **creates an imaginary situation** that allows the child to work through desires that are unrealizable.

 Andrew is learning as a three-year-old that he must wait for his turn many times in the preschool situation. He doesn't want to do this, and his imaginary play allows Andrew to work through these feelings.

Vygotsky also suggests that the second feature of play is that it **contains rules for behavior.** If children are to successfully complete a play scene, they must follow the accepted rules for social behavior in the situation they are enacting.

Kathryn wants to be the mommy and must conform to the rules of maternal behavior for the play sequence to work.

1. What is the zone of proximal development, and how does play create such a zone?
2. Compare and contrast Vygotsky's ideas on play with the contemporary theories of play discussed in this chapter.

first research investigation at the age of ten. He began his lifelong investigation of mankind's acquisition of knowledge shortly after completing his doctoral studies. Piaget took a job analyzing responses to standardized intelligence tests and was intrigued by children's incorrect answers. After carefully questioning and observing children (including his own), Piaget published his theories concerning intellectual development. These theories are often labeled **constructivist** (Kamii & Ewing, 1996) because they suggest that individuals actively construct knowledge on an ongoing basis. In other words, Piaget theorized that we are all constantly receiving new information and engaging in experiences that lead us to revise our understanding of the world.

Piaget's studies of children continue to influence contemporary educators in many ways. The best-known component of his research was the definition of **stages of intellectual development** (Piaget, 1950). Less well-known is Piaget's research on **moral development** in children (Piaget, 1965). Piaget also studied **play in childhood** (Piaget, 1962) and found that child development was enhanced through these experiences. His work is discussed in more detail in Chapter 4.

FOCUS ON . . .

The Constructivist Perspective on Learning

The constructivist perspective is based on Piaget's assertion that learners actively construct knowledge based on their own individual experiences and understanding.

In a constructivist learning environment, the child creates rather than receives knowledge, and the teacher guides or facilitates this process of discovery. Unlike a traditional classroom where the teacher might lecture or perform demonstrations in front of a group of passive students, the students in a constructivist environment actively learn by doing.

For early childhood educators, this approach makes a lot of sense. After all, children learn a great deal without being formally taught. They are able to understand, communicate, move, and function in the world around them long before they encounter schoolteachers, handouts, tests, homework, and report cards. They learn all these things by simply interacting with their environment.

Here are some characteristics of a constructivist learning environment:

• Learning is a **social and collaborative** endeavor rather than a solitary activity.

• Activities are **learner-centered** rather than teacher-centered.

• Activities are often **cross-disciplinary,** encouraging students to make connections and integrate information, rather than compartmentalize it.

• Topics for inquiry are **driven by students' interests** rather than strict adherence to a fixed curriculum.

• Emphasis is on **understanding and application** rather than rote memorization or copying.

• Assessment is through **authentic measures** rather than traditional or standardized testing.

1. *Spend some time observing in an early childhood classroom, looking for evidence of children learning through the constructivist approach. Describe your findings to others in your class.*

2. *Do you think constructivist learning requires more or less effort on the part of the classroom teacher? Discuss your thoughts with others.*

American Influences

The twentieth century ushered in a period of rapid growth and improvement in American education. Several theorists and practitioners from the early 1900s have had a significant impact on the direction of early childhood education today. These educators relied heavily upon their European predecessors while striking out in new directions to influence young children and their development.

John Dewey (1859–1952).   Dewey's career began as a teacher of philosophy at the university level. After time at several institutions, he settled at the University of Chicago in 1894. It was here that Dewey began to apply his philosophical ideas to the study of education. As his concepts took shape, Dewey's fame spread, and the **Progressive Movement** in American education was born.

John Dewey

The last half of the nineteenth century was a period of rapid growth in the availability of education in America. This was a major step forward, yet at the start of the twentieth century, many were questioning the generally accepted methods and content of schooling. Dewey's ideas were a catalyst for the reform efforts of progressive education in the 1920s and 1930s.

Although his philosophy was embraced by many educators of his day, Dewey was also often misunderstood by his supporters. Braun and Edwards (1972) summarize the major ideas associated with Dewey as follows:

- *Education should be integrated with life.* To make education meaningful, it must be associated with real-life events.
- *Education should preserve social values.* The common values of the culture need to be taught and supported by the schools.
- *True education occurs in social situations.* Dewey felt very strongly that learning was strengthened through social interactions with peers and adults.

- *Children's instincts and powers create starting points for education.* An understanding of child development and individual needs and interests is necessary for teachers planning learning experiences for children.
- *Active learning is essential.* Children must be intellectually and physically involved in their classrooms to truly learn from their experiences.

Arnold Gesell (1880–1961).   With medical training and a doctorate in psychology, Arnold Gesell had unique qualifications for his work in early childhood education. Gesell used his education to research the development of children. Interested in studying their maturational characteristics, he spent thirty years as director of the Yale Clinic of Child Development. In this position, he created a comprehensive collection of data describing normal child development. For children from birth through adolescence, Gesell identified observable changes in growth and behavior categorized into ten major areas.

Gesell authored or co-authored several books (see, e.g., Gesell & Ilg, 1949), which summarize for readers the typical or normative behaviors of children. This information became very popular with parents and teachers who needed clear descriptions of normal child behaviors. Gesell's descriptions continue to be used and are discussed further in Chapter 4.

Patty Smith Hill (1868–1946).   Hill, originally trained in Froebel's methods of kindergarten education, was strongly influenced by the work of John Dewey. By blending the thinking of these two different but compatible philosophies, she was able to create a strong curriculum for young children. Hill's educational efforts became the backbone of kindergarten practice in the United States.

Hill is credited with two very important innovations. First, she helped found the laboratory nursery school at Columbia University Teachers College in 1921. This model program helped train many fine teachers of young children while providing a research site for faculty at the college. Her second contribution was to help organize the National Association for Nursery Education. This group was later renamed the National Association for the Education of Young Children (NAEYC), today's largest and most influential organization of early childhood educators.

Lucy Sprague Mitchell (1878–1967).   While Patty Smith Hill worked at Columbia Teachers College, Lucy Sprague Mitchell labored under similar circumstances, also in New York. Mitchell is credited with helping start the laboratory nursery school at the Bureau of Educational Experiments in 1919. She initiated an excellent model program for young children where researchers could study children and their development. She also trained prospective teachers who left to start their own nursery school programs in other locations. The Bureau of Educational Experiments was later renamed the Bank Street College of Education. This program has been very influential over the years in defining important directions for early childhood education (see Chapter 3 for more information).

Abigail Eliot (1892–1992).   Abigail Eliot made important contributions to early childhood education through her work with low-income nursery school children. After working with the McMillan sisters in their Open-Air Nursery in London, Eliot served as director of the Ruggles Street Nursery in Boston beginning in 1922. In many ways, this nursery school became an early model for the Head Start program.

The Ruggles Street Nursery had the following characteristics:

- *Child-sized equipment*
- *Comprehensive program* (including health care, meeting the needs of the whole child)
- *Variety of materials* (Froebelian, Montessori, and McMillan materials)
- *Full-day program* (including nap)
- *Work with parents*

Historical Events Influencing Early Education

The insights of many early educators have enriched the teaching and learning of young children over the past several centuries. However, historical events as well as people have influenced the directions of early education. During the twentieth century in America, several key events have significantly shaped the ways in which we teach and care for young children, and these are described next.

Child Study Movement

The end of the nineteenth century and beginning of the twentieth century brought a rapidly growing interest in studying children and their development (Weber, 1984). This period is known as the Child Study movement. It may surprise you to know that the main reason for this new-found urge to understand children was the realization that children are qualitatively different from adults. Although we accept this today as common knowledge, for much of the history of mankind, children were viewed simply as miniature adults (Aries, 1962). As teachers and researchers began to recognize that differences existed between children and adults, they were forced to investigate these variations. The Child Study movement was born.

This research effort was important to early childhood education for two main reasons. First, the interest in studying children generated a great deal of very useful **child development information.** People like Arnold Gesell were observing children and carefully documenting data about typical development and the variations between children. This information is still very much in use as an initial planning guide for teachers of young children.

The child study movement was also an important catalyst in the growth of **laboratory nursery schools.** To better understand young children, colleges and universities throughout the nation created nursery schools as research sites for faculty. Some key programs begun during this period include (Braun & Edwards, 1972)

- *Columbia Teachers College:* Under the direction of Patty Smith Hill, this program began in 1921.
- *Merrill-Palmer Institute:* Edna Noble White was this program's first director, beginning in 1922.
- *Yale Guidance Nursery:* Arnold Gesell was instrumental in this nursery program, started in 1926.
- *Bureau of Educational Experiments:* Lucy Sprague Mitchell was the guiding force behind this program, which began in 1919. Eventually, this became the Bank Street College of Education in New York.

In addition to providing research sites for the Child Study movement, the laboratory nursery schools were models of excellence in early education and also stirred interest in prekindergarten programs. As adults learned of these opportunities and recognized the benefits for the development of children, more options became available across the country. Preschool programs for disadvantaged children and cooperative nursery schools are two examples of this increased interest.

The Great Depression

Surprisingly, the depression of the 1930s in the United States had an important impact on early childhood education. Major federal efforts to put people back to work ended up promoting the cause of prekindergarten education. The Works Progress Administration (WPA) took unemployed school teachers, custodians, cooks, and nurses and gave them jobs in government-sponsored preschool programs (Steiner, 1976). The main benefit of these efforts was that nursery education became more widely recognized. With this recognition came acceptance by the American public. Early efforts at parent education were another important spinoff of the WPA programs.

Unfortunately, significant problems also surfaced as a result of the WPA nursery schools. The unemployed educators put to work teaching in the nursery programs were given little or no training for their new roles. The assumption (a false one) was that because they knew how to teach older students, they could easily manage younger children. Teachers were also paid very low wages for their services. The WPA was able to pay teachers only a fraction of their prior salaries. The perception that began to develop during this period was that teachers of young children didn't need much training or salary.

One of the most significant issues facing early childhood education is the problem of low salaries for those providing care and services for young children and their families. While many people are attracted to working with prekindergarten children in preschool and day care situations, few can afford the low salaries and poor benefits associated with the occupation.

Based on data from the Bureau of Labor Statistics, in 1994, child care workers were the lowest-paid workers of the forty-nine occupations studied (National Center for the Early Childhood Work Force, 1995). On a weekly basis, the median salary for child care workers was reported as $158. This income lags behind all others, including janitors ($293), hairdressers ($285), and waiters and waitresses ($256). Elementary school teachers' median weekly salary, on the other hand, is a more reasonable $624.

Here are three things you can consider doing to improve teacher salaries:

Participate in Union Activities.
Some child care workers are beginning to organize into local unions or affiliate with existing groups (National Center for the Early Childhood Work Force, 1995). Early childhood teachers working in public schools can get involved in either the American Federation of Teachers or the National Education Association and their local affiliates.

Seek Program Accreditation.
Since the summer of 1985, early childhood programs have engaged in a process of self-evaluation and growth leading to accreditation by the National Academy of Early Childhood Programs (Bredekamp & Glowacki, 1996; National Association for the Education of Young Children, 1991). Receiving accreditation should help programs make a stronger case for higher teacher salaries.

Promote the Importance of Good Salaries.
Those in the field need to spend time educating the general public about the low pay of early childhood caregivers and the importance of quality care for children. The Worthy Wage Campaign, a national organization, works to create a unified national voice for early childhood workers; to improve the wages, benefits, and working conditions of those working with young children; and to make quality early childhood programs more affordable for all families. Contact them at

National Center for the Early Childhood
Work Force
733 15th Street, NW, Suite 1037
Washington, DC 20005-2112
(202)737-7700
(800)U-R-WORTHY

 _____

1. *Find out the date for this year's Worthy Wage Day, and plan to participate.*

2. *Brainstorm ways in which you could promote the cause of better wages for those working in early childhood education.*

World War II

As America reluctantly became involved in World War II, those left at home were called upon to keep the economy running. The government gave special priority to war-related industries to make sure the equipment needed for the war effort was produced on time. Both government and industry encouraged many women with young children to work in these industries, creating a temporary need for child care. The Lanham Act made federal money available to provide this care.

The most famous child care program from this period was located at the Kaiser Shipyards in Portland, Oregon (Hymes, 1978). Under the guidance of James Hymes, this program implemented many innovations:

- *A building was designed from the beginning for child care.*
- *Child care centers were located at the work site.*
- *Programs were open twenty-four hours a day.*
- *Children could attend when parents needed a night to themselves.*
- *Centers had an infirmary for sick children.*
- *A family consultant was available to assist parents with local community resources.*
- *A home food service allowed parents to pick up a hot meal to take with them.*

These innovations continue to be a model for present-day child care programs.

The Launching of Sputnik

In 1957, the launching of Russia's first satellite into space created a great uproar in America. Sputnik was a visual image that represented to many our failure as a society. We were behind the Russians in the race to conquer this new frontier. Something must be done, people said, to reverse this truly alarming situation. The consensus that emerged from this discussion was that we needed to do a better job of educating children so that American scientists could eventually catch up with their Russian counterparts (Braun & Edwards, 1972).

This attitude led to both positive and negative results. One clear benefit was a renewed interest in preschool education. The general thinking seemed to be that if we started earlier, we could better educate our children. The early years began to be recognized as an important developmental period that needed to be taken advantage of and carefully studied. Another positive result was the increased public support for early education. People were more willing to provide financial assistance for programs that showed promise. More federal money, in particular, was available during the 1960s and 1970s to demonstrate new models of early education and for research on teaching and learning.

Unfortunately, there were also negative outcomes in education, stemming from the launching of Sputnik. One of the most problematic was an overemphasis on intellectual performance. The concern over lagging abilities in mathematics and science in particular led many early educators and the general public to place

VIDEO CASE STUDY:
Early Head Start

Watch the ABC News video segment "Early Head Start" and consider these excerpts:

"Ron Lally studied what makes kids tick and learn for more than 30 years. His theory is that children exposed from day one to a wide range of stimulating activities learn faster and perform better in school . . . In 1970, Lally began studying two groups of infants from Syracuse, New York. One group was placed in daily child care and exposed to intense brain stimulation for nearly four years. The other group was left in the care of their own families. Lally has tracked the groups ever since. What Lally found validated his original theory. The children in the program . . . were more successful, excelled in school, and were four times less likely to get into trouble with the law. Lally says the benefits to society are obvious: less teenage pregnancy, drug use, and crime, which saves us billions every year."

— *Bill Ritter, ABC Correspondent*

"If [children] don't have the proper brain development, they're going to enter into the learning environment, such as school, unprepared and unready to learn. And the result of that is what you see already in our school system. You see numerous kids who are tracked in special ed. You see behavior problems in the school. Eventually, you're going to see dropout rates."

— *Portia Kennel,
Early Head Start Program Director, Chicago*

"I was a single mom. I was raising a child. The [Early Head Start] program was more than just the child care . . . She was learning the whole time that she was in the program. She was learning, and then they did follow-up with all the parents. So we were able to learn how to be better parents."

— *Janice Wagner, Mother*

VIDEO CASE STUDY: **Early Head Start**

Now that you have seen the ABC News video segment, consider the strategy behind Early Head Start programs and the services they provide, as described by the Administration for Children and Families, a division of the Department of Health and Human Services.

Established in 1994, the Early Head Start program benefits low-income families with children under three and pregnant women. Currently, approximately 38,000 children and their families a year receive services; however, new legislation proposes to more than double the number of children in Early Head Start over the next 5 years.

Early Head Start recognizes the powerful research evidence showing that the period from birth to age three is critical to healthy growth and development and to later success in school and in life. As a result, Early Head Start provides early, continuous, intensive, and comprehensive child development and family support services to low-income families with children under the age of three. The goals of the program are to:

- enhance children's physical, social, emotional, and cognitive development

- enable parents to be better caregivers of and teachers to their children

- help parents meet their own goals, including that of economic independence.

The services provided by Early Head Start programs are designed to reinforce and respond to the unique strengths and needs of each child and family. Services include the following:

- quality early education in and out of the home

- home visits, especially for families with newborns and other infants

- parent education, including parent-child activities

- comprehensive health services, including services to women before, during, and after pregnancy

- nutrition education

- ongoing support for parents through case management and peer support groups.

[Based on information provided by the Administration for Children and Families at http://www.acf.dhhs.gov/, a division of the Department of Health and Human Services.]

Early Head Start

Act

Although the focus of the Early Head Start program is providing services and support to children under three and their families in low-income brackets, as a teacher and caregiver, you will be responsible for providing services, support, and information to children and families to some degree in any early childhood environment.

Consider the specific needs of either the neighborhood in which you live or the one you grew up in, the strengths and needs of the children you interact with and their families, and your own talents and interests. Then re-examine the list of services that Early Head Start programs offer (previous page), and devise an outreach activity or service that could help a school or care-giving facility provide services and information to children and their families.

too much importance on the intellectual activities of young children. While the traditional preschool emphasized all aspects of the child's development, the growing expectation was for programs that could demonstrate improved intellectual performance. A second problem associated with Sputnik's launch was the expectation for quick and lasting results. The American public, while providing support for new educational efforts, anticipated speedy solutions that would rapidly help us catch up with the Russians—a wholly unrealistic expectation.

The War on Poverty

The presidencies of John F. Kennedy and Lyndon Johnson increased emphasis on helping low-income families break free from the grip of poverty. The cornerstone of this War on Poverty was federal support for early childhood programs designed to assist young disadvantaged children (Hymes, 1978). The thinking of policy makers was that the cycle of poverty could only be broken by providing quality educational experiences for children from low-income families. These children would then end up in better-paying jobs, and all of society would benefit. Beginning in 1965, the federal government provided money to local sites for preschool-aged children from low-income families.

The most well-known option for disadvantaged children to come out of this period was the Head Start program (see Chapter 1). The early research conducted on the effectiveness of Head Start (J. Coleman, 1966) was disappointing, with minimal initial success in improving children's intelligence scores and with the gains eventually washing out by the time children reached the third grade.

But Head Start officials survived the criticisms that came with these results by reemphasizing the comprehensive nature of the program. Over the years, it has been effective in serving the needs of the low-income children enrolled. Head Start's emphases on developing the whole child and working closely with families are important elements to be modeled by others in early education and care.

The inability of Head Start and other compensatory education programs to produce long-term IQ score gains in their students led many to believe that a more concentrated effort over a longer period of time was needed. **Project Follow Through,** begun in 1969, was funded by the federal government as a way to continue this assistance to low-income children in the primary grades. A variety of model programs were funded at sites across the country, and research was conducted to determine their effectiveness. Although the research results continued to be disappointing, Project Follow Through had a significant impact on early education.

Other federally funded **compensatory education programs** for disadvantaged children were also initiated during the War on Poverty. These programs were each designed to assist low-income children to catch up with their more advantaged peers in intellectual functioning. The model programs developed during this period still continue to influence thinking and practice today. Most importantly, these programs created a stronger link between preschool and primary education.

Most of the models used many of the same techniques that had been successful at the preschool level to assist primary children in their development. Early childhood educators began to view children from birth through age eight as similar in many ways and started planning educational experiences that reflected this perspective.

Summary

This chapter introduced key historical figures who have had a significant impact on early childhood education. Major figures from Europe are Martin Luther, John Amos Comenius, Jean Jacques Rousseau, Johann Pestalozzi, Friedrich Froebel, Maria Montessori, Margaret McMillan, Lev Vygotsky, and Jean Piaget. In the United States, John Dewey, Arnold Gesell, Patty Smith Hill, Lucy Sprague Mitchell, and Abigail Eliot had a significant impact on early education.

The Child Study movement, America's depression of the 1930s, World War II, the launching of Sputnik, and the War on Poverty begun in the 1960s were important events influencing early education.

∾ For Discussion and Action

1. Choose a historical figure discussed in this chapter who interests you, and spend some time reflecting on his or her contributions to early education today. Share your thoughts with others in your class.

2. Read a portion of a text by one of the historical figures mentioned in this chapter. What did you learn about this person from this task? Share your findings with others.

3. Investigate one of the historical events discussed in this chapter in more detail. What did you learn?

∾ Building Your Personal Library

Braun, S., & Edwards, E. (1972). *History and theory of early childhood education*. Belmont, CA: Wadsworth. This is probably the best text to overview historical people and events that have influenced early childhood education. It includes extensive quotes from the works of famous early childhood theorists and practitioners.

Weber, E. (1984). *Ideas influencing early childhood education*. New York: Teachers College Press. This scholarly text is an excellent resource describing many of the historical people and events discussed in this chapter and presents others for further study.

Wortham, S. (1992). *Childhood 1892–1992*. Wheaton, MD: Association for Childhood Education International. An interesting look at the history of childhood over approximately the last hundred years. The book provides important insights into changes that have occurred during that time.

3 Types of Programs

In this chapter you will

- Identify the diverse types of program models associated with early education.

- Study the Montessori model and its implications for teaching young children.

- Investigate the High/Scope curriculum as it is used in preschool and primary classrooms.

- Look at the Bank Street model for early education.

- Understand the elements of the Reggio Emilia program and its applications in the United States.

Amanda is taking her first course in early childhood education and is trying to make sense of all that she is learning. The issue she is currently struggling with concerns early childhood program models. Amanda has learned about Montessori education, the High/Scope model, the Bank Street program, and the Reggio Emilia approach. Is one better than the others for young children?

The programs that she has studied share many similarities, which makes it more difficult to sort out her thoughts. Amanda's thinking is further complicated by the fact that she likes different elements of each model. Additional information would be helpful to her as she evaluates the options. It would be nice, for example, to see each of the programs in action, but the local early childhood centers don't clearly identify themselves with the specific models Amanda has studied. ∿

The issues you will face as you read this chapter will probably mirror those that Amanda identified in the preceding scenario. Several clearly defined models for early childhood education are currently in practice; making conclusive judgments about them without in-depth study is difficult. Also, pure models of the different approaches are hard to find, making it unlikely that you can compare each of the models in action.

You need to be aware of the different program models being promoted for educating young children and to understand their similarities and differences. Think about what appeals to you personally, and plan to learn more later about these models. Remember, this is just the beginning point for your understanding of early childhood education.

This chapter presents an overview of the four major program models for early childhood education, discussing the key elements of each. These options significantly influence the philosophy behind and teaching in early childhood programs across the country. Figure 3–1 summarizes the key features of each approach.

Program	Key Features
Montessori education	Work experiences rather than play. Special materials for specific learning tasks. Carefully prepared classroom environment.
High/Scope program	Based on the theory of Jean Piaget. Use of a plan–do–review sequence. Classroom organized into centers. Emphasis on cognitive development.
Bank Street model	All aspects of child development are addressed in the curriculum. The work of Freud, Erikson, Piaget, and Dewey all influence the model. Commercial equipment is supplemented with teacher-made and child-made materials. Emphasis is on an integrated curriculum.
Reggio Emilia approach	Emphasis is on in-depth projects to facilitate learning. A special workshop area is used to record in visual form what is learned. Parents are expected to share responsibilities in educating children. Strong collaboration among staff members is encouraged.

The Montessori Program

The teaching and writing of Maria Montessori led to a unique model for early learning that has had a significant influence on early childhood education. The Montessori approach has both strong supporters and vocal critics (Roopnarine & Johnson, 1993).

One major difference between Montessori education and many other early childhood programs in the United States is the emphasis on work experiences rather than play times. Although these concepts share similarities, the differences are significant.

Montessori's Work Experiences

Montessori described children's interactions with materials in the classroom as **work tasks** (Montessori, 1965). Although children are free to choose the materials they want to spend time with, these items are used in very specific ways. Before the child is allowed to work on a task, the teacher demonstrates how the materials are to be used. Precise steps are clearly presented, and any deviations from these procedures result in a new demonstration by the teacher or guidance into a different activity.

In classrooms based on Maria Montessori's approach to teaching, children are free to choose from a variety of tasks that she called *work experiences.* Two examples of these tasks follow:

Cylinder Blocks

One popular Montessori work task is the cylinder block. Several different types are used, some varying only in the depth of the cylinder, others only in the diameter. The more difficult ones require the child to differentiate both depth and diameter. Children take the cylinders out and place them carefully on the table and then replace them in the appropriate holes.

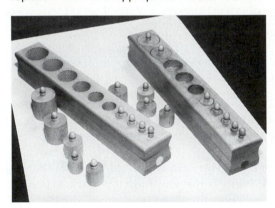

Buttoning Frames

Montessori developed several types of buttoning and tying frames, expecting children to unbutton/untie the frame contents and then reconnect them, which develops fine motor skills.

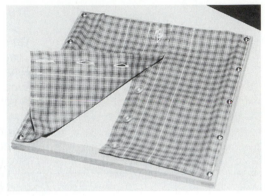

1. *What are the educational benefits of these work tasks? Would you include them in the early childhood classroom? Why or why not?*

2. *How do Montessori's work experiences compare with the play options presented in Chapter 5? Identify the similarities and differences.*

An example of a work task used in Montessori classrooms is the spooning of dried peas. On a child-sized tray, the Montessori teacher organizes two bowls (one filled with dried peas) and a spoon. When a child shows interest in these materials, the teacher carefully demonstrates how the child should place the bowls, hold the spoon, and spoon peas from one bowl to the next without spilling. The child is then free to engage in this work task as often as he wants.

Play Times

Play experiences, on the other hand, are much more open-ended. Children have many choices of interesting materials and use those toys and equipment in their own unique ways. Play materials usually don't require demonstration by the teacher. Children understand their use and simply take them from their storage location and engage in play. A set of wooden blocks, for example, is an excellent play material that leads to building castles, roads, towers, or anything else that comes to mind.

Characteristics of the Montessori Classroom

Montessori's ideas of work and play and her views of child growth and development (discussed in Chapter 4) provide a clear rationale for the materials in the Montessori classroom, the organization of the classroom environment, and the teacher's role in a child's education.

Montessori Materials. Because of her work with poor children in the slums of Rome (see Chapter 2 for a brief biographical sketch), Montessori felt very strongly that the materials used in her classrooms should be beautiful (Lillard, 1996). They were constructed with care from only the finest woods and other materials and carefully finished to look and feel good to children. For many of her students, this equipment was one of very few contacts with truly beautiful materials.

Montessori designed her equipment with other specific characteristics in mind as well (Standing, 1962):

- *Careful attention to concept development.* Each piece of equipment was designed to teach specific concepts to children as they used them.
- *Graduated difficulty/complexity.* As children develop, they need increasingly challenging materials to stimulate their continued growth.
- *Self-correcting.* Whenever possible, Montessori-designed materials are self-correcting, eliminating the need to consult an adult.
- *Sensory-oriented.* Montessori considered all of the senses to be important, and she designed her materials to stimulate their use as part of the learning process.

Classroom Organization. Montessori carefully organized her materials and equipment in her classroom so that children could easily and effectively use them (Lillard, 1996). One characteristic of this organization is the **child-sized equipment** she used. She designed tables and chairs with young children's bodies in mind. She also designed storage shelves, sinks, drinking fountains, toilets, and other equipment at the appropriate height so that children could easily use them.

This Montessori teacher shows students how to trace letters made from sandpaper.

Precise organization is another characteristic of the work tasks in a Montessori classroom. The teacher stores each activity in a specific place and carefully organizes the materials for easy use by students. The teacher stores many of the work tasks on trays so that children can take them to their own work space and use the materials and return them easily to their proper storage spot. The washing-up tray, for example, is stored on a shelf in the home living center and typically contains a child-sized pitcher, bowl, washcloth, soap, soap dish, and apron all neatly organized for use by children.

A third characteristic of organization in the Montessori classroom is the use of **individual work space** for each child. Typically, a small rug or mat defines the personal space children need for their work tasks. During work time, children bring out their rug, place it on the floor or at a table, and then select the task they want to use. These mats encourage children to focus their energies on the work before them.

Montessori classrooms are loosely organized into centers that differ somewhat from the typical early childhood classroom. Lillard (1972) identifies four categories of materials that are used in each of these centers:

• *Daily living materials.* These materials involve the physical care of the person or the environment. A child-sized dustpan and broom are examples of this type.

- *Sensorial materials.* Montessori saw the development of all the senses as an important way to help young children learn. These materials help refine the senses while assisting in intellectual development. Montessori's sound cylinders, which the teacher uses to help children discriminate between sounds of different materials placed in wooden cylinders, are examples of this type.

- *Academic materials.* The teacher uses these materials to teach language arts, mathematics, geography, and science. Children naturally progress from the sensorial to the academic materials. Montessori classrooms provide numerous metal shapes that students trace as they develop the physical skills necessary for later writing tasks.

- *Cultural and artistic materials.* This area contains materials that help prepare children for later artistic expression. For example, Montessori teachers believe that children need practice in walking a line on the floor as they prepare for future music and dance expression. As children develop their sense of balance and learn to better control hands and feet, they develop the skills needed for rhythm and dance experiences.

Role of the Teacher. The formal training of Montessori teachers is an extensive process. Prospective candidates must thoroughly study child development, understand the educational values of all the materials used in the classroom, become sensitive to the appropriate times to present work tasks to students, and gain experience in interacting with children.

Teachers in a Montessori classroom operate on three basic principles (Roopnarine & Johnson, 1993):

- A *carefully prepared environment.* The first and most important role for a Montessori teacher is the thorough preparation of the classroom environment. When children can work with materials that meet their developmental needs, they can spend many productive hours engaged in work tasks.

- An *attitude of humility.* Montessori teachers recognize that children's inner needs are very difficult to understand. At the same time, adult attempts to assist in meeting needs are often misguided. Truly effective teachers must approach their roles humbly and constantly evaluate their own motives and interactions with children.

- *Respect for children's individuality.* A thorough understanding of child development and individual differences is essential for the Montessori teacher. Knowing and respecting these differences between children helps the teacher focus on the positive characteristics each child possesses.

Montessori's ideas and materials have a relatively small but loyal group of supporters both in the United States and around the world. The strong emphasis on highly structured work-oriented tasks, however, is generally in conflict with the play orientation of most American early childhood classrooms. Montessori's approach is most popular with parents of gifted children who seek a structured learning environment to stimulate their children.

FOCUS ON...
Montessori Options

Montessori education began as a program for low-income children from four to seven years of age. Today, the principles of this approach are being used with preschool-through high school-aged students. Although most of these options are private schools for mostly middle-class students, growing numbers of public school programs are using the Montessori method (Chattin-McNichols, 1992).

Montessori programs in the United States are generally associated with one of two major associations. The **American Montessori Society** is a group dedicated to implementing the ideas of Montessori in the United States. This association has adapted Montessori's methods and materials for use in American schools, in an attempt to make the approach more widely accepted here. The association is headquartered in New York:

American Montessori Society
150 5th Avenue
New York, NY 10011

The more traditional methods and materials Montessori developed are promoted through the **Association Montessori Internationale.** Montessori programs throughout Europe, India, and the rest of the world generally associate themselves with this organization. A portion of American programs also affiliate with the international association. The address for this group is:

Association Montessori Internationale
U.S. Branch
170 W. Schofield
Rochester, NY 14617

1. Search the Internet for more information about either of these organizations. Share what you found with your classmates.

2. Talk to a teacher or administrator in a Montessori program, and find out about their affiliation. Discuss differences between associations with this person.

The High/Scope Curriculum

The High/Scope curriculum model has had a major influence on early childhood education for over thirty years (Bredekamp, 1996). David Weikart and others created the Perry Preschool Program in the 1960s as a model approach to helping disadvantaged preschool children develop the skills needed to succeed in the public school system. The program continues to emphasize the cognitive understanding required for academic success in reading and mathematics (DeVries & Kohlberg, 1987).

After several years of federal funding, a private organization called the High/Scope foundation took over responsibility for continuing the model. This curricular approach, although originally designed for preschool-aged children, has been successfully used with primary children in recent years (Bredekamp, 1996).

FOCUS ON . . .
Constructivist Early Childhood Education Programs

Constructivist education developed in response to Jean Piaget's theory of intellectual development (see Chapters 2 and 4). Basically, Piaget felt that children learn by actively constructing understanding based on their interactions with the people and objects around them. Young children learn basic properties of water, for example, by playing with water in the sink, tub, and creek outdoors.

The application of Piaget's ideas have led to several programs that have been termed *constructivist.* The High/Scope model described in this chapter is one such program. Rheta DeVries, George Forman, and Constance Kamii have each described their thoughts on constructivist education in separate books. Although it is beyond the scope of this text to describe the similarities and differences here, the citations for each perspective follow so that you can study these programs in more detail:

- DeVries, R., & Kohlberg, L. (1987). *Constructivist early education: Overview and comparison with other programs.* Washington, DC: National Association for the Education of Young Children.
- Forman, G., & Hill, F. (1984). *Constructive play: Applying Piaget in the preschool.* Menlo Park, CA: Addison-Wesley.
- Kamii, C., & DeVries, R. (1978). *Physical knowledge in preschool education: Implications of Piaget's theory.* Upper Saddle River, NJ: Merrill/Prentice Hall.

1. *Observe young children as they play in an early childhood classroom. Does their activity appear to be a process of constructing knowledge? Why or why not?*
2. *Can young children learn in other ways besides constructing knowledge? If so, describe how this is done. If not, why not?*

Theoretical Basis

The High/Scope curriculum is grounded in the theoretical perspectives of Jean Piaget, who believed that children learn best when they build understanding through direct experiences with people and objects in the world around them. While emphasizing the development of the whole child, this program focuses on strengthening children's cognitive skills through active, hands-on learning experiences. This cognitively oriented curriculum is founded on the belief that children cannot understand themselves without first being able to place themselves in time and space and to classify and order objects and events (Weikart, Rogers, Adcock, & McClelland, 1971, p. 6).

The High/Scope program is designed to help children develop logico-mathematical and spatiotemporal understanding of the world around them

(M. Hohmann & Weikart, 1995). **Logicomathematical relationships** include organizing objects into groups according to common characteristics and ordering items from smallest to largest. These tasks are based on Piaget's studies of logic and number. **Spatiotemporal relationships** focus on helping children understand relational concepts such as up/down, over/under, and inside/outside. Event sequences and cause-and-effect relationships are also emphasized.

The Plan–Do–Review Sequence

To help children develop stronger conceptual understandings, the High/Scope curriculum uses a procedure called the **plan–do–review sequence** (M. Hohmann & Weikart, 1995). The teacher encourages children to plan the tasks they want to accomplish during free choice time, engage in those activities, and then spend time later in the day reflecting on what they learned.

Children typically engage in **planning time** in small groups of four or five, working with a teacher. Children identify activities they would like to try during work time, and the teacher helps them refine their thinking to produce a clear, structured plan for the work period ahead. The teacher uses a variety of motivational strategies to assist children in making decisions about their school day. For example, a set of pretend walkie-talkies could be used to help children communicate their plans to others.

During do time *in the High/Scope curriculum, children spend their* work time *carrying out activities that they have planned.*

Teachers often refer to the **do time** in the High/Scope curriculum as *work time;* it directly follows the planning period. In this model, teachers organize classroom space into areas where children spend their work time with blocks, art projects, quiet activities, and dramatic play. Teachers give children a large block of time (usually forty to sixty minutes) to carry out their planned activities.

The **review time** is the last of the three components of the plan–do–review sequence and typically follows the work period cleanup. Teachers can conduct this recall time either in small groups or as a whole class. Again, teachers assist the children in reviewing their work experiences in a variety of developmentally appropriate ways. Drawing a picture of the block structure built, discussing who they spent time with, and reviewing the plans made earlier in the day are examples of the techniques used during this period.

The Curriculum

Teachers in the High/Scope program emphasize eight **key experiences** as they plan for their time with children (Weikart et al., 1971):

1. **Active learning.** Teachers expect children to initiate and carry out their own tasks in the classroom. Teachers encourage manipulation of materials in all areas of the High/Scope classroom.
2. **Using language.** Teachers emphasize oral and written language. Teachers encourage children to talk with others about their experiences and feelings as they go through the school day.
3. **Experiencing and representing.** Children need many opportunities to experience through their senses and represent those activities through music, movement, art, and role playing.
4. **Classification.** The ability to notice similarities and differences among objects grows during the early childhood years. Teachers provide many opportunities for children to grow in their understanding of classification because of its importance in later mathematical learning.
5. **Seriation.** Another important foundation for mathematics is the ability to order objects from smallest to largest on the basis of some criteria such as length, weight, or width.
6. **Number concepts.** Understanding what *fiveness* means is another mathematical concept that High/Scope teachers promote.
7. **Spatial relationships.** Children gain understandings of concepts such as under/over, up/down, and in/out as they interact with materials in their environment.
8. **Time.** Although the concept of time develops slowly, children gradually learn concepts about seasons, past and future events, and the order of activities as they work with tasks and communicate their results to adults and others.

Starting from its beginnings as the Perry Preschool Project, the High/Scope program has researched the effectiveness of the model. Because of the diligence of the program founders, some of the best long-term research on the effectiveness of early childhood programs for low-income children comes from High/Scope. Having kept track of former students for nearly thirty years, the program research provides very convincing evidence of the values of early education. Schweinhart and Weikart (1993) summarize these findings from interviews with students at age twenty-seven:

- A higher percentage of High/Scope students had completed high school than nonprogram students.

- Fewer students had been arrested by the police.

- More young adults from High/Scope had a job at age nineteen than those not attending the program.

- A greater percentage of these young people were self-supporting as young adults.

- Nearly three times as many former students owned their own homes.

- Fewer students had been classified as special education students.

These results translate into considerable savings to the public. Lower costs for special education, jails, and police interventions; higher income levels; and less reliance on welfare services all mean that early intervention programs can be highly cost-effective. Schweinhart and Weikart (1993) estimate a savings of approximately seven dollars for every dollar invested in early intervention programs.

1. Read Schweinhart and Weikart (1993), and discuss the implications of this research for early childhood education.

2. If early intervention is so effective, why aren't more options available to young children? Talk this over with someone not working in the education community.

Structure of the Class Day

The High/Scope model emphasizes that the best learning experiences occur when children have a consistent classroom routine. Teachers carefully plan special events such as field trips and discuss them with children ahead of time. This adherence to a planned sequence of events helps give children the control they need to successfully learn from the people and materials in their environment (M. Hohmann & Weikart, 1995).

A typical half-day classroom schedule in the High/Scope program includes the following elements:

- *Planning time.* The day begins with time in small groups where children plan their work experiences with the assistance of a teacher. Children have consistent opportunities to share with teachers their ideas and plans and then learn to act on their choices.

- *Work time.* This period is generally the longest time children spend in any one activity during the day. Children select their activities for this time based on the planning conducted earlier and engage in the tasks at their own pace. Teachers during this time are there to observe and assist where needed.

- *Cleanup time.* This period is a time to restore order to the classroom environment following the preceding work experiences. It also becomes additional learning time as children sort and return materials to their proper storage locations.

- *Recall time.* Children have the opportunity each day to summarize what they have learned during the work period. This recall period helps bring closure to the earlier planning and work times and assists children in building stronger conceptual understandings.

- *Small-group time.* Teachers carefully plan this structured activity and conduct it with four or five children in a small-group setting. While teachers expect children to participate in these activities, drawn from their backgrounds and experiences, teachers encourage children to add their own insights along the way.

- *Large-group circle time.* This component of the class day consists of ten to fifteen minutes of games, songs, finger plays, sharing, and a short story. This helps children develop group social skills as they engage in a variety of motivating experiences.

A full-day High/Scope program includes additional elements (C. Hohmann, 1996). Outside time provides children with opportunities for play and work experiences in that setting. Meal times are valuable opportunities for learning in addition to being necessary for physical well-being. Most full-day programs provide both breakfast and lunch for students. A nap/quiet time gives children the chance to rest and prepare for further learning later in the day.

The Teacher's Role

Teachers in a High/Scope program work with children to strengthen their overall development, while specifically emphasizing cognitive skills. Roopnarine and Johnson (1993) identify four key components to these interactions with young children:

- *Teachers as active learners.* High/Scope teachers are active learners themselves as they work with children. By modeling excitement and interest in learning, they encourage children to do the same. This attitude also helps teachers prepare more interesting activities and materials for use in the classroom.

- *Careful observers.* Good teachers need to make thorough, detailed observations of children to understand their developmental abilities and plan motivating activities for them. The High/Scope program has developed an observation guide called the Child Observation Record (COR) to assist teachers in this effort (Schweinhart, 1993).

- *Plan and organize the environment.* A key role for teachers is preparing the classroom for students' work and play activities. Although teachers maintain overall consistency in the environment, students need new materials to stimulate their

Observation is an important tool for the early childhood educator. Teachers use observation to assess children's developmental understanding, gain insight into behavioral patterns, and evaluate the effectiveness of the materials and activities in the early childhood classroom. The High/Scope Foundation developed an observation tool to help teachers in their efforts to better understand children.

The Child Observation Record (COR) requires training to use accurately. It is designed to assess each child's behavior in six categories (Schweinhart, 1993):

- *Initiative*—the ability to make and carry out choices, engaging in complex play scenarios
- *Creative representation*—constructing with manipulatives, expression through art activities, pretending
- *Social relationships*—how effectively children relate to adults; the ability to make and keep friends
- *Music and movement*—the ability to move to music, engaging in rhythmic activities; making music

- *Language and literacy*—interest in, and understanding of, the beginning reading and writing processes
- *Logic and mathematics*—the ability to sort, understand number concepts, and sequence using different criteria

Beginning six to eight weeks into the school year, teachers observe each child in each of these six categories. Teachers record brief notes describing the child's behavior and then evaluate the students in relation to the COR standards. By repeating this process two or three additional times during the year, teachers develop a clear picture of each child's understanding and progress. This approach is much more useful as an evaluation tool than the more traditional tests and grades used in most elementary schools.

1. *Talk to an early childhood educator, and find out how she uses observation as a tool in understanding the child's development.*
2. *Can you identify either strengths or potential weaknesses of using observation in the early childhood classroom?*

growth and development. Minor modifications each week help keep children involved in their school day.

- *Positive interactions with children.* High/Scope teachers work hard to communicate effectively with children. These positive interactions include being a good listener, asking challenging open-ended questions, and motivating children to reach higher levels of understanding.

The Bank Street Model

A third important model for early childhood education is called the **Bank Street approach,** which was developed at the Bank Street College in New York. Initially designed in the 1930s at what was then called the Bureau of Educational Experiments, this model continues to have a strong influence on theory and practice in the field.

Although this program also promotes a constructivist approach similar to the emphasis in the High/Scope curriculum, Bank Street is best described as a **developmental interactionalist model** (Weber, 1984). The Bank Street curriculum addresses all aspects of child development in a setting that encourages both interpersonal interactions and learning experiences that integrate intellectual, social, and emotional understandings.

Theoretical Underpinnings

The Bank Street approach identifies three major theoretical perspectives that form the foundation for the model (A. Mitchell & David, 1992):

- *The psychoanalytic perspective.* The writings of Freud and others, particularly Erik Erikson (see Chapter 4 for further details), clarify children's psychological/social/emotional development. This information guides the Bank Street teacher's activities for these aspects of development.
- *Piaget's cognitive developmental theory.* Piaget's ideas on how human intelligence changes during the early childhood years are the basis for this component of the Bank Street curriculum.
- *John Dewey and progressive education.* Dewey emphasized the importance of social learning experiences and the values of active involvement of children in the educational process. Both of these ideas strongly influence the Bank Street model.

Program Goals

The Bank Street program has four broad goals (DeVries & Kohlberg, 1987). The first of these is to **enhance competence.** This goal includes building not only children's knowledge and skills but also the more subjective elements of competence, such as self-esteem, resourcefulness, and resilience.

A second broad goal of the program is to develop **individuality, or identity.** Teachers encourage children to develop qualities of self-hood. Teachers assist children in the process of learning what makes them unique and building on individual strengths. The program fosters an attitude of independence by allowing children to make choices, develop preferences, and learn from their mistakes.

A third objective is to positively influence **socialization.** Young children need considerable practice and assistance as they work through the complex process of becoming a social being. Learning to recognize and respond appropriately to the points of view of others is one major challenge faced. The ability to use a variety of communication strategies to interact positively with adults and other children in work and play situations requires much additional practice.

The final goal of the Bank Street model is an **integration of functions.** Children are guided in understanding the inter-relatedness of things and people in

FOCUS ON . . .
The Behaviorist Perspective

Dewey's progressive movement began as an alternative to what is now referred to as the *behaviorist perspective*. Based on the theories of people such as Watson (1924) and Skinner (1974), this approach continues to be popular in elementary and secondary schools across the country. The behaviorist perspective is at odds, however, with the developmentally appropriate approach emphasized in this book.

The Behaviorist Teacher

- Deals only with observable behaviors.
- Breaks a learning task down into its smallest components and teaches them to children in the appropriate sequence.
- Plans the curriculum first and then matches children with those plans.
- Spends most of her time engaged in direct instruction: sharing information with children in small- and large-group settings.
- Uses positive reinforcement, punishment, and ignoring as primary tools of management and discipline.

The Developmentally Appropriate Teacher

- Deals with observable behaviors and also with motives for behaviors and with feelings.

- Often allows children to discover appropriate steps in learning.
- Understands each child's developmental abilities and then plans the curriculum.
- Spends much of her time facilitating children's hands-on learning through playful experiences.
- Uses a variety of techniques for guidance and discipline, many of which emphasize counseling and communication strategies.

The behavioristic ideas presented here are worthwhile when used in moderation but should not be considered the primary methods for teaching and learning in a developmentally appropriate classroom.

1. *Spend some time observing in a primary classroom. Did you see any of the behaviorist's ideas presented here? Discuss your findings with your peers.*

2. *Which of these strategies would be easier for you to implement as a classroom teacher: the behaviorist approach or a developmentally appropriate one? Discuss this issue with others.*

---

the world around them. For example, rather than compartmentalizing the teaching of mathematics or science, the Bank Street program integrates these subjects into the study of topics such as recycling or aging.

Governing Principles

Understanding child development and then using that information in the planning of activities for young children is essential in the Bank Street model.

Given an exciting environment that can be freely explored, children will actively engage in learning about the world around them.

A. Mitchell and David (1992) identify six general developmental principles that guide the program:

- *Child development is a complex process.* Some general concepts are helpful in describing this process, such as stages of development and moving from simple to more complex behaviors. It is important to realize, however, that each child differs from the average and that development varies between children.

- *Behavior varies and is often unpredictable.* Although it would be nice to have a checklist that allows us to predict what children will do next, many factors may cause children to engage in more mature behavior today and in less-advanced interactions tomorrow.

- *Developmental progress includes both stability and instability.* Periods of stability allow children the opportunity to consolidate their understandings and refine concepts. As children approach developmental milestones and are challenged to develop new understandings, they face times of uncertainty and instability in their knowledge. Both are necessary for healthy development.

- *Motivation to learn about the world lies within each child.* Given an exciting environment that can be freely explored, children will actively engage in learning about the world around them.

- *Developing a sense of self is essential.* Critical to overall development is the process of learning about capabilities and understanding one's uniqueness. Children who develop a positive self-concept become active, independent learners.

- *Conflict is necessary for development.* As children mature, their ideas and wants come in conflict with others. Children need strategies for dealing with these natural conflicts in positive ways.

Although none of the programs described in this chapter are designed exclusively for students who are gifted and talented, each can accommodate these students and provide quality educational experiences for them. Typically, three approaches to gifted education can be found in the United States (Piirto, 1999):

• *Separate education.* In this option, children who are identified as gifted and talented are isolated from other students and taught in a separate classroom within the school. While providing potential benefits, this option runs counter to the current emphasis on integrating children with special needs into the regular classroom.

• *Accelerated education.* In this type of program, children who are gifted and talented either skip grades in the public school system, work with older children and their teacher to learn more advanced topics, or use more accelerated materials more independently in their regular classroom. Although it moves gifted and talented children more rapidly through required subjects,

this approach may fail to stimulate and challenge these students.

• *Enrichment education.* Children in this program type remain in their regular classroom and receive experiences that extend and expand learning through special projects and activities. This option allows children who are gifted and talented to socialize and interact more normally with their peers while still receiving the stimulation they need for exciting learning experiences. Enrichment programs support the effort to integrate all children with special needs in the regular classroom.

1. *Talk to a primary teacher about how she deals with students who are gifted and talented. Which of the three options described here best describes the teacher's responses? Discuss your findings with others.*

2. *Do some reading on gifted education. What issues did you encounter? Share your insights with classmates.*

Curriculum and Materials

The activities and materials found in a Bank Street classroom reflect the goals and principles described previously here. One essential characteristic is a learning environment that allows children to choose their preferred activities and materials (DeVries & Kohlberg, 1987). Areas for building with blocks, dress-up, sand and water play, books, and art are typical in this model. During much of the class day, children are allowed to choose the activities and materials that they want to use for play and work experiences.

Although commercial toys and equipment are common in Bank Street programs, classrooms also use **teacher-made and child-made materials** (A. Mitchell & David, 1992). Some simple rhythm instruments made by the teacher, for example, could be selected by children during choice time for exploration and use. In addition, teachers in the Bank Street program encourage children to make their own books, read them to others, and then place them in the book area for others to enjoy.

Another important characteristic of the Bank Street model is its emphasis on an **integrated curriculum** (Weber, 1984). Rather than attempting to separate mathematics, science, and literacy topics, for example, teachers work hard to integrate these content areas into experiences that center around thematic studies of interest to children. A field trip to a local park for a group of second-grade children might lead to a discussion of the problems associated with litter and the broader topic of what happens to our garbage. This theme could be developed by the teacher into several activities that combine mathematical, science, and literacy skills.

Strong **two-way communication with parents** is yet another valued component of the Bank Street program (A. Mitchell & David, 1992). Parents are important allies in the educational process. They provide teachers with much useful information about attitudes, feelings, and stressors, while assisting in essential ways with developmental progress. Effective communication between home and school is the foundation needed for taking full advantage of all that parents have to offer.

The Reggio Emilia Program

In recent years, the preschool programs of Reggio Emilia, Italy, have captured the imaginations of early childhood educators in the United States. Often referred to as a **project approach** because of the emphasis on in-depth investigations of topics of interest to children and teachers, the educational experiences these preschools provide are truly remarkable (New, 1990). With adult help, children in Reggio Emilia schools document their learning through conversations, photographs, and artwork that are insightful and detailed.

An exhibit that includes photographs and projects completed by children in the Reggio Emilia schools and is titled "The Hundred Languages of Children" has been touring the United States for the past several years and provides many examples of experiences in the Reggio Emilia classroom.

> Few walk away unmoved by its visual impact. They remember the carefully selected photographs, most often grouped in sequences, that are vibrant records of children's experiences and explorations as they investigate various aspects of a particular theme. Even more beguiling are the extraordinary pictures and objects made by the children themselves. (Hendrick, 1997, p. 28)

What makes the Reggio Emilia program so remarkable? According to program founders, it is a combination of fundamental ideas that must all be present for the model to be successful (Gandini, 1993). Many of these components are present in other programs for young children. The difference may be in the intensity with which they are applied in Reggio schools (Bredekamp, 1993). The following sections describe the key elements of this unique program.

A project is an extended study of a topic usually undertaken by a group of children, sometimes by a whole class, and occasionally by an individual child. The study is an investigation into various aspects of a topic that is of interest to the participating children and judged worthy of their attention by their teachers. (Roopnarine & Johnson, 1993, p. 209)

Although the Reggio Emilia program is the most recent example of the project approach in early education, the methods have been a part of educational experiences since at least the 1920s and the work of John Dewey. More recently, the "open education" movement in the United States in the 1960s and 1970s relied on project work.

Four key steps are involved in implementing project work (Roopnarine & Johnson, 1993):

- *Selecting a topic.* This is a very important step that generally requires considerable guidance from the classroom teacher. The topic possibilities are limited only by the imaginations of children and teachers but should be based on children's own firsthand experiences. They should also be topics that children can investigate in the school setting.
- *Beginning the project.* Teachers encourage children to share their own understanding of the topic through drawings, writings, or dramatic play. This helps everyone involved start with a common understanding of the issue being studied.
- *Doing the project.* Children and teachers engage in gathering new information on the topic primarily through real-world experiences. Taking field trips, carefully observing and manipulating objects, and talking directly with people who have additional information on the topic can all be productive ways of collecting new knowledge.
- *Ending the project.* Children need procedures for consolidating the new information they have gathered. Children can summarize what they have learned through artwork, photographs, displays, or a discussion with others not involved in the project.

1. *Discuss with your classmates project work you have been involved in or have seen in the classroom.*
2. *Talk to a teacher about the use of project work. What did she see as the strengths and problems with this approach?*

The Environment

The physical space in a Reggio Emilia school is designed to foster communication and relationships. Children are encouraged to learn from each other, the teacher, and parents in a setting that is discovery-oriented and attractive to them. The basic message teachers attempt to convey as they set up the environment is that learning is a pleasurable, social activity (Hendrick, 1997).

Reggio Emilia classrooms are full of children's own work. Although this is true of many early childhood programs in the United States, the differences are in the breadth and depth of these representations by children of what they have learned. Paintings, collages, sculptures, drawings, mobiles, and photographs are present in every nook and cranny of the classroom. They are displayed so that parents, teachers, and other children can better understand the process of children's thinking.

One special space found in Reggio classrooms is called the **atelier.** The teacher sets aside this special workshop area as an area for recording in visual form what students learn as they engage in projects of their own choosing (C. Edwards, Gandini, & Forman, 1993). The atelier contains a wealth of tools and resource materials that children can use for their documentations. Under the direction of a trained specialist, children work cooperatively to construct summaries of their learning experiences.

Children, Parents, and Teachers

Reggio Emilia teachers view children as active, curious, and eager learners. When interesting materials and activities are present and when adults give children thoughtful guidance, children can engage in quality educational experiences.

Parents are considered essential in the Reggio Emilia approach and are expected to share responsibilities in educating children (New, 1990). Some parents participate regularly in the classroom, while others are involved in special events or engage in parent education activities. Strong parental support and communication help maximize child growth and development in the early years.

Reggio Emilia teachers are partners with children and parents in the educational process. Careful observation and strong communication skills allow teachers to develop plans for assisting the learning experiences for each child in the classroom. In addition, teachers see themselves as learners and continue to grow in understanding along with children.

Cooperation, Collaboration, and Organization

Additional key elements of the Reggio Emilia model are the cooperation and collaboration between staff members in each school and throughout the system (Gandini, 1993). Teachers work in pairs in Reggio classrooms and view themselves as equal partners in gathering information about children and in making plans to enhance students' growth and development. Through active cooperation, teachers and administrators make it possible for students to achieve the lofty goals of the program.

Cooperation and collaboration are more effective in a system that is highly organized. Reggio Emilia teachers work within a structured system that is designed to make planning and discussions about children more effective. The program sets aside a minimum of six hours each week for teacher meetings, preparing the environment for children, parent meetings, and in-service training (Hendrick, 1997).

In the Reggio Emilia model the atelier, *with its tools and art materials, is the site where the* atelierista *guides teachers and children in documenting learning.*

The Atelierista

A specialist trained in the visual arts referred to as the **atelierista** is hired for each Reggio Emilia school and works with the other teachers and children to assist them in the development of projects summarizing learning experiences (Edwards et al., 1993). The atelier (workshop/studio area), with its tools and art materials, is the focal point for the atelierista's efforts. By guiding teachers and children as they proceed through several refinements of their projects, the atelierista contributes significantly to the work effort in the Reggio Emilia classroom.

The Importance of Documentation

A critical part of schooling in the Reggio Emilia model is the process of **documenting learning experiences** (Hendrick, 1997). Students are expected to describe for others the work they have accomplished and the processes they have used in discovering new knowledge. This documentation can take a variety of forms, including

- Transcriptions of children's remarks and discussions
- Photographs of activities in and around the classroom
- Art media representations of experiences (group murals, sculptures, paintings, drawings, etc.)

Documentation serves several important functions (Hendrick, 1997). First, it helps parents become more aware of children's learning and development. In addition, teachers use these representations of learning to better understand children and to assess their own teaching strategies. Reviewing documentation with other teachers serves another valuable function by encouraging a sharing of ideas and promoting professional growth. Children benefit as well, seeing that their efforts are valued by adults and consolidating their understandings by being able to communicate them to others.

Projects

The central learning experiences of the Reggio Emilia approach are organized around in-depth projects that are often several weeks in length and captivate the interests of both children and adults. Ideas for these projects come from the experiences of both children and adults and lead children to advanced understanding of the world around them.

Hendrick (1997) describes how children and teachers in a Reggio Emilia classroom developed a project related to birds on the playground. Teachers remembered how children during the previous school year were very interested in promoting birds visiting the playground and had built a small lake and bird houses as projects. The teachers then prepared questions and possibilities to present to children to see if the students were interested in following up on these earlier efforts.

> Then they had the first meeting with the children. The children's conversation was full of ideas and surprises as, in the course of it, they became more and more involved. First, they explored the idea of repairing what had been constructed the previous year, and then they thought of improving the area by adding several amenities for the birds to make them feel welcome in their playground. Finally, they became very enthusiastic about the idea expressed by one child of constructing an amusement park for the birds on the playground of the school. (Hendrick, 1997, p. 23)

This discussion led to several children drawing what they thought should be included in the amusement park for birds. The teachers discussed the idea further and presented more questions and suggestions to the children, and gradually the idea began to take shape. A project was born and eventually implemented by children and adults in the Reggio Emilia classroom.

Summary

This chapter introduced four distinct program models in early childhood education. In Montessori education, children choose from a variety of work options and learn through experiences with these materials. The High/Scope program is based on the theory of Piaget and emphasizes cognitive development. The Bank Street approach stresses all aspects of the child's development and uses an integrated curriculum. In the Reggio Emilia program, students engage in extensive projects and often record their learnings in detailed artwork. Each of these programs has had a significant influence on the practices seen in early childhood programs throughout the United States.

For Discussion and Action

1. Read further about one of the models discussed in this chapter. Share your findings with classmates.

2. Choose one idea from Montessori's approach that you like, and describe how this concept would influence the way in which you would teach young children.

3. Brainstorm with your classmates three or four examples of how children construct knowledge of the world around them.

4. What are the strengths of integrating the curriculum across disciplines? Are any weaknesses associated with this approach?

5. Check out your community to see if any early childhood programs follow one of the four models presented in this chapter. If so, take some time to observe in that program, and share your insights with your class. If not, talk to an early childhood teacher, and see which models she is familiar with and how these models influence teaching and learning in that classroom. Share results with your class.

Building Your Personal Library

Epstein, A., Schweinhart, L., & McAdoo, L. (1996). *Models of early childhood education.* Ypsilanti, MI: High/Scope Press. This book presents six models of early education and discusses the curriculum, training, and research materials of each.

Hendrick, J. (Ed.). (1997). *First steps toward teaching the Reggio way.* Upper Saddle River, NJ: Merrill/Prentice Hall. This recent book is an excellent overview of the Reggio Emilia approach to early education. In addition to describing the key elements of this model, several educators discuss the implications of Reggio Emilia for American early education.

Hohmann, M., & Weikart, D. *Educating young children: Active learning practices for preschool and child care programs.* Ypsilanti, MI: High/Scope Press. This is the most recent book by High/Scope to describe its program. It follows two earlier texts (Weikart, Rogers, Adcock, & McClelland, 1971; Hohmann, Banet, & Weikart, 1979) that also provide valuable information on this program.

Lillard, P. (1996). *Montessori today. A comprehensive approach to education from birth through adulthood.* New York: Schocken Books. This book is an update of a classic that has been in use for nearly thirty years (Lillard, 1972). It provides an excellent overview of the theory and practices associated with the Montessori method.

Mitchell, A., & David, J. (Eds.). (1992). *Explorations with young children.* Mt. Rainier, MD: Gryphon House. This text describes the Bank Street approach to early education. Although it is designed as a curriculum guide for Bank Street classrooms, it does not provide specific lessons or activities to use; rather, it identifies the processes teachers use in order to develop materials and activities for early childhood classrooms.

II

Foundations

 ~ 4

Understanding How a Child Develops and Learns

 ~ 5

Play in Childhood

 ~ 6

Guiding Young Children

 ~ 7

Working with Parents, Families, and Communities

 ~ 8

Diversity Issues and Young Children

In this chapter you will

■ Learn about developmentally appropriate practice.

■ Gain insight into the relationships between child development, learning, and teaching.

■ Study differing perspectives on development.

■ Review characteristics of children at different ages and stages of development.

■ Identify strategies for learning about children and their development.

It is time for another school year to begin, and you sit down to study the class list for your second-grade students. Patrick's name is a familiar one to you. Other teachers have warned that he is a handful and that you should be prepared for a very busy, bright, sensitive, easily excitable child. Patrick has been tested and qualifies for the school's gifted program, yet often is off-task and into trouble. But Patrick's name isn't the only one you recognize. From the additional twenty-five names on the list, three are on medication for attention-deficit/hyperactivity disorder, two others are receiving special education assistance, and four more students on the list come to you with very low reading scores. And this is considered a normal classroom. What can you as their teacher do to prepare for this diverse mix of children? How will you meet Patrick's need for challenging experiences while working effectively with the children in your class who have special needs? The remaining students on the roster also have diverse abilities that require your teaching expertise. This is no small task. ∾

As difficult and challenging as the preceding scenario appears, this classroom experience is manageable. Good teachers across the country face these dilemmas each year and consistently find creative ways to deal with them. One essential ingredient for success in this process is an understanding of the overall patterns of child development and learning. The more you know about normal child development and variations from these typical patterns, the better able you will be to plan appropriate learning experiences for your class. In the same way, an understanding of different theoretical perspectives on how children learn and develop allows you to see children through new eyes and create lessons and activities that meet the needs of all your students.

The Developmentally Appropriate Classroom

Basing the curriculum on an in-depth understanding of child development and learning is often referred to as **developmentally appropriate practice.** Rather than focusing first on what is to be learned, in a developmentally appropriate classroom, the teacher begins by working hard to understand the developmental abilities of his class and then makes decisions about what should be taught. This philosophical approach to teaching and learning is at the heart of most early childhood classrooms. The National Association for the Education of Young Children (NAEYC) has published a book outlining the characteristics of developmentally appropriate practice (Bredekamp, 1987) for children birth through age eight.

Educators should be aware of two dimensions to developmentally appropriate practice. The first is referred to as **age appropriateness,** what is appropriate for the age of the child based on developmental averages (called *norms*) for that age. When a kindergarten teacher selects a game that requires the child to count to ten, he is using knowledge of age appropriateness to choose a game within the developmental abilities of the typical five-year-old. The second dimension to developmentally appropriate practice is called **individual appropriateness.** This aspect takes into account what is appropriate for each child based on his unique personality and experiences. When Sarah's mom shares with you her interest in collecting rocks, and you decide to have some books in your third-grade classroom about different kinds of rocks, you are using individual appropriateness as you plan your curriculum.

Developmentally appropriate classrooms have many other characteristics (Bredekamp, 1987). An essential one is that *learning is viewed as an active process.* Children in a developmentally appropriate classroom are busy exploring their indoor and outdoor environments and interacting with other children and adults. Play is considered a vital element of this active learning: "child-initiated, child-directed, teacher-supported play is an essential component of developmentally appropriate practice" (Bredekamp, 1987, p. 3).

Another characteristic of developmentally appropriate practice is that it *considers all aspects of the child's development.* The child's physical, emotional, and social development are valued just as highly as cognitive development. All areas of development are integrated into the activities planned for the early childhood classroom (Gestwicki, 1995).

Active **parent involvement** in the education process is also considered critical to developmentally appropriate practice. Parents can contribute time and talents both at home and in the classroom to assist the teacher in the learning process. Parents' knowledge of their own children's developmental histories provides the teacher with invaluable information to assist in planning individually appropriate activities (Gestwicki, 1995).

Teachers should provide **multicultural, nonsexist materials and experiences** in developmentally appropriate classrooms. Citing a variety of research studies, Banks (1993) identifies the early childhood years as critical to the development of multicultural and nonsexist attitudes. Chapter 8 provides specific advice on how teachers of young children can empower their students in this important area.

Key Perspectives on Learning and Development

Many attempts have been made over the years to explain child development and learning. It should come as no surprise that there are no easy answers to these complex issues. But armed with the insights from a variety of theorists, early educators can have a much better understanding of developmental processes in childhood. Several key theorists stand out as sharing perspectives that are essential for those who work in the field of early childhood education. The works of Bowlby, Maslow, Gardner, Gesell, Montessori, Vygotsky, Erikson, and Piaget provide a wealth of insights into child development and learning.

John Bowlby (1907–   )

Early in his work in child guidance, British researcher John Bowlby became concerned about the ability of children raised in institutions to form lasting relationships with others. He developed an explanation for these behaviors that is referred to as an **ethological theory** (Crain, 1985) because he studied relationship building within an evolutionary context. Bowlby proposed that children who grew up in orphanages were unable to love because they had not had the opportunity to form a solid attachment to a mother-figure early in life (Bowlby, 1969). This **attachment** is an emotional bond that occurs between two people and is essential to healthy relationship building. Bowlby's work led him to suggest that this bonding process begins at birth and is well under way by about six months of age. During this time, infants typically attach themselves to their primary caregiver. From about six to eighteen months, a young child separated from an attachment figure (often the mother) will be quite upset and frequently engage in much crying. Fear of strangers is another common behavior during this period. (See Figure 4–1.)

Although infants develop a primary attachment to one caregiver, other attachment bonds can also be very significant. Fathers, siblings, relatives, and other important caregivers can be attachment figures to the young child. Mary Ainsworth, a key American researcher to study attachment, describes these as secondary attachments (Ainsworth, 1973) and discusses the importance of these bonds.

Bowlby (1969) also describes the more positive aspects of this attachment relationship. As the infant/toddler becomes more confident in his caregiver bonding, he becomes more able to use the attached person as a base from which to explore. If, for example, a mother and her one-year-old son go to the park for the afternoon, the strongly attached child will typically remain close for a short time and then move off to briefly explore his new surroundings. This sense of confidence and competence allows young children to learn more about the world around them and continue to grow stronger emotionally and intellectually.

Clearly, the attachment relationship has important implications for the early childhood classroom. Teachers of infants/toddlers in particular need to be aware of the importance of attachment and be prepared to deal with the separation problems that many children will face when attached caregivers leave. Another issue is the effect of high turnover rates in child care centers on secondary attachments. Raikes (1993) found that children who spent at least nine months with a high-quality teacher were more likely to develop a secure relationship and that attachment security was enhanced.

> **Figure 4–1** *Stages in Attachment*

- **Preattachment (Phase I)** lasts from birth to approximately twelve weeks of age. During this time, children make little distinction between people in their vicinity. turn toward them, follow with their eyes, and are generally more contented when others are around.
- **Attachment-in-the-making (Phase II)** is the period from about twelve weeks to six months of age. At this point, children continue to be interested in people around them. They do not express concern when strangers are introduced during this period. The main change at this phase is that infants become more enthusiastic in their responses to their primary caregivers. They begin to clearly prefer that key person who is providing for their basic needs.
- **Clear-cut attachment (Phase III)** begins around six months of age and continues to about two years. Now, the young child clearly discriminates between people who provide primary care and others. As children begin to explore the world around them, they use the attached person as a secure base from which they move out to interact with people and things. The bonds between primary caregivers and the child are strong, and it is hard for the child to be separated from these attachment figures. Strangers produce more anxiety and concern for children during this phase as well.
- **Goal-corrected partnership (Phase IV)** finds the two-year-old beginning to develop relationships with attached persons that are more complex and that start to recognize the goals and plans of the attached adults. Up to this point, the child has focused on having needs met, and the attachment bond is a rather one-sided relationship. Slowly, these partnerships mature, and the increased opportunities for reciprocal interactions benefit both the child and the adult.

Note. Adapted from *Social and Personality Development: Infancy through Adolescence* by W. Damon, 1983, New York: W. W. Norton.

Abraham Maslow (1908–1970)

Maslow's ideas about human development are often referred to as a **humanistic theory** (Thomas, 1985) because of the emphasis on the development of self. He proposes that people have needs that must be met in order to become and stay healthy. Maslow's **hierarchy of human needs** is depicted as a pyramid in Figure 4–2, with the most basic needs starting at the bottom and progressing up the pyramid to higher-level needs. The first two levels of needs are often referred to as **deficiency needs** (Maslow, 1968), because their absence causes physical illness. Healthy growth requires that physiological, safety, and security needs be met. The top three levels of needs are called **growth needs** and are the individual's attempts at becoming a more satisfied and healthy person.

Maslow emphasizes the fact that the lower-level deficiency needs must be met before the higher-level growth needs can be addressed. The traditional role of nurturing the child's intellect may be very difficult if other more basic needs are not being met. Because lower-level needs must be met before higher-level needs, the child who comes to school without breakfast is unlikely to be excited about the learning process. Once deficiency needs are met, academic learning helps meet the growth needs of self-respect and self-actualization.

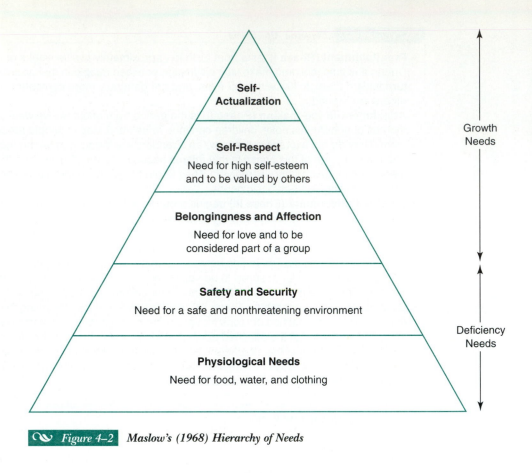

Self-
Actualization

Self-Respect
Need for high self-esteem
and to be valued by others

Belongingness and Affection
Need for love and to be
considered part of a group

Safety and Security
Need for a safe and nonthreatening environment

Physiological Needs
Need for food, water, and clothing

Growth
Needs

Deficiency
Needs

Figure 4–2 *Maslow's (1968) Hierarchy of Needs*

Maslow's theory provides hope for children who come from very difficult circumstances. He suggests that when unmet basic needs are met, the child can move ahead and develop more normally. Clearly, the child who lives in a physically abusive home is under incredible stress and is likely to experience many difficulties in school. Yet, if this child is removed from the abusive environment or if the abuse is eliminated, healthy growth is again possible. This encouraging perspective has support in the research literature (Skeels, 1966) and should help teachers be more optimistic toward even the most difficult circumstances.

Maslow's theory makes it clear that teaching is much more complicated than many people believe. Rather than focusing solely on academics, teachers must also be concerned with children's needs and must do their best to make sure these needs are consistently being met. Although it is not possible for any one teacher to meet all of the needs of each student, it is necessary to work to meet as many needs as possible. Teachers must begin by being aware of any needs that children have that are unmet.

Howard Gardner (1943–   )

As a faculty member at Harvard University, Howard Gardner has been prob-
ing in his many writings a new view of intelligence. Rather than seeing intelligence as a single, general capacity that each of us possesses, he suggests that we
have at least eight distinct types of intelligence. This **theory of multiple intelligences** (Gardner, 1993) has prompted many to rethink the ways in which learning takes place and the techniques used to measure intelligence.

Gardner identifies eight intelligences that people possess to greater or lesser
degrees (Gardner, 1983; Shores, 1995). **Linguistic intelligence** is seen in people
who speak or write creatively and with relative ease. A person with strengths in **logical-mathematical intelligence** is able to reason effectively and engage in mathematical and scientific inquiry. **Spatial intelligence** allows people like engineers and
sculptors to form refined mental models of the spatial world around them. Other
people are especially talented in singing or playing a musical instrument and have
strong **musical intelligence. Bodily kinesthetic intelligence** helps people solve problems and fashion products using their body or body parts. Athletes and dancers
have high bodily kinesthetic intelligence. Two additional intelligences are referred
to as the **personal intelligences: Interpersonal intelligence** is the ability to understand other people, while **intrapersonal intelligence** allows a person to understand
himself. Finally, **naturalistic intelligence** was recently added to the original seven
categories (Shores, 1995). The person strong in this intelligence has special abilities in recognizing differences in the natural world.

Gardner's notion of multiple intelligences reminds us that children come to
the classroom with many different talents and skills and that we as teachers need
to recognize and respect these abilities. Too often, schools prize linguistic and
logical-mathematical intelligences and overlook the rest (Gardner, 1983). When
we are sensitive to the other intelligences, children see themselves as more successful and competent.

Recognizing a variety of intelligences also means that teachers must plan their
curriculum differently. Campbell (1992) describes his attempts at implementing
thematic learning centers designed to take advantage of the different kinds of
intelligence into his third- through fifth-grade multiage classroom.

Arnold Gesell (1880–1961)

Through thirty-seven years as director of the Yale Clinic of Child Development
(later renamed the Gesell Institute of Child Development), Arnold Gesell pursued
the task of observing and recording the changes in child growth and development
from infancy through adolescence. Gesell is a **maturationist;** his descriptions of
developmental patterns in childhood emphasize physical and mental growth determined primarily by heredity. By carefully observing children in his campus school,
Gesell established norms or typical behaviors of children throughout childhood.
He categorized these **gradients of growth** into ten major areas (Gesell & Ilg, 1949):

1. *Motor characteristics* (bodily activity, eyes and hands)

2. *Personal hygiene* (eating, sleeping, elimination, bathing and dressing, health and somatic complaints, tensional outlets)
3. *Emotional expression* (affective attitudes, crying, assertion, and anger)
4. *Fears and dreams*
5. *Self and sex*
6. *Interpersonal relations* (mother–child; child–child; groupings in play)
7. *Play and pastimes* (general interests; reading; music, radio, and cinema)
8. *School life* (adjustment to school, classroom demeanor, reading, writing, arithmetic)
9. *Ethical sense* (blaming and alibiing; response to direction, punishment, praise; response to reason; sense of good and bad; truth and property)
10. *Philosophic outlook* (time, space, language and thought, war, death, deity)

Gesell and his staff created an extensive list of normative information that remains very popular with and useful to parents and teachers. A parent or teacher concerned about what is normal behavior for a given age can refer to Gesell's growth gradients for specific information. In his books, he summarizes the statistical data into statements of what a child is like at a given age. For example, here is his statement about two-year-olds and their eating:

> Appetite—Fair to moderately good. Breakfast is now relatively small. The noon meal is usually the best, but with some the one good meal is supper. (Gesell & Ilg, 1943, p. 164)

Maria Montessori (1870–1952)

Another maturationist is Maria Montessori. Through her teaching of young children in Italy, she developed an intriguing theory and many practical strategies that have significantly influenced early childhood education. Based on her readings and observations of children, Montessori believed that children pass through numerous **sensitive periods** during their progress to adulthood (Montessori, 1949/1967). She viewed these periods as genetically programmed blocks of time when young children are especially eager and able to master certain tasks. For example, Montessori suggested that there is a sensitive period for walking when the infant/toddler spends considerable time and effort in learning to walk. As most parents can attest, it becomes almost an obsession for children as they struggle to master this important task.

Another important idea that Montessori promoted was the concept of the **unity of the mental and physical** (Lillard, 1972). Until Montessori, Western educational thought had been influenced by Descartes, who viewed mankind as divided into two parts: the intellectual and physical. Her readings and work with children led Montessori to the opposite conclusion. That is, full development of the intellect is not possible without physical activity. Learning through doing is a cornerstone of Montessori's educational approach.

Montessori also believed that, during the first three years of life, children have **absorbent minds** (Montessori, 1949/1967). Because children's minds are not fully formed during these years, she reasoned that they must learn in ways different from adults. Montessori believed that children unconsciously absorb information from the environment around them and, like a sponge, simply soak up information into their developing minds. This information also forms their minds in preparation for later, more advanced thought.

Montessori also felt that children pass through stages in their growth and development. She described five specific periods of growth:

- *Birth to age three.* During this period, children unconsciously absorb information from the world around them.

- *Three to six.* Gradually, children bring the knowledge of the unconscious to a conscious level.

- *Six to nine.* Children build the academic and artistic skills necessary for success in life.

- *Nine to twelve.* A knowledge of the universe gradually opens up to children during this period.

- *Twelve to eighteen.* Children explore areas of special interest in more depth (Lillard, 1972).

Lev Vygotsky (1896–1934)

Although he lived a short life, Vygotsky's theory of development has had a significant impact in his homeland of Russia and more recently is gaining influence in the United States. Often referred to as a **sociocultural theorist** (Berk, 1994), Vygotsky believed that development is primarily influenced by the social and cultural activities in which the individual grows up. Interactions with other children and adults are the primary vehicles children have for learning about the world around them. Language becomes a crucial tool for learning because it is the primary way we communicate and interact with others. It allows us to talk about our social interactions and is essential in the thinking process.

The major focus of Vygotsky's research was the relationship between language and thought. He concluded after much study that this relationship changes over time. Initially, there is little connection between the two. They are like two circles that do not touch. Over time, however, language and thought partially overlap to form **verbal thought.** The child now learns concepts that also have word labels (Thomas, 1985). Language and thought never totally merge, however; both children and adults continue to use nonverbal thought and nonconceptual speech. Figure 4–3 provides a diagram of these relationships.

Vygotsky (1962) is perhaps best known for a concept referred to as the *zone of proximal development.* This is the gap between the child's independent performance of a task and that which he can perform with a more skilled peer or adult's help. The child builds knowledge of the world when he is in this zone of proximal development and receives assistance from a more skilled peer or an adult. Vygotsky felt

 *Figure 4–3*

Vygotsky (1962) on Language and Thought

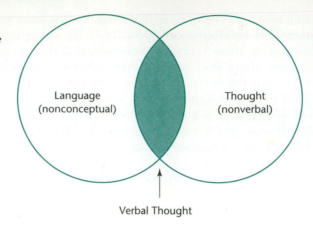

that educational tasks should be planned to challenge each child at the top of his zone of proximal development.

As with the other theorists identified, Vygotsky's ideas have many practical implications for the classroom teacher. First, if the child's social and cultural experiences play such a major role in development, it is critical to understand and build on the experiences children bring to the early childhood classroom. Also, because relationships with peers and adults are so critical to development, the classroom teacher must work hard to foster strong teacher–student and peer relations. Teaching strategies such as project learning in which small groups of peers work together to attain a common goal (see Chapter 3 for more information) are also very compatible with Vygotsky's theory.

Erik Erikson (1902–1994)

Erikson's theory of human development is one of the few to describe human behavior from birth through old age. It is often called a **psychosocial theory** because of its emphasis on psychological development through the person's interactions within his social environment (Thomas, 1985). Erikson proposes that humans pass through a series of eight stages from birth to old age. Each stage has a major issue that must be addressed, which Erikson refers to as a **psychosocial crisis** for that time of life (Erikson, 1963). Successful resolution of the psychosocial crisis of the current stage provides a stronger foundation for approaching the next crisis.

The first four of Erikson's stages are important for early childhood education and are briefly discussed next. The title for each stage identifies the psychosocial crisis for that stage, with the first descriptor representing the positive resolution of the crisis.

- *Stage 1: Trust versus Mistrust.* For the first year of life, children are dealing with the trustworthiness of their primary caregivers. If parents and others provide consistent care and meet the child's physical and emotional needs, a sense of trust begins to develop, and the young child can start to trust others.

- *Stage 2: Autonomy versus Shame and Doubt.* From approximately one to three [...]
of age, young children make initial attempts at doing some things for ther [...]
Wanting to dress and feed themselves helps give them a sense of indepe [...]
When not allowed to engage in these activities, children may develop a sense [...]
they are not capable and experience what Erikson calls shame and doubt.

- *Stage 3: Initiative versus Guilt.* During the preschool and kindergarten years, children are developing a sense of initiative by making plans, setting goals, and
working hard to accomplish tasks. Parents and teachers need to encourage the
child's natural curiosity to allow this growing initiative to blossom.

- *Stage 4: Industry versus Inferiority.* The elementary school years (ages six to twelve)
are spent in Erikson's fourth stage of psychosocial development. A child develops a sense of industry through learning the skills necessary to be successful in
society. Children begin comparing themselves with others and identifying their
own particular strengths and weaknesses (Crain, 1985).

Teachers and parents play key roles in assisting children with successful resolution of each of these psychosocial crises. Adults must be constantly aware of the
impact of their words and actions on young children. Demonstrating trustworthiness, allowing some independence, encouraging planning and exploration, and
praising children's accomplishments help ensure positive resolutions to each of
these stages of psychosocial development.

Jean Piaget (1896–1980)

Piaget's long and very productive career is difficult to summarize, because of the
breadth of his writing and research. In general, Piaget was interested in studying
how knowledge develops in human beings. Through very careful observations, and
ingenious experiments with children, he proposed that we all pass through a series
of four stages in gaining knowledge about our world.

Regardless of age, Piaget suggests that people form mental concepts about our
world that he refers to as **schemas.** These schemas are general ways of thinking
about or interacting with things in our environment. As we take in new information
from the world around us, we can **assimilate** that information into already existing
schemas to strengthen our understanding of that mental concept. A three-year-old,
for example, may already have a schema for *dog* that includes experiences with short-
haired dogs such as Dalmations, Labradors, and boxers. Upon meeting a new breed
of short-haired dog such as the dachshund, the child can assimilate that new information into his schema for dog. When new information doesn't fit already existing
schema, however, then the schema must be modified to **accommodate** this new
knowledge. The same three-year-old, upon meeting a curly haired poodle, must
change or modify his schema for dog to accommodate this new bit of information.

The best-known and most influential aspect of Piaget's work is his four **stages
of intellectual development** (Flavell, 1963). Piaget states that everyone passes
through each of these stages at approximately the same ages and that ways of
knowing about the world vary significantly from one stage to the next.

FOCUS ON ...
Piaget's Conservation Experiments

Piaget suggests that young children don't understand that quantities such as number, length, and mass remain unchanged despite transformations in their appearance. Children begin to understand *conservation* when they enter the stage of concrete operations. Piaget developed simple but effective tasks to determine if children understand this principle. Two examples follow:

Conservation of Number

The experimenter in this situation presents children with two rows of pennies or checkers, which are equally spaced and in one-to-one correspondence. Then the adult asks "Does your row have more, does mine, or are they both the same?" One row is then spread out as indicated in the picture, and the same question is repeated. Children until about age six say the longer row has more.

Conservation of Volume

In this task, children are presented with two identical clear glasses filled with equal amounts of water and asked, "Does your glass have more, does mine, or are they the same?" Then (as in the picture), the water from one glass is poured into another glass of different diameter (smaller diameter and taller), and children are asked the same question. Again, younger children think the taller glass has more water.

1. *Try one or both of these experiments with children. Consider using two children three to four years old, two children five to six years old, and two children seven to eight years old. Discuss your results with classmates.*

2. *These experiments have been criticized as ineffective in measuring a child's true understanding of conservation. What issues might be involved in these criticisms?*

- *Sensorimotor intelligence.* From birth to about age two, children are in Piaget's stage of sensorimotor intelligence. During this time, children learn about the world through sensory experiences and motoric activity. The infant's sucking and shaking of various objects are examples of early ways of learning about things in his environment through physical manipulation and sensory exploration.

- *Preoperational intelligence.* Children from approximately two to seven years of age (most of the early childhood years) engage in preoperational thinking. During this stage, children begin to use symbolic thinking rather than exclusively learning through sensory and motor interactions with the world. Preoperational children make initial attempts to be logical but are unsuccessful by adult standards. **Egocentric** in their thinking, children have a difficult time seeing things from any perspective other than their own. Taking things literally is another characteristic of this stage.

- *Concrete operations.* From seven to twelve years, children engage in concrete operational thinking. The child becomes more successful in thinking logically and systematically, especially when dealing with concrete objects. At this stage, the child understands **conservation,** recognizing that matter doesn't change in quantity or mass, when moved or manipulated. Children are less egocentric and more able to see the perspectives of others.

- *Formal operations.* Piaget suggests that, from adolescence on, we enter the stage of formal operations. At this point, the abstract and logical thinking necessary for scientific investigation are possible.

Piaget's constructivist approach has had a significant impact on education in general and on early childhood education specifically. Although he spent little time in defining the educational implications of his theory, others have suggested many connections. Piaget's theory implies active learning during the early childhood years. Hands-on manipulation of materials and objects in the world provides the child with much information to assimilate and accommodate. Understanding how children gain knowledge about their world is essential to planning for future learning (Kamii & Ewing, 1996). The learning environment must allow for manipulation of objects and interactions with other children and adults.

Children: Developmental Similarities and Differences

Imagine for a moment the process a creative chef uses for cooking a culinary delight. Although the process may not be conscious, the knowledgeable cook understands the characteristics of each of the foods used in a recipe. Length of time needed to cook, properties when mixed with other ingredients, consistency, color, and aroma are just some of the bits of information the creative chef relies on before beginning the process of cooking. In much the same way, a creative teacher must know a great deal about children and their typical developmental patterns before beginning the teaching process. This information becomes the basis for the planning and teaching that will follow. And, unfortunately, there are very few recipes to follow in order to succeed in the classroom.

From study and experience working with children, the best teachers know what is normal for a group of young children. A kindergarten teacher, for example, knows that a typical five-year-old child should be able to string a set of ten beads and has the fine motor skills to begin to enjoy the writing process (Charlesworth, 1996). Preschool teachers have learned that many young children have difficulty separating from their parents when they arrive at school (Hendrick, 1994). The tears and clinging are normal reactions to the stress of leaving loving parents. Third-grade teachers understand the importance of peer relationships

INTO PRACTICE . . .

What Children Can't Do . . . Yet

Although young children are capable of many things at an early age, it is also important to keep in mind what they are unable to do . . . yet. Dan Hodgins (1996) has developed a list of significant considerations, some of which are presented here:

- *I can't share.* This is an important skill that teachers should encourage, and many young children will continue to struggle with sharing throughout the early childhood years.

- *I can't say I'm sorry and mean it.* It is difficult for young children to see things from another person's perspective. Therefore, saying "I'm sorry" has little meaning at this age.

- *I can't focus on more than one task at a time.* Developmentally, young children have difficulty holding in memory more than one direction at a time. It is only toward the end of the early childhood years that they are ready for two or more directions presented together.

- *I don't process negative commands.* Saying "Don't slam the door!" or "Don't run in the hallway!" generally produces poor results in young children. It is hard for them to process this

information. It is much more productive to state things more positively, "Please walk in the hallways."

- *I can't sit still for very long.* Controlling the very natural tendency to move is difficult for young children. So, sitting still in a chair or on the floor won't last for long during the early childhood years.

- *I can't tell the difference between reality and fantasy.* From the violence viewed on television to the fantasy world of masks and costumes, the young child has difficulty sorting through what is real and what is not. This confusion may lead to fear, frustration, or tears.

- *I can't express myself in words very well.* Physical means of communication are easier for young children because they haven't yet developed strong verbal skills. They need assistance in learning to use appropriate words to take the place of physical actions.

- *I can't wait.* Taking turns with a toy or piece of equipment is difficult at this age. Children should not be kept waiting for long periods of time.

---

and work hard to encourage positive interactions among students. In these, and many other similar ways, teachers use their knowledge of child development to begin the process of planning and teaching.

Knowledge of what is typical for a given group of children must be supplemented with an understanding of the variations that exist among children of the same age. Children develop at different rates. The reasons for these deviations are complex but are some combination of genetic factors and environmental influences (Bee, 1995). Finding and using this information about individual differences among children is very useful to the teacher in planning the curriculum. Talking to a three-year-old child's parents, for example, could help a teacher to understand that this child's delay in climbing may be partially due to a broken leg at age two. Observing kindergarten children at play, a teacher may discover that a child needs help in making friends. Or the second-grade teacher who analyzes a fairy tale that her student has written may learn of the child's special writing talents.

The longer a teacher works with children, the more sensitive she becomes to the general patterns of development and the subtle variations between children. These building blocks of knowledge and understanding form the foundations for good teaching and learning.

The following characteristics describe typical behaviors of infants and toddlers. They are meant as a guide in understanding the patterns of development at these ages.

Physical

Grasps objects (4 months)
Sits and crawls (6–7 months)
Feeds self (10 months)
Walks (12 months)
Up and down stairs (toddlers)
Scribbles (toddlers)

Language

Cries to express needs (0–1 months)
Babbles sounds (3 months)
Understands words (8–10 months)
First words (12 months)
Two-word phrases (toddlers)
Up to fifty words (toddlers)

Cognitive

Smiles of recognition (4 months)
Object permanence (8 months)
Plays pat-a-cake (12 months)
Block towers, 3–4 (toddlers)
Identifies book pictures (toddlers)
Follows one direction (toddlers)

Social-Emotional

Recognizes familiar faces (3 months)
Attachment begins (6 months)
Stranger anxiety begins (6 months)
Does things by self (toddlers)
Plays by self (toddlers)
Active, curious (toddlers)

Infants and Toddlers

The first three years of life are characterized by very rapid growth. The young child moves from being totally dependent on others to someone able to walk and talk and begin to interact with others. This period is also a critical foundation for all of the development that is to follow. Parents and caregivers need to understand the developmental patterns of this period. (See Figure 4–4.)

Infant Development.   Newborn Jenny has just arrived home and is already causing quite a stir in the household. She seems so helpless and unaware of her surroundings. Yet, Jenny is quickly learning about her parents and the world around her. Although her first movements are reflexive, she quickly begins to develop more purposeful activities. Nursing is quickly mastered, and Jenny's cries take on a variety of meanings from "I'm wet" to "feed me!" She is learning about her world through her senses and motor activities, so dropping, squeezing, sucking, seeing, and hearing are some of the many ways in which Jenny is making sense of her world.

By the middle of her first year, Jenny is sitting up when propped, grasping objects, and rolling over. Her understanding of language is growing rapidly, and she is babbling the sounds used to make up words. At this point, Jenny is also attached to her significant caregivers and becomes upset when they are not with her.

As Jenny's first birthday approaches, she is taking her first steps and speaking her first words. These are major milestones that change dramatically her interactions with others. No longer dependent on others to get from one place to another, Jenny is free to explore her environment more independently. Words

This young toddler is more confident and stable in his gait than he was at twelve months of age. By age two, he will be able to run.

open up a new and more precise way of communicating with others, and Jenny is using this tool to her full advantage. Jenny's total dependence on caregivers has changed significantly over the past twelve months.

One-Year-Olds.   Matt has just turned one and is already off exploring his environment. From his first shaky steps just a few weeks ago, he is now becoming more confident and stable in his gait. By the end of his second year of life, he is able to run and effectively navigate up and down stairs. This newfound mobility allows Matt to expand his horizons and learn even more about his growing world.

Matt's language is also growing by leaps and bounds. Beginning the year with just a few words that were understandable mostly to parents, Matt's vocabulary will expand to approximately 300 words by year's end. He is also now able to put together words and form simple two-word sentences. Matt understands much more of the verbal communications from others than he is able to repeat himself.

Toward the end of this year, Matt will be able to mentally represent objects and events as symbols. Although he still learns much from his senses and motor activity, he is now able to engage in symbolic thought. Matt can now imitate the actions of others and get involved in simple make-believe play.

Matt's push toward more independence can be difficult for his parents and caregivers. Although he wants to do as much as he can by himself, he still needs and wants closeness and assistance. Finding that delicate balance between independence and assistance is often difficult for both Matt and his parents. Patience and calmness are virtues for adults at this point.

Two-Year-Olds.   As a two-year-old, Serena is making the transition from babyhood to childhood. She continues to gain body control, with improved walking and running and small muscle development. Serena spends considerable energy in refining her skills by repeating over and over again the things she is learning. For example, she will put together a simple puzzle many times before she is ready to move on to the next activity.

Serena's language continues to grow exponentially. Her vocabulary will triple by year's end to approximately 1,000 words. Serena's sentences have grown as well, with many including three or more words. Conversations with others become more interactive, with Serena able to listen and talk in appropriate contexts.

Along with her growing language abilities, Serena is developing deeper conceptual understandings of her world. She remains curious and excited about exploring the natural world around her. Serena has a lively imagination and enjoys using it in her play with others.

Although Serena's social skills are growing, she is still likely to play side by side, rather than with other children. And rather than ask for a toy, Serena may well just take it. Her newly acquired ability to communicate more effectively is often not enough in many situations to avoid conflict, and Serena reverts to throwing a temper tantrum.

Children Age Three to Five: The Preschool Years

The years from three to five are often referred to as the *preschool years*. Many young children are entering a school-like setting for the first time. Although growth has slowed somewhat from the frantic pace of the earlier years, development is still rapid during this period. A three-year-old is very different developmentally from his five-year-old friend, and each year brings new milestones. (See Figure 4–5.)

Three-Year-Olds.   Mario is three and very much a child and no longer a baby. He has lost most of the baby fat that gave him that chubby look of younger children. Mario's physical skills have grown, and he is able to balance on one foot, unbutton and button clothing, and ride a tricycle. He has achieved bowel and bladder control and can use the toilet with limited supervision.

Mario's language continues to develop, with increased vocabulary and sentence structure. He is better able to engage in a real conversation with others, talking *with* rather than just *to* others. Mario is full of questions about his world and constantly asks for information about the people and things around him.

During this year, Mario is developing conceptual understanding through playing with people and things. His pretend play has become more complex, and Mario

Figure 4–5 *Development of Children Age Three to Five: The Preschool Years*

The following characteristics describe typical behaviors of children three to five. They are meant as a guide to understanding the patterns of development at these ages.

Physical

Losing baby fat (3 years)
Can ride a tricycle (3 years)
Hops and skips (4 years)
Draws stick figures (4 years)
Ties bow knot (5 years)
Rides a bicycle (5 years)

Cognitive

"Why?" questions common (3 years)
Names basic colors (3 years)
Understands concept of *three* (4 years)
Curious about how things work (4 years)
Sorts by color, shape (5 years)
Calendar has meaning (5 years)

Language

Three- to four-word sentences (3 years)
Correctly uses past tense (3 years)
Plays with words (4 years)
Uses talk to solve some conflicts (4 years)
Up to 1,500 words (5 years)
Dictates stories (5 years)

Social-Emotional

Often imitates adults in play (3 years)
Sex-role stereotypes form (3 years)
Can work in groups of two or three (4 years)
Has special friends (4 years)
Feelings can easily be hurt by others (5 years)
Likes group games (5 years)

can now include two or three other children in the scenarios he creates. Although his attention span is still relatively short, Mario can use his lively imagination to play out complex themes, especially those in which he imitates adult roles. In the block corner, Mario often constructs and then names what he has made.

Socially and emotionally, Mario continues to make significant progress. He now is able to establish and maintain short-term friendships with others and begins to enjoy playing *with* rather than *near* his buddies. Mario is learning to use social skills such as taking turns, but he finds it difficult to consistently use these emerging skills. His imaginary friend, Buffy, is often included in play themes around home and in school. Mario is often frightened by large dogs and horses and needs comforting when he encounters these animals.

Four-Year-Olds. Mary is a very active and confident four-year-old. Having mastered the basics of movement, she is constantly testing her physical limits to improve upon her skills. Mary climbs higher, runs faster, and pumps vigorously on the swing to challenge her motor skills.

Mary's language has now matured to the point that she can communicate with others using fairly sophisticated words and sentences. Language becomes a plaything for Mary, and she loves rhyming and nonsense words. Bathroom talk, tall tales, and swearing are also parts of her experimentation with language.

Highly interested in how things work, Mary is constantly asking questions that challenge the adults who work with her. Her interest in the concepts of life and death lead her to explore the world of insects and small animals. Mary will often name her artwork and begins to draw and paint objects that represent things and

Mary, age four, enjoys the challenge of a puzzle.

people in the world. Number concepts are beginning to develop, and Mary enjoys games and songs that incorporate them. Mary understands time as a sequence of events and appreciates a consistent routine to her day.

Mary's friendships are becoming stronger, and she has clear preferences for playmates. These special friends do change regularly, however. Play has now become a truly social activity during most times with others. Occasionally, however, Mary still likes to go off by herself for some quiet time. Turn taking and sharing are becoming easier for Mary because she is beginning to recognize the value of cooperation. On the other hand, her growing skills and confidence often lead Mary into confrontations with others. She wants to be the leader and is bossy and assertive in her relationships with peers.

Five-Year-Olds.   Abdul has calmed down a bit from a few short months ago. He is now much more interested in fine motor activities and spends considerable time building with Legos, cutting paper, making artwork, and engaging in beginning writing activities. Abdul's interest in swinging, climbing, and running is still strong, and he engages in these activities in a fluid, coordinated, confident manner. He also has fun throwing and catching from short distances.

Abdul's language use is now fully developed, with a vocabulary of several thousand words. He is able to construct complex sentences and accurately use grammatical forms in communicating. Abdul eagerly learns new words that give him labels for the increasingly widening world he is exploring.

Socially, Abdul has solidified his friendships at school and in the neighborhood. Although he will play with others, his strong preference is to be with his special friends. Cooperative play themes, in which children take on roles, is a common component of Abdul's activity. He is aware of rules and begins to enjoy simple games.

Abdul's conceptual knowledge is expanding rapidly. His understanding of number has improved, and he can now accurately count ten objects and count by rote to twenty. Abdul can sort objects by either color or shape. He knows the purpose for a calendar and can tell time by the hour. Abdul also understands the concepts of *tomorrow* and *yesterday*.

Children Age Six through Eight: The Primary School Years

Although the life of a primary-aged child has changed dramatically with the introduction of formal schooling, developmental characteristics through this period closely resemble those of earlier years. Children are still working hard to understand and construct social relationships, deal with their emotions, and learn about their world through hands-on manipulation of objects and interactions with peers and adults. (See Figure 4–6.)

Six-Year-Olds.   Christy is a normal, busy six-year-old who enjoys practicing newly acquired skills. Although her physical growth has slowed, she likes to test the limits

---

Figure 4–6 *Development of Children Age Six through Eight: The Primary School Years*

The following characteristics describe typical behaviors of children six through eight. They are meant as a guide in understanding the patterns of development at these ages.

Physical

Permanent teeth appear (6 years)
Likes rough-and-tumble play (6 years)
Works at mastery of physical skills
(7 years)
Growth slows (7 years)
Body proportions more adult-like
(8 years)
Healthier, less fatigued (8 years)

Language

Learning to write (6 years)
Understands conventions of conversation
(6 years)
Likes to write own stories (7 years)
Spelling lags behind reading (7 years)
Masters reading (8 years)
Written stories more complex, detailed
(8 years)

Cognitive

Interested in reading (6 years)
Enjoys collecting (6 years)
Able to sequence events (7 years)
Understands beginning arithmetic skills
(7 years)
Eager to learn about happenings around
the world (8 years)
Games with rules popular (8 years)

Social-Emotional

Nightmares common (6 years)
Same-sex friendships (6 years)
Compares self with peers (7 years)
Wants more time to self (7 years)
Special friendships develop (8 years)
Most fears conquered (8 years)

of her body with challenging activities such as acrobatics and jump rope. Christy just got a new bicycle and is working hard to master two-wheeling. Other activities that require good balance such as skating and skiing are also fun for her.

Christy has many friends, most of whom are other girls. Her playmates change regularly, however, with new friends being added and old ones set aside. Christy is making comparisons between herself and her peers, which is leading her to recognize personal strengths and weaknesses.

Although Christy still has some minor articulation errors, she is eager to talk with adults and others. It is hard to get her to be quiet long enough to enter the conversation. Christy is making significant progress in putting her thoughts into writing and enjoys practicing this new-found skill.

Christy's school days are filled with learning to read and developing early math skills. She is making steady progress with these very complex tasks.

Christy collects rocks and enjoys sorting and classifying them.

Although she enjoys simple games in school and at home, winning and losing are very difficult for Christy, and she is happier when they are deemphasized.

Seven-Year-Olds.   At seven, Gordon values his and others' physical competence. Sports figures like Michael Jordan and Ken Griffey, Jr., are important to him. Gordon is a typical boisterous seven-year-old and enjoys rough and tumble play with his friends. He needs daily opportunities to engage in active play. Sitting still doesn't seem to be a part of Gordon's makeup.

Gordon's rate of vocabulary development has slowed, but language learning remains significant. Gordon is learning Spanish in an after-school enrichment program and is finding this a fun activity. His ability to communicate in writing is improving steadily, and Gordon enjoys writing long, fantasy-oriented stories to share with his friends and parents.

The overriding desire of seven-year-olds is to be part of the group.

Although Gordon likes to work alone, his overriding desire is to be part of the group. Peer pressure to conform to the in-group expectations is growing. Mood swings are common for Gordon, with complaints of not being liked and concerns over competence when he compares himself to peers.

Gordon's thirst for knowledge about the world around him appears boundless. He wants to know how the real things he encounters work, and he spends considerable energy on tasks that interest him. Gordon has mastered the basics of reading and has learned the arithmetic operations of addition, subtraction, and multiplication.

Eight-Year-Olds. Marissa is beginning to look more adult-like in her physical appearance. Her body proportions are subtly changing in preparation for the more dramatic changes of puberty just ahead. Marissa's movements are now quite fluid and graceful, and she uses good posture when seated. She is in general healthier and less easily fatigued than she was as a seven-year-old.

Marissa is very aware of the differences between herself and the boys in her class, and she works hard to separate herself from "those geeks." Her friends are all girls, and she likes it that way. Her group of friends is becoming more exclusive, and it is difficult for them to add new members. Although closeness with her parents at home is still important to her, Marissa is beginning to separate herself from her teacher and finds this relationship less important than it was a year ago.

Marissa's hungry mind is eager to know more information about her expanding world. In addition to her desire to know more about people and relationships in her family and neighborhood, Marissa can conceptualize nations around the world and is curious about life there. She has an Internet pen pal in Australia and enjoys learning about school and family life there. Marissa is beginning to show an interest in historical events and can conceptualize and discuss future events.

Children with Special Needs

Children with special needs can be categorized as disabled, at-risk, or gifted.

Children with Disabilities. A child who is **disabled** is unable to do something or has difficulty with a specific task (Hallahan & Kauffman, 1994). Seven-year-old Angela uses a wheelchair and is unable to walk. She is considered physically disabled. All other aspects of Angela's development are normal, however. Other disabilities can influence more than one aspect of development. Brian has a significant hearing loss and is delayed in his oral language development. Because he has difficulty hearing others and communicating with them, Brian also struggles with social relationships. The types and severities of disabilities children possess are many and varied. Some children experience mild disabilities, while others are faced with moderate to severe ones. At age seven, Aretha has trouble distinguishing between letters such as *b* and *d* as she reads. She has been diagnosed as having a mild learning disability. Jason has Down syndrome, congenital heart defects, and severe mental retardation. His disabilities are much more damaging to his overall development.

Classrooms consist of children with many, varied special needs: children with disabilities, those who are at risk for failure, and those who are gifted.

Wolery and Wilbers (1994) have suggested the following categories of disabilities often encountered by teachers of young children:

- *Speech and language:* hard-of-hearing, deafness, stuttering, cleft palate, chronic voice disorders, learning disabilities
- *Physical-motor:* visual impairment, blindness, hearing impairments, orthopedic disabilities (cerebral palsy, loss of limbs, muscular dystrophy, etc.)
- *Intellectual:* mental retardation, brain injury, brain dysfunction, dyslexia, learning disabilities
- *Social-emotional:* self-destructive behavior, severe withdrawal, dangerous aggression, noncommunicativeness, attention-deficit/hyperactivity disorder, depression, phobias, autism
- *Health impairments:* severe asthma, epilepsy, hemophilia, congenital heart defects, malnutrition, diabetes, cystic fibrosis, Down syndrome, sickle-cell anemia

Two categories of disabilities currently receiving considerable attention by educators at all levels are **learning disabilities** and **attention-deficit/hyperactivity disorder (ADHD).** Children with learning disabilities are found in almost every classroom. Although they have no outward signs of problems, these children struggle

Children who used to be classified as hyperactive are now described as having attention-deficit/hyperactivity disorder (ADHD). Statistics indicate that up to 5 percent of all children under eighteen may be affected by this disorder (Wallis, 1994). Boys tend to be diagnosed more often with this disorder. A drug called Ritalin is frequently prescribed by physicians to counteract the problems of this behavior pattern. Unfortunately, significant side effects are associated with Ritalin, and its overuse is questioned by many. Appetite and sleep disturbances, increased heart rate and blood pressure, and growth retardation have all been associated with Ritalin use (Anselmo & Franz, 1995).

Characteristics of Children with ADHD

- Impulsive (acting without thinking of the consequences)
- Short attention spans (difficulty concentrating on a task or activity)
- Difficulty in organizing thoughts and work

- Easily distracted from the task at hand
- In constant motion (finds it hard to sit still and refrain from fidgeting)

Guidance Considerations

- Provide consistent routines in school day.
- Keep the child away from distracting noises and active areas.
- Make eye contact while giving clear directions.
- Create a signal that reminds the child to get back on task.

1. *Review two recent articles on ADHD, and discuss the authors' perspectives on this disorder. What suggestions were made regarding the teacher or parent's role in assisting these children?*

2. *Can you see some problems associated with classifying children in this way? What are your concerns? What are the benefits?*

with one or more basic learning tasks. Educators are attempting to define, identify, and remediate children with learning disabilities. Allen, at age eight, has considerable difficulty remembering his basic computational facts. Addition, subtraction, and multiplication facts all seem to go in one ear and out the other. He has a learning disability relating to memorization skills. Allen shows normal developmental patterns in other aspects of his schoolwork.

ADHD is characterized by a short attention span and a tendency to be restless and impulsive.

     Rasheen is a very likeable five-year-old who seems to be in constant motion. At group time in his kindergarten classroom, he finds it very difficult to focus on what the teacher is saying and often needs another adult next to him to remain seated and involved in the group activity. Rasheen's family doctor diagnosed him as having ADHD, and Rasheen is taking a drug called Ritalin to help him deal with his disability.

Although treatment with Ritalin is common for ADHD, many educators are concerned that we are overmedicating children and that other options may be more helpful in working with these children.

Children at Risk.   Children who are **at risk** may experience delay in development due to negative genetic or environmental factors such as poverty, low birth weight, or maternal diabetes. These children have not been identified as having disabilities, but they may develop problems without adequate intervention. For example, Joy, only a few days old, is experiencing neonatal abstinence syndrome (Anselmo & Franz, 1995) because of her addiction to cocaine. She became addicted during the prenatal period and is at risk in her future development. Joy needs to receive special assistance to help her through this difficult beginning.

Early childhood education has long been involved in helping at-risk children prepare for success in the formal schooling process. Head Start and other similar programs, for example, were created to meet the needs of young at-risk children.

Particularly during the prekindergarten years, educators are reluctant to classify children as having particular disabilities. Developmental patterns at these early ages vary greatly. Yet, children who have experienced early risk factors often need assistance to develop more normally and avoid later intervention. Either biological or environmental factors can lead to the child being identified as at-risk. Biological risk factors may occur either during pregnancy or after birth. Premature birth, low birth weight, maternal diabetes, and severe illnesses are all biological factors that may place children at risk in their development.

> *At age two, Monica got into the cleaning agents under her mom's sink and swallowed samples of several types. After an emergency visit to the hospital for a stomach pump, she has been recovering nicely. Her day care center has been asked to carefully watch for signs of longer-term problems associated with this traumatic event. Monica is considered at risk for at least the short term.*

Environmental factors play a major role in creating at-risk conditions for children. Poverty, homelessness, child abuse, and poor parenting are all key factors that can cause children to be at risk in their development.

> *Andrew is three years old and has just begun to attend the local Head Start program. His mother is eighteen, a single parent on welfare, and struggling to get her life together. Andrew's overall development is lagging behind his peers, and he is considered at risk.*
>
> *Five-year-old Bonnie has just been placed in temporary foster care. Her parents are suspected of neglect. Bonnie frequently comes to school dirty, unkempt, hungry, and tired. The school staff has been notified, and she is being watched for signs of problems in her overall development.*

Gifted Children.   Children who are **gifted** demonstrate excellence in an aspect of development well beyond most children of the same age (Bee, 1995). Armon taught himself to read at four, and at age six, he is reading long chapter books

FOCUS ON . . .
The Well-Being of Children

It may surprise you to learn that children in the United States don't do well on several measures of well-being. The Annie E. Casey Foundation (1996) has identified several indicators that children may be at risk, four of which follow:

Low Birth Weight Babies

Children weighing less than about 5.5 pounds at birth have a high probability of experiencing developmental problems. The percentage of babies in this category has grown since the mid-1980s. Low birth weight is often associated with mothers who have not had adequate prenatal care, often because of a lack of health care. Hispanic Americans, African Americans, and people living in poverty more frequently fit this category.

Infant Mortality Rates

The infant mortality rate for children born into poor families is more than 50 percent higher than that for children born into more affluent homes. More than twenty-five countries worldwide have lower infant mortality rates than the United States.

Teen Birth Rate (Ages Fifteen to Seventeen)

Teenage childbearing is problematic for both the newborn and the young parent. The teen is typically unmarried and has not finished high school. A child born into this situation is ten times as likely to be living in poverty.

Children Living in Poverty

In the 1990s, the percentage of children living in poverty in the United States has grown to over 20 percent. Children in most other developed countries fare better on this measure than do those in the United States.

1. *Discuss these indicators with your classmates. What does this tell you about America's commitment to children?*

2. *What are the implications of these indicators for those working in early childhood education? How would you try to compensate for them?*

found challenging by many ten- to twelve-year-olds. He is enrolled in a gifted program at his elementary school. Traditionally, IQ tests have been used to identify giftedness, and very high intellectual functioning is seen by many as the true mark of a gifted person. More recently, people such as Howard Gardner (Gardner, 1983) have suggested that intelligence comes in many forms and that high levels of expertise in music, art, sports, and relationships are also evidence of giftedness. Taylor began piano instruction at age three and now at five is reading and playing classical music for pleasure. Her musical giftedness is obvious to all who listen to her play.

Giftedness is a complex concept that is difficult to define. One popular description follows:

Gifted and talented children are those identified by professionally qualified persons who, by virtue of outstanding abilities, are capable of high performance.

INTO PRACTICE . . .

Signs of Giftedness in Preschoolers

Giftedness comes in many different forms and often can be detected at an early age. It is important to encourage talents exhibited without applying pressure to excel that can overwhelm the young child. The American Association for Gifted Children (1998) has developed a set of characteristics that indicate giftedness. These traits can help adults identify gifted children. If some of the following signs of giftedness are present during the preschool years, then the child may be gifted. The gifted preschooler

- Learns quickly and remembers easily.
- Uses a large vocabulary and shows an unusual interest in reading.
- Seems mature for his age.
- Experiments readily and often to solve problems.
- Prefers older playmates.
- Seems more sensitive than others his age.
- Shows a high level of intellectual curiosity.
- Questions others in authority.

- Seems to get bored easily.
- Shows a special talent in music, art, dance, or drama.
- Displays a more mature sense of humor.
- Has a high energy level.

If a child shows signs of giftedness, then parents and teachers can work to assist growth and development. Reading books of interest to the child, spending time in storytelling activities, encouraging writing experiences, and taking trips to interesting places are just a few of the options that might be considered. Those interested in more information on gifted children can call or write

The American Association for Gifted Children
Duke University
1121 W. Main Street, Suite 100
Durham, North Carolina 27701
(919) 683-1400

Internet address:
http://www.jayi.com/jayi/aagc/gifted.html

These are children who require differentiated educational programs and services beyond those normally provided by the regular program in order to realize their contribution to self and society. Children capable of high performance include those with demonstrated achievement and/or potential ability in any of the following areas: (1) general intellectual ability; (2) specific academic aptitude; (3) creative or productive thinking; (4) leadership ability; (5) the visual and performing arts; and (6) psychomotor ability. (Marland, 1972, p. 10)

No one list of characteristics describes children who are gifted. Certain traits and abilities, however, do seem to be common to many (Deiner, 1993). Unusually strong language skills may indicate giftedness. These children frequently have a very large and complex vocabulary and are able to use their words to create elaborate oral stories, songs, and rhymes. Early reading and writing are often demonstrated as well.

Strong skills of observation enable gifted children to pay attention to details that allow them to master concepts more quickly. Four-year-old Amy, for example, notices many differences in the colors and body parts of the ladybug caught on the playground this morning. She asks her teacher many questions and is eager to look through the book in the library center that describes bugs.

These children are often more willing to take risks and problem solve as they learn about their world. Curiosity and a willingness to explore the possibilities make these children eager to grow in their understanding of people and things. Eight-year-old Aaron is constructing a castle out of blocks after reading a story about medieval times. He is having difficulty constructing a roof that meets his expectations and tries several possibilities before getting it the way he wants it.

Learning About Children

The task of understanding children and their development is definitely an important one. It is not, however, an easy process. A teacher must study a great deal and consider many factors in learning about children. How, then, does the busy teacher work this task into an already overcrowded life? The answer lies in beginning now and in working hard to become more knowledgeable over time. As you read about and study child development, make careful observations of children, and work closely with parents, the task becomes more manageable.

Studying Development and Learning

This chapter has provided a brief overview of child development and learning. It is merely a beginning point for further study and investigation. You will need to understand the work of each theorist presented and every developmental milestone in more depth in preparation for working with children. Acquiring a thorough understanding of Vygotsky's theory, for example, requires more in-depth reading, study, and discussion with others. Similarly, the concept of attachment is more complex than presented here. Most teacher preparation programs generally require courses in child development and learning, and these are an important component of the learning process for understanding these issues. In addition to this more formal learning process, most teachers continue to refine their knowledge of these topics through advanced readings and discussions with others.

Observation: Tool for Understanding

Another essential avenue for learning about children and their development is to spend time carefully observing them. This time-honored technique can provide the insightful teacher with a great deal of useful information about children individually and collectively (see Chapter 11 for more information). The time invested in observing pays big dividends.

Communicating with Parents

There are many good reasons for working with parents (see Chapter 7). One very important one is that parents know a great deal about their own children and can often share their insights with interested teachers. Although parents usually aren't experts in child development, they do have a wealth of knowledge about their own children that is frequently useful in the classroom.

> ∿ *Tenesha's parents meet with you for the fall parent–teacher conference. You learn that this bright, capable four-year-old has been struggling to get to sleep at night, fearful that there are alligators under her bed. It is clearer why Tenesha has been tearful and easily stressed this past week in day care.*
>
> *Brian has been diagnosed as having autism and struggles to interact socially with other children in your third-grade classroom. In talking to his parents, you discover that he is gifted musically and that opportunities to express himself on the piano help him engage in more appropriate social behaviors.*

With strong parent–teacher relationships, it is possible to learn and use parents' valuable insights regarding their own children's learning and development.

Summary

The characteristics of developmentally appropriate practice are a cornerstone of early childhood education. Teachers also need to understand the theories and concepts of John Bowlby (attachment), Abraham Maslow (hierarchy of needs), Howard Gardner (multiple intelligences), Arnold Gesell (gradients of growth), Maria Montessori (maturationist theory), Lev Vygotsky (sociocultural theory), Erik Erikson (psychosocial theory), and Jean Piaget (stages of intellectual development). An understanding of the developmental characteristics of children from infancy through eight years of age allows teachers to successfully prepare materials and activities for young children. Children with special needs (disabled, at-risk, and gifted) are an important part of early education; teachers need to understand and prepare for educating these children. Finally, academic study, observation, and communication with parents are all important ways of learning about children.

∿ For Discussion and Action

1. Does the concept of developmentally appropriate practice make sense? Would you be comfortable promoting it with parents? Discuss your questions, likes, and dislikes regarding developmentally appropriate practice with your peers.

2. When you recognize that children come into the classroom with unmet needs, it makes your job as teacher more difficult. What are your responsibilities in helping meet these needs? What do you do when you can't meet a child's needs?

3. Pick an aspect of development (such as the development of sex role identity), and discuss the influences of heredity and environment on the process.

4. Spend time observing a child in the early childhood years. Look for evidence of how this child constructs knowledge from playing with people and things. Discuss your insights with classmates.

5. Each of the theories outlined in this chapter (such as Erikson's psychosocial theory) have significant implications for the ways in which you teach in an early childhood classroom. Choose one theory, and discuss specific ways in which it would affect your teaching.

6. Interview a special education teacher. Without using names, ask the teacher to describe for you one child with special needs included in the regular classroom. Find out why the child has been classified as having special needs, what behaviors the child displays, and how the special education teacher works with the child during the regular school day.

❧ *Building Your Personal Library*

Anselmo, S., & Franz, W. (1995). *Early childhood development: Prenatal through age eight* (2nd ed.). Upper Saddle River, NJ: Merrill/Prentice Hall. This book provides much good additional information on child growth and development during the early childhood years. It provides much more detail than was possible in this chapter.

Berk, L. (1994). *Child development* (3rd ed.). Boston: Allyn & Bacon. Another excellent book describing child growth and development throughout the early childhood years.

Gesell, A., & Ilg, F. (1949). *Child development: An introduction to the study of human growth.* New York: Harper & Brothers. This classic book presents a wealth of information collected on children's developmental patterns. The normative data provided here are still very much in use to describe typical development of children.

Hallahan, D., & Kauffman, J. (1994). *Exceptional children: Introduction to special education* (6th ed.). Boston: Allyn & Bacon. This text describes the field of special education and what it is like to teach children with special needs. It details the types of children with special needs and ways to work with them.

5 *Play in Childhood*

In this chapter you will

- Study definitions of childhood play.
- Review theories explaining why children play.
- Learn about social and cognitive play types.
- Understand the benefits of play to all aspects of the child's development.
- Identify the adult's role in facilitating childhood play.

Your kindergarten children have just been dismissed for their morning recess. Rather than head down to the teacher's lounge today, you spend a few minutes watching your students engage in play just outside your classroom windows. It's amazing how busy they have become. Two minutes ago, they were quietly listening to the story you had chosen, but now the playground supervisor has her hands full. Phillip and John are already rolling around on the grass, enjoying the spring weather and the chance to engage in rough-and-tumble play. Maria and Chelsea are laughing and talking as they swing back and forth with their friends. Charlie and Andy are playing cops and robbers and chasing several girls excitedly around the playground. Joe is new to your class and is currently just observing the actions of others. The sandbox has attracted Albert and Amy, who are planning the castle they intend to build. Eric and Austin are climbing and swinging from the monkey bars, trying to outdo one another. The excitement and enthusiasm are evident. What is less obvious is all the learning that is taking place through the varied play experiences. If only others knew how valuable play can be during childhood, it would be much easier to include it as part of your school day. Just yesterday, a parent was quizzing you about the importance of play in the classroom, and once again you were explaining the many benefits of this natural part of childhood.

Unfortunately, the most common perception of play is that it is a fun but rather frivolous activity. Many parents, the general public, and some teachers and administrators view play as a nice treat for children who have spent time engaged in more serious learning tasks. But include it as an important part of the early childhood curriculum? That is a more difficult task to accomplish. This chapter is designed to provide you with a solid understanding of the benefits of childhood play. It will also help you develop a strong rationale for including play in the early childhood curriculum and clarify others' misconceptions about childhood play. As research continues to identify its many benefits (Fromberg, 1990), it is hoped childhood play will be accepted for its important role in development and learning.

It is perhaps surprising to realize that childhood play is actually a very difficult term to define. Garvey (1990) helps us understand the challenges of defining play through the following imaginary dialog between a mother and her son:

> *"Tom, I want to clean this room. Go out and play."*
>
> *"What do you mean, 'go out and play'?"*
>
> *"You know what I mean."*
>
> *"No, I don't."*
>
> *"Well, just go out and do whatever you do when you're having too much fun to come in to dinner."*
>
> *"You mean toss the tennis ball against the garage? Finish painting my bike? Practice standing on my head? Tease Andy's sister? Check out the robin eggs?" (p. 2)*

The broad umbrella of play also includes a great variety of other behaviors, such as swinging, sliding, running, digging in the dirt, building with blocks, dancing to music, making up nonsense rhyming words, dressing up, and pretending. As a result of this variety, several different definitions of play exist.

Characteristics of Childhood Play

One approach frequently used to define play is to list common characteristics of these experiences. Four such attributes stand out as essential to our understanding of the term. First, play is **active.** When children play, movement often involves both large and small muscles. Children are using their bodies and manipulating the natural and human-made materials that they find in their play environments. Rather than passively taking in information, children involved in play are engaged in learning about the world by constructing knowledge through active interaction with people and things (Chaille & Silvern, 1996).

Another characteristic of childhood play is that it is **child selected** (Bredekamp & Copple, 1997). Quality play experiences are ones that the child chooses to participate in. Consider, for example, a parent who tells her six-year-old child to clean her room. For most children, that request to clean something would be met with groans and protests, and it would not be thought of as a playful event. That same child, however, could choose to clean her bike in preparation for an upcoming ride and find the task enjoyable and generally playful. When the child chooses the task, it becomes fun and rewarding and is more likely to fit a broad definition of play.

Play is also **process oriented** rather than product oriented (Bruner, 1972). Seven-year-old Michael is constructing a castle out of blocks. He uses the building process to represent his new-found knowledge of medieval times. Once he has built the castle and shown it to his classmates, Michael will be ready to dismantle it

INTO PRACTICE . . .
Games from Other Cultures

Orlick (1978) suggests that one good way to better understand different cultures is to play childhood games from around the world. He also feels strongly about options that rely on cooperation rather than competition among players. The following two examples are just a few of the possibilities that early childhood teachers can consider.

Pin.   This game of cooperation is played by Native American children in Guatemala. A wooden pin is set up at a moderate distance from a throwing line. (The group can decide the length.) The object is for the team to work together to get the first ball that is rolled (lead ball) to touch the pin without knocking the pin over. The first player rolls her ball, and the subsequent team members try to roll their balls so that

they nudge the lead ball closer to the pin. The game is won when the lead ball is touching the pin. If the pin is knocked over, the player who knocked it over starts a new game by rolling the first ball (Orlick, 1978, p. 76).

Muk (Silence).   This game comes from the Inuit people in Alaska and centers around laughter. Players begin by sitting in a circle. One player moves into the middle of the circle. She then chooses another player, who must say "Muk" and then remain silent and straight-faced. The person in the middle uses comical expressions and gestures to try to "break the muk." The player to break the muk is dubbed with a comical name and replaces the person in the middle (Orlick, 1978, p. 81).

and move on to other projects. This process orientation gives children in play the freedom to explore and experiment without fear of failure. There is no right or wrong way to play, so children can try a variety of play options, knowing that it is the road traveled rather than the destination that is the most important aspect of this activity.

A final characteristic of play is that it usually requires a **suspension of reality.** When children play, they set aside the realities of their world and enjoy activities that are often silly but fun. For example, the child who makes up nonsense rhyming words knows that they are not "real" words, but she still enjoys the process of creating them. Piaget (1962) calls this a *ludic set.* This ludic (or playful) mind-set allows children to suspend their knowledge of reality and engage in activities that are creative, spontaneous, and fun. Children who pretend to be astronauts or characters from their favorite movies are creating a ludic set to engage in this play.

Definitions of Play

Other attempts at defining play have been more traditional descriptions of this complex activity. Definitions from key historical and modern figures follow in order to provide additional insights into the complexities of childhood play. Friedrich Froebel, described in Chapter 2 as the father of the modern kindergarten, defines play as "the natural unfolding of the germinal leaves of childhood" (E. Mitchell & Mason, 1948, p. 103). Although this description gives few specifics, Froebel gives us a beautiful metaphor for childhood play. He characterizes it as an essential and necessary component of childhood. Play is part of the fabric of children's lives and leads to healthy growth and development.

John Dewey suggests that play consists of activities not consciously performed for the sake of any result beyond themselves (Dewey, 1929). When children play, they do so because the process is meaningful to them. The doing of the activity gives it value. The end product, if any, holds little meaning for the child. A child painting at the easel often has a goal in mind as she covers the page with vibrant colors, but the real joy of the activity is just engaging in the painting process itself. Once the painting is completed, she is ready to move on to the next challenge.

Several writers have defined play by contrasting it with work. One such definition comes from Erik Erikson (1963), who suggests:

> When man plays he must intermingle with things and people in a similarly uninvolved and light fashion. He must do something which he has chosen to do without being compelled by urgent interests or impelled by strong passion. He must feel entertained and free of any fear or hope of serious consequences. He is on vacation from social and economic reality—or as is most commonly emphasized: he *does not work.* (p. 212)

Another well-known psychologist, Jerome Bruner (1972), writes the following about childhood play:

> Play appears to serve several centrally important functions. First, it is a means of minimizing the consequences of one's actions and of learning, therefore, in a less risky situation. . . . Second, play provides an excellent opportunity to try combinations of behavior that would, under functional pressure, never be tried. (p. 693)

Play, according to Bruner, can be seen as a prime opportunity for children to take risks without fear of failure. Bruner's definition also suggests that childhood play and creative activity are closely linked. When fear of failure is low and children can explore and experiment in their play, the possibilities for creative outcomes are greatly enhanced. For example, a young girl building with Legos can creatively explore and experiment without fear of failure. There is no right or wrong way to build with these materials.

One final definition of play comes from the work of David Elkind (1981b). He states, "Basically, play is nature's way of dealing with stress for children as well as adults" (p. 197). This perspective may be initially surprising, and it clearly does not describe all play behaviors, but for a significant portion of children's activities, stress reduction is an important function.

> ❧ *Seven-year-old Robert's mother is pregnant. Getting ready for a new brother or sister is stressful. Mom and dad are busy making preparations, there is less time and energy for the other children, and just making sense of the upcoming changes takes considerable time and energy. Robert is going to need some good ways to release the stress being experienced.*

Examples abound of this kind of situation and the value that play holds in allowing children to reduce their stress levels.

None of the definitions presented here is sufficient, in and of itself, to fully explain this complex phenomenon we call *play*. But each adds a little insight to help us in our understanding of play. Collectively, they paint a clearer picture of this important concept.

Why Children Play: Theories

Just as there are a variety of definitions of play, many different theories have been proposed to explain why children engage in this activity. Although no one theory is fully satisfying, together they add much to our understanding of a child's motivation to play. M. Ellis (1973) organizes theories of play into two categories: classical and contemporary. The classical theories are older and generally less complex in their explanations of why children play. Contemporary theories are relatively recent and provide a more detailed rationale for this childhood activity.

Classical Theories

An early explanation for why children play is the **surplus energy theory.** It is based on the notion that each of us generates a finite level of energy that must be expended. Our first priority is to use that energy on survival. What is left over accumulates until it reaches a point where it must be used up. Play becomes the vehicle for expending that extra energy. This theory suggests that children play more than adults because they are not burdened with survival tasks. This theory has considerable appeal. Mothers and fathers often tell their children something like, "You need to go outside and burn off a little of that extra energy." Teachers play games with their children to "get the wiggles out." Many times, children seem to need to use up their surplus energy. Yet, at other times, children clearly are operating on reserve energy but still very much want to continue in their play.

A second classical explanation of play is the **relaxation theory.** In essence, it is the opposite of the surplus energy theory. This theory suggests that people play because of a deficit of energy. When we engage in tasks that are relatively new to us or that are demanding in some way, fatigue sets in, and relaxation is needed to replenish our energy. Because children encounter more new tasks and challenges than adults do, they need to spend more time relaxing in play.

This theory clearly has application for children in the elementary school years. With the many new academic tasks they face, play becomes an important opportunity for rest and recuperation. Recess and indoor play breaks give children much-needed opportunities to get away from work-like experiences and re-energize. At the same time, this theory seems to be less effective in explaining the play of preschool-aged children. At this age, children have few work-like tasks to escape from. New and demanding tasks are generally encountered *in* play during these years.

A final early explanation for play is the **preexercise theory.** Play is seen as an opportunity to practice skills necessary for adult life. When puppies, for example, engage in play fighting, they are practicing survival skills that they need in adult life. A young boy who pretends to be daddy is also developing abilities for his future role

Play becomes an important opportunity for rest and recuperation for elementary school children facing many new academic tasks.

as a parent. This theory proposes that through their play children practice dealing with such things as fear, anger, curiosity, assertion, and submission. Although this may provide a rationale for a limited scope of childhood play behaviors, this theory seems less helpful in explaining much of what children do in their play.

Contemporary Theories

A more recent description of why children play is the **psychoanalytic theory** of play. Many have contributed to this perspective, but it is based on the work of Sigmund Freud. He suggests that play is motivated by what he calls the *pleasure principle* (Freud, 1938). Pleasure is achieved, according to Freud, through wish fulfillment in play. When seven-year-old Maya pretends to be an astronaut, she is gaining pleasure by becoming that important person for a short period of time. Play provides an opportunity for children to bend reality and gain gratification.

This theory also suggests that play has significant therapeutic value. When children encounter unpleasant situations or stressful circumstances, play becomes the child's vehicle for mastering them. By playing out mom and dad fighting, five-year-old Brent can begin to make sense of this unpleasant event and eventually set it aside and move on to other play themes. A specific branch of therapy for children who have experienced severe stress is based on this premise and is called *play therapy* (see, e.g., Axline, 1947). Trained therapists use this approach to help victims of child abuse and other traumatic events come to grips with very difficult and complex experiences.

Other theorists have expanded upon Freud's ideas concerning childhood play. One such person is Waelder (1933), who added the concept of the *repetition compulsion*. He identified the almost compulsive way in which many children will repeat an unpleasant experience in their play over and over again. Waelder states that children may find some events too difficult to assimilate all at once. They often need to play it out over and over again, until finally diminishing the intensity of the experience. N. Brown, Curry, and Tittnich (1971) describe an event in which several kindergarten children observed a man who was critically injured on the street adjacent to their playground. In observations of later play experiences, it was clear to the writers that these children needed to repeat this very unpleasant and difficult event over and over in order to make better sense of it. Throughout the school year, this accident-related play theme reappeared regularly as children worked through their feelings.

Another more recent theory that has been proposed to explain why children play is called **play as arousal seeking.** M. Ellis (1973) developed this theory from a number of research studies that make a case for a new drive—the drive for optimal arousal. In an attempt to avoid boredom on the one hand, and overstimulation on the other, people strive to reach just the right level of excitement. Each of us is engaged in behavior that can be called stimulus seeking. Play is a major opportunity for most of us to be stimulated. Not all stimulus seeking, however, is play. When five-year-old Angie challenges herself to climb one level higher on the climber or four-year-old Jamal jumps off a three-foot-high box, each is doing a bit of thrill seeking. These behaviors are a little risky and therefore more exciting for the children engaged in them. Although this theory again does not explain all of children's play, it applies readily to many childhood activities.

A final theory discussed here comes from the work of Piaget (1962). He explains play in terms of children's **cognitive structures.** As the child learns about the world, she is adding to her **schema** or conceptual understandings. These schema are strengthened through the dual processes of **assimilation** (taking in information from the environment and fitting it into an already existing schema) and **accommodation** (adjusting schema to take into account new input from the environment that does not fit existing structures). Piaget suggests that when children play they are engaging primarily in the process of assimilation. As children take in information during play, they are unconsciously growing in their understanding of the world.

Piaget also proposes that the play children engage in is strongly influenced by their intellectual stage of development. For each of his first three stages (see Chapter 4), there is a corresponding type of play the child primarily exhibits. For example, Piaget suggests that, during the sensorimotor stage of intellectual development, children engage primarily in functional play. These simple, repetitive muscle movements match the cognitive functioning of the child during the sensorimotor period. Piaget's play stages have been expanded upon by Smilansky (1968) and are described in more detail in the next section of this chapter.

INTO PRACTICE . . .

A Pretend Grocery Store

When given the time and appropriate materials, young children can have great fun pretending as they play out a theme you have prepared as the classroom teacher. One example of this type of activity is to set up a grocery store in the classroom. The basic ingredients needed are

Grocery bags

Empty food containers (soup and vegetable cans, cereal boxes, etc.—use your imagination)

Pictures or posters of food items

Telephone

Assorted baskets

Plastic foods

Play money (coins and paper)

Note pads for making out grocery lists

Sticky notes for pricing groceries

Writing utensils

Cash register

Adding machine

Shelves for storing foods

Checkout table

Although this is just a starting point for collecting materials for this play theme, it should be clear that with some work by the teacher some very creative play can take place. Children who are provided with these materials can take on the roles of shoppers, grocery checkers, and clerks. Some can price the groceries while others shop for bargains on a budget. As they do so, they are having fun while they practice prereading and writing skills, counting, learning more about money, and interacting with others in a social setting.

Cognitive Play Types

People who have studied childhood play generally categorize it according to either its cognitive or social elements. **Cognitive play** categories identify the intellectual functioning of children during play. **Social play** types describe how children gradually become more able to relate effectively with others as they play.

As suggested earlier, Piaget (1962) developed cognitive play categories that match each of his first three intellectual stages of development. Smilansky (1968) modified these stages by adding a fourth cognitive play category. Her cognitive play stages have been widely accepted as an effective way to understand and study childhood play. From birth to about age two, children engage in **functional play.** Characterized by simple, repetitive muscle movements, this play develops physical skills and is done because the activity is pleasurable. The toddler who is learning to walk spends considerable time practicing the muscle movements necessary to get from one spot to the next. An infant shaking a rattle is also engaging in functional play. This play type is the predominant one during the first two years, but it does not end at that time. Elementary children swinging on swings or running happily across the playfield are participating in functional play.

Smilansky suggests that children from about two to three years of age are involved primarily in **construction play.** This play type is characterized by the child actually making something out of the materials available. For example, when using a set of blocks, Alyssa can now begin to create simple structures such as towers. The intellectual skills needed for building are a step above those required for functional play. Older children also engage in construction play, but it is the two-year-old's primary cognitive play type.

CELEBRATING PLAY . . .
Children's Invented Games

After their second-grade teacher's discussion of the procedures for creating a board game, Rebecca and Latoya decide to give it a try. During free time, they begin the process of planning a board game around the theme of horse racing. For the next week, these girls spend all of their spare moments avidly constructing their game and then sharing it with the rest of the class. Given the opportunity, primary children seem to love the chance to invent their own games. Castle (1990) describes several benefits of this activity:

- *Practice academic skills* such as writing and reading and mathematics. Children use writing skills, for example, to label game parts and create game instructions.

- *Develop organizational skills* like having a plan and putting it to work. Planning the game sequence requires the use of organizational abilities.

- *Cooperate* with other children and adults. Through the planning and construction process, children must take into account the perspectives of others and learn to adjust their game accordingly.

- *Solve problems* as children encounter differing opinions about how the game should proceed. Once a prototype is constructed, children practice problem solving as they debug the difficulties they encounter when playing.

1. *Try constructing your own game to discover the challenges this task may require of children. Share your game with others, and then modify your game as needed.*

2. *Would this activity be appropriate for preschool children? Why or why not?*

When the child enters what Piaget calls the preoperational stage of intellectual development, **dramatic play** becomes the preferred play type. From about age three to seven, children pretend that one object is something else or take on a role other than being children. Four-year-old Lisa pretends to be a teacher and imitates what she has seen her preschool teacher do by encouraging her playmates to try new pretend foods in the housekeeping center. She must use considerable intellectual skill to imagine the sequence she plays out with her peers. Research indicates that this play type is very important as a foundation for later academic learning (Smilansky, 1968) and should be encouraged both at the preschool and early elementary levels.

At approximately seven years of age, children enter Piaget's stage of concrete operations and begin to engage in **games with rules.** These activities require children to agree to a set of rules before beginning play and accept the defined penalties for breaking the rules. Piaget spent considerable time observing children playing marbles and learned much not only about this particular game with rules but also about children's social and moral development (Piaget, 1965). Although the game of marbles is less common today, other organized games such as basketball and soccer are very popular with children of all ages.

Social Play Types

A number of researchers and writers have suggested different categories to describe children's social play. The work of Mildred Parten (1933), however, has stood the test of time as one of the best and most descriptive summaries of the development of children's socialization skills in play. Parten states that, until about two-and-a-half years of age, children engage in **solitary play.** They play alone, with toys that are different from those of children playing nearby. Children at this stage make no attempt to get close to or interact with others. Clearly, the level of social interaction at this point is very low. It is important, however, to realize that, despite its lack of social value, solitary play should be encouraged as a part of the young child's activities. Much of an elementary child's day, for example, is spent in independent seat work. Children who have learned to be comfortable in solitary play are more likely to succeed in working independently.

Parten (1933) defined the next social play category as **parallel play.** From about two-and-a-half to three-and-a-half years, children continue to play independently, but now they are among their peers and use toys that are similar to those of the children around them. Just as parallel lines run side-by-side, children in this play stage play beside, but not with, others. There is an awareness of the children nearby but little interaction. Andre and Kelly are playing with play dough at the art center in their preschool classroom. They occasionally glance at each other's efforts, but spend most of their time just molding their chunks of dough. They are engaging in parallel play.

As children continue to mature, they begin to engage in **associative play** at about three-and-a-half years. This play type is characterized as one in which children truly play with others. Children borrow and loan play materials, and the group members are engaged in similar activities. Parten suggests that, at this point, the associations are more important than the play activity itself. Children begin to form small play groups and spend considerable time moving from one activity to the next, with playmates remaining together. Watch children of this age swinging on swings, for example. They enjoy the swinging but spend more of their efforts talking and laughing with their friends. When a group leader decides it is time to move on, others make the move as well. Being with the other children has become more important than the activity itself.

Parten (1933) calls the final social play type **cooperative play,** which begins to appear at about four-and-a-half years of age. Parten describes this as the highest level of social play; it is characterized by children playing in groups as they did in associative play. But now, the children demonstrate division of labor, working on a group product or cooperating to attain a common goal. When four kindergarten children decide to build a town with blocks, and each takes a specific part of the town to build, play has become cooperative. It is important to note that although cooperative play requires practicing important social skills, it is not always a desired play type. Think about three preschool children who decide to torment a fellow classmate. Although each takes on a separate role and the children are working toward a common goal, the play is unpleasant for the targeted child.

Although Parten (1933) observed preschool-aged children, others have studied the social play of older children. Seagoe (1970), for example, identified a

In parallel play, children play beside, but not with, others.

social play type for children beginning at about age seven or eight. **Cooperative-competitive play** involves play activities that are formally patterned toward team victory. Organized team sports such as soccer and baseball are examples of this play type. The social understanding needed for cooperative-competitive play is more advanced than that required for the cooperative play described by Parten.

Benefits of Play

> ∿ *Jay and Aaron are excitedly rummaging through the play junk pile on the preschool playground. This collection of bricks, boards, old tires, and assorted building materials has them thinking of the many different structures they might construct. There is no thought in their minds of the learning potential of these tasks. These two young boys are merely playing. Yet, mathematics, language usage, social skills, basic physics principles, and more may all be enhanced as they play out their fantasies.*

Unfortunately, it takes a thorough educational effort for parents, other teachers, administrators, and the general public to recognize the many benefits of play. Every aspect of the child's development is enhanced through play. It is just not obvious to many people at first glance. Figure 5–1 summarizes the benefits of play discussed next.

Intellectual growth
    Engage in multisensory experiences
    Have opportunities for problem solving
    Master abstract symbolism

Build social skills
    Learn social roles
    Decrease egocentrism
    Understand the rules of social interaction

Language and literacy development
    Play with language
    Engage in metacommunication
    Engage in pretend communication

Physical development
    Develop gross motor skills
    Develop fine motor skills
    Become aware of body, space, and direction

Emotional development
    Master emotional issues
    Feel good about themselves

Play and creativity
    Have opportunities to be creative

Intellectual Growth through Play

Because many people assume that the primary goal of schooling is to feed the intellect, this discussion on the benefits of play begins with some information on how play enhances cognitive development. Using Piaget's terminology, *cognitive development* is the process of building more elaborate schema or concepts about the workings of the world. Both Bruner (1966) and Piaget (Piaget & Inhelder, 1969) stress that **multisensory experiences** with things and people in the child's environment lead to conceptual development. Play provides the most natural and enjoyable opportunities for these experiences and therefore is a major tool that children use to understand their world. When seven-year-olds David and Jessica construct cardboard castles during free choice time, they are internalizing the information they read in their social studies text. Their play has expanded and solidified several existing schema.

The ability to effectively problem solve is seen as a major asset in intellectual development. Children who can make sense of the problems they face and work through them are adding greatly to their understanding of the world and their ability to work through future problems. Evidence points to a clear link between play and problem solving. Children who engage in creative play experiences are better at convergent (Vandenberg, 1980) and divergent (Pepler & Ross, 1981) problem solving. Play frees up children to explore and experiment in ways that lead to important intellectual understanding.

> ⌒ When four-year-olds Kelly and Sarah play in the dramatic play area, they discover that they don't have the props they need to become pilots. After yesterday's field trip to the airport, they are very excited about this play theme. Kelly discovers a headset from the listening center and decides it can be used "for one of those things pilots listen and talk through." Sarah arranges several child-sized chairs into rows for the passengers. After several minutes of preparation, they have created the basic props they need for their play, and they begin the process of acting out their respective roles.

During play, children encounter and master new problems as well. Play provides many chances for practicing problem solving.

A third major way in which play assists in intellectual development is by helping children **master abstract symbolism.** This is especially true when children engage in dramatic play. As they pretend, children arbitrarily assign meaning to objects they are using in their play. A block is temporarily viewed as a door to the castle, child-sized chairs in rows become passenger seating on an airplane, or a magnifying glass becomes "that thing doctors use." Objects become arbitrary, abstract symbols for real things needed for dramatic play. Nourot and Van Hoorn (1991) state this same concept as follows: "In its complex forms play is characterized by the use of symbols to represent objects, ideas, and situations not present in the immediate time and place" (p. 41).

Children who are able to manipulate abstract symbols in their play are more likely to succeed in managing symbols in school. Both reading and mathematics are fundamental components of formal education that require frequent manipulation of arbitrary and abstract symbol systems. Smilansky and Shefatya (1990) emphasize that children who are good at dramatic play are going to be more successful with these and other academic tasks.

Building Social Skills

In addition to its role in cognitive development, play is an important tool for strengthening social skills. As they play, children have many opportunities to learn about the social world in which they live. The give and take that occurs as children interact helps them **learn about social roles.** Following a trip to the fire station, a group of first graders try out this role in their play outdoors. They are consolidating and integrating their understandings of this important work situation.

Piaget describes children in the preoperational stage of intellectual development (approximately two through seven years of age) as egocentric. By this he means that it is difficult for children this age to see things from another person's perspective. Play provides children with many opportunities to **decrease egocentrism** (Piaget, 1962). To maintain a play sequence, children are forced to acknowledge other viewpoints and modify or adapt the activity accordingly. For example, Ariel and Katy are playing train conductors. Ariel is upset because "only boys wear the conductor's hat." Katy, on the other hand, feels that girls can too. These two will need to recognize their differing perspectives and work out a solution in order to continue the play sequence. Gradually, as children experience a variety of perspectives through their play, egocentrism becomes less of a factor in relating to others.

Play also allows children to **understand the rules of social interaction.** While playing with others, children learn and practice the principles that underlie all social exchanges (F. Hughes, 1995). Such tasks as listening, speaking, taking turns, leading, and following are all guided by commonly understood rules. For example, we all understand that if several people in a group have something to contribute to the conversation, only one can speak at a time. To do otherwise would lead to mass confusion. Children learn this and other similar rules for social interactions as they become involved in their many play experiences.

FOCUS ON...

Making a Case for Play

One of the major challenges for teachers interested in including play in the early childhood classroom is convincing others of its value. Having a collection of resources that provide well-written arguments describing the benefits of play is a must. The following articles should help you begin the process of resource collecting. Many more are available, so use these to begin a strong resource file that you can use to convince parents, other teachers, and administrators of the value of play.

Foreman, G. (1996). A child constructs an understanding of a water wheel in five media. *Childhood Education, 72*(5), 269–273. This article is a detailed account of a young child playing and learning. It describes in clear terms how the child is constructing his knowledge of a water wheel through a variety of play experiences.

Nourot, P., & Van Hoorn, J. (1991). Symbolic play in preschool and primary settings. *Young Children, 46*(1), 40–50. The authors review recent research on symbolic (dramatic) play and make a strong case for the importance of this activity in the preschool and primary classroom.

Stone, S. (1995). Wanted: Advocates for play in the primary grades. *Young Children, 50*(6), 45–54. Sandra Stone makes many excellent points about the importance of play in the primary curriculum and gives concrete suggestions about how teachers can be true advocates for childhood play.

Wasserman, S. (1992). Serious play in the classroom. How messing around can win you the Nobel Prize. *Childhood Education, 68*(3), 133–139. This article is a personal favorite. Wasserman helps us understand how important play is in the creative process. Society needs creative individuals to address the many complex issues that are a part of life today. Play is a major way in which children gain confidence in their ability to be creative and solve problems.

1. *Can you find three additional articles in the professional literature that talk about the importance of childhood play? Try to locate recent articles that could be added to your resource file.*

2. *Quite a few books also are available on childhood play. The section "Building Your Personal Library," at the end of this chapter, lists four good resources. Find two more.*

Karen and Rachel both want to be teacher as they play during free time in kindergarten. As they realize that it works best to have only one teacher at a time, the girls practice the art of negotiation and compromise so that the play may continue. They learn social rules in a safe and enjoyable way as they proceed.

Language and Literacy Development

Through play, children also enhance oral and written language skills. Garvey (1990) suggests that every aspect of language can be better understood through

"Would you like to come to my house for dinner?" "Yes, that would be loooovvvely."

play. Phonology (sounds of language), grammar, and meaning are all playfully explored as children engage in their free choice activities. Garvey proposes four different types of play with language:

1. *Play with sounds and noises.* Children explore the sounds used to form words and experiment with putting them together in creative and fun ways.
2. *Play with the linguistic system.* In their play, children begin to understand how sounds combine to form words and recognize the structure and ordering of words in sentences.
3. *Spontaneous rhyming and word play.* Through simple rhyming games, children learn about the structure of words and their meanings.
4. *Play with the conventions of speech.* By using and breaking the rules for conversation, children learn how to effectively communicate.

In addition to playing with language, children use language in and around their play experiences. **Metacommunication statements** are used to structure and organize play. "Let's pretend this rope is a snake." "First we'll go to the market, then the toy store." **Pretend communication statements** are appropriate to the roles children have adopted. "Hush, baby! Mom is on the telephone!"

During the preschool and primary school years, children learn about the written language around them as well. Play can provide many opportunities to facilitate literacy development.

> 🐛 *Cindy and Erik, both age four years, are playing in the restaurant set up in the dramatic play center at their day care center. Erik takes orders by scribbling on a notepad and passing the orders on to Cindy, who cooks up some imaginary foods.*

> ❧ *Anook has built a town out of blocks modeled after the story he has just read in his second-grade classroom. Once the town is completed, he writes an imaginary tale describing life in his town.*

When appropriate props are available, play becomes a rich resource for literacy learning (Vukelich, 1990).

Physical Development

For many, play is epitomized by children running, climbing, jumping, and moving. The pure joy of these simple physical activities is warmly remembered. Children using their large muscles in these activities are strengthening their **gross motor development** (Gallahue, 1982). Beginning in infancy, children improve neuromuscular coordination through repeated use of their large muscles. Batting at a mobile as an infant, walking during early toddlerhood, running and climbing at the preschool level, and swinging and skipping in the primary years are all examples of how play enhances gross motor development.

Play activities also include use of smaller muscles for a variety of tasks. **Fine motor development** is refined through cutting, lacing, buttoning, painting, and writing experiences in play. Building with Legos, putting together puzzles, sand and water play, woodworking projects, play dough, and dressing dolls are additional examples of play activities that promote fine motor development.

In addition, play allows children to develop a better awareness of body, space, and direction. As they move their bodies, children learn about up, down, in, out, over, under, left, right, and more as they climb, swing, crawl, and run. Playing in the gym or outdoors is particularly good for body awareness learning.

As children mature, they use their muscles in continuingly more complex ways, integrating large and fine muscle movements with visual perception. Play allows frequent practice of these complicated actions. Hitting and catching a ball, jumping rope, playing hopscotch, and using the monkey bars are all examples of these more difficult coordinated movements.

Emotional Development

Play is an excellent vehicle for helping children with their emotional (also called *affective*) development (Trawick-Smith, 1994). In their play, children can master emotional issues such as anxiety, frustration, normal developmental conflicts, traumatic situations, unfamiliar concepts, and overwhelming experiences.

> ❧ *Four-year-old Alan just had a very exciting trip to the museum. His initial experience, however, was a bit overwhelming. Just inside the door to the museum was a huge skeleton of a* Tyrannosaurus rex *dinosaur. When his father told Alan that this was once a living animal, he was shocked. How could anything that big ever have lived? During the days and weeks ahead in preschool, Alan plays out his*

Frost and Jacobs (1995) talk about a variety of factors that have caused children to have fewer opportunities for creative free play experiences:

- *Lack of time.* Most children today lead such busy lives that they have little time left over for play. Sports, music, school, and child care arrangements are just a few of the time constraints that take away from play opportunities.

- *Fewer safe places to play.* In the past, children could just go outside and engage in many creative play experiences. Traffic, congestion, and the increased risks of abduction now make it difficult for many parents to feel comfortable in sending their children out to play.

- *Television, movies, and video games.* Children spend large blocks of time today engaging in these activities, which again take time away from play. In addition, the violence and sexual themes that children are exposed to are difficult to understand and are undesirable models of how people should relate socially.

Frost and Jacobs suggest that because children are engaging in fewer quality play experiences, they are unable to learn appropriate social skills to replace the models of violence they see in the world around them. Clark (1995) reviews research on play and also emphasizes its importance in understanding and dealing with violence. Further long-term research is needed to verify this connection, but it is strong and should provide educators with further reasons to promote the values of play.

1. Are children involved in fewer play experiences today than they were just a few years ago? What can be done to improve this situation?

2. Do you see a connection between play deprivation and youth violence? Why or why not?

wonderment by making dinosaurs with play dough, drawing dinosaurs, building dinosaur cages with the blocks, and fighting dinosaurs on the playground. It will take him many weeks to play through this interest, but when it is completed, Alan will have mastered a complex emotional issue.

Another major emotional benefit of play is that it gives children numerous opportunities to feel good about themselves. Because there is no right or wrong way to play, children have successful experiences that positively influence their self-concept.

  Annette, age eighteen months, is playing with a set of nesting blocks in her toddler class, experimenting with building a tower. Although this was not the intended use for this toy, Annette has managed a stack of three blocks—her tallest yet. Her success is evident in the huge smile that seems to fill her whole face. She is feeling very good about herself right now.

Play and Creativity

Sometimes, thoughts of the creative process bring to mind those rare individuals who invent marvelous new products or play a musical instrument better than anyone else. These truly gifted individuals certainly add richness to the lives of those around them. Yet, each of us has creative potential that can be expressed in different and enjoyable ways. Teachers of young children need to look for and nurture this aspect of each child's personality.

During the early years, play provides many opportunities to express and develop a child's creative talents. In free play, children experiment with things and ideas and create new combinations not experienced before. Wasserman (1992) states it this way: "The creation of new ideas does not come from minds trained to follow doggedly what is already known. Creation comes from tinkering and playing around, from which new forms emerge" (p. 134).

Goertzel and Goertzel (1962) studied the early years of four hundred famous adults and discovered that a common thread for these creative individuals was the opportunity to explore their areas of interest and play with things and ideas. For example, Frank Lloyd Wright was encouraged by his mother from an early age to play with colored papers and cubes of wood. She felt that these play experiences would stimulate his intellectual development.

Clearly, play will not make a creative genius out of every child. But it does help stimulate each person's creative talents.

> ❧ *Paul is having fun painting in his second-grade classroom. As he deftly strokes paint on the paper, he gains a sense of control over the elements he is working with. Paul feels good about himself and his artwork. When he gets positive feedback from his classmates and the teacher, his pleasure increases even further. Paul's continued success in art will bolster his attitude about school and increase his willingness to try out his skills in other aspects of school life.*

Facilitating Childhood Play

Play seems such a natural part of childhood that it is difficult to imagine children needing help with this part of their lives. But the many hours spent in front of the television, the overscheduling of children's lives, and a reluctance of many parents to let their children go outside and play for safety reasons have all taken their toll on many children's play abilities. Children today often need the help and support of caring adults to engage in quality play experiences.

Preparing the Play Environments

One important role teachers have in facilitating play is to prepare the places where children play. Teachers and administrators need to make materials and spaces available for play both indoors and outdoors if quality experiences are to take place there (Henniger, 1985). Time and energy must be spent in carefully planning

Teachers should change materials in the students' environment regularly so that children have opportunities to play with new materials often.

these environments. Materials should change regularly, so that children have opportunities to play with new materials often. A variety of challenges should be available for the diverse abilities that children bring with them to their play. As a general rule of thumb, each child needs at least one-and-a-half play options, both indoors and outside. For a class of twenty-five kindergarten children, this means that between forty and fifty play options should be available so that each child has a variety of choices.

Creating a Climate for Play

Another important role for the teacher is to create a classroom atmosphere that lets children know that play is valued. One way in which this can be accomplished is to allow plenty of time for play (Ward, 1996). Quality play experiences can seldom be completed in ten or fifteen minutes. A minimum of thirty minutes (more is better) is needed for creative indoor and outdoor play.

> *As Rick begins his second-grade art project, he first needs a few minutes to see what is available today in the way of materials, time to settle on an idea, and then additional opportunity to do his art activity. Once his project is complete, Rick needs time to share ideas with others in the art center and clean up before moving on to the next activity.*

Figure 5–2 *Adult Interventions in Play*

Parallel playing	Adult plays beside children, using similar materials.
Co-playing	Teacher enters children's play but lets children lead.
Play tutoring	Adult takes brief control of play and gives directions/suggestions.
Artist apprentice	Teacher removes clutter from play environment and adds needed props.
Peacemaker	Adult helps children resolve conflicts.
Guardian of the gate	Teacher works to get new children involved in an ongoing sequence.
Matchmaker	Adult encourages specific children to play together.

Note. Adapted from *Play at the Center of the Curriculum* by J. Van Hoorn, P. Nourot, B. Scales, and K. Alward, 1993, Upper Saddle River, NJ: Merrill/Prentice Hall.

A teacher's responses to children as they play also strongly influence the climate for play. Making encouraging statements to children for sharing, commenting on the positive uses of play materials, and just being nearby to assist as needed all help children know that play is valued. "Philip, thank you for sharing the blocks with Cheri! The two of you are creating some amazing structures!" "Casandra, I like the way you combined the blue and yellow paints in this part of your picture. It makes an interesting contrast to the rest of your work." A teacher's comments and actions are essential in promoting quality play experiences.

Adult Involvement in Play

Many children experience times when the teacher needs to become more directly involved in play to enrich the experience or move it in a different direction. This is not something the teacher should take on lightly, because an adult's participation can actually undermine the child's creativity, spontaneity, and choices for play. After carefully assessing the need for involvement in play, the teacher should participate at the lowest level possible. Figure 5–2 summarizes several techniques to consider when intervening in children's play.

Johnson, Christie, and Yawkey (1987) describe three levels of adult involvement in children's play. They call the lowest level of intervention **parallel playing.** When an adult plays beside, but not with, children and uses the same materials as the other participants, she is engaging in parallel play.

Hermoine notices that several toddlers in her program are having difficulty finding productive ways to use the play dough in the art center. She sits down at the table, tears off a piece of dough, and begins to roll it out into long snakes while quietly humming to herself.

This play type allows children to see the teacher model positive play behaviors without directly intervening in the children's activities.

The next level of play involvement is referred to as **co-playing.** In this instance, the teacher actually enters the children's play but allows them to control the activities. By taking on a needed role and, again, modeling appropriate play responses, the adult can subtly influence the direction and complexity of the play.

> ❧ *As Arthur watches the play in the dress-up corner of his kindergarten classroom, he notices that children are struggling with the role of patient at the doctor's office. Walking into the center, he volunteers to be the next patient and helps children see how this person should interact with the doctors and nurses by playing out the role.*

The highest level of involvement in play by the teacher is called **play tutoring.** Taken from the work of Sara Smilansky (1968), this form of participation requires the adult to take at least partial control of the play situation. The teacher now gives children directions or suggestions that lead the play into new areas. It is possible to engage in play tutoring while participating in the children's play or to guide from outside the play sequence. In either instance, the teacher must be sensitive to intervene in such a way that children can learn from the suggestions being made and reinitiate leadership of the play events.

> ❧ *As Ellen passes by the block center in her third-grade classroom, she notices that Awesta and Carrie are struggling with the castle they are trying to build. She states: "Before you two go any further in your building, perhaps you should review the book you have and then sketch the castle you would like to construct. That may give you the ideas you need to continue your project."*

Van Hoorn, Nourot, Scales, and Alward (1993) suggest additional roles for adults in guiding play. Again, the authors suggest using these strategies with care so that adult direction is kept to a minimum. Their proposed roles include

- *The artist apprentice.* The adult guides play through the subtle removal of clutter in the physical space and the provision of props needed to continue the theme, much like a set assistant would do for a theatrical production.

- *The peacemaker.* Adults assuming this role help children resolve conflicts over toys and equipment, suggest alternatives when disputes over roles occur, and invent new roles to extend the play.

- *Guardian of the gate.* Teachers can also help children enter an existing play episode. By introducing an accessory that requires a new player or suggesting an additional role, the adult can involve other children without violating the rights of those who initiated the activity.

- *Matchmaker.* Adults may also choose to group players in pairs or small groups to stimulate more involved play sequences. Matching more skilled players with those who need assistance may encourage children to help one another as they play.

Summary

The characteristics and definitions of childhood play help clarify the meaning and value of this complex concept. An understanding of theories, both classical and contemporary, adds further insights into why children play. The cognitive play types of Piaget and Smilansky and the social play categories defined by Parten describe increasingly complex stages of play behaviors. The intellectual, social, linguistic, physical, and emotional benefits of play define a strong rationale for including play in the early childhood classroom. The adult's role in facilitating play includes preparing both the indoor and outdoor environments, creating a climate for quality play, and techniques for adult intervention/involvement.

✑ For Discussion and Action

1. Spend time observing children at play (at least two hours would be best). Describe what you saw. Compare your observations with the information presented in this chapter.

2. Choose a theory of play that is most helpful to you in explaining why children play. Make a case to your classmates for the values of this theory.

3. Play a game designed for young children (like Candy Land) with a child five or younger. Describe the way in which the child played. Does this tell you anything about games with rules and young children?

4. A parent wants to know why you are encouraging play in your classroom. What will you tell that parent?

5. Talk to a teacher who includes play in an early childhood classroom. What does this teacher do to facilitate quality play?

✑ Building Your Personal Library

Frost, J. (1992). *Play and playscapes*. Albany, NY: Delmar. This book has a balanced discussion of play in indoor and outdoor settings. There is much good information about how to plan and prepare for quality outdoor play experiences.

Garvey, C. (1990). *Play*. Cambridge, MA: Harvard University Press. A scholarly but very readable book that describes many of the advantages of childhood play. The discussion of social and linguistic benefits is particularly useful.

Van Hoorn, J., Nourot, P., Scales, B., & Alward, K. (1993). *Play at the center of the curriculum*. Upper Saddle River, NJ: Merrill/Prentice Hall. The authors have a nice blend of theory and practical suggestions about how to make play the focus of the early childhood curriculum. Separate chapters on play and the electronic media and play as a tool for assessment are particularly helpful.

Wasserman, S. (1990). *Serious players in the primary classroom*. New York: Teachers College Press. This is one of only a few books examining the importance of play in the primary classroom. Wasserman makes a strong case for encouraging play at this level and provides many good ideas on how this can be accomplished.

6 Guiding Young Children

In this chapter you will

- Define guidance and differentiate it from discipline.

- Study basic principles of guidance.

- Understand the importance of routines in the early childhood classroom and learn how to deal with them.

- Develop strategies to assist children in understanding and responding to their feelings.

- Identify techniques for guiding social interactions.

- Learn about guiding groups of young children.

Free choice time has just begun in your preschool classroom. Nineteen four-year-olds are busily engaged in play in the different centers, and things are moving along nicely. Suddenly, you hear Tasha and Ariel arguing over an accessory in the block center. Going over to investigate, you discover that they both want to use the same toy elephant in their separate block-building activities. Just as you finish helping them work through this dilemma, you notice Hector standing near the edge of the manipulative center watching the other children playing there. After bending down and resting a hand on his shoulder, you suggest some play options that you think might help him get involved in the classroom activities. Moments later, Christa is screaming and pounding the floor in the art center. She has accidently mixed the blue and yellow tempera paints on her easel paper and she is very upset. Christa is so mad that your only option is a brief time-out so that she can get herself back together and continue playing. Group time is next on your schedule, and everything is going well until you mention your new pet cat. Now everyone wants to talk at once, and it takes several minutes to get the discussion back on track. This is proving to be another typical day, with many opportunities to practice your guidance skills.   ❧

Although the preceding scenario might sound unusual, it is really a pretty average day in the life of an early childhood teacher. Young children are learning a great deal more than just conceptual knowledge as they grow and develop. The guidance skills needed by teachers of young children are many. These skills don't come naturally to most people and require both understanding and practice. This chapter is designed to help start you on the road to understanding and using these techniques.

What Is Guidance?

Sometimes, the words you use make a big difference in the message heard by others. Think about the words *guidance* and *discipline,* for example. When you hear the word *discipline,* what comes to mind? For most people, it brings thoughts of what you do when children have done something wrong. Guidance, on the other hand, often conjures up images of helping and assisting children in their growth and development. Although both words have much in common and in many contexts could be used interchangeably, **guidance** is generally considered a broader concept, incorporating all the adult does or says to influence the behavior of the child (Hildebrand, 1994). **Discipline,** then, is a smaller but important component of the guidance process dealing with children who misbehave.

Building Self-Esteem

One important aspect of guidance is the process of helping young children strengthen their feelings of self-worth. Kostelnik, Stein, Whiren, and Soderman (1993) identify three dimensions to self-esteem: competence, worth, and control. They define **competence** as the belief that you can accomplish tasks and achieve goals. **Worth** can be viewed as the extent to which you like and value yourself. **Control** is the degree to which people feel they can influence the events around them. In many ways, the development of self-esteem is a life-long venture. The teacher plays a critical role in the child's early efforts in esteem building.

> *Aretha is new to your preschool program and hesitates when it is her turn to pour juice for snack time. When you encourage her to do so, she can serve herself without spilling. Aretha has added a bit to her sense of competence and will likely continue to expand her horizons as she becomes more involved in preschool activities.*

> *Although Mica struggles with mathematics in your third-grade classroom, you know that he does excellent artwork. You have just complimented him for the clay pot he has made. The ready smile and obvious pleasure he displays help you know that Mica's sense of competence has been enhanced.*

Dealing with Social/Emotional Issues

Learning to relate socially to other people is a difficult and complex task. Children in the early childhood years are constantly struggling with appropriate ways to interact with others (Trawick-Smith, 1997). Teachers must regularly take time to assist children in this important process.

> *As Darla enters the block center in her kindergarten classroom, Mark blurts out, "Go away, Darla! We don't want any girls in the block area!" Clearly, the classroom teacher will need to help Mark develop better ways to communicate with Darla.*

Emotionally, children are also just beginning to make sense of the many different feelings they experience. Children during the early childhood years need help from adults to identify their feelings and then learn appropriate ways in which they can deal with them (Reynolds, 1996).

Two-year-old Randall has just fallen off the climber on the playground, scraped his elbow, and is crying. The classroom teacher sits down, holds Randall, and says, "That must have hurt and scared you when you fell off the climber. It's okay to cry. I'm just going to hold you for a minute before we go in for a bandage."

Adults who give children labels for the feelings they see them express and then suggest effective ways for children to manage their emotions are providing critical guidance.

Growing toward Independence and Self-Control

Another important goal of the guidance process is to help children make good decisions and interact with others without adult assistance. Good guidance should eventually create within children the ability to guide themselves (Hildebrand, 1994). This independence and self-control develop slowly and painfully in most people over a long period of time. Yet, these elements are important to becoming healthy, fully functioning adults. For example, the influence of peers becomes very strong during the middle school years. It is essential that we help young children become more independent so that they can resist the negative push to experiment with drugs and other potentially harmful activities that present themselves during these years. We also need children to be able to demonstrate self-control as they manage their anger and frustrations in positive ways rather than resorting to the increasingly more common aggression and violence, which many are using to deal with feelings (Beaty, 1995).

Teachers of young children need to create an atmosphere that encourages independence. Sometimes that means stepping back and letting children work things out themselves. It may take longer, and be a more difficult task, but when children learn that they can do it on their own, they gain independence (Trawick-Smith, 1997).

Armondo and Dee are two members of a cooperative learning group in your second-grade classroom that are working on gathering information on sea life. They have just asked you for assistance in learning about whales, a special interest of yours. It would be easier (and probably more fun) to spend some time helping them with this task, but since you know that they can find this information in the resources you have provided, you direct them to the books and computer software you have in the science center.

Self-control can also be encouraged in the early childhood classroom. One important way in which teachers do this is by demonstrating their own methods for managing difficult situations (Fields & Boesser, 1998). When the teacher remains calm in dealing with his feelings and shows children constructive ways to express them, he is inviting children to engage in similar activities.

Two four-year-olds in the block area need your assistance. Briana just hit Rory with a block. After placing Briana in time-out and comforting Rory, you

Creating rules for the classroom is an important task that will help establish the atmosphere of the learning environment and assist children in their independence and self-control. Having a short list of clear, positively stated rules that both children and teachers understand and agree with makes the start to the school year more positive. As much as possible, it makes good sense to involve children in the process of making the rules they are to live by.

The following guidelines should be helpful as you develop rules for your classroom:

• Keep your list of rules short. Only four or five broad, clearly stated rules are needed.

• Make your rules positive statements, rather than negative ones. Change "don'ts" to "do" statements.

• Rules should preserve each child's dignity by being supportive rather than harsh.

• All rules apply to adults as well as children. Be sure to model appropriate behaviors for students.

• Make sure students understand the rules and your specific expectations for each.

• The consequences for breaking the rules need to be identified and clearly understood by students.

1. *Develop a list of rules that you think might be appropriate for a group of preschool or primary children. Discuss this list with a friend.*

2. *Talk to a teacher about his classroom rules and how they were developed. Be sure to ask about the students' roles in creating the rules.*

---

return and say, *"Briana, I am angry with you right now. You hit Rory with that block and it really hurt him! I'm too angry to discuss it right now, so we will talk about this when the others leave for lunch in five minutes."*

Gradually, with continued verbal guidance and appropriate modeling, children begin to learn appropriate options for self-control.

Principles of Guidance

As indicated earlier, guidance is everything the teacher does or says either directly or indirectly to influence the behavior of the child. Therefore, planning and organizing the physical space in the classroom, the materials available to children, the activities and lessons for learning, and what the teacher says and does all are included under the broad heading of guidance. Here are some basic principles that will help conceptualize and define guidance.

Initial Considerations

Before becoming more specific about what is involved when the teacher engages in guidance, some reminders about children and teachers are needed. First, it is essential to remember that *each child is unique.* Just look around any early childhood classroom, and you can see many of the more obvious differences between children. What may not be quite so clear are the varying responses they have to guidance techniques.

> 🌊 *Two-year-old Marissa is quite happy to have you take her by the hand and gently lead her to the next play event when she struggles to get involved. Four-year-old Greg, on the other hand, is more likely to respond positively when given two options from which he can choose.*

Adding to the complexity of guidance decisions is that *every situation is unique.* Good teachers must have a variety of guidance options available so that they can meet the needs of each child and the unique situations they create in their day-to-day interactions.

> 🌊 *Today, Taylor and Pam are fighting over the paints available at the easel. Because of their relative maturity levels, you decide to remind them that they need to share and ask them to try to work it out themselves. Yesterday, when Craig and Josh were having trouble using one of the manipulative toys together, you stepped in and helped them work through their conflict. You decided that they needed your help to work through the issues involved.*

Not only are guidance techniques different because children and situations vary, but it is also important to remember that *every teacher is unique.* There is no one right way to teach and no one ideal teacher. Excellent teachers come with all sorts of different personalities and techniques that work for them.

> 🌊 *Alicia is a new second-grade teacher who spends many extra hours organizing her class day. By carefully planning her activities, Alicia finds that she is more confident and her students are actively engaged in learning. Mary, on the other hand, is more spontaneous and gets really excited about her teaching. She is always coming up with crazy (but fun) ways to get her third-grade students involved in the learning process. Both are highly capable teachers with very different strengths that they bring to their classrooms. It shouldn't be surprising to find that these two teachers tend to use a different mix of guidance strategies as they teach children.*

Indirect Guidance

Much of what a teacher does to influence children's behaviors is indirect. The behind-the-scenes work and planning help prevent problems in the first place. By managing the space, equipment, materials, and people in the child's environment, teachers can eliminate many potential conflicts. Hildebrand (1994) provides several principles of indirect guidance:

- Carefully plan the daily schedule to meet the interests and abilities of the children.
- Arrange classroom spaces so that there are clues to help children know what to do there (pictures on the wall, pillows for reading, etc.).

The teacher of these two young students placed this water table in an area of the classroom where the contents wouldn't splash other children or surrounding materials and left enough space around the table for the students to move.

- Plan activities and lessons that are varied and exciting to children and that motivate them to learn.
- Arrange activities in an interesting way that invites children to participate.
- Prepare materials so that children can use them safely and with a minimum of adult help.
- Store out of sight those materials you do not want children to use (dangerous materials should be stored outside the classroom).
- Observe children to develop a basic understanding of each child's behavior and needs.
- Talk to parents to gain a deeper understanding of each child and learn ways to effectively relate to them.

Time spent in indirect guidance is very profitable, indeed. A smooth-running and pleasant classroom is well worth the effort required.

Building Relationships

An important key to effective guidance and discipline is the relationships teachers establish with students, parents, and other teachers and administrators throughout the school building. Glasser (1990) talks about the importance of **building a friendly workplace.** If teachers are to create what Glasser calls a quality school, it must begin with the many key relationships that teachers establish with others. Student–teacher interactions head the list in terms of importance. Teachers who want to succeed in guiding their students must establish strong working relations with their students. This can be accomplished in part through the positive interactions with children that teachers have throughout the school day. A pat on the back for a job well done, an engaging smile when greeting each child in the morning, and words of encouragement are all examples of relationship-building interactions. Sometimes, however, it is important to plan contrived situations to get better acquainted with students. Name-game activities at the start of the school year to get better acquainted with students are examples of this type of interaction.

Establishing quality relationships with parents is also important to good guidance in the early childhood classroom (Hildebrand, 1994). When parents know the teacher and support at home the activities occurring in the classroom, children develop a stronger sense of the importance of education. This helps make guidance easier to implement in the classroom. Good communication is the key to strong home–school relationships and is thoroughly described in the next chapter.

When an entire school works to create an atmosphere of cooperation and support as a staff, children once again benefit (Glasser, 1990). When the school has created a friendly workplace, students are much more likely to want to be there. Children who are motivated to be in school and learn are less likely to create discipline problems for teachers. Furthermore, when problems do occur, the school staff can work together to address the issues and help children move forward in positive directions.

Physically Guiding Children

Teachers at all levels are becoming much more cautious about touching children in their classrooms. Many are avoiding physical contact entirely, even at the preschool level (Lewis, 1994). From one perspective, it is understandable why teachers are taking this stance; they are scared. The threat of lawsuits and possible job loss are strong deterrents. Despite these complications, however, and despite all that has been written recently about the inappropriate ways in which teachers and other adults touch young children, it is very important to use good touch as a guidance strategy. What better way is there to let children know that we care about them and want to help them deal with the many problems they will face? One expert writes:

> A scraped knee, a bruised ego, or a lost lunch box each brings on the same reaction: a fountain of tears. And even though the school nurse doles out bandages liberally and kindly, the act of healing is seldom complete without an additional "it'll be all right" kind of hug. Nothing kinky. Nothing amorous. Just a quick, reassuring connection that indicates our link as two human beings, one who needs comfort and another who is willing to give it. (Delisle, 1994, p. 33)

VIDEO CASE STUDY:
Building Brains

Watch the ABC News video segment "Building Brains" and consider these excerpts:

"There is nothing in nature quite as complex or full of promise as the brain of a human baby. Any analogy then, is bound to be a poor one, but imagine for a moment that you are in a house. Leading from this house there are thousands upon thousands of paths and streams, roads and rivers, highways and air routes. They can take you anywhere in the world you might want to go during the rest of your life. But if they are to remain open, you will have to key them in one by one, indicating an intention to use that particular road. Failure to do so will result in the disappearance of that artery. You have a few years to do the job. As I said, it's a poor analogy, because a baby's brain has about 100 billion neurons that are connected to one another by literally trillions of synapses. But if during the first few years of life, those synapses, those connectors remain unused, they'll be eliminated. Use them and they're there for life. But if they remain unstimulated by sight or sound or touch, by the flood of sensory experiences, then, in the extreme, the brain of the infant will literally shrink."

— Ted Koppel, ABC Anchorperson

"Here in Vermont, they believe if you spend money early, when a child's brain is most changeable, you can save money later in special education, foster care, even in prisons."

— Deborah Amos, ABC Correspondent

"Education just doesn't start at kindergarten. It starts a long time before that, and I think schools of the future need to think about that, and we need to get out of the box, and begin to engage very early with young children."

— Ray McNulty, School Superintendent

"As early as when Harry Harlowe did his first studies we knew that robbing babies of close, safe, secure relationships with adults was going to lead to drastic negative outcomes. What all of this wonderful brain science has done for us is to give us the tools to see how that was working in the brain."

— Megan Gunner, Researcher

"If you came from outer space, you would look down and you'd say 'Gee, this is the time in life when they're most changeable, early in life. That's when their brains are most modifiable, yet somehow they choose to spend all of their time and effort trying to modify and influence brain organization after age five.' You know, we have to discuss these things as a society and look at what our real values are."

— Dr. Bruce Perry, Texas Children's Hospital

Now that you have seen the ABC News video segment, consider the position of Ted Koppel's studio guest, Dr. Stanley Greenspan, a professor of psychiatry and pediatrics. Based on his research findings published in *The Growth of the Mind* (1996), Greenspan suggests that there are six types of experiences in early life that help to promote a child's intelligence and sense of self.

- Making Sense of Sensations: The ability *to attend*—to show emotional interest in various sights and sounds

- Intimacy and Relating: The ability *to engage*—to experience joy, pleasure, and emotional warmth in the presence of another

- Buds of Intentionality: The ability *to be intentional*—to create and direct desire

- Purpose and Interaction: The ability *to form complex interactive intentional patterns*—to connect personal, emotional signals with those of others in interactions

- Images, Ideas, and Symbols: The ability *to create images, symbols, and ideas*—to think and communicate symbolically

- Emotional Thinking: The ability *to connect images and symbols*—to sense personal feelings and intuitively grasp the feelings and desires of another

A child's success in social and educational environments depends upon the extent to which she has successfully mastered these developmental milestones. Therefore, caregivers and teachers are responsible for tailoring their interaction with infants and young children to account for the developmental stages they go through, and for helping to scaffold a child's growth and development. To accomplish this, Greenspan recommends that parents, caregivers, and teachers:

1. Tune into the child's own developmental level.

2. Present children not with information to assimilate, but with problems to solve through active initiative and participation.

3. Take the child's natural inclinations and perspectives seriously.

4. Present activities and material in steps and at a pace appropriate to the child's cognitive abilities and learning style.

5. Establish structure and limits.

VIDEO CASE STUDY: **Building Brains**

As a teacher and caregiver, you will be responsible for nurturing young children as they grow and develop socially, emotionally, and intellectually. Think about what you know about how children learn and grow, and using Dr. Greenspan's recommendations as a guide, describe what you might observe and how you should respond using the following table. You can complete this exercise individually, or compare your responses with a group.

Dr. Greenspan's Recommendation	Educational Implication	What You Might Observe	How You Might Respond
Tune into the child's own developmental level.	Use observation and assessment to know each child as an individual and determine which developmental skills each child has mastered and which need work.	Spencer, a toddler in your group, is thirsty after playing outside and has declared to your new teacher's aide "Spence want juice." She pours him a cup and sits it on the table in front of him. Spencer, who has had some difficulty with his coordination, tries to pick up the cup to drink. Before it reaches his mouth, he spills it, splashing juice down his shirt front. He looks down at his wet shirt front and lets out a huge wail.	
Present children with problems to solve through active initiative and participation.	Include developmentally appropriate hands-on tasks, experiments, field trips, writing projects, and similar techniques that encourage the child to engage with others and the material, and that capitalize on the child's energy and curiosity.	You notice that for the past few days, Rosa has been spending her outdoor play time watching the family of birds that has made a nest in a nearby tree, and has been "flying" around the playground, arms outstretched, playing "birdies" with Seth and Marta.	
Take the child's perspectives seriously.	Provide examples from the child's daily life, and/or see the material through the eyes of the child, at the particular developmental level and in the terms she understands it.	Whenever Tessa's parents drop her off at preschool, she clings to their legs and cries and screams as they leave. You almost have to pry her off of them. It's almost as if she thinks that when they leave, she'll never see them again.	
Present activities and material in steps and at a pace appropriate to the child's cognitive abilities and learning style.	Use observation and assessment to determine the appropriate pace, method of delivery, and level of difficulty for each child.	The children in your toddler class are learning the names of body parts. You are sitting in a circle, and when you point to a specific part of your body, the child whose turn it is says the correct name for it. You notice that Micah has been fidgeting, and right before his turn comes, he pulls Jenna's hair hard enough to make her cry. You speak with him firmly and give him a "time out." As he sits in the corner, you realize that he has successfully avoided speaking aloud in front of the class once again.	
Set structure and enforce limits.	Establish rules for children that are clear and reasonable, and that carry automatic sanctions that penalize but do not humiliate. Limits should be accompanied by support so that the child can understand and do better next time.	Mei-Lin and Jeffrey are playing happily with blocks in the manipulatives center. Suddenly, Jeffrey shrieks! Mei-Lin has bitten him because he used a block for his tower that she had been intending to use in her elaborately constructed doll house. And now Jeffrey has knocked over the entire doll house to retaliate!	

Physically guiding young children is much more than the important hug. It includes such things as just being close to a child who is struggling to stay on task. **Physical proximity** of the teacher does make a difference in children's behaviors. **Gesturing and body language** are other aspects of physical guidance. We send children many messages about what we expect when we smile, raise an eyebrow, or point with a finger. Taking a child by the hand and leading him to a more positive activity is an effective strategy for many children. Physically turning a child gently at the shoulders and **redirecting** him toward a desired activity also work well during the early childhood years.

Teachers and children vary in their comfort levels with physical touch. Not every adult wants to hold children close in an embrace or encourages children to sit on his lap. But a gentle pat on the shoulder, "high fives," and handshakes all communicate to children that we care. Children also differ in their need for touch. Teachers must be sensitive to these variances and respond accordingly.

Verbal Guidance Strategies

Verbal communication is a major element of child guidance. The words we use as adults strongly influence the behaviors of young children. An excellent beginning for effective verbal communication is the ability of the adult to be a good listener. **Active listening** is a technique that helps the adult be more effective in the communication process (Reynolds, 1996). The teacher begins by being open and approachable and listens carefully to what the child is saying and doing. Then, in his own words, the teacher repeats back what he has heard the child say. "It sounds like you are sad right now, Damion. You wanted to use the truck that Audrie is playing with." When the teacher uses active listening, he lets children know he is trying hard to help them identify the feelings they have and respond to those emotions in appropriate ways.

Another form of verbal guidance is called **redirection.** Two-year-old Andrew is fascinated by climbing and is preparing to move from his chair to the nearby table. His teacher, knowing Andrew's love of books, takes him by the hand and says, "Andrew, let's go find a book to read." Marion (1995) suggests that for the youngest children, redirection becomes a way to divert or distract the child from an undesirable behavior into a more appropriate activity. For older children, teachers can verbalize a substitute for the problem behavior. "Rachelle, you will need to get your own blocks from the shelf. Martin is using those."

When teachers initiate verbal messages, they should use **positive directions,** telling the child what to do, rather than what *not* to do (D. Miller, 1996). When an adult says "Don't jump off the table!", it's almost as if the child doesn't hear the "don't" and is further encouraged to engage in the inappropriate behavior. In addition, *don't* statements fail to tell the child what it is you would rather have him do. The statement "Climb down off the table, please" clearly identifies what it is you expect and makes it easier for most children to comply.

Teachers can also strengthen verbal communication by making it clear when **children have choices** (Marion, 1995). Many times, choices are appropriate and

It is choice time in your second-grade classroom, and Mrs. Hanson, your elementary school principal, has just walked in the door. Children are actively engaged in creative play in the three centers you have set up, but the noise level is rather high. Matt, Carolee, and Arlene are busy talking and constructing a southern plantation based on their social studies unit. Norm, Sandy, Molly, and Kareena are animatedly discussing their play options in the art center. Several others are engaged in productive but noisy tasks throughout the room. You can tell that Mrs. Hanson is distracted by the sounds of busy players. She is probably wondering, "Is all this noise really necessary?"

Hakeem and Albert have just asked your permission as their preschool teacher to get a bucket of water and make mud pies in the sandbox. It is a beautiful spring day and you have just consented. But now you are beginning to wonder about your decision. Both children are having a great time but are covered from head to foot with wet sand. You are very hopeful that no parents drop by before you can get the boys cleaned up. It always seems to be a challenge to keep children from getting too messy when they are involved in creative play experiences.

These are not isolated incidents but are fairly typical of many play situations. Noise and mess do seem to be a normal part of children's play. That doesn't mean, however, that there are no limits. Noise levels can become too high, and children may need to be reminded of appropriate voices for play indoors and out. A certain amount of messiness is also typical of most play. Creative art projects, block structures in progress, and manipulatives being used all create a cluttered environment. Children learn rather quickly, however, that at the end of a play sequence, things can and should be picked up before the next activity is begun. The mess from play should be temporary and manageable.

1. What could you say to Mrs. Hanson to help her understand the need for some noise as children play?
2. How do you feel about noise and messiness? Do you think your attitudes may influence children's play activities?

useful to children in developing independence and decision-making skills. "Gary, would you like to use the computer now that Carla has finished, or are you interested in continuing with your math project?" Other times, however, adults inadvertently give children choices when they really don't mean to do so. Young children think more literally than adults do, so when they hear phrases like "Would you like to sit down now for group time?" they may well assume that you have given them a choice. Another common problem many teachers have is ending their statements with "okay?" "Philip, it's cleanup time now, *okay*?" Without meaning to do so, adults have given children an implied choice by the words they have used.

Hildebrand (1994) gives additional suggestions for making verbal guidance more effective with young children:

I Message	I, followed by feelings experienced by the adult, ending with what behavior caused the feelings.
Natural consequences	A naturally occurring result of the child's behavior.
Logical consequences	The teacher establishes a consequence that has a logical link to the child's behavior.
Positive reinforcement	Anything that follows a behavior and increases the likelihood it will occur again.
Punishment	Anything that follows a behavior and decreases the likelihood it will occur again.
Ignoring	Avoiding verbal and nonverbal responses to attention-seeking behavior.
Problem solving	Using techniques of counseling, the teacher and student work together to resolve difficulties.

- Get down on the child's level, speak quietly and directly as you make eye contact.
- Place the action part of your guidance statement at the beginning ("Hold tight, or you might fall out of the swing").
- Give directions at the time and place you want behavior to occur.
- Give logical and accurate reasons for your requests.
- Keep competition to a minimum in your verbal guidance.

Discipline Strategies

Despite the best intentions of the teacher to prevent problems from occurring, children will still engage in behaviors that require some form of discipline. Teachers can use a variety of strategies to deal with these issues as they arise. The appropriate option depends not only on the situation and children involved but also on the teacher's personality. Knowing about, and being able to effectively use, several discipline options allows the creative teacher to make good choices in many different situations. Figure 6–1 summarizes the discipline techniques described next.

One strategy recommended by Thomas Gordon (1974) is to use what he calls an **I Message.** This communication statement includes the personal pronoun *I,* the feelings experienced by the adult, and what caused those feelings. The I Message itself is frequently followed by a brief explanation from the adult to help explain why the feelings are important.

> ᐁ *Kelsey has just come in late from recess for the second time this week and you decide to use an I Message. "Kelsey, I get frustrated when you come in late from recess. You distract the rest of the class and miss many of my initial directions for the next lesson."*

Rather than criticizing a child for an undesirable behavior, an I Message identifies the feelings of the teacher and helps the child see how his behavior influences others. If the relationship between teacher and student is strong, many children will voluntarily change their behavior and act more responsibly in the classroom.

Dreikurs, Grunwald, and Pepper (1982) propose the use of **natural and logical consequences** as an effective discipline strategy. Both options make a clear link between the child's inappropriate behavior and the consequence for that activity. With natural consequences, the teacher simply lets the inherent outcomes for certain actions take place.

> ➷ *On a cool, fall day, you remind your kindergarten children to put on their coats before heading out to the playground for recess. Larissa hears your reminder but decides to ignore it. After discussing the situation with her individually, you allow her to experience the natural consequence of going outdoors for a few minutes without her coat—she is cold.*

A major drawback to natural consequences is that many times they either don't occur or are potentially dangerous to the child. In those instances, a logical consequence is needed. The teacher establishes the consequence and makes a logical link between the child's behavior and the resulting discipline strategy. Karma runs down the hallway as students go to music class. A logical consequence would be to have her start over and walk down the hall at the teacher's side. If possible, it is best to discuss these consequences before they are implemented with a child. Furthermore, stating logical consequences in a choice format helps students make stronger connections between their behavior and its results. In discussing Karma's behavior with her before the next music class, the teacher could say, "Karma, you need to walk down the hallway to music or you can walk next to me. You choose."

Many educators use a group of discipline strategies referred to as **behavior modification.** Based on the theoretical perspectives of behaviorists such as B. F. Skinner (1974), three basic techniques are associated with this approach (Kameenui & Darch, 1995). These are positive reinforcement, punishment, and ignoring.

Positive reinforcement is anything that follows a behavior and increases the likelihood that it will occur in the future. Smiles, high fives, and positive comments are all considered positive reinforcers for children when they increase behaviors that precede them. Sometimes, things that adults would normally consider negative interactions may actually be reinforcing to some children. A stern talking to by the teacher may be reinforcing to certain children who really need to get any kind of attention from adults. On the other hand, a typically reinforcing action like a pat on the back may not be viewed as such by some children. Carefully watching the child's reactions to our interactions will help us know whether or not they are reinforcing.

Punishment is another strategy associated with behavior modification and is defined as any event or action that follows a behavior and decreases the likelihood that the behavior will occur again. A common punishment used by many early childhood educators is time-out.

> ➷ *Angie is an active first-grade student who tends to lose control of her emotions from time to time. Today she hit Carl as the class was lining up for recess. You decide to try time-out and place Angie in an isolated part of your classroom for five minutes to think about what she has done.*

The advantages of time-out are that it gives many children the time they often need to regain control of their emotions before dealing with the inappropriate behavior. If set up properly, time-out is also a boring experience that will help to deter children from engaging in the inappropriate behavior in the future. Many suggest that time-out is overused by many teachers (Betz, 1994). This option should be reserved for more severe acting out behaviors, and it needs to be implemented calmly by the adult and kept short. A good rule-of-thumb is one minute for every year of age. Time-out should be avoided for infants and toddlers because they don't understand why their behavior is inappropriate.

Some forms of punishment are widely viewed by early childhood experts as inappropriate in working with young children. Most agree that corporal punishment (spanking) is harmful to teacher–student relationships and creates a classroom atmosphere of fear and anxiety. Although spanking is a traditional approach in many homes, early childhood educators should never resort to corporal punishment in disciplining children. Humiliation and intimidation are two other potentially effective punishments that are extremely harmful to relationships and self-esteem. They, too, have no place in the early childhood classroom.

The third strategy typically associated with behavior modification is **ignoring.** Many times when children misbehave, they are seeking attention from adults. The class clown is typically engaging in attention-seeking behavior. Ignoring can be a very powerful strategy if the teacher can refrain from giving any verbal or nonverbal feedback for the inappropriate behavior. When adults can consistently ignore attention-getting behaviors that are not too disruptive to the rest of the class, children rather quickly learn that what worked in the past is no longer effective.

Another set of discipline options available to teachers is often referred to as **problem-solving strategies.** These are very different from the behavior modification techniques just described. Rather than being teacher-initiated and -directed, the problem-solving approach is a cooperative effort that engages both the student and teacher in together working through the issues of concern. Similar problem-solving approaches are presented by both Glasser (1969) and Gordon (1974). The basic approach used in problem solving is to work with children much as a counselor interacts with his clients. Built on a strong foundation of good communication and positive relationships, the teacher and student

- Work together to identify the problem behavior.
- Discuss the implications of the behavior.
- Brainstorm possible solutions.
- Agree on a plan.
- Check periodically to make sure the plan is working.

The process is relatively time-consuming and requires a private space and time to work through the issues, so teachers should reserve this technique for more problematic behaviors that can't be resolved in other ways. The dialogue in the accompanying "Focus On" box highlights the basic elements of the problem-solving method.

Cara is a second-grade student who has been consistently forgetting to do her math homework. After trying some simple reminders and then keeping Cara in for part of her recess period to finish her work, Mrs. Harper decides it is time to sit down and talk through the problem with her. Cara is asked to stay behind for a few minutes at recess to discuss this issue. See if you can identify each of the problem-solving steps used to help Cara get her homework completed:

Teacher: Cara, I hope you know how much I enjoy having you in my class this year! Your bright smile and excitement about school make you a real pleasure to be around. But we do have a problem that I've mentioned to you before. Do you know what it is?

Cara: Yeah, I'm not doing my math homework, right?

Teacher: You're right. It's the math homework. Why is this a problem, do you suppose?

Cara: I think it's because I'm not learning my math as well as I should.

Teacher: You've got it. What I'd like to do today is try to understand why you haven't been handing in your math assignments and try to figure out what we can do to get them completed. Can you tell me why you haven't done your math?

Cara: No, not really.

Teacher: Do you have time after school to finish your homework?

Cara: Yes. When I go to day care after school, they always ask me if I have homework. Then I sit down and work on it. But when I try to do the math, I always have trouble.

Teacher: I've noticed that you were having some difficulty in class. Do you think that could be the reason you are not getting the work done?

Cara: I guess that could be it.

Teacher: I have an idea. Your bus arrives about fifteen minutes before school begins. Would you be willing to come into the room early for the next week? Then we can spend a few minutes each day making sure you understand your math.

Cara: That sounds okay.

Teacher: Good! Let's try it for a week and then meet again to see how things are going.

Cara: Thanks, Mrs. M. Can I go out to recess now?

1. *What do you see as the strengths and weaknesses of the problem-solving approach in dealing with inappropriate student behaviors?*

2. *Make a list of the kinds of situations for which the problem-solving strategy may work.*

Guiding Routines

During the early childhood years, children's routines are an important part of their daily experiences. As they move through the school day, they encounter a variety of regularized events that often require adult assistance to successfully manage. When these components of the day are consistently managed and children know what to expect, they are more comfortable and relaxed in school (Hildebrand, 1994).

Arrival and Departure

The beginning and end of the day are important times for children. Teachers need to carefully plan for these times to reduce problems during these transitions. For many children in the infant/toddler and preschool years, leaving the security of their parents for the school setting can be a frightening experience. Greeting children at the door and guiding the less secure through a consistent routine help make the arrival time more positive. Even with older children, a consistent beginning to the school day helps ensure a productive start to the day. Similarly, at the end of the day, it is important to routinely take time to summarize what has taken place in the classroom and bring closure to the many things children have accomplished in a predictable and recognizable way. Helping children leave with a good feeling about the day also increases the chances for beginning the next class session on a positive note.

Transitions

At first glance, the times between the activities of the school day may seem unimportant. Often, however, they can be a prime time for problem behaviors if teachers fail to plan for them. Children need clear directions and procedures for transitioning from one event to the next. Think about a group of kindergarten children getting ready to move from group time to recess. If the classroom teacher were to say, "Okay, children, recess is next. Go get ready," children would likely respond in a variety of ways, many of which may be problematic. Several might head to the bathroom at the same time, making for crowded conditions there. Others could line up for a drink, while yet another group could head to their tables to finish up an art project before moving to the coat area. If expectations are not clearly explained, these transition times can be very confusing and frustrating to both children and adults. Good teachers know what they want children to do at transition times and clearly describe their expectations.

Snack/Meal Time

Another important routine that requires clear adult guidance is snack/meal time. For the infant/toddler, eating is a frequent and essential part of the day. Caregivers must work carefully with parents to understand each child's eating schedule, food preferences, and routines. In addition to regular meal times, preschool and primary children need a nutritious snack both midmorning and midafternoon to ensure high energy levels and involvement in classroom activities. Whether these snacks are prepared by school staff or brought from home, children need clear expectations for how snack time is to proceed. Should children sit together in small groups and visit with peers and an adult? Or do students pick up a snack, return to their desks, and continue working? What are the expectations for children serving themselves and cleaning up afterward? The teacher must address and the children must understand all these issues (and

Teachers must make sure children understand what behavior is expected of them at snack time.

more) in order to have a consistently pleasant snack time. Snack time should foster independent student behavior and create a relaxed atmosphere for eating and visiting with others.

Toileting

For the very youngest children, toileting in the early childhood classroom means diaper changing. Until approximately two years of age, most children have not developed the bladder and bowel control to use a toilet. Adult caregivers at the infant/toddler level must simply accept this aspect of young children as normal and natural and work to make these times as pleasant as possible. Talking, singing, and playing games as diapers get changed help make this time more interesting and enjoyable for all. As children begin the toilet-training process, teachers must work carefully with parents to consistently use similar toileting procedures and communicate about issues and problems as they arise. Well after toilet training has ended, some children will occasionally have accidents. How the teacher reacts to these situations will make a big difference in how the child feels about himself. A casual, calm approach will help minimize the embarrassment the child will likely feel.

Rest Times

The younger the child, the more significant the rest-time routine is in the child's life. Infants and toddlers need frequent nap times throughout the day. Each child will be different, with routines learned at home and differing sleep needs. Consistent communication with parents helps make this routine more successful with the youngest children. During the preschool years, rest/nap times are usually found only in full-day programs and occur in the early afternoon. Generally, it is best to have all children spend some quiet time on a mat or cot. During this time, some will actually nap while others rest. Caregivers must work hard to create an atmosphere in which sleep is possible for those who need it and rest time is pleasant for the rest. Back rubs, soft singing, reading a book, and quiet conversations all may help children during this time.

Dealing with Feelings and Emotions

Throughout the early childhood years, children are beginning the life-long process of recognizing and appropriately responding to their feelings. This difficult, yet extremely important, task requires insightful interventions by the adult. By helping children recognize and deal with their feelings, the caregiver is laying the groundwork for mature coping mechanisms in adulthood. Opportunities to deal with feelings come up regularly, as Furman (1995) indicates in the following example: Two policemen arrive at the door of a preschool lunchroom with a four- or five-year-old boy in tow. The officers had found the child wandering around near the school and had assumed he belonged there. After being told that he did not, the policemen went on their way, leaving behind many young children who had mixed emotions about this event. Rather than ignore this experience, teachers then spent time discussing children's concerns, making the visit a learning opportunity for them.

Accept Feelings as Valid

An important starting point in guiding children through the emotions they experience is to help them realize that feelings themselves are valid responses to life situations (D. Miller, 1996). A preschool child who is saddened by his father's departure at the beginning of the school day is not going to be helped by an adult attempting to talk him out of those feelings. Feelings are just that—feelings. They are neither right nor wrong, good nor bad; feelings simply exist. Helping children recognize this important concept makes it easier to deal with them.

Seven-year-old Andrea has just described to you through her tears the anger and frustration she feels because of an incident on the playground. Two of her friends have decided to exclude her from their play activities because of a perceived slight. Andrea is angry and hurt. Your response as her classroom teacher could

As a teacher, you can help children identify and label their basic feelings, such as sadness, fear, anger, excitement, and happiness.

begin with some variation of the following: "Andrea, I can understand your feelings of anger right now. It hurts when others treat you that way."

Be Calm and Direct

In many circumstances, emotions lead to turmoil. In childhood, that may mean such responses as tears, hitting, or screaming. Whether those reactions are directed toward the adult, other children, or are merely expressed, it is helpful for the teacher to remain calm and deal with these emotional responses as directly and simply as possible (Fields & Boesser, 1998). When the adult is calm, the child is more likely to regain control and begin to work through his emotions. Body language, words spoken, and tone of voice all contribute to an appropriate adult response to children's emotional outbursts. Even when the child doesn't initially express a problem behavior, a calm demeanor will help ensure a better resolution to the feelings being experienced.

Help Child Verbalize Emotions

Although children experience emotions from a very early age, it takes considerable practice for them to identify and label these elusive feelings (Furman, 1995). For younger children, the basic feelings of sadness, fear, anger, excitement, and happiness need to be given names by caring adults.

Although it may sound easy, it is often a challenge to know what to say to children who express their feelings to you as an adult. While accepting the child's emotions as valid, the teacher must help clarify the feelings being exhibited and provide positive suggestions about how to deal with them. Try your hand at stating the actual words you would use to respond to the children in the situations described here:

 Sad Sarah. *Sarah is four years old and in preschool. She wanted to play with her friend Karen in the dress-up area. Karen, however, was involved in an art project and told Sarah she didn't want to play in the dress-up area with her. You overhear the conversation and recognize that Sarah is sad and hurt by the rejection. What are the actual words you would use to respond to the feelings you see in Sarah?*

 Frustrated Chad. *Chad is an active, busy, usually happy boy in your second-grade classroom. Today, however, he is feeling frustrated by his math assignment. You have just explained for the first time the process of borrowing for subtraction problems. What could you say or do to help Chad through this unpleasant experience?*

 Angry Elizabeth. *Several children in your kindergarten class seem to be especially aggressive today. The latest incident concerns Elizabeth. Two children raced through the art area, and one bumped her while she was painting at the easel. Elizabeth's brush jumped erratically across the paper, destroying her painting. Elizabeth is angry and in tears. Describe your response to her.*

 Excited Rob. *Your group of two-year-olds includes a young boy named Rob. He announced upon entering class today that he was "Going Grammy's." Rob's enthusiasm has been evident since his arrival. How can you verbalize to Rob the feelings you see him expressing?*

 _____

1. *Does this task tell you anything about the challenges of responding to children's feelings? What did you learn from the process?*
2. *What is missing from each of these scenarios that would greatly improve your ability to respond to each of these situations?*

 Four-year-old Krista is smiling broadly as you discuss the upcoming field trip at group time. "Krista, your face is telling me that you are excited about going on the field trip to the farm this afternoon!" By giving her feeling a name and describing what you are observing, you are helping Krista to gain experience in identifying her feelings.

Older children continue to benefit from this assistance, when adults verbalize the emotions children experience. Those children who have succeeded in identifying the more basic feelings can be assisted in identifying more subtle emotions such as loneliness, annoyance, and worry. This verbalization process is an important beginning point for eventual mastery and control of feelings.

Suggest Alternatives

Inappropriate responses to negative emotions are common in childhood. It is easier and perhaps more natural to strike out either physically or verbally rather than work through these feelings in a more mature way. Children need considerable help and practice in dealing with their emotions. In addition to serving as models for appropriate responses, teachers need to give children concrete suggestions for dealing with feelings (Hildebrand, 1994).

> *Two-year-old Meesha has just taken a toy truck away from Ben and caused him to cry. You suggest, "Meesha, I know you wanted that truck, but Ben was playing with it. When you want something Ben is using, you need to ask him for it." Most children will need many reminders from caring adults before they begin to understand that there are better ways to get what they want.*

As children get older, the teacher may try to get students more involved in this process of selecting appropriate alternatives for dealing with feelings. Rather than making a direct suggestion, the adult may ask the student for his ideas (Gordon, 1974).

> *Eduardo has just called his third-grade friend Allen a "geek" for not wanting to work together on a writing project. Allen's feelings are hurt, and Eduardo is mad at him. You respond to Eduardo, "Allen was hurt when you called him a 'geek'. Can you think of a better way to tell him that you are mad because he didn't want to work on the writing project with you?"*

Of course, it may still be necessary to help children at this age select appropriate strategies for dealing with their feelings.

Guiding Social Interactions

Throughout the early childhood years, children learn to relate socially to one another and to adults. Becoming social beings is a complex process that also requires considerable adult guidance for success. Good teachers make strong relationships a high priority for their early childhood classrooms.

Be a Careful Observer

An excellent starting point for dealing with many issues in education is to make thorough and regular observations of children. The more you know about children and their typical patterns of interaction, the better able you will be to help them in their social development (D. Miller, 1996). When direct observations are supplemented with information provided by other teachers and parents, the chances for success in guiding social interactions increase dramatically.

Many times, these observations can be informal and require little preparation. As preschool children play during center time, for example, the teacher can focus her attention on small groups of children and make brief notes about the ways in which they interact socially. With older children, the teacher may not have as many opportunities to stop and observe, but when important behaviors occur, the teacher can make a mental note and then record a short written statement at a later, more convenient time.

> ∾ *Matt's interruptions during reading group today is something you want to remember, but you don't have time to stop during the lesson. Later, after announcing snack break, you take a minute to jot down a note about his behavior for future reference.*

On other occasions, more formal observations may be necessary to clarify the behaviors you are concerned about. Techniques such as anecdotal records, running records, and checklists are described in Chapter 11. By choosing the appropriate observation method and creating an accurate picture of the child's activities, the teacher has taken the first step to help children improve their social interactions.

Can Children Solve Their Own Problems?

A major reason many people enter the teaching profession is that they like children and want to assist them in their growth and development. That desire to help is strong in good teachers and in most instances is a real asset. At times, however, this helping attitude actually can be harmful to children. It is useful to remember that even at very young ages, a major goal of guidance is to help children grow toward independence. This may mean stepping back a bit and allowing children to at least try to work issues through themselves. Gordon (1974) suggests that teachers should mind their own business more often and see what children can do to resolve their own problems. Perhaps just hesitating briefly before stepping in will allow children the time they need to successfully work through their social conflicts. It is sometimes difficult to do, but pausing before you intervene could pay big dividends in terms of encouraging more independent behavior among your students.

Define the Limits of Acceptable Behavior

Clearly, children do need help in many social interactions. Hurting others either physically or emotionally, for example, cannot be allowed. When the teacher recognizes the need for intervention, he needs to step in and provide assistance. Frequently, problems with social interactions create strong emotions, and the teacher can begin by following the strategies outlined in the previous section for helping children deal with their feelings. In addition, however, it is often useful for teachers to clearly define for students the limits of acceptable behavior (Hildebrand, 1994).

One way in which this can be accomplished is through the setting and consistent application of classroom rules (see "Into Practice . . . Rules for the Classroom," earlier in this chapter). As surprising as it may first seem, children actually are far more comfortable in an environment where rules are clearly understood and consistently enforced. Their need to test the limits is less, and they are then free to explore and experiment within the known boundaries. With a few well-chosen and easy-to-understand rules, the teacher can create a classroom climate that is consistent and fair. More effective social interactions are one positive result of these clearly defined rules.

Another aspect of defining limits is to help children understand through examples which social behaviors are acceptable and which are not. Children learn rather quickly the clearly inappropriate social interactions. They know that hitting, biting, kicking, and swearing are unacceptable. Unfortunately, many interactions are not so easily categorized as right or wrong. Take, for example, talking back. Although it is certainly acceptable for children to ask the teacher for clarification on an assignment or task, many other responses the child might make would be considered talking back.

> ❧ *Yolanda's second-grade teacher has just told her to clean up her desk and get ready for recess. If she responds by saying: "No, I'm not ready yet!" that would be talking back to her teacher. On the other hand, if she said: "Can I finish my story first?" that would be acceptable. The gray areas need to be carefully defined for students so that they clearly know what is acceptable and what is not.*

Group Guidance

When you gather young children together in groups, new guidance strategies need to be considered to ensure that these experiences are positive. Children must learn many new behaviors for small- and large-group times to go well. Taking turns speaking, listening while others are talking, and sitting without disturbing neighbors are all important social skills that require considerable practice and discussion before children can manage them successfully. With careful planning and preparation, the early childhood teacher can successfully manage these group experiences.

Consider the Physical Setting

The physical space used for group times is important (Marion, 1995). If children are too crowded or uncomfortable, they will be less likely to cooperate and enjoy the experience. Normally, a carpeted area with students seated on the floor is the best arrangement for a large-group meeting. Placing children in a circle also allows for better eye contact and a more intimate setting for communication. Some teachers find that for younger children, taping a circle on the rug is also helpful to visually remind students of the approximate size of the group circle. Removing unnecessary distractions also increases the likelihood that children will be able to focus their attentions on the teacher's agenda.

Small-group experiences are often held at tables seating four to six students. In some instances, the purpose for the small group may make it more appropriate for children to sit on the floor in a carpeted area of the classroom. The classroom teacher should position himself so that he can periodically **scan** the activities occurring in other areas. While his primary responsibilities are to the small group, taking

Placing children in a circle usually results in more cooperation because it allows for better eye contact and a more intimate setting for communication.

the time to look up briefly to notice what is happening in the rest of the room will help improve the teacher's understanding of total classroom functioning.

Careful Planning and Organization

The group experience requires thorough preparation and thought (A. Mitchell & David, 1992). The group time should include active and quiet components, times for children to participate, times for them to listen, and a fairly consistent routine to add stability. The length of time should be tailored to the age of the children, with ten to fifteen minutes being an adequate group time for three-year-olds and twenty or twenty-five minutes more workable for second graders. The actual activities will vary according to the purposes of the group time (see Chapter 11 for more information on this topic).

An opening group time for a first-grade classroom might look like this:

8:30 Greetings and opening song

8:35 Lunch count, weather, calendar

8:40 Action songs/story

8:45 Dismiss to desks for daily oral language

Although this seems to be a rather simple group experience, each individual component needs careful planning for productive use of the time.

INTO PRACTICE...

Circle Time

The practice of gathering children together for group activities and having them sit in a tight circle has been around for over a hundred years. Friedrich Froebel (discussed in Chapter 2) is generally credited with introducing this idea in his kindergarten classrooms in the mid 1800s. From his careful observations of young children, Froebel found that when they spontaneously gather together, children hold hands and stand or sit in a circle to play games and activities. Taking advantage of this natural tendency, Froebel found that group experiences seem to be more positive experiences when held in a circle.

Circle time has become a fixture in most early childhood classrooms today. This arrangement of students has a number of clear benefits:

• It creates a more intimate atmosphere for communicating and interacting with others.

• A circle makes it easier for children and adults to see what others in the group are doing. This helps young children pay better attention to the activities being presented.

• Many songs and games are easier to manage when children aren't distracted by others in front or back of them. Seeing the pictures in a storybook is also easier for most children when they sit in a circle.

• The teacher can more readily see potential discipline problems. Once the teacher observes a problem, a hand on the shoulder of a student seated nearby or direct eye contact may be all that is needed to keep the behavior from escalating further.

Mixing Active and Quiet Times

The activity level of young children is definitely high, making it difficult for them to sit still and listen to an adult for any length of time. Moving, touching, and talking to others are natural ways for children to learn about the world around them. So, although it is important for students to learn to manage their wiggles and listen for short periods to the teacher, these are not easy things for most children to do. Teachers can help this process along by making sure to allow for active involvement of children in group experiences (Dodge & Colker, 1992).

This can be accomplished in many good ways. Having students share their thoughts during group time can be one involvement technique. By asking appropriate questions and allowing time for children to respond, teachers engage the minds of classmates in the issues being discussed. Singing active songs is another favorite of many early childhood teachers. Movement and music mesh very well in the classroom and allow children to participate physically during the group time. Simple games and exercises also add movement and interest to group times. The traditional Simon Says is a time-honored favorite that can be added to a group experience to break up longer stretches of quiet sitting times. The best teachers have a long list of these fun activities that they can use as needed to add spice to group times throughout the day. Some examples include

• **Songs.** The Eensy Weensy Spider; Head and Shoulders, Knees, and Toes; The Hokey Pokey; The Wheels on the Bus

- **Activities.** Follow the Leader Stretching, Clapping to Music, Marching in Place to Music, Rolling a Ball inside the Circle of Children
- **Games.** Duck, Duck, Goose; Be My Mirror; Simon Says; Heads-Up, Seven-Up

Guidance for Children with Special Needs

In most cases, the problem behaviors exhibited by children with special needs are no different from those of other students. Although the frequency and intensity of their reactions may be greater, these children struggle with the same issues that other students their age face. For this reason, the guidance strategies described in this chapter for all students can also be effectively used with children with special needs (Hildebrand, 1994).

Even though the techniques remain the same, it is important for teachers of children with special needs to plan carefully for the implementation of these strategies. Working closely with parents can provide educators with the knowledge they need to better understand the child's motivation for engaging in inappropriate behaviors. Teachers of students with special needs can add further insights and work cooperatively with the classroom teacher in implementing effective guidance techniques. Other teachers who work with the special child may suggest new options. When the teacher spends the extra time necessary to discuss and plan guidance strategies for the child with special needs, this component of a comprehensive management system can be effectively implemented.

Summary

The major components of child guidance include nurturing each child's self-esteem, helping children develop skills in dealing with social-emotional issues, and allowing children to grow toward independence and self-control. Planning the physical environment and building relationships are important components of the guidance process. Physical and verbal guidance strategies help teachers deal effectively with young children. Discipline procedures such as I Messages, natural and logical consequences, behavior modification techniques, and problem-solving strategies are all useful in the early childhood classroom. It is important to develop procedures for dealing with routines such as arrival and departure, transitions, snack/meal time, toileting, and rest times.

Children are better able to deal with emotions when adults accept children's feelings as valid, when adults are calm and direct in dealing with feelings, when adults assist children in verbalizing their emotions, and when adults present alternative ways of dealing with emotions.

Careful observation, allowing children to resolve at least some of their own problems, and defining the limits of acceptable behavior are all important in guiding social interactions.

Guidance of children in groups is another important task for teachers of young children. The physical setting, careful planning and organization, and mixing active and quiet times all help make these experiences more effective.

For Discussion and Action

1. Observe in an early childhood classroom, looking for examples of guidance and discipline. Discuss what you observed with classmates.

2. Ask an early childhood teacher to describe the main discipline strategies used in the classroom. Make a list from your discussion, and compare it with the principles described in this chapter.

3. Discuss effective techniques you could use to build relationships with children in the early childhood classroom. Identify at least five you would consider using.

4. Are there circumstances for which it would be appropriate to show your emotions with children? Describe situations for which it may be acceptable, for example, to express your anger in the classroom. Identify at least one appropriate and one inappropriate way to express anger to children.

5. Watch a teacher conduct a group time experience with children. Pay careful attention to active/quiet times and how the teacher actively engages children in the planned activities. Discuss your findings with others.

Building Your Personal Library

Beaty, J. (1995). *Converting conflicts in preschool.* Ft. Worth, TX: Harcourt Brace. This book presents practical suggestions for dealing with a wide assortment of conflicts that early childhood teachers face. Such issues as attention-getting behaviors, power struggles, and aggressive play are addressed in separate chapters. Although the book focuses on preschool children, the principles presented apply well to the entire early childhood range.

Essa, E. (1995). *A practical guide to solving preschool behavior problems* (3rd ed.). Albany, NY: Delmar. After overviewing basic strategies for dealing with behavior problems, Essa describes specific ideas for dealing with aggressive, disruptive, destructive, and emotional behaviors.

Hildebrand, V. (1994). *Guiding young children* (5th ed.). Upper Saddle River, NJ: Merrill/Prentice Hall. This classic text presents important information about direct and indirect guidance in the early childhood classroom. Hildebrand's sensitivity to children and guidance issues makes this a must-read for those interested in knowing more about this important topic.

Miller, D. (1996). *Positive child guidance* (2nd ed.). Albany, NY: Delmar. Miller provides sound advice on how to prevent misbehavior. She adds a strong chapter on the importance of good communication for guidance and discipline.

In this chapter you will

- Learn about the diversity of family situations and their impact on education.

- Understand the importance of parent and community involvement.

- Study the elements of effective communication.

- Identify tools for quality communications with parents.

- Clarify the role of community members in early education.

Your third year of teaching first grade has just begun. *The content and materials for teaching are well organized. You are feeling comfortable with your guidance and discipline strategies. Perhaps this is the year to begin involving parents more consistently in their children's learning. You are already sending home a weekly letter, making telephone calls with positive comments, and holding parent–teacher conferences in the fall and spring, but you know that much more could be done. Having parents volunteer in the classroom is rather scary, but it is clear from what you have read and heard from others that this type of involvement has many benefits. Providing ways for parents who can't come in during the school day to participate at home would also be of significant value to you and the children in your classroom. If parents are interested, you could plan to have a social event such as a potluck to get families better acquainted. And you have been thinking about collecting and organizing information about community resources to assist parents with their many needs. It looks like this will be another very busy and productive year.* ❧

The importance of working cooperatively with parents and families cannot be overlooked in quality programs for young children. This idea is being embraced by educators and lawmakers at all levels. In March of 1994, President Clinton signed into law the Goals 2000: Educate America Act. This legislation contains eight essential goals to move American education into the twenty-first century. One of these goals states: "By the year 2000, every school will promote partnerships that will increase parental involvement and participation in promoting the social, emotional, and academic growth of children" (Early, 1994, p. 3).

Teachers must recognize that although they do have a major influence on the lives of children, their impact pales in comparison to the significance of parental interactions. For one thing, parents have spent, and will continue to spend, far more time with their children than teachers can ever do. And the bonds created between parents and children are hard to match in the classroom setting. Teachers need to recognize this fact and work with parents and families to make sure that children have the best opportunities for growth and development. As teachers understand family situations and plan strategies for working with them, everyone benefits.

It is essential to involve parents in the educational process. Neglecting this important element will definitely influence the quality of early education. Parents have much to offer the schools in terms of support, insights, and skills. The effort expended in establishing strong working relationships with parents will pay big dividends.

Family Life Today

It doesn't take too much insight to realize that families today look much different from the way they did just a generation ago. The idyllic picture of mom, dad, and two or three children living happily in the house down the street with the white picket fence is just not as likely to be found today. Family situations vary widely, and educators not only must know what those possibilities look like but must be ready to work effectively with diverse family patterns (Barbour & Barbour, 1997; M. Coleman, 1991).

> ∾ *Margaret Smith's third-grade classroom has parents who had children as young teens and others who waited until much later in life. There is a homeless family, several who qualify for food stamps, and a few who are upper middle class. Several single-parent families, remarriages, and one gay couple add variety to her family configurations. Ethnic and religious differences create an even more diverse mix of values, attitudes, and traditions among her families.*

The Missing Extended Family

Not too many years ago, it was fairly common to find families and relatives living in the same community or general area. Aunts, uncles, and grandparents were available to help with child care and give advice on how to parent. This support system was often very helpful, especially to new parents as they struggled with the many challenges of raising children. Although some of these extended families still exist, they are now the exception rather than the rule. Despite the fact that many parents still need and want the support the extended family provided, few have found an adequate replacement (Eisenberg, 1990). Teachers and schools can assist in this process by helping parents create a network with other families in similar situations to provide one another with support.

Divorce and Single-Parent Families

One of the most significant family situations that teachers will encounter is the single-parent family. National statistics indicate that more than 27 percent of children under eighteen are living in families with only one parent (Children's Defense Fund, 1997). These families are also far more likely to be living at or below the poverty level (Annie E. Casey Foundation, 1996). It is estimated that approximately 43 percent of all single-parent families headed by women are poor, compared to only about 7 percent of two-parent families (National Commission

CELEBRATING DIVERSITY . . .
Families Today

Families today differ from those of only a few short years ago. That doesn't make the modern family bad, just different. Many of these changes influence early childhood education. Specifically, four characteristics of American families have created either greater needs for early education or changes in programming:

- *More single parents.* Divorce has led to growing numbers of single parents in this country. The Children's Defense Fund (1997) estimates that one in two children will live with a single parent at some point in their childhood. Because most single parents still need to work, they need child care for their young children.

- *Increasing numbers of working mothers.* The number of working mothers with school-aged children has grown over the last thirty years and is projected to increase even further in the next few years. In 1992, 75 percent of mothers worked, and this number should grow to 83 percent by 2005 (Center for the Future of Children, 1995). As more mothers work, the need for child care continues to grow.

- *More families living in poverty.* During the past three decades, the number of families living in relative poverty has increased significantly (Center for the Future of Children, 1995). Although these families need child care for their young children, their incomes make child care very difficult to obtain. Increased state and federal support for these families are needed.

- *Growing racial and ethnic diversity.* Without question, the number of diverse families is growing in America (Archer, 1996). Issues of poverty, language barriers, and cultural differences must be addressed by those engaged in early education.

1. *Pick one of the factors presented here, and brainstorm the potential impact on early childhood education. Be as specific as possible.*

2. *Talk to a teacher of young children to get her perspectives on changes in the family and their impact on working with families.*

on Children, 1991). Single parents tend to be very busy with work commitments and child-rearing responsibilities, leaving less time for things like parent–teacher conferences and helping out in the schools. Teachers need to be sensitive to these time constraints and work to find ways to creatively work with single parents and their children.

Blended Families

Arthur is a new four-year-old in your classroom. His mother and his new stepfather have brought together four children, two each from previous marriages. This new family has been working hard to redefine roles and responsibilities. Although many positive attributes are in this blended family, everyone is struggling to adjust.

FOCUS ON . . .

Kids Count: Ranking the States

How do various states compare in terms of the support they provide to children? The Annie E. Casey Foundation has collected information on this topic and published a book titled, *Kids Count Data Book* (1996). The following list summarizes the differences that exist on the given indicators:

Measure	Best State	Worst State
Percent low birth weight babies	Alaska	Mississippi
Infant mortality rate	New Hampshire	Mississippi
Child death rate	New Hampshire	Alaska
Percent of births to teens	New Hampshire	Mississippi
Juvenile violent crimes	Vermont	New York
Graduation from high school	Connecticut	Louisiana
Percent children in poverty	Delaware	Louisiana
Children with single parents	Utah	Louisiana

Note. From *Kids Count Data Book,* by the Annie E. Casey Foundation, 1996, Baltimore, MD: The Annie E. Casey Foundation. Copyright 1996 by The Annie E. Casey Foundation. Adapted with permission.

1. *It is clear that states vary greatly in terms of their commitments to children and families. Does this suggest any initiatives that may be important at the national level to help meet the needs of children and families?*

2. *What can or should you do as a future teacher of young children to help children and families in your community deal with these difficult issues?*

Divorce leaves children without one of their parents and creates many stresses for children and parents; the eventual remarriage that frequently occurs leads to other new challenges. Approximately 16 percent of all families include a stepchild or stepchildren (Dainton, 1993). While adults are learning to mesh parenting styles and combine efforts to manage complex households, children are adjusting to a variety of new relationships (Berger, 1995). Careful observation and sensitive interactions may be required of the teacher to assist children and families with these complex changes.

Two-Career Families

Today's economic realities find a great many intact families in which both parents have to work outside the home for financial reasons. In other two-parent families, both husband and wife have career aspirations and are also employed full-time outside the home. In either of these circumstances, children in recent generations tend to have less time to spend with their parents. It has been estimated that between 1960 and 1986 children spent ten fewer hours each week with their parents, primarily due to the increase in both parents working (Eisenberg, 1990). In addition to less family time, when both parents work outside the home, parents have fewer opportunities to be actively involved in school activities. Teachers of young children need to understand the complexities of this family type and make adjustments in their involvement strategies to ensure that busy lifestyles and limited flexible time can be managed.

Older and Younger Parents

Another change in family composition that impacts schools for young children is the age of the parents themselves. People are having children at both older and younger ages. Teen pregnancies and birth rates among unmarried women continue to rise, despite many efforts to make young people aware of the major challenges facing teen parents (Annie E. Casey Foundation, 1996).

> *Becky is a young single mother of six-year-old Brian. She got pregnant at fifteen and has worked hard to complete high school, keep a part-time job, and be a good mother to Brian. Becky has lived at home to make ends meet and is just now beginning to get herself together both financially and emotionally.*

At the same time, many couples are choosing to wait until later in life to begin families. This older group of parents tends to be well-educated and brings a diversity of life and work experiences to their interactions with schools.

> *Lisa and Mike postponed children for several years while getting established in their careers. Both returned to graduate school to strengthen their career mobility. At age thirty-eight, they decided to have their first child. Now in their mid-forties, they have two children, busy professional lives, and a secure financial outlook.*

With young parents, older parents, and every possible age combination in between, teachers find less common ground on which to base their interactions and communications with parents. Working with parents becomes a more individualized event, with more emphasis on the needs, interests, and abilities of the diversity of parents found in each classroom.

Ethnic/Cultural Diversity

Another fact of life today in the United States is that families continue to grow more diverse in terms of ethnic/cultural background (Fuller & Olsen, 1998). It is estimated, for example, that the non-Hispanic white population in this country will decrease from nearly 75 percent in 1980 to approximately 50 percent by the

Teachers of young children need to be sensitive to the ages and lifestyles of parents and make adjustment to ensure that parents have opportunities to be involved in the school.

year 2030 (Hernandez, 1995). During this same period, the Hispanic and Asian American populations will increase significantly.

In addition to modifications that need to occur in the curriculum because of these changes in demography (see Chapter 8), this increasing diversity will also influence the kinds of interactions that teachers have with parents and families. For example, Asian American parents tend to have high expectations for their children academically but also feel that the school should have considerable autonomy in dealing with academic and discipline-related issues (Fuller & Olsen, 1998). Consequently, they may be less likely to get involved in some aspects of school life. Adults working with young children and their families need to be aware of these cultural/ethnic differences and adjust to them as plans are made to involve parents and families in the educational process.

Family Mobility

One final characteristic of families today that significantly impacts teachers is the relocation of families in new communities (Barbour & Barbour, 1997). In some cases, this movement is brought about when parents are promoted to a higher position in a corporation or relocate to find a better job in a new community. For other families, moving may be the only way to keep one step ahead of creditors. Migrant workers who move around the country taking low-paying agricultural jobs are yet another reason many families are on the move. Whatever the reason, family mobility frequently leads to stress and can impact the family's willingness to be involved in school.

Is Involvement Worth the Effort?

Given the family situations described here and the complications they present, you may be wondering whether or not this whole task of involving parents is worth the effort it clearly will take. Despite the added time commitments, teachers and schools who take the time to work with families find the experience a richly rewarding one for all involved (Fuller & Olsen, 1998). The insight and support that parents can provide the schools simply have no substitute. Conversely, parents often find that they desperately need the support and assistance schools can offer. Parenting is an extremely difficult and complex task requiring much guidance and assistance (Stipek, Rosenblatt, & DiRocco, 1994). Children, too, benefit when parents and teachers work together. Working with families becomes a win-win situation where all participants benefit.

Benefits to Teachers

❧ *Mrs. Andreson teaches second grade at Northwest Academy. She has worked hard to involve parents in the educational process. Although it means some extra effort on her part, she clearly sees many advantages. Involved parents are important aides in the classroom and helpmates for field trips. In addition, parents who participate in their child's education extend learning into the home and are generally more supportive of the schools.*

When teachers make the effort necessary to involve parents and community members, they find that other adults have a greater appreciation of the challenges of working with young children. Parents and community members come to value and respect teachers' efforts and are more likely to speak positively with others about early education (Gestwicki, 1996). With added assistance, teachers can also do a better job in their teaching (Shartrand, Weiss, Kreider, & Lopez, 1997). While a parent or community member is busy with a small-group art project, for example, the teacher is freed up to work with other children in the classroom. Bringing in other adults with unique talents and abilities also adds to the excitement of the classroom and often leaves teachers feeling more satisfied with their work (Gestwicki, 1996). As teachers work to involve parents and community members, their relationships with children also tend to improve (Ehly & Dustin, 1994). With more time for each child, increased understanding, and a more exciting curriculum, children respond more positively to teachers.

Involving Parents in the Classroom

Many good reasons support involving parents in your classroom. One of the most important is that children benefit from more adult help and a richer curriculum. Here are a few suggestions for ways in which parents can effectively contribute to your classroom:

- Read books to individual children or small groups.
- Play an appropriate educational game with children.
- Prepare and organize materials for an upcoming classroom activity.
- Share a talent or interest with the class. An example might be a cooking activity.

- Assist the teacher in a planned field trip into the local community.
- Spend time with children on the playground as they engage in activities in that setting.
- Talk about your work world. Demonstrate the use of specialized equipment or talents needed for the job.
- Help children engage in an interesting science experiment that requires lots of helping hands.
- Tutor an individual child who needs assistance in mathematics.

Benefits to Parents and Families

The difficult task of parenting is often a struggle for many adults. When parents are involved in the schools, they find opportunities for support that make this task a little more manageable (Berger, 1995). Just knowing that other parents are struggling with the same issues is reassuring to many. Talking through parenting challenges with others gives parents new ideas and renewed motivation to manage their struggles with children. Conversations with teachers and opportunities to see them deal with similar issues in the classroom also provide parents with good options to try with their children at home (Gestwicki, 1996). Parents who get involved also gain new insights into their own children's lives in a different setting. All of this tends to strengthen their self-esteem and hone parenting skills. The Head Start program has many examples of parents who have gotten involved in school activities and gone on to improve their lives in a variety of ways ("Head Start Star," 1995).

Benefits to Children

> *Kendra has been struggling with reading in her first-grade classroom. After conferencing with her parents, Kendra's teacher has asked two parent volunteers to spend time each week listening to her read. At home, Kendra's parents have set aside twenty minutes each evening for family reading time. This combined effort is beginning to pay dividends, and Kendra's reading skills are slowly improving.*

When parents, community members, and teachers work together, children's lives are improved. Children who see a variety of concerned adults working to help them improve their school performance respond positively, leading to increased

Involving Parents at Home

It is important to have parents involved in your classroom to provide you and the children you work with the best possible classroom environment. But, many parents can't or won't be able to participate in your classroom activities during the school day. They can, however, support you in the home. The following list of possible activities is meant to get you thinking about the many possibilities that exist. You should consider creating your own list of options.

- Read good books to children regularly.
- Talk with children about the positive and negative influences of television while viewing together.

- Create a space at home for children to do projects related to school, and work with them to make sure they get done.
- Type the classroom newsletter, and prepare it for mailing to other parents.
- Prepare a game or activity that the teacher can use in the classroom.
- Call other parents to remind them of the upcoming field trip, and find volunteers to help with transportation.
- Let children know you think school is important and that they need to be active, positive participants.

achievement (Fuller & Olsen, 1998). This involvement makes it clear to children that schooling is important, and as a result, their motivation to succeed is strengthened. Just as with parents, children also tend to have improved self-concept when parents, community members, and teachers combine efforts on their behalf. It feels good to know so many important people care. Participation also benefits children by providing an enriched classroom environment (Gestwicki, 1996). When parents get involved in the classroom, more hands-on activities (which simply couldn't be managed without additional help) become possible. A trip to a local grocery store, for example, to learn about an important community business wouldn't be possible without parents and others to assist along the way.

Building Strong Two-Way Relationships

Healthy human relationships of all sorts have as a foundation strong communication. Friendships, marriages, and parent–child relationships all require regular and effective interactions to remain strong. This same basic premise is true for parent–teacher relationships as well. When teachers and parents engage in frequent verbal and/or written interactions, their relationships can grow and prosper (Fuller & Olsen, 1998).

Providing Mutual Support

When you think about the friendships you have with other adults, do you recognize the mutual give and take that is necessary to make these relationships work? Strong friendships require mutual support if they are to remain healthy. This same

Elements of Good Communication

The key to good parent–teacher relations is good communication, so what can you do to make it happen? Good communication has five key elements:

- *Your voice.* The loudness or softness of your voice, its pitch, the speed of delivery of your message, and the emotional tone all significantly influence your communication with another person.

- *Body language.* We send many messages with our bodies. For example, body language can reveal our insecurity or confidence in a communication situation or show our interest or boredom. It is important to make our nonverbal messages the same as our verbal ones.

- *Word choice.* Words are a major vehicle for sharing meaning with another person. The words we choose send important messages to others. For instance, *outspoken* and *blunt* have very similar meanings, but your word selection sends very different messages to parents.

- *Situational variables.* The physical context also strongly influences communication. Comfortable, adult-sized furniture, for example, makes the parent–teacher conference more positive. Also consider the fact that your clothing choices also send powerful messages to parents.

- *Listening skills.* Good communication also requires strong listening skills. It takes active involvement, comments, and appropriate questioning to make sure the speaker knows she has been heard and understood. Not an easy task.

idea applies to parent–teacher relationships as well. If we are to work with parents as partners in the educational process, we need to see our interactions as providing support for one another (Kasting, 1994). When parents spend time in the classroom, they are providing us with support in the educational process. Other parents support teachers when they assist their children with school-related projects at home. The options for parental support of teachers are many. Creative teachers will find a number of ways to find and use this support.

It is important, however, for teachers to support parents as well (Kasting, 1994). When we share parenting information with a concerned parent, listen to the struggles families face, or help locate a community resource to meet a parental need (Stephens, 1994), we are providing valued assistance that will strengthen our relationships with parents. This does not imply that teachers can meet all or even most of the needs of parents and families. Many times, the teacher's role is to simply know of resources available within the community and refer parents to them when needed (Stephens, 1994).

Communication: The Key

Without question, the key element needed for effective parent–teacher partnerships is strong communication. It is the beginning point and a continuing need in these relationships (Gestwicki, 1996). Calling Mrs. Jackson to mention the extra effort Zachary put into his mathematics today, a brief note to Jennifer's father to thank him for coming on the recent field trip, and just taking the time to say hello

Ms. Epstein calls Mrs. Jackson, a parent, to mention the effort that her son made in mathematics that week.

to Shaquille's mom when she drops him off for class are all simple, but important relationship-building communications. Effective understanding and positive interactions result from spending time getting to know one another via thoughtful, quality communications.

Epstein (1995) suggests that the best schools work to create partnerships between teachers, families, and communities. When members of these partnerships work together, children have the greatest opportunities for learning and development. These partnerships lead to six different types of involvement:

- **Parenting:** Help all families establish home environments to support children as students.
- **Communicating:** Design effective communication strategies to connect home and school.
- **Volunteering:** Recruit and organize parent and community volunteers.
- **Learning at home:** Provide parents with ideas that they can use to help their children at home.
- **Decision making:** Parents and community members participate in decisions about how the school operates.
- **Collaborating with community:** Identify and use community resources to strengthen school programs (Epstein, 1995).

Although only one of these six categories of involvement specifically addresses communication and its importance in home, school, and community relations, it isn't difficult to see that each type requires strong communication to be effective. The partnerships we seek with parents and community members are just not possible without good communication.

Effective Communication Methods

Given the importance of quality interactions between parents and teachers, it is critical for teachers of young children to be aware of a variety of communication techniques and the potential strengths and weaknesses of each. No one technique will meet all of a teacher's needs for communicating with parents. Several methods, used appropriately, will be necessary to build and maintain the partnerships between parents and teachers.

Telephone Calls

One simple but effective communication tool that teachers can put to good use is the telephone. It is a quick and easy way to communicate simple, positive messages to parents (Berger, 1995). A two-minute call to share with a parent something positive her child did today in school will pay big dividends in terms of relationship building. Every parent wants to hear these positive messages, so if you decide to use this communication strategy, make sure you contact each family with a positive message about their child.

Using the telephone in communicating with families has several other important benefits (Henniger, 1982). In general, the telephone is inexpensive and provides for two-way communications. Most parents are also more comfortable in communicating with teachers when they can do it from the comfort and convenience of their own homes. Teachers can fit in short telephone calls around already busy schedules, making it more likely to be something that gets done.

Despite the many benefits, telephone use has some potential drawbacks. Because a phone call has no nonverbal cues, the phone is not appropriate for more difficult messages that may need to be shared with parents. Remember, also, that you don't know what you may be interrupting when you call. It is always best to ask if you are calling at a convenient time. You may need to give the parent the chance to talk with you at a later time. Although the old-style party lines, where more than one family shared the same telephone line, are rare today, the telephone is still not a secure communication system. Others may listen when you talk, so the nature of the communications shared must again be carefully considered.

One final issue should be mentioned regarding telephone use. Consider whether or not you will want to give out your home telephone number so that parents can contact you outside school hours. Some teachers feel very strongly that their home life should not be interrupted by work-related business. Others, however, want parents to know that they have the opportunity to call when they have a need. If you choose to give out your number, you may want to let parents know the appropriate times to call.

Written Communications

A common strategy that teachers use to exchange information with parents is written communications. A wide variety of options are appropriate (Barbour & Barbour, 1997; Henniger, 1984).

The simplest may be the handwritten **notes** sent home with individual children. Much like the telephone calls mentioned earlier, these brief notes are simply a little pat on the back for the parent and child by sharing a positive event from the classroom day. Teachers also find many opportunities to send home written **notices** to all parents about an upcoming event such as a field trip to the zoo. One- or two-page **letters** home to parents are another possible written communication tool. An introductory letter sent home to parents before the school year begins is one very effective use of this strategy. A **newsletter** is a longer, more complicated written document that usually goes home to parents less regularly. It may contain several pages of information to parents, including such things as a calendar of events, articles of interest to parents, samples of student work, ideas for parents to use at home, and a wish list of materials that parents could collect for the classroom.

As more homes and schools develop computer linkages, **electronic communications** may well become a more common written strategy for parents and teachers. Electronic mail is one such option that is growing rapidly. In addition, many schools and/or teachers have developed home pages on the World Wide Web that allow for sharing of written materials. The ease and speed of communicating electronically will undoubtedly make it a popular option.

A final category of written materials are those that are **prepublished** through other sources. Many public agencies prepare brochures or other written materials that might be very useful to you in working with parents. Articles in newspapers and magazines (remember to obey copyright laws if you make multiple copies) are also helpful in communicating important information to parents.

As you think about using written communications with parents, consider the following issues. One of the difficulties many teachers face with any written material intended for parents is how to make sure it gets home. Children of any age need assistance in getting these messages to their parents. Another issue with written communications is that, although they provide parents with good information, they seldom encourage a response from the home. When this can be built in, the connection between home and school is stronger.

Perhaps the most important consideration when developing written communications is to make sure that your writing is of the very best quality. What kind of response would parents have to a letter from the teacher that had several spelling and grammatical errors? Often, the reaction is surprise, followed by frustration. Teachers are expected to be good models. Punctuation, grammar, and spelling errors send a negative message home that may be stronger than the more positive intent of the written communication. If writing is something you have to work hard at doing well, plan on spending the time that is necessary to ensure a well-written message.

Visual Communication Tools

Although written communications are an important part of interactions with parents, other options are available for teachers to use. One additional category of communication tools could be called *visual displays*. Videotapes and bulletin boards (Gestwicki, 1996) are two important types of visual displays discussed here. Many parents would like to know what is happening in their children's classrooms but don't have the chance to drop in on a regular basis. Consider making regular videotapes of the activities in your classroom and then loaning these to parents who want to catch a glimpse of their children's daily activities. Although both children and adults act differently when they know they are being videotaped, before long, normal behavior returns and parents have an accurate picture of what is happening in the classroom.

Bulletin boards are another form of visual communication that can be productively used in working with parents and families. A wide assortment of information can be shared on parent bulletin boards. Upcoming events, classroom activities, samples of children's work, articles on parenting or child development issues, and a wish list of materials parents could collect at home are a sampling of possible items that may be included. A thoughtful parent bulletin board will be read and appreciated by the parents who enter your classroom and have a few minutes to browse (Barbour & Barbour, 1997).

Although bulletin board use has many positive aspects, it is important to mention that bulletin boards do have their limitations. Perhaps the most obvious is the fact that those parents who don't come into your classroom will not be able to see them. Another potential drawback is that bulletin boards don't give parents much opportunity to communicate with the teacher. One-way communications definitely have inherent limitations. Finally, be aware that bulletin boards are time-consuming to create and require periodic updating to make sure the information remains current.

Home Visits

One of the best ways to get acquainted with parents and families is to take time to go out and meet with families in their homes (Rockwell, Andre, & Hawley, 1996). The teacher sets up an appointment, plans an agenda, and travels to the parent's home to meet and talk with the family. Home visits have been shown to be highly effective in teaching parents skills that they can use in working with their children (Bronfenbrenner, 1974) and for conducting parent–teacher conferences. Perhaps the best way, however, for most teachers to use home visits is to use them to get better acquainted with children and their families.

Many preschool teachers attempt to have home visits with all of their families before the school year actually begins. These getting acquainted visits typically last thirty to forty-five minutes and may include a variety of activities. Some teachers take a book or a simple activity with them to break the ice with the children who will be coming into their classrooms. Young children frequently want to lead the

Home visits are an ideal time to casually share with parents a bit about yourself and what you hope to accomplish during the school year.

teacher on a tour around the house and show off their bedrooms and favorite playthings. Home visits are an ideal time to share casually with parents a little bit about yourself as a person and what you hope to accomplish during the year as a teacher. Sharing in this way often encourages parents to open up to you about their lives as well. Refreshments, casual conversation, and an opportunity to get a feel for home life are other common elements of a getting acquainted home visit.

If you choose to make home visits, consider the following suggestions (Barbour & Barbour, 1997; Gestwicki, 1996):

- It is essential that you make an appointment with parents ahead of time and explain to them the purposes of the visit.
- Establish a time frame for the visit (typically thirty to forty-five minutes) so that parents know what to expect.
- Think carefully about what you will wear on the home visit. Remember that first impressions are important and that you want to appear professional but still approachable by parents.
- Avoid note taking during the home visit itself. Parents generally feel anxious when you do. Drive a few blocks away after the home visit, and then stop to make any needed notes about things you wanted to remember.

Parent Meetings

Getting together with parents in group settings is yet another possible communication strategy to be considered (Foster, 1994). A number of meeting types are useful. Some gatherings could simply be **social times,** when you have a chance to get to know the parents and help them meet other families in the class. The traditional potluck or a family fun night are examples of this meeting type. Many parent meetings are designed to be **educational** and focus on a topic of interest and importance to a larger number of parents. "Helping Prepare Children for Reading" might be one topic that would interest a variety of parents. Some additional parent meetings are needed to organize for a specific task or to deal with the management of the school. These **business meetings** can frequently be dull and uninspiring, so it may be best to try to combine this task with another more fun event. Finally, some parent meetings provide an opportunity for **child performances.** While not appropriate for the preschool and toddler years, a musical program or the presentation of a play can be a very enjoyable experience for primary children and their families.

If you plan on incorporating parent meetings into your collection of communication tools, be sure to plan carefully for them. Parents who give up precious evening time to come into your classroom will want to get a good return on their investment. Make sure the meeting topics are of interest to parents. A simple questionnaire can be used to determine what parents want and need for their group gatherings. Plan a variety of interesting activities that actively involve parents in discussion and learning. Have a planned agenda organized to keep events moving along smoothly. This careful planning will pay big dividends in terms of parent interest and involvement in your meetings.

Parent–Teacher Conferences

One of the most common communication tools used in early childhood classrooms is the parent–teacher conference (Lawler, 1991). Most schools expect teachers to conference with parents at least once each academic year and more commonly twice. A typical pattern is to have conferences fairly early in the fall and again in the spring. In many early childhood settings, schools will set aside one or two regular school days and additional evening times for conferencing.

Parent–teacher conferences should be a high priority. An important benefit of the conference situation is that it brings parents into the classroom. For some, this may be the only time they enter the school. When done well, the conference builds positive rapport with parents as the teacher and parent discuss the child's strengths, progress, and possible areas for improvement. Conferences allow for far greater detail to be shared about the child's progress than either a report card or written report can. In addition, when the conference is held in the classroom, the parent can actually see projects the child has completed and get a better sense for the learning experiences occurring there.

Although most parent–teacher conferences are pleasant and enjoyable for both the parent and teacher, many times, issues raised require the teacher to demonstrate quick thinking and tact to avoid possible problems. The following purely hypothetical excerpt from a conference situation highlights this issue:

> ⌘ *Margaret is the mother of five-year-old Louise. During the parent–teacher conference, Margaret announces: "You know, I am suspicious of anything Louise does. She has fooled me too many times. Oh, I have read all the books on child psychology, but it hasn't helped me much. I really don't know what to do with Louise. There are so many things wrong with her!"*
>
> *As Louise's teacher, you want to understand Margaret's concerns and work effectively with her while also helping the parent see the good things Louise does in your classroom—not an easy task. Think about how you might respond to this parent.*

Another major consideration for the parent–teacher conference is whether or not to include the child in the actual event (Berger, 1995). This is often referred to as a three-way conference and has both strengths and problems. When children are involved, their anxiety over what is being discussed is eliminated. They can also share their perspectives on conference issues and, along with the parent and teacher, can commit to any plans for improvement. Many times, seeing the interactions between parent and child in the three-way conference is also very insightful and provides the teacher with important information about family life.

The three-way conference has potential problems. For example, the teacher or parent may be less comfortable when the child is present. Each may wish to share information about family life or classroom interactions that is just not appropriate or helpful for children to hear. In other instances, the adults may downplay the child's problems when she is present. Adults can also make the child feel like she is an unimportant part of the conference process by talking over and around the child. Some argue that another potential problem with the three-way conference is that younger children may not understand or be ready to participate in the conference.

Despite these potential problems, you should consider including the child as you prepare for parent–teacher conferences. With careful preparation, even the youngest children can benefit from participation in at least part of your interactions with parents.

Factors Influencing Quality Involvement

Parent involvement doesn't just happen by magic. It requires a great deal of hard work. And, as indicated earlier, it requires frequent, quality communications between home and school. But other factors help ensure the success of parent involvement in schools. Williams and Chavkin (1989) have identified seven essential elements of parent involvement programs in schools. Although Williams and Chavkin identified these elements for schools, the concepts can be applied to individual classrooms as well. In addition to the notion of quality two-way communications, the authors found these elements to be essential:

- **Written policies:** Documents that legitimize the importance of parent involvement and provide guidelines for ways in which parents can expect to be involved.

- **Administrative support:** When the administration supports the concept, money is made available, materials and physical resources are provided, and people are assigned the task of carrying out the involvement tasks.

- **Training:** Teachers and parents both need training to make involvement a success. This training should occur over time and focus on developing partnerships between home and school.

- **Partnership approach:** Quality programs emphasize the importance of parents and teachers working as partners in the educational process. Each has much to share and much to learn from one another.

- **Networking:** Promising parent involvement programs network with other programs to share ideas, resources, and expertise.

- **Evaluation:** The best programs also take the time to have regular evaluations of parent involvement activities. Changes and improvements can then be implemented to make involvement activities even more successful.

Families Having Children with Special Needs

Families that have children with special needs are much the same and yet much different from other families. These parents love their children and want the very best for them educationally and socially. They are concerned about parenting strategies that work, want their children to learn and grow in healthy and safe environments, are thrilled when a new developmental milestone is reached, and worry about what is best for their children. At the same time, families that have children with special needs often face additional burdens and responsibilities that make parenting and family life a real struggle. Shepherd and Shepherd (1984) describe the range of emotions that many parents and families with special needs children experience. The following is a sampling of these possible feelings:

- It is a little like everything that everyone else has experienced; it is a lot like nothing anyone else has ever experienced.
- It is feeling like you want to kick in the TV screen every time you see the "Take care of your baby before it is born" public service commercial. I took care of myself when I was pregnant, and our child is handicapped.
- It is being afraid to ask for help because you are fearful that you cannot personally cope with any more blame or guilt.
- It is "dying" from the silence and stares of other people when they meet our son. It is wanting to announce to the whole world that you have a handicapped child and also simultaneously wanting to disappear from the face of the earth for a few moments.
- It is being afraid to even think, much less plan, concerning the future.
- It is dying a little when your son does something inappropriate and others laugh and say "You are so funny!"
- It is having three specialists all ask you during the same day if anyone in your family has ever been diagnosed as schizophrenic. (Shepherd & Shepherd, 1984, pp. 88–89)

Teachers and schools working with these parents and families must make every effort to be sensitive to the special needs and feelings of these families. Extra care must be taken to listen carefully, to communicate positively, and develop good working relationships with these parents. Remembering that each family unit is unique, teachers must work to understand the challenges these families face and stand ready to assist in whatever ways possible. In addition, families that have children with special needs want to feel needed and accepted as a part of the classroom experiences. Make sure they are welcomed with open arms.

Connecting with the Community

This chapter has focused primarily on involving parents and families in the educational process. And although parents are critical to the success of early education, community members can also provide many important benefits. A great many resources can be productively used to benefit young children (Rockwell et al., 1996). In terms of human resources, the local fireman, policewoman, or retired volunteer can share much with your class. Material resources also abound in most communities. Scrap paper, wood, and other recyclable materials can be located and used effectively. Community businesses are often generous in their donations of money and materials in support of local educational efforts. When community

Having a firefighter visit the school, or taking your class to a fire station, can enrich your lesson on fire safety.

members are involved in your classroom, they are also more likely to understand and support your program when talking to others. It makes good sense to work toward involving community members along with parents.

Involving the Community in the School

The community can be active in the early childhood school setting in many good ways (Barbour & Barbour, 1997). One possibility is to allow the school building to be used for appropriate community activities. Groups wanting to offer classes in jewelry making or woodworking, recreational activities such as ballroom dancing, or noncredit classes on such topics as health or psychology always need a place to conduct these activities. Community organizations may also need a meeting room and could benefit from a local school's willingness to provide space.

Another important way to involve community members in the early childhood classroom is to seek out and use resource people to strengthen the curriculum (Latimer, 1994). Community helpers such as doctors and dentists can come into the classroom and share information with children about good health and dental care. Workers from a variety of occupations can begin the process of career awareness with young children by coming in and demonstrating their expertise. Other community members may well be interested in simply volunteering their time and talents to help out in your classroom.

Finally, community members should be involved in the schools as part of the decision-making process. What is taught, who should serve as teachers, and decisions about purchases of equipment and supplies are all potential issues that community members should be involved in. The Head Start program requires that every local center have representation from parents and the community on its Advisory Board (U.S. Department of Health and Human Services, 1984). These boards make all the major decisions about Head Start activities. Local public schools also are managed by school boards made up of elected community members who agree to oversee the activities of the schools under its control.

Involving the School in the Community

Early childhood educators and children can also benefit from getting out into the local community (Dolan, 1996). By doing so, schools avoid the tendency of isolating themselves from the rest of life. Perhaps the most common way in which teachers and classrooms get involved with the community is through the traditional field trip. A well-planned visit to the local bakery could be a wonderful way to help children understand food production and distribution, for example.

With parental support, the community can also become a site for observation and learning separate from classroom-wide events. In some instances, teachers can provide parents and children with specific assignments to go out into the community and gain insights into business and community services. For example, a second-grade teacher could encourage parents and children to interview a local business person in preparation for an upcoming social studies unit. In other circumstances, providing parents with information about upcoming community events and services can lead to important opportunities to learn outside the traditional school setting and day.

Another option for involving the school in the community is to consider ways in which parents, children, and school personnel can give back to the community (Rockwell et al., 1996). Getting involved in a community service project such as planting seedling trees during an Arbor Day celebration could be one way to do this. Another possibility is to adopt a community park and spend time there on a regular basis cleaning and maintaining the grounds. Donating clothing and food to the local women's care facility could be yet another chance to help children and families feel that they are contributing to the community in positive ways.

Summary

The issues involved in working with parents, families, and communities begin with an understanding of family life today and the impact of diverse family situations on parent involvement. The many benefits of involvement for teachers, parents, and children need to be clearly understood. The key to working with parents is to build strong two-way relationships through mutual support and communication. Communication strategies such as telephone calls, written communications, visual communication tools, home visits, parent meetings, and parent–teacher conferences are essential to the relationship-building process. Several factors influence the quality of parental involvement, and teachers must address special issues in working with families having children with special needs. Teachers also need planned strategies for involving the community in the school and the school in the community.

∾ *For Discussion and Action*

1. Interview a parent with a child in the early childhood years. What does this parent see as the major hassles of family life? How does the parent feel about her child's school? Is the parent involved in the school? Come up with several specific interview questions, and see what kinds of responses you get.

2. Does parent participation make a difference? Do some reading on the subject, and make a case for why it is important to take the time to get parents involved.

3. This chapter discussed a variety of different family situations that you will encounter in your work with young children. Discuss how these variances in family structure could influence the ways in which you work with parents and families. Try to be as specific as possible.

4. How do you think you will use written communications in your work with parents? Identify two or three specific ideas that you may want to use.

5. Are you aware of community resources that may be available to help parents deal with some of the struggles they face? For example, if a parent confided in you that she needed some warm clothing for her children to make it through the winter, could you point her in the right direction? Find three community resources for this situation or a similar problem of your choosing.

∾ *Building Your Personal Library*

Barbour, C., & Barbour, N. (1997). *Families, schools, and communities: Building partnerships for educating children.* Upper Saddle River, NJ: Merrill/Prentice Hall. The authors provide a strong overview of home–school–community relations. In particular, separate chapters on community involvement and model parent involvement programs are very helpful.

Buzzell, J. B. (1996). *School and family partnerships: Case studies for regular and special educators.* Albany, NY: Delmar. This book is a collection of case situations in which teachers and parents communicate with each other about a variety of issues. Following each case, the author provides questions for discussion and follow-up.

Gestwicki, C. (1996). *Home, school and community relations* (3rd ed.). Albany, NY: Delmar. This book is an excellent overview of the issues involved in working with parents and families. It stresses the importance of effective communication in establishing and maintaining relationships.

Lawler, S. D. (1991). *Parent–teacher conferencing in early childhood education.* Washington, DC: National Education Association. This book focuses on conducting effective conferences and includes separate chapters on academic performance conferences, referral conferences, and conferences about discipline problems.

8 Diversity Issues and Young Children

In this chapter you will

- Study how young children develop conceptual understanding of diversity issues.

- Identify ways to encourage acceptance of diverse people.

- Discover methods for integrating diversity topics into the early childhood curriculum.

- Investigate options for working with parents and community members regarding diversity.

*"**What an interesting class** I have!" you think, as you prepare for next week's activities. "These children are unique in so many ways! In my class of twenty-seven third-grade children, I've got quite a mix. There is Dimitri, who comes to us from Russia. His English has improved by leaps and bounds over the last several months. Eduard and Angela are Hispanic and benefit so much from the warmth and support of their extended families. Shantel is African American, and Quen has Asian heritage. Each brings a unique personality to the classroom. Then there is Alex. Despite using a wheelchair from a very early age, he is one of the most active and happy children in the group. To complicate things even further, the class has a higher than normal percentage of boys. It will be even more important than usual to make sure the girls have access to some of the traditionally boy-dominated equipment in the classroom."* ❧

Although the preceding scenario may sound rather unusual, in reality, this level of diversity is more often the norm rather than the exception in many early childhood classrooms today. Adults working with children need to be prepared for this situation and be ready to assist children in understanding and appropriately responding to diversity issues.

Diversity as a Foundation

The topic of diversity is included in this section of the text because it directly influences the foundational elements of early childhood education presented in Chapters 4 through 7. Child development, play, guidance, and working with parents and families are all influenced by diversity issues. Some examples should help highlight this point:

- **Child development and diversity.** Children with physical disabilities such as hearing and eyesight problems acquire oral and written language differently; boys and girls have variations in their gross and fine motor development (Schickedanz, Schickedanz, Forsyth, & Forsyth, 1998).

- **Play and diversity.** Children who live in cultures that value competition play more competitive games (Sutton-Smith & Roberts, 1981); children with autism seldom engage in symbolic play (Atlas & Lapidus, 1987); boys and girls have different toy preferences (Nash & Fraleigh, 1993).

- **Diversity and guidance.** Children with attention deficits often need special guidance regarding instructions (Landau & McAninch, 1993); eye contact is considered impolite in some cultures, thus changing the way in which you guide some children (Hildebrand, 1994).

- **Working with diverse parents.** In African American families, it is common for aunts, uncles, grandparents, and other extended family members to informally adopt children, thus creating unique family constellations for the teacher to work with (Fuller & Olsen, 1998); the involvement of men in child care and education has increased and changes the mix of parents that teachers will be working with (Barbour & Barbour, 1997).

It should be clear from the preceding examples that diversity issues influence the way teachers work with children and families. As American society grows increasingly more diverse, the importance of this topic will continue to expand. A careful study of diversity will add to your understanding of the foundations of early childhood education.

Attitudes about Diversity

An important starting point in the study of diversity is to address the attitudes of children (and adults) toward people who are different from themselves. Without question, children notice the many distinctions that exist. For example, infants as young as six months notice skin color differences (Banks, 1993). By the age of two, children not only notice similarities and differences but also ask questions about their observations. Clearly, children find diversity topics interesting and want to talk about and understand these issues.

Racial/Cultural Attitudes

To understand children's attitudes about racial and cultural differences, it is necessary to begin with those held by adults. Children are strongly influenced by the comments and actions of the significant adults in their lives.

With the passage of the Civil Rights Act in 1964, many people assumed that racial discrimination would end relatively quickly and that attitudes about racial and cultural differences would improve greatly. This has not, however, been the case. Although many people accept and value the racial and cultural diversity of American life, many others do not. Unfortunately, many adults continue to pass on to children their misconceptions and negative attitudes about people who are different from themselves.

Children who are exposed to these adults begin to absorb these negative attitudes as early as two-and-a-half years of age (Banks, 1993). Through repeated exposure to parents, teachers, neighbors, television, and other media that regularly reinforce this disapproval of people different from themselves, children start to internalize these values. Because both positive and negative attitudes begin to develop early in the young child's life, it is essential for early educators to help guide children in the process of valuing diversity.

Attitudes about Gender

Efforts to provide women with equitable opportunities in all aspects of American life have been only slightly more successful than the results for racial/cultural minorities. Take, for example, gender equity in National College Athletic Association (NCAA) sports. A recent study by the NCAA indicates that even though equitable funding has been mandated for many years, it will probably be another decade before parity is reached (Tucker, 1997). Although most people talk about the importance of gender equity, the subtle (and not-so-subtle) behaviors of many adults indicate that women are often given lower status in American society. Children are again exposed to many parents, adults, and media events that promote gender inequities. This can often lead to childhood behaviors and budding attitudes that are less than desirable.

> ∾ *Mandy, Ariel, and DeForrest are playing in the dress-up area of their preschool classroom. Clothes and equipment are available for playing doctors and nurses. Mandy wants to dress up as a doctor and begins to gear up for her role. "Hey!" calls DeForrest. "You can't be the doctor! Girls have to be the nurses!"*

Preschool children's attitudes about gender roles (like the one just expressed) are often overgeneralizations made from their observations of, and interactions with, other adults. These early stereotypic responses can be modified by caregivers who provide children with more diverse examples of women's roles in society. Young children need early and frequent exposure to pictures, stories, and adult models that demonstrate more equitable opportunities for women in America.

People with Special Needs

With the passage of **Public Law (PL) 94–142** (the Education for All Handicapped Children Act) in 1975, children with special needs began to be mainstreamed into American public school classrooms. Children without disabilities began to work and play with students having special needs. Before this time, these groups rarely interacted. In 1986, **PL 99–457** mandated mainstreaming for children from three to five years of age, further encouraging contact between children with special needs and the general population. More recently, **PL 101–336** (known as the Americans with Disabilities Act) was enacted in 1990. Viewed as a major piece of civil rights legislation (Wolery & Wilbers, 1994), this law requires equal access to public and private services for individuals with disabilities. These services include the opportunity to participate in early childhood programs.

The passage of the Education for All Handicapped Children Act (PL 94–142) in 1975 allowed children with special needs to be mainstreamed into public school classrooms.

One result of the preceding legislation was that a definition of the different types of disabilities eligible for services evolved. The U.S. Department of Education (1996) has identified the following categories of individuals with disabilities:

- Specific learning disabilities
- Speech or language impairments
- Mental retardation
- Serious emotional disturbance
- Multiple disabilities
- Hearing impairments
- Orthopedic impairments
- Other health impairments
- Visual impairments
- Deaf-blindness
- Autism
- Traumatic brain injury

The opportunity for early and regular contact has led to many benefits for children with and without disabilities. Wolery and Wilbers (1994) list the following potential advantages:

Children with Disabilities

- Are spared the negative effects of separate, segregated education.
- Receive realistic life experiences that prepare them to live in the community.
- Have opportunities to develop friendships with typically developing peers.

Children without Disabilities

- Can develop more accurate views about individuals with disabilities.
- Have opportunities to develop positive attitudes about people who are different from themselves.
- Are provided with models of children who succeed despite many challenges.

It appears that an important system is in place that can help young children develop positive attitudes about people with special needs. Early childhood teachers need to take advantage of these naturally occurring interactions to help children grow in their understanding and acceptance of individuals with disabilities. By modeling appropriate interactions and encouraging children to do the same, adults can help ensure the development of healthy attitudes.

Encouraging an Acceptance of Diversity

It should be clear that teachers and caregivers must actively help children develop appropriate attitudes about diversity. The negative opinions children encounter in many hours of television viewing and through interactions with prejudiced adults require careful and frequent effort to overcome. This process should begin with the youngest children and continue throughout the early childhood years. Research indicates that many attitudes are firmly entrenched by nine years of age and may be very difficult to change after that time (Aboud, 1988).

Begin with Self-Analysis

An excellent place to begin this active process of influencing children's attitudes is with a self-analysis. Because the teacher is one of the most influential adults in the life of the child, an understanding of personal attitudes and behaviors is important (Bowman, 1994). Although most of us would like to think that we are not prejudiced against those different from ourselves, careful reflection often uncovers many areas that could be improved. One method for developing more accurate self-awareness is through individual reflection and journal writing. The support and assistance of a small group is strongly encouraged. A sampling of activities that could be useful in this process follows:

It is important for teachers to analyze their feelings about people different from themselves so that they do not project negative attitudes to their students.

- Think about how you would describe or define your racial/ethnic identity. Write about or discuss with others what you find important/not important about this aspect of yourself. Describe how you feel about your racial/ethnic identity.
- Repeat the preceding activity two more times, focusing first on your gender identity and next on differences in physical abilities.
- Think about and share either in writing or with a small group your views on race, ethnicity, gender, and ableness compared with those of your parents.
- Write down lists of acceptable and unacceptable behaviors for boys and girls, men and women. Discuss these lists with others (Derman-Sparks, 1989).

Again, these self-awareness activities are most effective when combined with a support group to help its members discuss and deal with the issues uncovered in this analysis. Often, the feelings encountered are painful and difficult to deal with. Help from others may be needed to work successfully through these concerns.

Talk about Differences

Good early childhood educators have always been effective in recognizing and building on children's natural interests. As captivating topics are identified by children, the creative teacher takes the opportunity to discuss them in detail. Through spontaneous dialogue and additional planned activities, children build important understandings of these issues.

Children recognize and want to know more about the differences between people. Whether during a trip through the grocery store, a church activity, community events, or an experience at school, children are very aware of racial, gender, and ableness issues to which they are exposed. Again, the insightful teacher or caregiver will recognize these experiences as opportunities for natural and effective discussion times regarding diversity.

Expose Children to Diversity

Engaging children in discussions about diversity issues is too important to be left to chance. Early childhood educators must plan for a variety of experiences with diversity that become a natural part of the daily activities of young children. Many toys, materials, pictures, books, and experiences can be woven into the curriculum to challenge children to question, compare, and contrast people and experiences different from themselves. An awareness of the need to plan for these options makes it much more likely that children will develop healthy understandings of diversity.

Inappropriate Responses to Diversity Issues

Before discussing positive ways of addressing diversity in the early childhood classroom, it is important to address two ineffective strategies that are commonly seen. Each has been used by teachers to avoid meaningful discussions of human differences with young children.

Ignore Diversity

One clearly inappropriate response to diversity issues is to deny they exist. A typical comment from a teacher ignoring diversity would be: "This multicultural education business doesn't make sense for my classroom. My class is all white, and anyway, kids don't notice differences at this age." Clearly, this approach is misguided. Children do recognize and talk about the differences they see. Teachers need to weave diversity issues into the curriculum during the early years.

The Tourist Approach

Another strategy employed by teachers to study cultural differences is to engage in a tourist-multicultural curriculum (Derman-Sparks, 1994). These well-meaning adults take a simplistic, often stereotypic look at different cultures by taking quick little curriculum visits to other parts of the world before returning to the more important European American focus for the majority of time.

Boutte and McCormick (1992) describe the tourist approach as follows: "cooking ethnic foods, examining Native American artifacts at Thanksgiving or discussing African American achievements during Black History month. Certainly, these lessons have merit; however, since they are often isolated and discontinuous, they are actually 'pseudomulticultural' activities" (p. 140).

Although this approach introduces children to aspects of different cultures, it does so in ways that lead children to believe that the European American focus is the most important and that other cultures are only tangentially significant. Often, these brief visits lead to stereotypic perceptions of other cultures and therefore sabotage the true goals of studying diversity (Boutte & McCormick, 1992).

The tourist approach to multicultural education tends to disconnect content learned in the quick trips from the main curriculum. The unintended outcome is to trivialize the contributions of different cultural groups. The unconscious thinking of children could be described as follows: "How can this content we are studying be important? It is only a small add-on to the main topics we are discussing. Studying differences can't be that important if that is all we are going to do to address it." Clearly, this is not the message we want children to receive through the study of multicultural issues.

Obviously, this tourist approach can also be used by well-meaning teachers to address gender and ableness issues as well. When either topic is treated as tangential to the main curriculum, students get the message that these are less important concerns. If diversity in general is to be a meaningful component of the early childhood classroom, this quick-fix strategy must be avoided.

Integrating Diversity throughout the Curriculum

To make diversity topics valuable additions to the curriculum, a more complex and thoughtful strategy than the tourist approach must be implemented. Issues relating to cultural differences, gender, and ableness must be made an integral part of the daily activities in the early childhood classroom (Henniger, 1995). Rather than brief diversions into interesting but less important areas, the curriculum must be infused with materials, activities, and people that provide regular opportunities for young children to come in contact with meaningful diversity issues.

The Antibias Curriculum

Louise Derman-Sparks (1989) suggests an appropriate title for a program that integrates diversity throughout the curriculum: the antibias curriculum. She states that, although specific techniques are associated with this approach, each teacher must take the general principles she presents and create an appropriate program for her specific group of children and families. The philosophy undergirding the antibias curriculum is value-based: "Differences are good; oppressive ideas and behaviors are not." The antibias curriculum "sets up a creative tension between respecting differences and not accepting unfair beliefs and acts" (Derman-Sparks, 1989, p. x). This approach requires careful planning, self-assessment, and communication with others to implement. It takes dedication and commitment but provides many rewards for children and adults alike.

Teachers interested in implementing an antibias curriculum should take a five-step approach (Derman-Sparks, 1989) to ensure success:

Step 1. Make a personal commitment. To make this curriculum a reality, teachers must spend considerable time and energy. Diversity issues must be a high priority.

Step 2. Organize a support group. The perspectives and feedback from peers are essential for rethinking the teaching of diversity.

Step 3. Do consciousness-raising (self-analysis) activities. Self-analysis was described earlier in the chapter. Teachers need to become aware of their own feelings toward cultural, racial, sexual, and ableness differences.

Step 4. Make a plan for implementing the curriculum. Through an evaluation of the physical environment, a critique of current activities, and observations of children, teachers can make plans for implementing antibias activities.

Step 5. Move slowly and carefully. Integrating diversity issues into the curriculum is hard work and requires careful planning. Moving more slowly helps ensure success.

Using Toys that Promote Diversity

One important way to encourage an acceptance of diversity in the early childhood classroom is through the provision of toys and equipment that portray similarities

This puppet show, which includes puppets with physical disabilities, helps children recognize and discuss similarities and differences among themselves.

and differences between people. Swiniarski (1991) suggests that toys are excellent ways to introduce young children to global education.

As children play with these materials and notice their similarities and differences across cultures, many opportunities for natural multicultural learning take place.

> ꙍ *Four-year-old Natalie is playing with a plastic replica of a giraffe in the block area. This is her first experience with the toy giraffe, so as the teacher stops to observe block play, Natalie asks about this animal. Where does it live? What does it eat? How big is it? Her curiosity leads to the teacher finding some picture books and other materials that describe the habitat of giraffes. Natalie is gaining understanding of a place with people and animals that are different from herself and her surroundings.*

A variety of toys are common worldwide (Swiniarski, 1991). They include

- Dolls
- Toy animals
- Musical instruments
- Puzzles

- Construction toys
- Movement toys (cars, trucks, planes)
- Puppets

The cultural uniqueness of these toys is generally in their presentation or decoration. By including toys from around the world as part of the play materials children can use in the classroom, children have many important opportunities to recognize and discuss their similarities and differences. Cultural discussions and understandings become a natural part of the day.

In addition to culture-specific toys, options are available for providing children with playthings that allow them to explore aspects of ableness. Dolls with disabilities, for example, are available through some toy vendors. Wheelchairs (both toy and real) are another possibility for the early childhood classroom. Other options are sure to present themselves to the teacher who is actively looking for these diversity options.

Toys and materials can also be purchased to encourage discussion and thinking regarding gender issues. One of the best examples of this is the variety of puzzles that are available depicting women in nontraditional work roles. Female doctors, police officers, and airline pilots are representative of this option. Some flannel-board sets and dolls provide additional opportunities for discussion of gender differences and roles.

Diversity through Games

Like the toys just described, many games from around the world can be used to enhance young children's understanding of different cultures. As with toys, games played by children around the world have more similarities than differences (Kirchner, 1991). Whether engaged in running and tag activities, ball games, or manipulative and guessing games, children play in very similar ways throughout the world. For example, the game Kick the Can, which has its origins in Canada, is played with slight variations in India (where it is called *Esha Desai*), Holland (*Burkuit*), Sweden (*Paven Bannlyser*), and Japan (*Kankai*) (Kirchner, 1991).

These games, in addition to being fun ways to spend time, provide opportunities for children to play out aspects of different cultures. For example, in the game Antelope in the Net (appropriate for seven- to ten-year-olds), which originated in the Congo, one child is chosen to be the antelope, and the rest form a circle (the net) around the antelope. Children forming the net hold hands and chant "Kasha Mu Bukondi! Kasha Mu Bukondi!" The antelope tries to break out of the net by crawling under, climbing over, or running through the tightly held hands. If the antelope is caught, the child who traps him or her becomes the new antelope (Hatcher, Pape, & Nicosia, 1988). In playing this type of game, children are naturally exposed to aspects of another culture and can begin to appreciate both the similarities and differences.

FOCUS ON . . .
Anatomically Correct Dolls

For many years now, companies have been producing limited quantities of dolls that have appropriate male and female genitalia. Their purpose is to naturally introduce children to the physical differences between female and male bodies. Particularly with some families, this option is controversial and unwanted. The arguments used for and against the use of these dolls go something like this:

Arguments for Anatomically Correct Dolls

1. Children learn a great deal from their play. One aspect of that learning should be the physical differences between boys and girls.
2. Physical differences should be discussed naturally and openly with children.
3. Anatomically correct dolls are more accurate representations of boys and girls, helping children develop more complete conceptual understandings of each.

Arguments against Anatomically Correct Dolls

1. Children don't notice or aren't interested in these physical differences.
2. The early childhood years are too early for discussions of sexual differences between boys and girls.
3. Anatomically correct dolls lead to discussions about sex, and sex education should be the responsibility of parents.

1. *Talk to a parent of a young child, and get his perspective on using anatomically correct dolls in the classroom.*
2. *What are your feelings on this topic? Make a case for the stand you take.*

Quality Children's Literature

Books for young children can be wonderful options for addressing diversity issues in the early childhood classroom. A good book can captivate the interests of children while introducing people and events that are new to them. Many times, books can lead to in-depth discussions and activities that help children understand the complexities of diversity topics (National Association for the Education of Young Children, 1993).

For example, to introduce the topic of diverse abilities, the book *Someone Special, Just Like You* (T. Brown, 1991) could be read and then discussed by young children. This book is a collection of photographs depicting children with special needs engaged in a variety of activities. The situations children have encountered will naturally lead to further discussions and activities, thus increasing awareness and understanding of this aspect of diversity.

Teachers of young children collect many different things that will be useful to them in the classroom. One such collection is often a picture file. Put on the walls in centers or used as discussion starters for different activities, these pictures should also include nonstereotypic people of color, pictures of individuals with disabilities, and examples of men and women in nontraditional roles.

Some potential sources of good photos for a diverse picture file include the following:

• *Magazines* such as *Life, Ms.,* or *Ebony* can provide many good pictures when carefully selected.

• *Calendars* made by organizations dealing with diversity issues may have excellent pictures that can be collected.

• *Photographs* of children and families in your classroom or community. Photos from your travels may also be useful.

• *UNICEF greeting cards* often portray diverse peoples and can be saved for a picture file.

• *Posters* from organizations focusing on children and families (such as the National Association for the Education of Young Children or the Council for Exceptional Children).

When selecting books on diversity, consider the following:

• Try to find books that represent children in your class.
• Books should introduce new information and ideas to children.
• Make sure to balance your selections to ensure that children are introduced to a variety of topics (Yokota, 1993).

The Visual-Aesthetic Environment

Another excellent way to increase opportunities to discuss diversity in the early childhood classroom is to use pictures and posters that depict these issues to decorate the room. These visual accessories should include people from different cultures and individuals with special needs engaging in real-world, everyday activities. Reproductions of artwork from around the world can also be used to decorate the early childhood classroom. All of these visual options can help children see that diversity is a natural part of their lives and can open new opportunities for discussing these important topics.

Artifacts from different cultures may also be used as visual displays to stimulate interest in discussing similarities and differences between people around the world. For example, a traditional African doll purchased by a parent during a recent visit could be introduced at group time and used to discuss dolls in different cultures. While these items may be too fragile or special to be put in a play center, using artifacts for group time experiences and then placing them on display can be a productive use of these materials.

The traditions surrounding holidays that are valued by different people are important opportunities for children to learn about diversity. Yet, it is often difficult to choose which holidays to celebrate and how to respect the cultures and religious perspectives represented by the children in your group. The National Association for the Education of Young Children (1996b) provides the following suggestions:

- Parents and teachers need to ask why children should learn about this holiday and whether it is developmentally appropriate.
- Celebrations should be connected to specific children and families within the group.
- Children should be encouraged to share their feelings and information about the celebrations they have.

- Every group (but not every holiday) represented within the classroom should be honored through celebration of a holiday.
- Activities should demonstrate respect for the customs of different cultures.
- Parents and teachers need to work together in planning these special events.

1. *Talk to an early childhood teacher to find out the different cultures and religious groups that are represented. What holidays does this teacher celebrate?*

2. *How do you feel about celebrating holidays that conflict with your religious/cultural heritage? Discuss these feelings with your peers.*

Music is yet another way in which children can be introduced to cultural similarities and differences. Simply playing a variety of musical styles during the day can be a good way of introducing children to an aspect of diversity. Discussing these musical pieces at group time may stimulate further understandings of people around the world.

Meaningful Diversity Experiences

Taking advantage of the cultural, gender, and ableness differences that exist within your classroom and community is an effective way to build meaningful experiences into the curriculum. By bringing diverse people into the classroom and having children interact with them, their awareness is heightened, and discussions of the similarities and differences noticed increases. These natural interactions while reading a book, working on a math problem, or building in the block corner can be important beginning steps in understanding diversity.

Informal interactions can be combined with other more focused activities to add meaningful diversity experiences to the curriculum. Having a parent whose first language is other than English come in to tutor children in their native language is one example of this more organized approach. Another option could be to have a community member help the class prepare a favorite meal that exemplifies his cultural heritage. When teachers locate people in their classrooms or communities that can add these experiences to the curriculum, everyone benefits.

Individuals with Special Needs

Despite the mainstreaming of children with special needs into the public schools across the United States over the last twenty years, individuals with disabilities are often misunderstood and only reluctantly accepted in classrooms by teachers and students alike. Much has yet to be done to more adequately integrate individuals with disabilities into American society. Early childhood educators must take important first steps in their classrooms to help this process along.

Developing Inclusive Environments

While many of the techniques, methods, and materials used with children who do not have disabilities are effective with children with disabilities as well, other strategies are often needed. The following four guidelines (Wolery & Wilbers, 1994) can help teachers of young children more effectively design the physical space for children with special needs:

1. *When needed, help children learn to play with toys and materials.* Some young children with disabilities may benefit from initial adult assistance in playing with typical early childhood materials. With sensitive guidance, these children, like children without disabilities, can greatly benefit from these play experiences.

2. *Select toys and materials that appeal to students.* Through careful observation, teachers can learn what play materials are enjoyed by their students with special needs. These should be provided on a regular basis to encourage creative play experiences.

3. *Provide play materials that engage children in playing, interacting, and learning.* When possible, toys and materials for children with disabilities should be selected to promote learning identified in their **Individualized Education Plans (IEPs).**

4. *Adapt toys and materials where needed.* Some toys and materials cannot be manipulated because of physical limitations. Adaptations such as battery-powered toys that can be manipulated with switches and wheelchair-accessible sand play areas outdoors help ensure that all children can benefit from quality play experiences.

Social Interactions in the Classroom

Creating a physical space that provides quality play experiences for all children is an important step in an inclusive classroom. Equally valuable are the social interactions that are encouraged. Adults must first be aware of the ways in which they relate to children with special needs. Many techniques such as observing, supporting, facilitating, and expanding children's play and interactions with others are useful with all students. Other more specialized techniques may be needed with some children. One adult interaction that is useful when teaching students with special needs is the use of **prompts.** A prompt can be defined as help given to assist a child in engaging in specific skills (Wolery & Wilbers, 1994). Prompts can be verbal, gestural, modeling, or physical assistance.

Interaction between children with disabilities and their typically developing peers is another dimension that teachers must work to enhance. Two important reasons support encouraging these exchanges. First, these social interactions help children understand one another better while establishing effective relationships that can grow with time. Second, when children with disabilities interact with others, they have peers who model appropriate and adaptive behaviors.

These interactions between children with special needs and other children don't simply happen, however. Teachers must support and encourage these exchanges. One strategy teachers can use is to encourage children to engage in social interactions in small-group, rather than large-group, settings. Whenever possible, children with special needs should be placed in small groups that contain peers who are especially competent in growth areas identified on the IEP.

Collaborating with Other Professionals

Joley is four years old and uses a wheelchair. Her mother is a single parent, so Joley spends almost nine hours each day in the Sunshine Day Care Center. In addition to the teachers she works with in the program, Joley spends time with a physical therapist twice a week, a psychologist works with her on anger control issues biweekly, and a school district special education teacher comes to the home once a month to assist her with oral language skills. Although Joley is benefiting from the assistance of a number of professionals, the coordination of these people and services is a challenge.

A variety of professionals frequently are involved in providing services for children with disabilities. Wolery and Wilbers (1994) describe the following disciplines as regular collaborators in caring for young children with special needs:

- Special education
- Psychology
- Speech/language pathology
- Occupational therapy
- Social work
- Nutrition
- Nursing
- Audiology
- Medicine

Although women have more commonly been discriminated against in the workplace, some evidence indicates public concern about men in early childhood education (Hill, 1996). Not only are men a very small minority in preschool and primary classrooms, others are often suspicious of them for wanting to work with young children. Some reactions noted by Hill include

- Parents may simply pull their children out of an early childhood classroom taught by a man.

- Female colleagues may feel that a man can't be nurturing enough to work with young children.

- Other adults may fear that a male teacher of young children is more likely to be sexually abusive in and around the classroom.

- Unflattering comments that imply men who teach in the early childhood classroom aren't capable enough to get a real job.

1. *Try to find a male teacher in early childhood education. Talk to him about the kinds of responses/interactions he has had with parents and others.*

2. *Are there good reasons to encourage men to be teachers in early childhood education? Discuss this issue with your classmates.*

The collaboration of these professions to provide support for young children with special needs has been mandated by legislation for many years. The IEP is one key area that requires this collaboration. Few teachers and other professionals, however, are prepared for the complexities of the interactions required. To succeed, all the professionals involved need to begin these collaborative efforts with an understanding of who should participate, what each professional's role should be, a willingness to communicate often and well, and a desire to adjust roles and responsibilities as needed in the best interests of the child (Spodek & Saracho, 1994).

Issues of Gender Equity

What are the components of gender equity that should concern us in the early childhood classroom? Do these include how we communicate with both sexes? Should we focus on equitable opportunities for boys and girls to participate in activities? What about adult perceptions of gender roles and how they influence interactions with children? Each question defines an important element of gender equity in the early childhood classroom and should be addressed by concerned educators.

Language

The words we use to communicate with children send powerful messages that influence many aspects of development, including attitudes about gender. Take, for example, the seemingly innocuous phrase: "Hey, you guys!" If addressed to a group of boys, there is obviously no problem. But what about using that same phrase to communicate with a mixed-sex group or a gathering of girls? Is there a hidden message here that may be inappropriate? A small thing perhaps, but it is often these finer nuances that children focus on as they make assessments about the relative value of being a boy or girl.

Language has other subtle influences on children as well. Consistently using words that suggest dependence, weakness, or submission to describe the behavior of girls and other descriptors that imply strength, independence, and dominance in relationship to male behaviors can lead to inappropriate gender definitions by young children. Although most of us support avoiding these categorical descriptions of boys and girls, the words we use to talk to young children may not be as generous. Careful self-assessment is needed to make sure we use appropriate terminology for both sexes.

Accessibility Issues

Research on the play behaviors of children in learning centers suggests that certain activities are dominated by boys and others by girls. Boys tend to take on more active/aggressive roles with cars and trucks, construction toys, and blocks. Girls, on the other hand, often are involved in dress-up activities, artwork, and housekeeping activities (F. Hughes, 1995). These gender differences are hardly surprising to most of us.

Although much of this natural interest among boys and girls can lead to productive play and learning, children should be encouraged to move out of their comfort zone to engage in other activities. For example, it is important for boys to be involved in doll play and housekeeping activities. Eventually, most will become fathers and need to learn appropriate nurturing behaviors. Similarly, girls need experiences with blocks so that they can begin developing foundational understanding for learning mathematics and science (Chaille & Silvern, 1996).

Without conscious adult intervention, however, most children will continue doing what they find comfortable. The early childhood teacher can help in three major ways:

1. Encourage children to try new activities. Making suggestions, pointing out interesting options, and redirecting children to play activities not normally chosen are effective for many children.

2. Provide materials that are more likely to attract children to areas not usually chosen. For example, marble painting or gluing and painting wood sculptures may be two activities that would encourage boys to play in the art center.

3. Model nontraditional play as an adult. Women teachers can spend time building with blocks, while men could engage in housekeeping roles, for example.

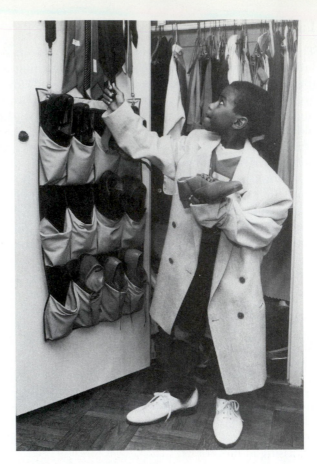

It is just as important for boys to be involved in playing "house" as girls since most boys will eventually be fathers and husbands.

Attitudes

Adult attitudes about gender are a complex mix of formal and informal learning experiences. Parental values, influential adult role models, experiences throughout the growing-up years, and the media all play important roles in the development of gender identity. And unless adults are particularly introspective, it is hard to identify their true attitudes. Yet, it is important to do so for the sake of young children. Our feelings about gender issues will strongly influence those we teach.

So, a key starting point is to raise our consciousness about attitudes toward gender. Although some may be obvious, others are much more subtle. As emphasized earlier, it is helpful to work with a support group to discuss these issues. For example, you might read the books *What Is a Girl?* and *What Is a Boy?* (Waxman, 1976a, 1976b) and then discuss your reactions with others. These books contain photos that show the anatomic differences between boys and girls and discuss problems associated with gender stereotyping. Would you feel comfortable reading these books to young children? Why or why not? As this kind of reflection takes place, you can begin to understand your own attitudes toward gender issues at a deeper level.

Working with Parents and the Community

Knowing the importance of the early childhood years in the development of attitudes toward diversity, it is essential to work with parents and gain their assistance in promoting equity. Similarly, communities provide many resources that can be useful in dealing with diversity issues.

Parent Involvement in Diversity Issues

Without question, parents play a major role in the attitudes children develop toward people who are different from themselves. If parents accept diversity and verbalize their feelings, young children are much more likely to develop positive attitudes themselves (Swick, Boutte, & van Scoy, 1995). Problems occur, however, when parents either don't address diversity issues or actively denigrate people because of their race, sex, or ableness. Teachers need to work hard to help parents understand the importance of discussing diversity and need to provide opportunities for changing inappropriate parental attitudes. Several strategies may be useful in this regard:

- **Parent education.** Teachers can help educate parents about diversity in many ways. Holding meetings about its importance, creating a lending library of books, and getting parents of different cultures and beliefs to interact either in the classroom or at school-sponsored events are some examples of this type.

- **Parent support.** Supporting families in their efforts to find resources and activities that encourage pride in their diversity can be a positive step for many parents.

- **Parent–teacher partnerships.** Parents can take an active role in the planning and implementation of a diversity curriculum. They can share their own experiences and family traditions as well as work to create a classroom atmosphere that is accepting of the differences between people (Swick et al., 1995).

Changing Attitudes

As teachers begin to work with parents whose attitudes toward diversity are problematic, it can be easy to become frustrated and give up on changing these deeply held beliefs. Parents may either openly or indirectly subvert your efforts to help children develop an attitude of acceptance toward diversity. The natural tendency is to become defensive and either angry or aloof in your relationship with those parents.

It may be helpful to remember that these parents' inappropriate beliefs have developed over long periods of time and through many experiences. Changing these attitudes will take patience and time. If teachers can take a longer-term view of this procedure, it may be helpful. Perhaps all a teacher can expect is to lay the groundwork for someone else to make progress in changing a parent's attitudes. Belief systems change slowly, despite our best efforts and careful planning.

Summary

Diversity should be considered a foundational component of early childhood education because of its importance to all the other foundations described in Chapters 4 through 7. Dealing with diversity begins with an understanding of attitudes about race/culture, gender, and people with special needs. Teachers can accept diversity issues in the early childhood classroom through self-analysis, a discussion of differences with children, and exposing children to diversity. It is inappropriate to ignore diversity or to teach using the tourist approach. Teachers can integrate diversity throughout the curriculum by using techniques proposed in the antibias curriculum, by including toys and games that promote diversity, by presenting diverse children's literature, by including diversity in the visual-aesthetic environment, and by providing meaningful diversity experiences.

Issues related to individuals with special needs and gender equity are important. Teachers must prepare inclusive environments, assist with social interactions in the classroom, and collaborate with other professionals working with children with special needs. Language issues, accessibility issues, and attitudes about gender equity are important for the early childhood teacher to understand.

Working with parents and community members in relationship to diversity issues is an important way to help bring about positive change. Parents can be closely involved in slowly changing attitudes about diversity.

∾ For Discussion and Action

1. What are your attitudes toward diversity? Go back to the section on attitudes, and try some of the activities suggested there. Discuss your thoughts with a small group of peers.

2. Take some time to browse through some toy and equipment catalogs for young children. What did you find that addresses diversity issues?

3. Find a children's book listed in the diversity bibliography of the National Association for the Education of Young Children (1993) and read it. Would you use it in working with young children? Why or why not?

4. Talk to a teacher of young children about his implementation of a diversity curriculum. What are the successes or problems this teacher had? Share your findings with your peers.

5. What is your biggest concern about implementing an antibias curriculum? Discuss this concern with others, and see if you can come up with ways to overcome this issue.

❧ Building Your Personal Library

Banks, J., & Banks, C. (Eds.). (1993). *Multicultural education: Issues and perspectives* (2nd ed.). Boston: Allyn & Bacon. As leading figures in the multicultural education movement, the editors of this text have brought together many key perspectives on implementing a multicultural curriculum. The book is an excellent beginning point for this topic.

Derman-Sparks, L. (1989). *Anti-bias curriculum: Tools for empowering young children.* Washington, DC: National Association for the Education of Young Children. A very practical guide for implementing a diversity curriculum. In addition to consciousness-raising activities, Derman-Sparks provides a review of children's literature dealing with diversity issues and suggests possible experiences that increase children's awarenesses and understanding of diversity.

King, E., Chipman, M., & Cruz-Janzen, M. (1994). *Educating young children in a diverse society.* Boston: Allyn & Bacon. This book provides some excellent anecdotes to illustrate concepts regarding diversity. Based on the authors' own experiences and those of others, these encounters with cultural, gender, and ableness issues bring their message to life.

Wolery, M., & Wilbers, J. (Eds.). (1994). *Including children with special needs in early childhood programs.* Washington, DC: National Association for the Education of Young Children. This book provides a strong overview of the issues involved in integrating children with special needs into the early childhood classroom.

III

Organizing for Instruction

 ∾ **9**
Planning the Physical Environment: Indoors

 ∾ **10**
Planning the Physical Environment: Outdoors

 ∾ **11**
Activity Planning and Assessment

9 *Planning the Physical Environment: Indoors*

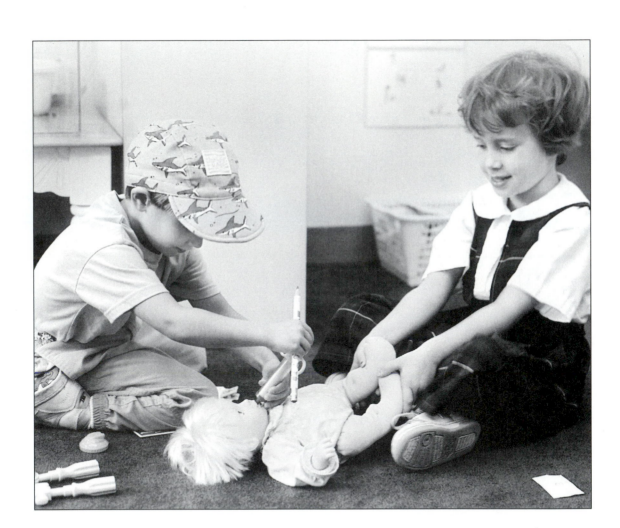

In this chapter you will

- Address basic issues related to planning an indoor environment for young children.

- Learn about the typical centers found in an early childhood classroom and the materials available in each.

- Investigate the indoor environments of infant/toddlers, preschoolers, and primary children.

- Understand criteria for selecting equipment and materials for the early childhood classroom.

- Study health and safety issues for young children.

It's planning time once again, and you are thinking through the past week with your four-year-old students in preparation for next week's activities. As usual, the children have engaged in much creative play in the different classroom centers. The block area has been home to the toy dinosaur collection, and children have been building fences and enclosures to hold their favorite creatures. After discussing block play with the assistant teachers, you decide to leave the dinosaurs out for another week. Interest is strong, and the toys are stimulating very imaginative play.

It is early in the school year, so the dramatic play center still contains fairly basic materials. Shirts, hats, dresses, and shoes have been available for dressing up. A mirror, stuffed chair, and chest of drawers are the major pieces of furniture in the center. For next week, you decide to add some jewelry, hair clips, and neckties for accessories.

The library center has had several books on dinosaurs over the past week. You have read them at group time and then made sure children could browse through them on their own. You will add two new books and a flannelboard story for the coming week.

In the manipulative center, three puzzles will replace some that the children haven't used recently. You will put away the Legos for a while and make Tinker Toys available. One of your assistants has agreed to make a new batch of play dough for this center as well. ❧

The planning in the preceding scenario exemplifies the efforts of early childhood teachers in their indoor environments. A major role of adult caregivers is to carefully and thoughtfully prepare the classroom for developmentally appropriate play. Because of the importance of child-initiated and -directed activities, young children need play spaces that stimulate creative experiences.

Planning Guidelines

Quality environments for young children don't just happen. They require careful planning and considerable work. A good place to start in this process is to understand the fundamentals of room organization.

Basic Considerations

The most basic factor in room organization is the **physical space** available. The National Association for the Education of Young Children (1991) suggests providing a minimum of thirty-five square feet of indoor space for each child in a preschool or primary classroom. In addition to the square footage available, the window placement, heating and cooling vents, doors, floor coverings (carpeting and vinyl), and other fixed elements influence your planning for children's indoor play spaces. Each of these elements has significant implications for the organization of the classroom. For example, the placement of doors for the room defines natural corridors for entrance and exit. These spaces must be left open for ease of use and for safety such as adequate fire escape routes. Teachers must consider these fixed aspects of the environment in the overall planning of play spaces.

A second basic consideration is the availability of **resources** in the classroom. The tables, chairs, room dividers, and storage cabinets strongly influence room design. Additional resources such as unit blocks, table toys, computers, and dramatic play equipment also impact the overall planning of the physical space.

> ✑ *Jamie is getting her kindergarten classroom ready for the coming school year. She has good storage units for the unit blocks, plenty of dividers for sectioning off space for centers, and enough chairs and tables for her expected enrollment. Dramatic play equipment is scarce; she will need to locate a child-sized stove and sink. In addition, as she looks through the manipulative toys available to her, it becomes obvious that she will need to carefully plan the use of the puzzles. With only ten sets, she will need to rotate puzzles in and out regularly to maintain interest. On the other hand, Jamie has an abundance of different construction sets like Legos. Her students will have many options available for this play type throughout the year.*

Teachers also need to consider the **goals for the program** before beginning plans for the indoor environment. If a top priority is the development of fine and gross motor skills, then equipment, materials, and centers need to promote these activities. Similarly, an emphasis on recognizing and appropriately responding to feelings leads to very different materials and planning of the physical space.

Active and Quiet Centers

As much as possible, teachers should physically separate incompatible activities. Some centers promote active, noisy play, while others encourage quieter times. Typically active/noisy centers include

- Blocks
- Music

- Housekeeping/dramatic play
- Woodworking
- Sand/water play

Centers that tend to stimulate quieter play are

- Art
- Books/library
- Computers
- Writing

Whenever possible, centers from these two categories should be separated. Having a noisy center like blocks near the library area creates unnecessary distractions for children. The banging of blocks and the creative discussion that often accompany the construction process may prevent a child who is concentrating on a book from becoming deeply involved in the story. It would be better to put the block area next to the dramatic play center, for example. These activities are more compatible in most early childhood classrooms.

Dry and Wet Centers

Similarly, some areas indoors should be kept dry while others are wet/messy centers. The areas that need to be dry should be separated from those that require water and other liquids. The art center—with paints, glue, marking pens, crayons, and other messy activities—needs to be placed away from the library corner, for example.

Spaces for Varying Group Sizes

Another factor in planning indoor environments is the provision of spaces to accommodate gatherings of different numbers of children. Generally, teachers set aside one area for whole-class meetings. In early childhood classrooms, this is usually referred to as **circle time,** which requires an area large enough for children and teachers to gather together in a circle formation, with everyone sitting on the floor. Often, this space is used for other activities (such as music and movement) outside of group times.

Small-group space is needed for many different activities in the early childhood classroom. For example, most programs have a snack time in the midmorning and again in the afternoon. The most common format for these food breaks is to have children gather together at tables, in groups of three to five, to enjoy a nutritious snack. When the early childhood classroom is set up in centers, teachers also create several small-group spaces that accommodate two to six children in various center activities.

Teachers often give children clues in the environment itself about the number of participants allowed in small-group activities. An art center, for example, with a table and five chairs effectively limits the number of children who can participate there at any given time. Another technique is to have a chart posted at the entrance to each center with the number of students allowed pictured in some way. A kindergarten math center chart with three smiley faces tells children the expected capacity for that area.

Indoor space also should make **solitary activities** a possibility for young children. Teachers tend to overlook this necessary element when planning classroom space. Healthy child development includes having many opportunities for social interactions with peers and adults. In addition, however, solitary time allows children the chance to reflect and regroup at different times during the day, before returning to the important tasks of socializing with others.

Although students tend to create their own solitary spaces, it is also useful for the classroom teacher to plan for this important activity. Some materials that are useful include

- Large pillows
- Clawfoot bathtub
- Reading loft
- Large cardboard boxes
- Beanbag chairs
- Child-sized stuffed chairs

By combining these materials with room dividers or placing them in strategic spots, adults can create cozy areas for children to get away from the busy activities in the rest of the classroom.

Personal Spaces

Both teachers and children also need to have areas that they can call their own. These personal spaces need not be large or complex but help create a home for materials that belong to individuals. Children benefit from having a spot to call their own (Readdick, 1993). At the prekindergarten level, a cubby for coats, boots, and classroom projects is a common element. At the primary level, desks provide an area for more personal items. And as children mature, the perceived importance of this private area increases. If desks are unavailable or undesirable, teachers should create other personal space for each child.

Teachers also need a spot for themselves for things like lunches, coats, purses, and umbrellas. Pictures of family members, a favorite coffee mug, and other personal items help create a more inviting working environment for adults. A desk or other work space can also be put to effective use in or near the early childhood classroom.

Cozy personal spaces such as this create inviting areas for a variety of student activities.

Assessing the Physical Space

One final consideration in planning the physical space is the need for assessment techniques to evaluate environmental quality. One option (Kritchevsky & Prescott, 1969) is to evaluate the **complexity of the play units.** Kritchevsky and Prescott have identified three different complexities in units:

- *Simple unit.* This play material or piece of equipment has only one use, and this is obvious to children. A toy truck or a stacking toy is an example of a simple unit.
- *Complex unit.* This play option has subparts, or different materials, that the child can manipulate. A sand table with digging equipment is a complex unit.
- *Superunit.* A superunit has three or more play materials juxtaposed. A block center that includes two different kinds of blocks and accessories such as toy trucks is a superunit.

Although all three unit types are valuable in the early childhood classroom, the more complex units are most attractive to children and hold their interest longest. Kritchevsky and Prescott (1969) suggest that by assigning a value of one to simple units, four to complex units, and eight to superunits, you can determine the total number of play spaces available in an indoor environment. Dividing that total number by the number of children gives the amount of options available to each child. Having two per child is considered highly desirable.

Harms and Clifford (1980) developed a second, more extensive, environmental assessment procedure. This well-respected rating scale has been recently revised (Harms, Clifford, & Cryer, 1998). Called the Early Childhood Environment Rating Scale, this assessment tool is organized into seven separate subcategories that allow the teacher to evaluate classroom space from inadequate (1) to excellent (7). The seven categories are

- *Personal care routines.* All routines that relate to children's health, comfort, and safety.
- *Furnishings and display for children.* Furniture, storage shelves, and display space to facilitate child growth and development.
- *Language-reasoning experiences.* Experiences, materials, and interactions to facilitate basic reasoning discussion among children about such things as cause and effect.
- *Fine and gross motor activities.* The use of small muscles in the hands and the larger muscles in the arms and legs.
- *Creative activities.* Open-ended activities and materials available in centers such as art, block, and dramatic play.
- *Social development.* Positive self-concepts and interaction skills.
- *Adult needs.* The needs of adults for a comfortable and efficient space for teaching.

With training and practice, the Early Childhood Environment Rating Scale can be an effective tool for assessing the indoor classroom. It can help identify both the strengths and limitations of the physical space.

The Centers-Based Classroom

Early childhood classrooms are often very individualized for the ages of children served and the educational setting. However, as described earlier in this chapter, classroom space is often defined by centers. Using low dividers, tables, child-sized furniture, and an assortment of storage units, caregivers create small areas within the room that children use for specific play- and work-oriented tasks. At the kindergarten level and below, classrooms are typically fully centers-based. Quality first- through third-grade environments can be partially or fully organized around centers. Although not all of the areas described next are found in every early childhood classroom, these centers are common to many indoor play spaces for young children.

Art Center

The art center is essential for the early childhood classroom. Located near a water source for easy cleanup, this area ideally should have a vinyl floor covering or other similar surface. Furniture typically includes a child-sized table and

The Art Center

Free exploration of materials in the art center provides many excellent opportunities for creative expression. Teachers should include fixed materials for young artists and other materials that change regularly:

Fixed Materials	*Materials that Change*
Easel(s)	Scrap paper for collages
Scissors	Water colors
Crayons	Fingerpainting materials
Rulers	Screen painting
Staplers	Sponge painting
Scrap paper	Tissue paper collages
Washable marking pens	Wood scraps, glue, paint

Some children will spend a large percentage of their choice time in art activities. By providing consistency and change at the same time, this center becomes an inviting one for children.

chairs, storage shelves for art supplies, and an easel. A quality art area includes some materials that are available daily and other materials that change regularly. This combination of consistency and change helps make the art center a popular place for play.

Manipulative Center

The manipulative area (also called table toys) usually consists of a table and chairs, open shelves for storage, and an assortment of materials that children can use for construction and manipulation. Small baskets or plastic storage units are available for ease of movement to and from the play table. If a separate space for a computer is unavailable, computer activities are compatible with the activities in the manipulative center. Developing fine motor skills, enhancing early mathematical understanding, and encouraging creative expression are typical goals for this center. Dodge and Colker (1992) identify four categories of toys found in manipulative areas:

- *Self-correcting toys* fit together in a way that lets children know when they have used the materials correctly. Puzzles are good examples of this type of toy, as are most Montessori materials.
- *Open-ended toys* are unstructured in their use. Creative exploration is stimulated. Legos, Lincoln Logs, and Bristle Blocks all fit this category.

- *Collectibles* are scrounged materials that children use in open-ended ways. Parents, children, and teachers can save plastic bottle caps, buttons, and old keys for sorting, matching, and comparing activities.
- *Cooperative games* engage children in pairs or small groups in simple activities that deemphasize winning and losing. Lotto games, concentration activities, and matching toys provide additional opportunities for quality play in this center.

Book/Quiet Center

A library center should be a quiet oasis for children to engage in early reading and writing experiences. The main ingredients for this area include comfortable spots for children to sit and read, storage/display shelves for books, a table, and a collection of quality children's literature. In addition to books, an assortment of emergent literacy activities such as flannelboard story figures, a listening center (with head sets), and magnetic board letters help stimulate the language arts.

Block Center

Blocks have tremendous potential for creative play and learning. This center is an essential for every early childhood classroom, including primary education (Harris, 1994). The basic elements needed for this area are a set of wooden unit blocks, a collection of large hollow blocks (often constructed of wood), a carpeted floor for building, low shelves for organized storage of blocks and ease of access, and accessories such as toy trucks or animals that the teacher rotates in and out of the center regularly.

INTO PRACTICE...
Unit Blocks

Unit blocks are generally made from smooth, sanded hardwood and come in sizes that are proportional in length and width to the basic unit, which is 5 1/2 × 2 3/4 × 1 3/8 inches. Every other block has a mathematical relationship to this basic unit. This proportionality allows for creative building and many inherent math and science learnings. Yet, as Hirsch (1974) states: "The pleasure of blocks stems primarily from the esthetic experience. It involves the whole person—muscles and senses, intellect and emotion, individual growth and social interaction" (p. iii). Some of the typical shapes found in a quality set of unit blocks are shown here:

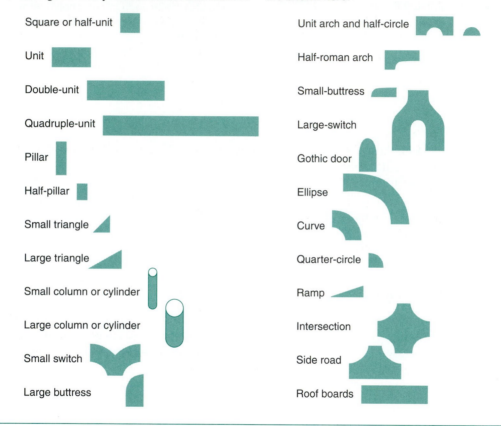

Square or half-unit

Unit

Double-unit

Quadruple-unit

Pillar

Half-pillar

Small triangle

Large triangle

Small column or cylinder

Large column or cylinder

Small switch

Large buttress

Unit arch and half-circle

Half-roman arch

Small-buttress

Large-switch

Gothic door

Ellipse

Curve

Quarter-circle

Ramp

Intersection

Side road

Roof boards

Although children use unit blocks imaginatively, added accessories help stimulate further creative play in this area. The teacher should rotate these props in and out of the center weekly to encourage play related to the current classroom theme. Some examples of accessories that are often used include

- Toy farm animals
- Transportation toys (trucks, airplanes, etc.)
- Small wooden or plastic people/figures
- Dollhouse furniture

- Zoo animals
- Hats (construction, police, etc.)
- Play money
- Writing materials (for signs)

Housekeeping Center

As the name implies, the housekeeping center is designed for young children to engage in dramatic play focused on home themes. Typically, the housekeeping area contains materials such as a child-sized sink, stove, refrigerator, china cupboard, table and chairs, toy dishes, silverware, pots and pans, a telephone, and a small broom and dustpan set. The teacher can rotate accessories such as pretend foods (empty cans/boxes or plastic food), pictures of people engaged in housekeeping tasks, and additional cooking utensils in and out of this area to create new interest in playing here.

Younger children (ages four and below) are particularly attracted to the housekeeping center, and including it as a permanent option with little change to the basic equipment makes good sense. If space is limited, or children are somewhat older, the housekeeping area may be effectively combined with the dramatic play center.

Dramatic Play Center

The importance of imaginative play has been clearly documented (Singer & Singer, 1990), and this type of play needs to be incorporated into the early childhood classroom at every opportunity. Although imaginative play can be found in any center, a separate space devoted to dramatic activities is very important. When located next to, or combined with, the housekeeping center, an imaginative play area is a popular addition to the early childhood classroom. Teachers often begin the school year with a few dress-up clothes, a mirror, dolls and doll beds, a chest of drawers, and a coat rack as the staples for this area. Gradually new accessories such as jewelry and hats can be added to stimulate more interest; later, thematic materials can be presented.

A common practice for teachers of young children is the creation of prop boxes of materials needed for specific dramatic play themes (Myhre, 1993). Because these boxes are portable, teachers can organize materials that children can easily use either indoors or outside. Some examples of prop box themes include

- Supermarket
- Shoe store
- Repair shop
- Office
- Camping
- Airplane

Prop boxes are a convenient way to organize the materials needed for dramatic play themes. When sturdy boxes of consistent size are used, the props can be easily stored when not in use. Tape a list of needed materials on the inside lid of the box so that a quick check can be made for missing items before using the box. Here are some sample ideas for specific prop boxes (Myhre, 1993):

Office Prop Box	*Beach Party Prop Box*
Telephone	Beach towels
Typewriter/keyboard	Sunglasses
Pads of paper	Straw hats
Desk accessories	Water bottles
Paper	Life preserver
File folders	Air mattresses
Envelopes	Picnic accessories
Repair Shop Box	*Grocery Store Prop Box*
Clipboard	Cash register
Wrenches and screwdrivers	Plastic foods
Safety glasses	Play money
Nuts and bolts	Empty food containers
Toolbox	Grocery bags
Scrap wood	Grocery cart
Workbench	Baskets

The Music Center

Musical experiences are important learning opportunities for young children and create a more pleasant environment. Group times that include singing, movement to music, and the use of instruments are common in most classrooms. In addition, however, it is important to encourage other experiences with music. A center can often be incorporated into the classroom for this purpose. A tape/CD player, an open, carpeted area, storage shelves, an assortment of music-making materials, and a piano are common items found in this area. It is best to start the year with one or two instruments on the shelf and gradually add more as the year progresses. Many teachers stock the group time area with music materials so that these are available for circle activities in addition to free choice options.

As with every center, the teacher should move instruments and musical options in and out of the area to maintain interest and use. Materials that teachers can rotate through this center include

- Rhythm sticks
- Cymbals

Music-making experiences are an important part of the early childhood curriculum.

- Triangles
- Bells
- Drums
- Autoharp
- Scarves (for movement to music)

Discovery Center

A discovery area provides opportunities for young children to develop important science understandings. Teachers can productively use a small table with displays of interesting materials for children to explore and to learn basic scientific principles and information. Additional storage space for other science-oriented materials is useful in this center as well. Materials to consider for the science area include

- Plants
- Rocks
- Shells
- Magnifying glass
- Balance scales
- Aquarium
- Animal/insect cages
- Small appliances to take apart and explore

Other Creative Center Options

Although the preceding areas are considered essentials in the early childhood classroom, several other possibilities can be incorporated as well. These centers provide many play opportunities that can't be easily duplicated in other ways. Space limitations are often the major reason for not including them.

Woodworking Center.   Real, child-sized saws and hammers, wood, nails, safety goggles, a woodworking table with built-in vises, and hand drills are the basic ingredients for the woodworking center. Additional accessories could include an old stump for simple nailing practice, glue, c-clamps, and wood rasps. For younger children, or just for a change, styrofoam can be substituted for wood.

Some teachers prefer to have this activity take place outdoors, but with enough space and proper supervision, it can be effectively managed indoors. Also, the noise, mess, and potential safety issues tend to frighten some teachers of young children away from providing woodworking activities. With preparation and careful adult supervision, however, this center can be an exciting and safe place for children.

Sand/Water Play Center.   The attraction of natural materials such as sand and water is very strong with prekindergarten children. The sensory nature of the experience and the flexible uses of these materials make them very popular in the early childhood classroom. Sand and water play should be considered essential for the outdoor setting and, if space permits, are important options indoors.

Child-sized sand/water tables are available commercially to hold either sand or water. A vinyl floor (or protective covering), water-repelling smocks, and accessories for mixing and pouring sand or water complete this center. Sample accessories include

- Funnels
- Measuring cups
- Water wheel
- Spoons
- Small buckets
- Hand trowels
- Basters
- Pitchers

Writing Center.   Providing many opportunities for early writing experiences is essential for the literacy development of young children. Having writing materials in the art, block, dramatic play, and library centers greatly increases the likelihood that children will incorporate writing into their play (Christie, Enz, &

Vukelich, 1997). In addition, older children should have a separate center that focuses specifically on writing activities.

The materials needed for a writing center are relatively simple: a variety of writing instruments, such as pencils, pens, crayons, and markers; recycled paper for rough drafts; lined paper; and heavier-weighted paper for book covers. Children could also productively use a dictionary or word file, staplers, an old typewriter, or the classroom computer.

Computer Center. Although some controversy surrounds computer use for young children (see Chapter 17), most early educators feel that when properly used, computers can be an important activity for the early childhood classroom. With quality, play-oriented software, children can learn a great deal and have fun at the same time (Haugland & Shade, 1994).

Probably the biggest drawback to computer use is the high cost of the hardware. Many prekindergarten programs in particular have very limited budgets, and committing $1,500 or more to a good-quality computer is difficult. Despite their many benefits, computers should not be a higher priority than an ample collection of unit blocks, for example.

To provide maximum benefit from a computer, the teacher should place the computer in the classroom (rather than in a separate computer room shared by the entire school). The computer should be available to children as another play choice during center time. With two or three chairs at the computer, several children can use it cooperatively.

Age-Related Considerations

Although most of the centers described here can be found in classrooms for children throughout the early childhood age range, teachers need to be aware of special considerations needed in planning these indoor spaces for each age. This section discusses these issues.

Infant/Toddler Classrooms

Figure 9–1 provides an example of the elements in an infant/toddler classroom. Because most infants and toddlers learn a great deal by putting things in their mouths, significant issues for this age are the **safety and cleanliness** of play materials. Teachers must not supply toys that may break or splinter when chewed or that are small enough to swallow. Because regular cleaning is necessary as well, equipment should be durable enough to withstand frequent washing.

Much of a young child's day is spent in routines. Eating, sleeping, and toileting activities are significant parts of the curriculum. **Special areas for routines** are important in infant/toddler programs. A changing area with a table and access to

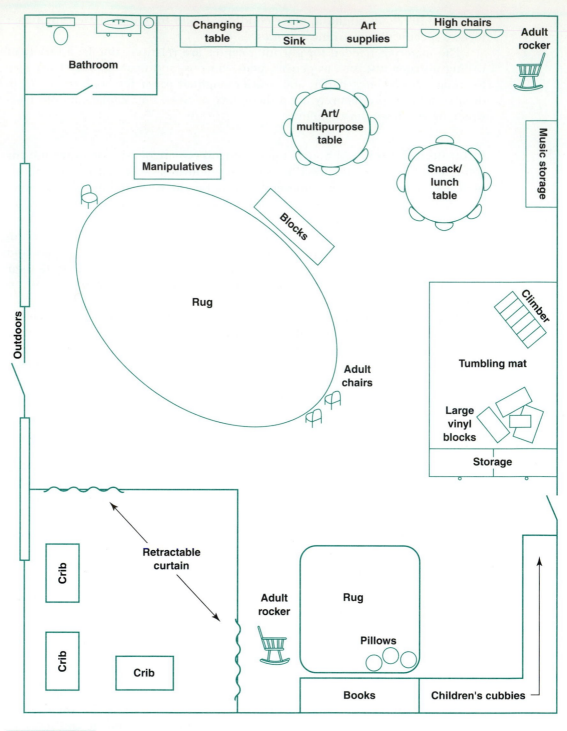

Bathroom

Changing table

Sink

Art supplies

High chairs

Adult rocker

Art/ multipurpose table

Manipulatives

Snack/ lunch table

Music storage

Blocks

Rug

Outdoors

Adult chairs

Climber

Tumbling mat

Large vinyl blocks

Storage

Retractable curtain

Crib

Crib

Crib

Adult rocker

Rug

Pillows

Books

Children's cubbies

∾ Figure 9–1   *Infant/Toddler Classroom*

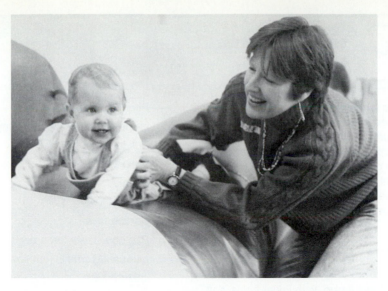

Commercial materials for climbing and crawling over are important for infants and toddlers.

water, for example, is a necessity. Separating it from the eating and play centers also makes good sense. Establishing similar spaces for sleeping and eating that can be used throughout the day are also necessary.

Comfortable adult seating should also be a part of the infant/toddler classroom. The importance of holding and cuddling at this age cannot be overstated. Children need frequent touch for healthy emotional development (Delise, 1994; Montagu, 1978). Rocking chairs, couches, and comfortable adult chairs help encourage this important activity.

Children at this age are in what Piaget calls the stage of sensorimotor intelligence (see Chapter 4). These young children learn about their world through sight, sound, taste, smell, and touch. **Sensory materials** that these children can easily manipulate are important.

In addition to sensory learning, young children learn about themselves and their environment through physical movement. Infant/toddler programs need materials that stimulate **motor development.** Climbing, crawling, walking, and stacking activities address the developmental interests of this age.

Children Three through Five

Figure 9–2 diagrams a typical classroom for preschool and kindergarten children. As discussed earlier, play is a primary vehicle for learning during these years. Almost without exception, classrooms for this age are organized around **centers.** These classrooms include areas for art, books/quiet activities, blocks,

Toys for children at the infant/toddler age need to be appealing to the senses, safe, and durable. Because of the importance of routines, teachers should provide materials for play in cribs, during diapering, as well as during general play time. The following is a sampling of toys that can be valuable in an infant/toddler program:

Crib Toys

Beads (large, bright, on sturdy cord)

Clutch balls (large, with finger holds, soft material)

Cradle gyms (things to push, pull, manipulate)

Mobiles

Rattles

Squeeze toys

Play Equipment

Large soft blocks for stacking and climbing

Pull toys

Stacking toys

Mirrors

Musical toys

Sorting toys

Peg board with large pegs

Interesting smells (cut flowers, spices, etc.)

Texture balls

1. *Spend some time observing in an infant/ toddler program. What kinds of materials were children using in their play?*

2. *What special health and safety issues are associated with working with infant/toddlers in group settings?*

manipulatives, housekeeping, and dramatic play. They also regularly include sand/water play, music, and discovery centers. Children have regular opportunities for spending large blocks of time in play activities that they select in these centers.

As children move toward greater and greater autonomy, classroom experiences and materials must allow for **increasing independence.** For example, child-sized pitchers allow children to pour their own juice, and a drying rack for artwork located at child level encourages independent behavior in that center. Materials that are self-correcting, such as puzzles, also require fewer adult interventions.

Too much change can be stressful for all children, including those from age three to five. One simple strategy to help reduce stress from change is to have **consistency in the environment.** Although accessories should change weekly, the general layout of the classroom and the basic structure of each center often remain

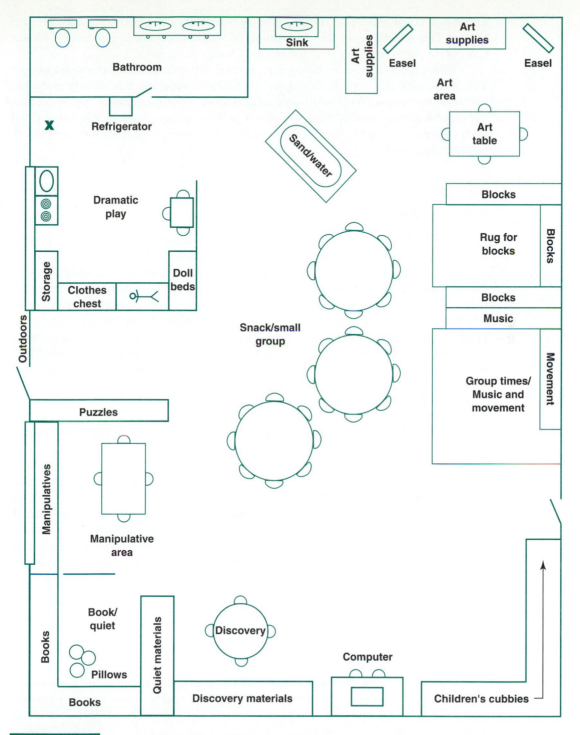

Bathroom

Sink

Art supplies

Easel

Art supplies

Easel

Art area

Art table

X

Refrigerator

Sand/water

Dramatic play

Blocks

Rug for blocks

Blocks

Storage

Doll beds

Clothes chest

Blocks

Music

Outdoors

Snack/small group

Group times/ Music and movement

Movement

Puzzles

Manipulatives

Manipulative area

Book/ quiet

Quiet materials

Discovery

Computer

Books

Pillows

Children's cubbies

Books

Discovery materials

∾ Figure 9–2 *Preschool/Kindergarten Classroom*

unchanged. For example, the block area contains low shelves to store the unit blocks. This shelving and the positioning of blocks on them often remain consistent, while the accessories (like toy trucks) change each week.

Children often begin to engage in pretend activities at about two years of age. This important play type is stimulated by **realistic materials** that clearly resemble the real-world item. With additional experience, more **ambiguous toys** are effective in stimulating quality dramatic play. Children at age three to five often need both realistic and ambiguous types of equipment, because of their different developmental abilities.

Primary Children

Figure 9–3 gives an example of a good indoor space for primary children. It combines some centers with more traditional work space for this age.

A quick look at most first- through third-grade environments indicates that centers are not in widespread use. One or two areas at most may be available for free choice activities. Many teachers, administrators, and parents of children at this level are yet to be convinced of the learning potential inherent in centers and playful experiences. Children, however, benefit significantly from these opportunities (Wasserman, 1990), and teachers need to **slowly add centers** to their classrooms. This process (which may take several years to complete) allows for careful preparation of each area and time to educate other adults about the benefits of centers and play.

A good starting point for centers in a primary classroom is to provide activities that allow children to **practice academic skills.** Mathematics, library, and writing centers can be readily linked to the elementary school curriculum and provide children with quality play experiences that extend their understanding in these important areas. Center use can then be expanded to include equally important centers such as blocks, dramatic play, art, and music.

The primary classroom also needs spaces for **cooperative learning** and small-group activities. Clustering four to six desks together is a practical arrangement for teachers who want their children to engage in frequent small-group work. With these small groups in the central portion of the classroom, the centers can be on the periphery, and children can use the centers when not engaged in large- and small-group activities.

Selecting Equipment and Materials

An important role of the early childhood teacher is the selection of appropriate equipment and materials for center activities. The combination of many choices and limited budgets makes it essential for adults to make good decisions about play materials for the classroom.

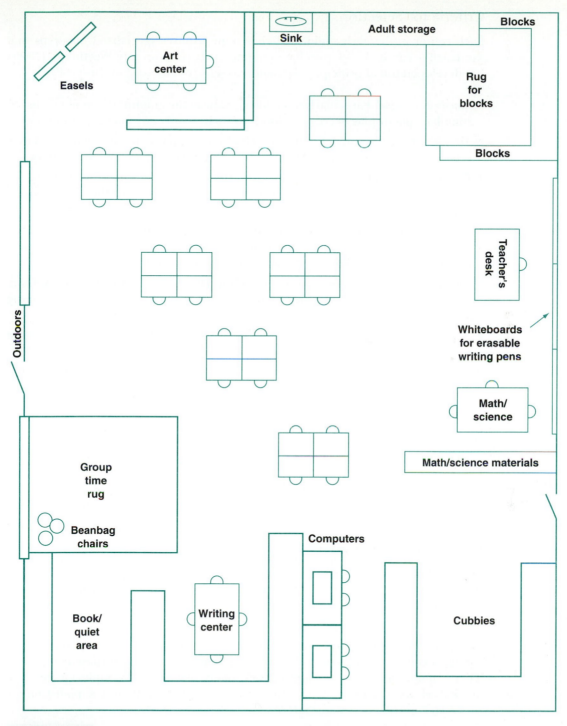

Easels

Art
center

Sink

Adult storage

Blocks

Rug
for
blocks

Blocks

Outdoors

Teacher's
desk

Whiteboards
for erasable
writing pens

Math/
science

Math/science materials

Group
time
rug

Beanbag
chairs

Computers

Book/
quiet
area

Writing
center

Cubbies

Figure 9–3 *Primary Classroom*

Criteria for Selection

Each center in the early childhood classroom requires specialized materials that the teacher can make or purchase commercially. Community Playthings (1990) has developed broad principles for materials selection to assist in this process:

- *Simplicity of detail.* Particularly as children mature, the amount of detail needed to stimulate quality play decreases. Good play materials keep detail to a minimum.
- *Versatility in use.* Equipment that allows children to explore/use in open-ended ways is best. More creativity is possible, and children tend to use the materials longer.
- *Easy to use and understand.* Quality materials require little or no explanation by adults to use. They are also of appropriate size for the ages of the children playing with them.
- *Involve the child in play.* Good toys are so inviting and interesting that children can't resist playing with them. Good toys stimulate the use of imaginations, language, cognition, and both large and small muscle movement.
- *Encourage cooperative play.* Because one of the goals of early education is to stimulate social learning, most play materials should promote interaction among small groups of children.
- *Materials look and feel good.* Play is more likely when children have equipment that is attractive to look at and feels good to the touch.
- *Durability.* Classroom materials receive frequent use and must be durable enough to withstand frequent cleaning and the banging, dropping, and general wear-and-tear by young children.
- *Safety.* Teachers should not purchase toys made of toxic materials, toys that can splinter or break, equipment that can pinch or cut, and materials that easily catch fire.
- *Value-priced.* With limited budgets, most early childhood teachers are interested in equipment that provides the best play value at the lowest cost.

Commercial Materials

Many different commercial companies produce toys and equipment for use in the early childhood classroom. They can be categorized as general purpose, specialty, and multicultural companies.

General Purpose Companies. Companies that produce and sell equipment for every center in the early childhood classroom are general purpose companies. Their catalogs are extensive and provide many selections. Examples of this type are Lakeshore Learning Materials, Constructive Playthings, and Kaplan Companies (see Figure 9–4 for more information).

General Purpose Companies	
Lakeshore Learning Materials	(800) 421-5354
Constructive Playthings	(800) 448-4115
Kaplan Companies	(800) 334-2014
Specialty Companies	
Nienhuis Montessori USA	(800) 942-8697
Creative Educational Surplus	(800) 886-6428
Cuisenaire Company of America	(800) 237-0338
Judy/Instructo	(800) 321-3106
Playtime Props	(800) 782-8697
Multicultural Companies	
Asia for Kids	(800) 765-5885
People of Every Stripe	(503) 282-0612
Remo, Inc.	(818) 983-2600

Specialty Companies. Companies that produce materials that either fit a specific approach to early childhood education or focus on limited aspects of the curriculum are specialty companies. An example of the former type is Nienhuis Montessori USA, which produces materials for the Montessori classroom. Other companies that specialize in aspects of the early childhood curriculum include Creative Educational Surplus (surplus materials that can be used in art and construction activities), Cuisenaire Company of America (hands-on math and science materials), Judy/Instructo (puzzles and other manipulatives), and Playtime Props (play frames to stimulate dramatic play). More information on these companies is provided in Figure 9–4.

Multicultural Companies. Some relatively new companies focus their energies on promoting multicultural play materials for the early childhood classroom. These companies are generally smaller but provide many unique options for play equipment. Some examples include Asia for Kids(books, dolls, games), People of Every Stripe (dolls of all sorts), and Remo, Inc. (multicultural musical instruments). See Figure 9–4 for more information.

Teacher-Made Equipment

To save money, many early childhood teachers make their own materials. Teacher-developed equipment can also be more closely matched to the developmental

Building with good manipulative materials is an enjoyable learning experience.

needs and interests of a specific group of children. Ideas for these options come from a variety of sources:

- Imitations of commercial equipment
- Ideas from other teachers
- Curriculum books for early childhood education

Although teachers are generally the source of ideas for noncommercial play materials, parents and other volunteers can be a big help in the actual construction of these items. Using carefully planned instructions, these adults can work on projects for the classroom in their spare time and greatly reduce the teacher's time commitment.

FOCUS ON . . .
Teacher-Made Materials

Teacher-made materials for young children have several advantages over commercial materials. One major plus is the low cost. Most programs on a limited budget cannot afford to purchase the many materials available through equipment companies. A second reason for considering this option is that it allows the teacher to custom-make items that best meet the needs and interests of children. A great many books are available that give good ideas and practical tips on constructing materials for use in the early childhood classroom. Here is a sampling of these books:

Hamilton, D., Flemming, B., & Hicks, J. (1990). *Resources for creative teaching in early childhood education* (2nd ed.). San Diego, CA: Harcourt Brace & Jovanovich.

Herr, J., & Libby, Y. (1995). *Creative resources for the early childhood classroom* (2nd ed.). New York: Delmar.

Mayesky, M. (1995). *Creative activities for young children* (5th ed.). New York: Delmar.

Trostle, S., & Yawkey, T. (1990). *Integrated learning activities for young children*. Boston: Allyn & Bacon.

1. *Browse through an activity book like those identified here, and find two or three ideas that appeal to you. Share those ideas with your classmates.*

2. *Talk to an early childhood teacher about the kinds of resources and ideas she finds useful in the classroom.*

Children with Special Needs

> *Katie is an outgoing four-year-old with cerebral palsy. She loves her preschool friends and enjoys her play opportunities there. At times, however, Katie becomes frustrated with the indoor environment. The braces she needs to walk make it difficult for her to move in and out of some centers and to get play items off the shelves. Her teachers are working to make the classroom more usable for Katie.*

As increasing numbers of early childhood programs include children like Katie, it is important to consider the accommodations necessary for creative play experiences. Winter, Bell, and Dempsey (1994) identify three fundamental elements for true inclusion of children with special needs.

The first element is **accessibility.** Every child should be able to physically enter each center in the early childhood classroom and use the materials found there. For example, a child in a wheelchair should be able to enter the block center and have easy access to its materials.

A second important component is the **ability to engage in activities** within each center. Having access to the art center, for example, is not enough. Special tools and equipment may be needed, for example, if a child with cerebral palsy is to succeed in using art materials. Children with special needs must have the opportunity to take an active part in the art projects provided there.

A third fundamental component of an inclusive play environment is **developmental appropriateness.** While materials provided in centers may be age appropriate, they may not be effective in meeting the individual needs of some children with special needs. A broader range of materials can better assist children with varying abilities to enjoy quality play experiences.

Changing the Physical Environment

Children's play can be characterized as fluid and changing. It mirrors the interests, developmental needs, and growth of those engaging in play. Sensitive early childhood teachers continually plan for changes in the indoor environment to facilitate these important experiences for individual children. Each week, adults should critique the uses of existing play equipment and make decisions about what should be kept out or put away and about whether any new materials should be added. By carefully observing children at play, teachers can plan centers that are stimulating and developmentally appropriate.

Balancing Consistency and Change

This planning process for young children's play environments must include careful thought about the need for both consistency and change. A consistent classroom gives young children a sense of security and comfort. In their home away from home, they need to experience a familiar routine and activities that are interesting without being overwhelmingly different: the younger the child, the greater the need for consistency.

Teachers create this familiar, comfortable environment in the following ways:

- Consistency in the general arrangement of furniture in each center
- Some materials that are always available to children (e.g., basic art materials in the art center)
- Routines for use and storage of play materials that are well-defined and known to children (e.g., blocks stored in clearly marked places on shelves that children can reach)
- Consistent blocks of time for daily creative play experiences

Although it is important to create a consistent environment for children, early childhood educators must also provide for variety and change. This helps maintain interest in and enthusiasm for the play environment. Teachers maintain children's involvement by the following:

- Discuss new toys and equipment at group times.

- Engage in play with children, using materials that have been overlooked or underutilized.
- Give children ideas about how to use toys or materials in their play.
- Casually leave materials out at the beginning of an activity period to remind children of their availability.

Rotating Materials through Centers

Providing for change in the early childhood classroom also means adding new play materials each week and removing other items that have served their current purposes. Teachers often meet weekly to discuss each center and make decisions about equipment changes. Some guidelines for determining toy needs for each center include the following:

- Make sure materials are available in centers to challenge each child in the classroom to higher levels of development.
- Provide options that build on student interests.
- Change no more than a third of the materials available in each center each week.
- Make sure equipment and toys match the curricular goals and themes established for the classroom.

Observe and Listen to Children

To effectively plan play environments for young children, adults need to carefully observe what children are doing as they interact with toys and each other. In the dramatic play center, for example, which clothes and accessories are the children using? What play themes are the children enacting? What are the children saying as they play? This information is invaluable to teachers in making decisions about toys and equipment to add or put away. If children are playing out travel themes in the dramatic play center, the teacher could put out props like suitcases and travel brochures to further stimulate this play type.

Often, adults working with a group of children meet to discuss the play experiences observed before planning for the next week. This sharing of information can be very beneficial in selecting center materials and activities. Specifics about individual children and general patterns of behavior become more obvious and make curricular decisions easier.

Health and Safety Issues

The health and safety of children are essential for optimal development, and teachers must consider these when planning the indoor environment (Marotz, Cross, & Rush, 1993). By taking responsibility for these issues, adults free children to actively interact with the people and objects around them.

Hand washing is generally considered the most effective procedure in controlling the spread of illnesses and disease in the early childhood classroom. Adults should practice this form of hygiene throughout the day (Marotz et al., 1993):

- Upon arrival or return to the child care setting
- Before preparing or eating foods
- After assisting with toileting or changing diapers
- Following the administration of child medication
- After handling mucus or blood

Teachers should also be prepared to teach younger children (and remind older ones) proper hand-washing techniques. Initial rinsing, followed by soaping, scrubbing, rinsing again, and drying with a paper towel are necessary for cleanliness. Turning off the faucet with the paper towel just used also helps prevent recontamination.

Planning a Healthy Environment

When considering materials for the early childhood classroom, teachers must avoid any materials that would lead to **potential health risks.** For example, many infant/toddler programs substitute corn meal or rice for sand because of the tendency for children of this age to put everything into their mouths. Similarly, nontoxic markers and crayons should be used. Lead poisoning from old paint (prior to 1977), contaminated drinking water, and some imported dishware are continuing problems for young children that can be prevented by adults' planning (Marotz et al., 1993).

Providing a **sanitary environment** for young children is also important in minimizing health-related diseases in the classroom. The more common problems such as colds and influenza can be better controlled with regular cleaning of the physical environment and careful hand-washing techniques. Other communicable diseases such as hepatitis and pinworm infestation also require attention to good hygiene for successful management. Concerns over dealing with children infected with human immunodeficiency virus/acquired immune deficiency syndrome (HIV/AIDS) (Seidel, 1992) have led to the use of disposable gloves and careful hand washing when dealing with children's body fluids.

Safety Concerns

The organization of the physical environment can assist in **accident prevention.** Due to limited experiences and developing physical skills, many children need careful preparation of the classroom. Electrical outlets, stoves, air-circulating fans, and climbing equipment are some examples of equipment that require planning and education for effective use. Medicines, cleaning agents, and insecticides are other materials that teachers must store out of the reach of children or outside the classroom to avoid accidental poisonings.

In many circumstances, adults need to demonstrate or teach children **safe use of equipment.** For example, assisting children in holding and properly using a sharp knife in a cooking activity helps promote safety. Providing safety goggles for the woodworking bench and demonstrating good sawing techniques will also help prevent accidents in that area. Although this advanced preparation won't prevent all problems from occurring, it helps create an environment where children can explore and experiment with greater freedom.

A Place for Parents?

Space in most early childhood classrooms is at a premium. It is often difficult to find room for every desired option. Despite this major problem, if teachers of young children want to help parents and other volunteers feel welcome in the classroom, having a parent corner makes good sense. The combination of a parent bulletin board, comfortable chair(s), educational information for parents, and possibly a hot water dispenser for coffee and tea creates a welcoming environment for visiting adults. It may be possible for this space to be used by teachers as a break area, enhancing its usefulness.

Summary

Planning a stimulating indoor environment for young children is complex. The teacher should separate active/quiet areas and dry/wet spaces, include areas for different sizes of groups, and evaluate the quality of the physical space. The indoor environment typically includes many different centers, and each must be individually planned. Special considerations are necessary for planning infant/toddler, preschool, and primary classrooms. Several commercial resources are available for useful equipment and materials; these can also be teacher-made. Adaptations are required for children with special needs. When changing the indoor setting to stimulate the children by providing variety, the teacher may find that the rationale and procedures discussed here are useful. Finally, teachers must consider health and safety issues. Teachers also may wish to create a special place in the classroom for parents.

✎ For Discussion and Action

1. Sketch to scale an early childhood classroom. Compare what you found with the guidelines presented in this chapter.
2. Observe children playing in an early childhood center. What were they doing and saying? Discuss your observations with your peers.

3. Your principal is concerned about your plans to add centers to your primary classroom. Make a case for the benefits of centers and play for children.

4. Take a careful look at an early childhood center. Make a list of all the equipment you found. Discuss with your classmates.

5. Research, make, and demonstrate to others a simple game or material that could be used for play in an early childhood center.

6. Spend some time in an early childhood classroom looking for ways in which the teacher has dealt with safety issues. Make a list of your findings.

∾ Building Your Personal Library

Dodge, D., & Colker, L. (1992). *The creative curriculum* (3rd ed.). Washington, DC: Teaching Strategies, Inc. This is a well-respected book describing the importance of play and a centers-based classroom. Special emphasis is on the prekindergarten age range.

Marotz, L., Cross, M., & Rush, J. (1993). *Health, safety and nutrition for the young child* (3rd ed.). Albany, NY: Delmar. This book provides a thorough description of health, safety, and nutrition issues for early childhood classrooms and playgrounds.

Mitchell, A., & David, J. (Eds.). (1992). *Explorations with young children*. Mt. Rainier, MD: Gryphon House. This book was prepared as a curriculum guide for early childhood classrooms by the Bank Street College of Education. It describes the Bank Street approach, which is a framework for developmentally appropriate practice for children from birth through age eight.

Wasserman, S. (1990). *Serious players in the primary classroom*. New York: Teachers College Press. An excellent rationale for the inclusion of play in the primary classroom, this book also presents many practical tips for implementing a primary program that is oriented toward play.

10 Planning the Physical Environment: Outdoors

In this chapter you will

- Gain knowledge about the importance of outdoor play.
- Get ideas for planning the outdoor play environment.
- Develop a rationale for stimulating a variety of play types outdoors.
- Address the teacher's role in preparing for outdoor play.
- Review information related to playground health and safety.

Marika and Nikky are excited about spending some time outdoors today and are ready to get started. These eager third graders have been planning to do some gardening activities for several days. The story about growing things and the visit from an expert gardener seem to have stimulated their interest. During project time over the past week, they have been formulating their plans. After reading portions of several books on gardening, they drew a map to scale of the portion of the garden area assigned to them and indicated the vegetables they will grow. Marika wrote a list of procedures for the planting and care of their vegetables, while Nikky gathered from her gardening parents all the seeds they will use and identified the proper planting depths for each. With shovels, trowels, row markers and seeds in hand, they are ready to begin. It is exciting to see how children's interests can become the basis for playful learning opportunities in the outdoor setting. ❧

Given opportunities to do so, most young children eagerly engage in creative experiences outdoors. The chance to explore the natural wonders found outside the classroom—combined with opportunities to run, jump, climb, and shout—makes this setting a valuable experience for children. Early educators need to be sensitive to the importance of this environment and plan for creative play experiences there.

Importance of Outdoor Play

Think about a favorite play experience you remember from your own childhood. What were you doing? Were you playing alone or with others? Were you indoors or outside? In a study of college students, over 75 percent remembered favorite play experiences that occurred outdoors (Henniger, 1994a). What makes the outdoor play experience so memorable for many adults?

A variety of possible explanations may help us to understand this finding. The sensory experiences associated with playing outdoors is certainly one possible explanation. Sights, sounds, smells, and textures found outside are very attractive to children and make that setting more interesting to them. The greater sense of freedom associated with the outdoors is another possible reason many of us remember outdoor play experiences so vividly (Rivkin, 1995). Running, jumping, shouting, and getting involved in messy activities can be accomplished outdoors with minimum adult involvement. A third possibility is that outdoor play gives children more opportunities for risk taking. Smith (1990) suggests that this is one of the main reasons that children play outdoors. Risk taking is exciting and motivates many children to play.

In addition to children's interests in this setting, there are other reasons for promoting outdoor play. The National Association for the Education of Young Children (NAEYC; Bredekamp & Copple, 1997) emphasizes the importance of outdoor play as an integral part of developmentally appropriate practices for young children. Daily outdoor play experiences for all children from birth through age eight is considered essential. They provide opportunities to use large and small muscles, learn from materials outdoors, and experience the freedom only the outdoors can allow (Bredekamp & Copple, 1997).

> *Arturo and Cindy are swinging side by side on their preschool playground. As they move back and forth, Cindy talks of her new baby brother. Mandy joins them, and as they swing, the children decide to pretend to be mom, dad, and baby out for a picnic in the park.*

These and other outdoor activities provide many opportunities for learning and development. A creative, well-planned playground can stimulate a wide variety of positive play experiences for young children (Henniger, 1985). Swings, slides, and wide-open spaces encourage functional play outdoors and help develop the young child's gross motor skills. A sandbox with digging tools and accessories can stimulate creative construction activities, and children can use an old boat for a variety of sociodramatic play themes. In fact, every aspect of the child's development can be enhanced when adults develop quality outdoor play spaces (Guddemi & Eriksen, 1992). With careful planning and preparation of the playground, children have rich and memorable experiences there.

Planning Guidelines

If outdoor play is to live up to its potential, teachers must commit time and energy to planning and preparing this space (Henniger, 1994c). The playground should be viewed as an extension of the indoor classroom and must be an important part of the teacher's planning efforts (Esbensen, 1987).

Basic Guidelines

Several considerations help make the outdoor play space a quality one for young children. These guidelines provide the basic ingredients children need for positive playground experiences:

- The playground should be located next to the classroom.
- Provide at least one hundred square feet of outdoor space for each child.
- A balance of sunny and shady areas will help the play yard appeal to the greatest number of students.
- Large, grassy areas should be included for children's games and large muscle activities.
- A tall, sturdy fence helps children feel safe and secure in the outdoor setting.
- A covered area provides opportunities for play during very hot or rainy weather.
- Playgrounds should have areas encouraging both group activities and private places when children need time to themselves.

Fixed Equipment

Playgrounds contain a variety of equipment and materials to stimulate children's play. The most commonly found structures on playgrounds today are pieces of fixed equipment such as swings, slides, and climbers (Frost, Bowers, & Wortham, 1990). These larger pieces of equipment are designed to be permanent and immovable and add important play opportunities for children. An ideal playground environment should include a variety of fixed equipment that children can use in creative ways. Swings, slides, climbers, a sandbox, dramatic play structures, and permanent storage facilities are all important pieces of fixed equipment needed for exciting outdoor play.

Swings provide children with many opportunities to practice coordinating large muscle movements as they pump vigorously with arms and legs. The exhilarating experience of moving back and forth on a swing as fresh air blows briskly over the child's face adds excitement and pleasure to this activity. When more than one swing is available, children will often gather at the swing set to talk and enjoy good friendships as they glide through the air. For other children, swinging can be an opportunity to separate themselves from the crowd and spend time thinking or regaining composure following a difficult experience elsewhere.

Slides and climbers are found on most playgrounds and provide many play opportunities for children.

> *Dottie has just reached the top of the largest climber on her elementary playground for the first time. She can't wait to tell her older brother, who has been "bugging" his first-grade sister to "climb the mountain," as he calls it.*

The challenge of moving step by step to the top of an imposing structure and then looking down at the rest of the world is an important one for the young child and can give a sense of power and accomplishment. Many modern slide structures provide children with several different ways to reach the top of the slide and challenge children to try them as they build confidence in their climbing abilities. Sliding itself provides other risk-taking opportunities and sensory experiences that are pleasurable for children.

The **sandbox** is another traditional piece of fixed equipment found on most playgrounds that adds important play options for children. In the sandbox, children spend many happy hours building, tearing down, and building again using simple child-sized tools and accessories such as spoons, scoops, and sifters (Baker, 1966). The joy of digging in the dirt, mixing sand and water, and creating a child-sized world of hills and valleys or a pretend lunch of molded sand is often a richly rewarding experience for children. The sandbox tends to draw children together and encourages them to play near or with others in creative ways. It allows the shy child opportunities to engage in parallel play in preparation for more social activities in the future.

Fixed equipment that encourages children to engage in dramatic play is also valuable on the playground. A **playhouse** stocked with child-sized furniture is one example of a creative piece of equipment that is useful in stimulating dramatic play. An old boat or small car that has been carefully prepared by adults could also provide children with many happy hours of dramatic play. Although not commonly found on most playgrounds for young children (Frost et al., 1990), these dramatic play structures help stimulate the important play types that can and should occur in the playground environment.

Another essential piece of fixed equipment needed on playgrounds for young children is the **storage shed.** A lockable building at least 10 × 12 feet is the minimum size needed. If the outdoor environment is to reach its true potential, some way of storing loose parts is needed (Henniger, 1994c). Making the outdoor environment an extension of the classroom requires storage spaces similar to those found indoors. The following items can be effectively stored outdoors for children's use:

- Construction materials (large and small)
- Dramatic play props
- Sand toys and digging equipment
- Materials for children's games
- Wheeled toys

A storage shed allows the teacher to change the materials available to children so that the new items stimulate increased interest and involvement.

Movable Equipment

Although the fixed playground equipment described here provides many valuable options for children, movable materials are also needed. Remember how children learn during their early years. Hands-on manipulation of toys and

Playing in the Gutters

Sue Dinwiddie (1993) suggests a simple and creative way to provide children with quality materials that they can move and manipulate outdoors. For her preschool program for children two-and-one-half to five, teachers introduced children to plastic rain gutters. After purchasing three ten-foot segments of gutter at their local lumber yard, Dinwiddie cut these pieces into different lengths with a hacksaw:

- Two 5-foot sections
- Three sections approximately 3¹/2 feet in length
- One section 7¹/2 feet; the remaining piece, 2¹/2 feet long

Initially, the teachers set up the gutters ahead of time in such a way that the gutters sloped down to the sand box and the water table. The teachers placed pitchers, pots, and buckets near the gutters for children to use. The children were then free to experiment with pouring sand and water down the gutters.

As you might expect, this activity attracted many children and held their interest for extended periods. They experimented with different slopes for the gutters and tried a creative assortment of materials such as balls and boats to send down the gutters. This inexpensive, durable option is an excellent example of a type of movable equipment that can be very productively used by young children.

---

equipment in their world provides young children with many opportunities for growth and development (Kamii & DeVries, 1978). When teachers of young children plan for learning indoors, they create centers that are rich with materials children can manipulate (see Chapter 9). Similar opportunities for manipulating materials are needed outdoors so that children can learn from doing in this setting as well.

> ❧ *Gordy, Brianna, and Meghan are busily moving lightweight sections of plastic rain gutter to create a series of ramps to roll their tennis balls through. These children are learning basic physics properties as they manipulate this outdoor equipment*

See Dinwiddie (1993) and the accompanying "Into Practice" box for more information on rain gutters as a play material.

Although most playgrounds for young children currently have limited options for manipulation (Frost et al., 1990), these materials can and should be added. In addition to the tricycles, old tires, and sandboxes typically found on playgrounds, children can effectively use other materials such as child-sized cable spools, commercially produced outdoor blocks, and gardening tools.

The **Adventure Playgrounds** of Europe provide other examples of movable equipment that children can effectively use outdoors (Frost, 1992). A trained play leader guides children in their outdoor experiences. Children can play with scrap lumber, bricks, tires, rope, hammers, nails, saws, a fire pit, and animals (for petting, feeding, and care). Teachers can include similar materials for even the youngest children on the early childhood playground.

Children get an extra measure of satisfaction when they can move equipment and change their play environment.

Variety of Play Options

Traditional playgrounds were designed to stimulate **physical/motor play** (Frost & Wortham, 1988). Although this is an important goal, playgrounds can encourage many other play types. Research on children's playground behaviors indicates that this environment, when properly prepared, can stimulate a wide assortment of play types (Rivkin, 1990).

In addition to active physical/motor play, the outdoor environment can allow for **solitary play** opportunities. Cardboard and wooden boxes that children can crawl inside, barrels, and natural plantings help create a small place for one or two children to briefly get away from it all. Construction play can also be encouraged when the teacher provides a variety of building materials. The teacher can also place outdoors prop boxes containing dress-up materials and dramatic-play toys to stimulate imaginative play themes. Teachers can encourage **games with rules** for children who are ready for this play type, by providing any needed equipment and adult guidance.

Play Areas Outdoors

Many educators view the playground as an outdoor classroom. These teachers carefully organize this environment to provide children with the best possible play experiences. Just as the classroom is divided into centers to encourage different play types, the playground can be similarly organized. Esbensen (1987) suggests organizing the outdoors into seven play zones: transition zone, manipulative/creative zone, projective/fantasy zone, focal/social zone, social/dramatic zone, physical zone, and natural element zone. The playground areas identified next are modifications of the play zones defined by Esbensen.

Transition Area

Shawna has just walked out the classroom door and is slowly scanning the playground to see what others are doing. She often needs time to warm up to the idea of playing outdoors.

As children leave the relatively quiet indoor environment to engage in more active outdoor play, a transition area helps many children adjust. This area could include quieter activities such as painting and water play (Esbensen, 1987). If possible, the transition area should be covered (making it more usable in poor weather conditions) and have child-sized tables and chairs for sit-down activities.

Manipulative/Construction Area

Another important space on the early childhood playground is the manipulative/construction area. Fine motor development can be enhanced by providing puzzles, small blocks, beads, and other manipulative materials typically found indoors. The addition of a woodworking bench and other building materials would also encourage construction play in this area. Creative materials such as play dough, clay, and art activities can stimulate other important play experiences (Esbensen, 1987).

Storage is an important concern for this outdoor area, to keep materials safe when they are not in use. A storage shed can be effectively used for many of these items. An already existing piece of outdoor equipment may also have a handy corner that might be used as a storage nook. Another possibility is to store construction materials indoors and bring them outside when needed.

CELEBRATING PLAY . . .
Play and Risk Taking

Smith (1990) suggests that a major attraction of playing outdoors is the opportunity to take risks. It's exciting to engage in play that *might* lead to accident or injury. Children don't want to be injured, but the possibility makes play more fun. This attitude is certainly contrary to what most adults want children to experience. That may be one reason why adults are frequently absent when children engage in their favorite play experiences outdoors. Kids want to take risks; adults prize safety in play.

1. Think back to your favorite play experiences outdoors, and try to remember any that had elements of risk taking. Do you think that the risks you took were an important reason why you enjoyed this play so much?

2. Do you think playgrounds for young children should include risk-taking opportunities? If you do, what could you include that would provide this element?

3. Observe a community or school playground. Did you see any examples of healthy risk-taking opportunities? Any ideas of ways in which you could add these options to the existing equipment?

4. There is probably a difference between healthy and unhealthy risk taking on the playground. Can you give some examples of unhealthy risks that we can and should eliminate from outdoor play?

Dramatic Play Area

Trentin and Tessa are excitedly playing commuter on the preschool playground. After filling their trikes with gas from the toy gas pump, they both motor over to the play house to end their busy work days and play with their families.

While dramatic play does occur spontaneously on the playground, providing creative props will stimulate even higher levels of this important play type. Boys, in particular, seem to engage in more pretend play in this setting when quality materials are available (Henniger, 1985). A permanent structure such as a play house could serve as a valuable gathering spot for the dramatic play area. If possible, this structure should also have storage space to accommodate the many props needed for creative dramatic play. Other structures, such as a small stripped car body or a steering wheel mounted in a wooden box, also encourage imaginative play experiences for young children.

Physical Area

The development of large muscles can be encouraged outdoors in many ways. Mounds, hills, grassy areas, asphalt or concrete surfacing, and winding, figure-eight

Water play is an enticing activity throughout the early childhood years.

tricycle paths challenge children to use their large muscles in new and interesting ways. Tricycle paths should be a minimum width of four feet to allow children to pass each other as they meet. Open spaces for running, skipping, and simple games are useful. Climbers, slides, and swings all help develop physical skills as well. This area should allow risk taking by children and challenge them with a variety of options and levels as they mature physically. When making decisions about where to locate this area, be sure to separate it from the quieter activities found elsewhere.

Sand/Water Play Area

The sandbox has been a traditional and important part of early childhood playgrounds. From Margaret McMillan's Open Air Nursery (Braun & Edwards, 1972) in the nineteenth century to the present time, sandbox play has been encouraged outdoors. This area should be large enough to accommodate several children at the same time. A variety of digging, mixing, and pouring utensils enrich the play experiences children can have there. Other accessories such as toy trucks, boats, plastic animals, and human figures add to the creative play potential of the sandbox. A permanent cover for the sandbox helps protect this area from animal use during nonplay periods. Ideally, the sandbox should also be near a water source so that children can combine these two elements for messy but thoroughly enjoyable play experiences.

Natural Areas

After several weeks of spring rains, today is a beautiful, sunny day. Awesta and Chrissy are skipping joyfully across the open grassy area of the playground, laughing and talking along the way. The dew on newly budding leaves sparkles in the sunlight, while the fragrant aromas of spring fill the air.

Part of the wonder and joy experienced by children outdoors comes from the natural elements found there (Rivkin, 1995). The sights, smells, and textures of this environment are unique and exciting for children. To enhance this aspect of outdoor play, adults should provide a variety of trees, bushes, and plantings. Taking care to choose flowering shrubs and trees for spring blooms, other trees for shade in the warmer seasons, and yet other plantings for vivid fall colors will help make the outdoor setting of continued interest throughout the year. An assortment of natural materials also allows children to experience different textures, leaf sizes, colors, and smells throughout the growing season. Rather than a single, large grouping of natural plantings in one area, several smaller groupings of trees and plants throughout the play yard can add interest and beauty to this environment. Parents and interested community members may assist in planning, planting, and caring for these natural elements.

A garden/digging spot that is separate from the sandbox can also be included in the natural area. Child-sized shovels, rakes, and gardening tools allow children to dig, plant, and care for an assortment of interesting plantings. Young children can enjoyably grow a variety of flowers, fruits, and vegetables in a garden plot.

Developmental Considerations

Just as indoor environments reflect the developmental abilities and interests of children, playground planners must consider these important characteristics in their planning. An infant/toddler playground will look much different from a play space created with four- and five-year-old children in mind. Similarly, before children with special needs can engage in outdoor play, the playground planner must understand their physical conditions, and must alter equipment and space to allow equal access.

Infant/Toddler Play Spaces

You may be surprised to learn that outdoor time is very important for children even at the infant/toddler stage. Recently, educators have begun to focus on outdoor play environments for infants and toddlers and have discovered that children this age find the outdoor setting richly rewarding (Wortham, 1989). Because infants and toddlers learn a great deal through the use of their senses, the playground provides many new opportunities for extending learning. Figure 10–1 provides a sample design for an infant/toddler playground.

Developmentally, infants and toddlers are growing daily in their locomotor skills. They perfect sitting, crawling, standing, and walking as they interact with people and objects in their environment. Socially, these very young children are becoming aware of others and beginning to interact with them. They are developing language and intellectual skills through playful exchanges with adults, other children, and playthings. Although indoor settings certainly enhance these developing abilities, the outdoors is another rich opportunity for growth.

Outdoor play environments for the infant and toddler should not be simply scaled-down versions of the complex play structures found on playgrounds for older children. Many simple additions can be made to the natural elements found outdoors for use by this age group. Small hills, ramps, low steps, and tunnels may all be useful in facilitating physical development. A pathway with different textures to walk on and touch is another creative option (Greenman, 1988). Infants and toddlers often select push toys, riding toys, dolls, and toy vehicles that help stimulate creative play (Winter, 1985). Children this age also productively use sand—or an edible substitute for the youngest children.

Children Three through Five

During the preschool and kindergarten years, children are developing greater social awareness and increasingly want to interact with their peers. Playground equipment for this age should help facilitate social skills by bringing children together for play experiences. A complex, multifunctional superstructure (Frost, 1994) that includes steps, slides, suspended bridges, ramps, and climbers can be useful for this purpose. Figure 10–2 provides a sample playground design for children three through five years of age.

> ∾ *Darren is a typical four-year-old. He loves running, climbing, and swinging activities on the playground. Darren also spends large blocks of time in the sandbox and riding tricycles.*

Physical skills during the preschool years are developing rapidly. These children need equipment that challenges their abilities in running, climbing, and complex tasks such as throwing a ball. Three- to five-year-old children need a variety of equipment choices that encourage them to expand their skills to a new level.

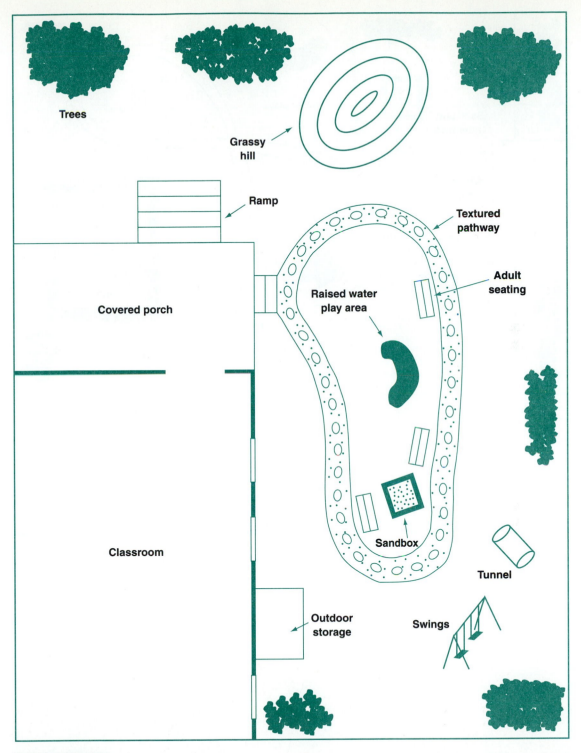

Trees

Grassy hill

Ramp

Textured pathway

Adult seating

Covered porch

Raised water play area

Classroom

Sandbox

Tunnel

Outdoor storage

Swings

Figure 10–1   *Infant/Toddler Playground*

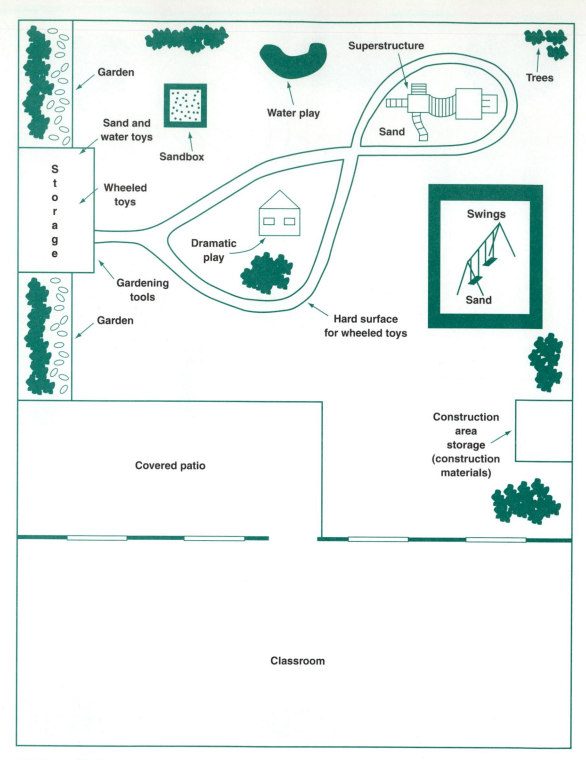

Garden

Sand and
water toys

Sandbox

Water play

Superstructure

Sand

Trees

Storage

Wheeled
toys

Gardening
tools

Garden

Dramatic
play

Hard surface
for wheeled toys

Swings

Sand

Construction
area
storage
(construction
materials)

Covered patio

Classroom

Figure 10–2 *Preschool Playground Design*

258

Equipment that can be adjusted or that has built-in varying levels of physical challenge are best suited for this age group.

Preschool and kindergarten children are actively engaged in pretend play sequences, and materials that encourage dramatic play themes are important inclusions. A variety of materials to stimulate this play behavior are essential. Children this age can creatively use fixed equipment such as an old boat or car body. Smaller props such as dress-up clothes and theme-related toys can also promote valuable dramatic play.

Primary Children

Although many primary-age children are beginning to show interest in other play activities, growing evidence indicates that children this age still need, and should be encouraged to engage in, dramatic play experiences (Smilansky & Shefatya, 1990). The materials and equipment described previously for dramatic play should also be available for the primary-age child. Figure 10–3 gives an example of a playground for children five through eight years of age.

Primary children continue to benefit from quality outdoor play experiences.

> ✍ *Carla is an active second-grade child who loves to play jump-rope games and hopscotch and to create her own challenges while twirling on the bars during outdoor time. She and her friends can spend long periods engaged in these activities.*

Piaget suggests that primary children are transitioning into the stage of concrete operations. As this process takes place, children become more interested in, and more able to play, games with rules (Piaget, 1962). Teachers can effectively introduce traditional team games such as soccer, baseball, and basketball, especially if competition is minimized. With an emphasis on skill building and enjoyment of the game, many children can benefit from these more structured play events. More spontaneous games that have entertained children for generations can also be productively introduced to young children during the primary grades. Multicultural games from around the world can open up additional playful alternatives for children (Kirchner, 1991).

The Child with Special Needs

Teachers of young children should also prepare the outdoor environment to accommodate the child with special needs. Playground experiences are important for these children as well. Two basic considerations should be kept in mind for this group.

First, the teacher must be aware that his involvement and assistance are essential when working with children with special needs (Karnes, 1994). Although these

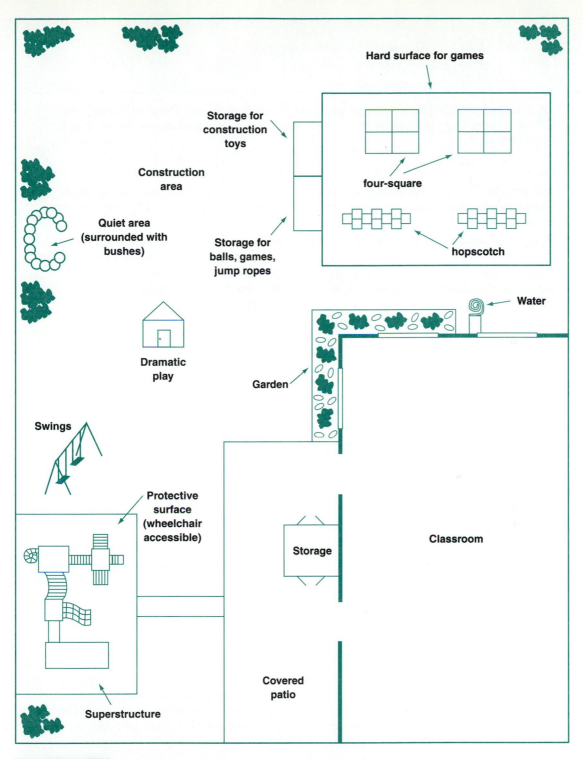

Hard surface for games

Storage for
construction
toys

Construction
area

four-square

Quiet area
(surrounded with
bushes)

Storage for
balls, games,
jump ropes

hopscotch

Water

Dramatic
play

Garden

Swings

Protective
surface
(wheelchair
accessible)

Classroom

Storage

Superstructure

Covered
patio

❧ *Figure 10–3* **Sample Primary Playground**

CELEBRATING DIVERSITY . . .
Outdoor Play for Children with Special Needs

All children, including those with special needs, benefit from playing outdoors. The following list of suggestions (Karnes, 1994) may help in planning quality outdoor play experiences for these children.

Do

Talk with children's physical therapists about making the playground safe and appropriate for each child.

Provide choices of materials based on children's abilities and interests.

Prepare children with special needs to use the play area before they encounter it with other children.

Make sure that children with special needs understand safety rules.

Don't

Expect that all children with special needs will play spontaneously. They may need ideas and assistance.

Make play choices for children with special needs. Let them make decisions for themselves.

Overprotect children with special needs. They are capable of taking an active part in outdoor play.

1. *Take a look at a playground for young children. What did you see that would indicate accommodations for children with special needs? Share your findings with classmates.*

2. *What special safety issues may you face with children with special needs on the playground? How would you deal with these safety concerns?*

children can playfully engage in activities outdoors that stimulate their physical, intellectual, and social/emotional development, they often need more modeling, encouragement, and reinforcement than other children. The teacher should provide this helping hand to ensure that these children get the most out of their play situations.

Second, the child with special needs must be able to use the available equipment. Many playground surfaces, for example, make it very difficult for children in wheelchairs to get near enough to use the equipment. Sand is a great shock-absorbing material under and around the swings, but it makes it very difficult for a student in a wheelchair to use them. Depending on the nature of the disabilities, other playground modifications may be necessary if we are to make the outdoor environment truly accessible to children with special needs.

Selecting Equipment and Materials

As opportunities arise for adding equipment to the outdoor environment, teachers should consider several options. Commercial materials, donated items, and adult-made equipment all can enhance the play value of the outdoor setting.

Commercial Equipment

Commercial equipment for outdoor gross motor play is readily available for early childhood settings. Many playground companies provide large permanent structures that cost from $2,000 to $10,000 or more. If you purchase all of your materials through commercial providers, the playground will be an expensive area to equip. When estimating costs for commercial structures, make sure to include the cost of the structure itself, installation costs (typically, 35 to 40 percent of the purchase price), and surfacing costs for the material placed under and around the equipment for safety purposes. In addition to the larger permanent play structures, commercial companies also sell some smaller movable equipment such as metal climbers, plastic interlocking panels, and tricycles. Figure 10–4 lists several commercial companies that supply outdoor equipment for young children.

Donated Materials

Even if your budget for outdoor equipment is small, you should not let the expense of commercial options stop you from creating an exciting playground for children. Other free or inexpensive options exist. With some creative thinking, you can locate and have donated to your program quality materials for outdoor play. Some commonly found materials that can be effectively used on the playground include old car and truck tires, boards, small cable spools (the kind that hardware stores use to hold chain and rope before sale), PVC pipe and connectors, and lumber for woodworking projects. Other larger items could include large tires from earth-moving equipment, wooden pallets used for storing materials in warehouses, and cargo netting from overseas shipping activities. Creative adults who get excited about the possibilities of outdoor play can undoubtedly come up with a much longer list than this. The key is to think imaginatively about the materials in your community that could be effectively used by young children on the playground and then get the community involved in providing them for your playground.

Adult-Made Equipment

Many of the materials that businesses and others may wish to donate to your early childhood program can be used to construct low-cost equipment that can serve the same purposes as the more expensive commercial playground structures. For

The following list of commercial companies that provide playground equipment for young children is a sampling of those available. It is not comprehensive but should give you an idea of the many options for purchasing equipment for playgrounds. Most companies will sell and install on your site the permanent equipment they offer.

Big Toys
7717 New Market St.
Olympia, WA 98501
(800) 426-9788

Grounds for Play, Inc.
3501 Ave. E East
Arlington, TX 76011
(800) 552-PLAY (7529)

Kompan, Inc.
R.D.#2, Box 249
Marathon, NY 13803
(800) 553-2446

Little Tikes Company
2180 Barlow Road
Hudson, OH 44236
(800) 321-4424

Constructive Playthings
12227 E. 119th St.
Grandview, MO 64030
(800) 448-4115

Iron Mountain Forge
P.O. Box 897
Farmington, MO 63640
(800) 325-8828

Landscape Structures, Inc.
Rt. 3, 601 7th St. S.
Delano, MN 55328
(800) 328-0035

Play Designs
P.O. Box 427
New Berlin, PA 17855
(800) 327-7571

example, a simple tire swing can be constructed from donated materials and have just as much play potential as the more expensive options available through commercial companies (Marston, 1984). More complicated structures like a slide/fort can be constructed with the assistance of knowledgeable parents and community members (Hewes, 1975).

Movable equipment can also be constructed by interested parents and others with skills in metal and/or woodworking. Such items as wooden boxes of different sizes, cleated boards to connect smaller pieces of equipment, a steering wheel mounted in a wooden box, and 55-gallon barrels with stands are a few examples of simple equipment that most parent or school groups can effectively design and build.

Hewes (1975) suggests a five-step approach when building your own equipment for outdoor use:

1. Consider the site for the playground equipment. What equipment could be constructed to complement the natural elements and the currently existing options?

2. Once you have commitments for donated materials, determine the amount of money you have for purchasing materials that haven't been donated.

3. After resources have been determined, develop a construction plan. The more detailed and accurate the plan, the more likely it will be that the rest of your project will unfold smoothly.

4. Select materials that are durable and safe for young children so that the structures constructed will stand the test of time.

5. Finally, you are ready to involve children, parents, and community members in the process of actually building your structure.

Planning for Change in the Outdoor Environment

Kate Ortega is a committed, hard-working kindergarten teacher. She understands the importance of planning for creative play and takes time each week to change her centers indoors to stimulate student interest. Recently, she realized that the outdoor environment also requires change. Kate now includes time to plan special materials and activities for use on the playground as well.

If we are to make the outdoor setting a true extension of the indoor environment, we must plan and prepare the outdoor environment with the same care and concern as for the indoor setting. Teachers must change materials and equipment used outdoors on a regular basis so that children approach playing outdoors with the same sense of excitement and joy as they do indoor explorations.

For example, when preparing for classroom play in the manipulative center, teachers decide which new puzzles and manipulative materials to place on the shelves so that children can have new and interesting opportunities on a regular basis. Other items can then be put away until later in the school year.

This same planning process must occur for the outdoor setting as well. The provision of outdoor prop boxes, teacher-movable equipment, and child-movable materials that change regularly help create the newness and challenge that are so important to a quality playground.

Outdoor Prop Boxes

A prop box is a collection of materials organized around a chosen theme to stimulate creative play. The selected props are typically put in a sturdy box that can be easily stored when not in use. Prop box themes and materials are limited only by the imaginations and creativity of the adults doing the planning. Jelks and Dukes (1985) describe prop boxes for the outdoor setting.

Prop boxes can have important benefits when used on the playground:

• The additional props stimulate more dramatic play outdoors.

• Prop boxes make it easy to add change to the outdoor setting.

• They are versatile and can be used effectively both indoors and outdoors.

Hatcher, Nicosia, and Pape (1994) make several suggestions for planning and constructing prop boxes for use in the early childhood classroom, and these also apply to outdoor prop boxes. The box itself should be clearly labeled on the outside

By moving larger pieces of equipment around periodically, teachers can help stimulate new interest in outdoor play.

to help the teacher locate the needed materials. A theme-related picture attached to the outside of the box can help stimulate children's thinking regarding the topic, just as pictures on the walls in the classroom give children ideas about play in early childhood centers. Inside the lid, an itemized list of props and ideas for setup and use can be included. This can be particularly helpful when prop boxes are shared between several classrooms in larger programs. To aid in storage, all the props should fit in the box and all boxes should be of a uniform size and shape. Finally, making the prop boxes accessible to children and easy to move in and out of designated play areas will make it possible for children to determine their own themes and select the needed play materials.

Teacher-Movable Equipment

As mentioned, when planning for indoor play, teachers must consider the physical arrangement of the larger equipment and make periodic adjustments to ensure that children have change and interesting new play options on a regular basis. The sand table may be emptied and refilled with water, for example.

This same philosophy can be implemented on the playground; at least some of the materials and equipment can be moved by adults. Placing aluminum climbing equipment in an interesting arrangement near a fixed piece of playground equipment can encourage new interest in this play area. Making a woodworking table and related materials available will stimulate more construction play activities. Moving a portable set of large wooden boxes to a new location on the playground and rearranging them in an interesting pattern can create a quiet space for one or two children for another play option on the playground. Rearranging these movable materials will increase the creative play potential outdoors.

Child-Movable Equipment

In addition to larger, adult-movable equipment, it is important to have smaller pieces that children can manipulate. Commercial options are available through various providers. Outdoor blocks, larger building sets (often plastic for durability and weather resistance), tricycles, and wheeled toys are examples of these materials. Children also can move donated materials such as small cable spools, used tires, and cardboard boxes. For example, when tires are available on the playground, children can use them to roll, sit in, or wash, or as part of their pretend play themes.

By moving equipment themselves, children gain important understanding about their world and see themselves as more competent and capable. Children begin to feel in charge of this environment, just as they do when they manipulate materials indoors. This sense of power and accomplishment is very important in the child's development and must be encouraged as much as possible throughout the curriculum of the early childhood classroom.

Health and Safety on the Playground

> *The elementary school nurse has been working overtime to patch up children's scrapes and bruises from playing outdoors. A kindergarten girl fell and scraped the palms of both hands on the asphalt. Another child cut her head on a metal brace while playfully running under the slide. A third-grade boy sprained his ankle when he slipped and fell off the climber and landed on a log border around the structure.*

Despite the many potential health and safety hazards found on most playgrounds, the preceding scenario does not occur regularly. Yet, if the outdoor setting is to meet its potential for stimulating creative play, it not only must be rich with materials and equipment but also must be constructed and maintained to protect children from unnecessary health and safety problems. Currently, many outdoor play spaces for young children fail miserably in this category. Playground injuries and health-related problems are common. As adults become more aware of the issues and change playground construction, many of the following problems can be avoided.

Playground Injuries

The United States has been concerned about injuries on playgrounds since approximately the mid-1970s. The Consumer Product Safety Commission (CPSC) coordinated studies of playground safety (Frost & Henniger, 1979) and found a variety of problems that needed correction. By far, the biggest problem then and now is the surfacing under and around play equipment. Large numbers of children

⚓ Table 10–1   *Protecting against Falls*

Shock-absorbing materials under and around play equipment help prevent injuries from falls. Typical options include wood chips, sand, and pea gravel. But how much is needed to protect against falls of different heights? The following statistics from the Consumer Product Safety Commission provide some initial guidelines. The commission's manual (1990) provides more specifics.

Material	Uncompressed Depth of Material*		
	6 inches	9 inches	12 inches
Wood chips	6 feet	7 feet	12 feet
Fine sand	5 feet	5 feet	9 feet
Fine gravel	6 feet	7 feet	10 feet

*Protects falls up to this height.
Note: From *Handbook for Public Playground Safety,* by the Consumer Product Safety Commission, 1990, Washington, DC: Consumer Product Safety Commission.

nation-wide are falling from playground equipment onto hard-packed surfaces and receiving injuries that range from scrapes and bruises to concussions (and worse). Another finding was that equipment on many playgrounds was not appropriate to the developmental abilities of children. Injuries often result when children attempt to use slides, climbers, and swings designed for older students. Equipment design problems in which exposed bolts, sharp edges, and pinch/crush points caused unnecessary injuries were also common. Early studies also found that placing pieces of equipment too close together was causing injuries as children moved around the playground.

Unfortunately, current statistics indicate that playground injuries today are similar in number to those from the 1970s. Frost (1992) indicates that 154,828 children were treated in hospital emergency rooms in 1980 for injuries associated with playgrounds. Despite an improved understanding of the problem, this number increased to 208,488 in 1985 and has remained fairly constant since then. Continued efforts clearly must be made to further reduce these preventable injuries on the playground. Table 10–1 provides information on how to reduce the most serious problem—falls onto hard surfaces.

Safety Guidelines

Because of the injuries described previously, the CPSC developed a set of safety guidelines (1990). They are designed to assist playground equipment manufacturers and concerned adults in creating outdoor environments that are safer places for children to play. Although these guidelines are voluntary, equipment manufacturers and others are strongly encouraged to follow them. To date, compliance has been mixed (Frost, 1992). Equipment that is less than ideal in terms of safety is still being produced and placed on playgrounds for children.

Health Considerations

In addition to creating playgrounds that are free from unnecessary safety hazards, planners must consider health-related issues. One such potential problem is the use of toxic materials on the playground (Frost, 1992). Chemicals sprayed on plants and coatings on wood surfaces are two examples of problem areas. Poisonous plants are also more common than might be expected and should be excluded from playgrounds. Consult an expert in your area for specific information on plants to avoid. Another consideration is to provide regular maintenance of the playground. Picking up trash and litter will help prevent unwanted injuries and infections from these materials. Standing water can also attract insects and disease agents and should be removed from the play yard. Sandbox areas should be covered when not in use to protect them from animal droppings. Regular cleaning of the sand can also protect children from potential risks in this area.

The Teacher's Role

Teachers have an important role to play in assisting children on the playground. When actively involved in facilitating outdoor play, teachers can substantially reduce potential injuries. The following list outlines some important considerations in creating a climate for quality outdoor play:

- Allow plenty of time for outdoor play (thirty minutes or more are needed for creative play experiences).
- Plan with children for creative playground use (talk to them about how the equipment can be used).
- Take time to prepare the outdoors for children (this will mean that more acceptable and new options will be available to children on a regular basis).
- Let children know what is acceptable and unacceptable behaviors outdoors.
- Spend time interacting with children in this setting.

Parent and Community Involvement

∾ *After the school-wide meeting last night on the condition of the playground, several parents expressed their interest in helping improve the creative play options outdoors. Marcus's dad is a building contractor and is willing to coordinate the construction of playground structures. Two other families own businesses that can donate some construction materials. The Parent–Teacher Association (PTA) is*

INTO PRACTICE . . .

Cleaning Sand

Because the sand children play with in the sandbox and elsewhere on the playground is often accessible to animals when children are not present, it is a good idea to clean the sand regularly to help prevent unnecessary risk of disease and illness (Esbensen, 1987). The following cleaning method has been successfully used in Great Britain for many years. You may wish to check with local health officials for similar methods for your area.

Cleaning Solution

Mix 220 milliliters of fluid chloride of lime to 18 liters of water for each 10 cubic meters of sand.

How to Use

After mixing this solution, pour it into a watering can, which can then be used to distribute the mixture evenly over the sandbox. Use a stick to mix the sand and disinfectant. Following the application of the solution, hose down the sandbox so that the disinfectant will penetrate the sand at lower levels. Before allowing children to use the sandbox area, turn the sand over one shovel deep to ensure even mixing.

looking for fund-raising projects and agreed to discuss the playground situation at its upcoming meeting. Perhaps there is hope after all for the much-needed improvements that have been discussed for the playground.

Parents and community members can play an important role in planning and preparing the outdoor environment. A big challenge, however, is to first convince them that this is a valuable activity for children. Can something so uninhibited and joyful as outdoor play also be a quality learning experience? Teachers need to convince the doubters that the outdoor setting is indeed a rich opportunity for growth. Research and writing supporting the importance of outdoor play for young children are limited. Therefore, concerned teachers will need to provide time for adults to observe and/or discuss this option before many will feel comfortable supporting play outdoors.

Once convinced of its importance, parents and community members can be invaluable in helping prepare a quality playground environment for young children. Through donations of money, materials, and the time needed to construct basic equipment, major improvements in the outdoor play equipment available to children can be made (Jambor, 1994a). With careful planning, this option can provide safe, durable, and creative play options at a fraction of the cost of commercial equipment.

When thinking of parent and community support, it is also helpful to remember that extra pairs of hands are very valuable outdoors as well. Woodworking experiences, for example, frequently require that an adult be present or nearby for safety reasons. These projects are less likely to be available if the teacher is alone outdoors. Consider the benefits of having an adult assist with

VIDEO CASE STUDY:
Playgrounds

Watch the ABC News video segment "Playgrounds" and consider these excerpts:

"Can it be that this place is hazardous? A child's playground, dangerous? Well, 185,000 Americans, virtually all of them children, get hurt on playgrounds every year. Fifteen are killed."

— Jed Duvall, ABC Correspondent

"By one count, there are more than 1,000 lawsuits in California courts alone involving injuries and playground equipment. In Colorado, a Health Department survey of 72 playgrounds turned up unsafe conditions in 95% of them. These things are wrong, many now think, in the traditional playground: the sandbox is dirty; the monkey bars are slippery; the swings are in the wrong place—a kid swinging can slam into one walking."

— Jed Duvall, ABC Correspondent

VIDEO CASE STUDY: Playgrounds

Now that you have seen the ABC News video segment, consider this information from the Consumer Product Safety Commission (CPSC) and The National Playground Safety Institute (NPSI). They have identified twelve of the leading causes of injury on playgrounds, and have issued the following guidelines for playground safety:

1. Improper Protective Surfacing

The surface or ground under and around the playground equipment should be soft enough to cushion a fall. Improper surfacing material under playground equipment is the leading cause of playground-related injuries. Since over seventy percent of all accidents on playgrounds are from children falling, maintaining protective surfacing under and around all playground equipment is the most critical safety factor on playgrounds.

Hard surfaces are not acceptable under play equipment. Concrete and blacktop do not have any shock absorbing properties, and packed earth or grass loses its ability to absorb shock during a fall through wear and environmental conditions. A fall onto one of these hard surfaces could be life threatening.

There are many surfaces that offer protection from falls. **Acceptable surfaces are hardwood fiber/mulch, sand, and pea gravel. These surfaces must be maintained at a depth of twelve inches, be free of standing water and debris, and not be allowed to become compacted**. There are also synthetic or rubber tiles and mats that are appropriate for use under play equipment.

2. Inadequate Fall Zone

A fall zone or use zone is the area under and around the playground equipment where a child might fall. **A fall zone should be covered with protective surfacing material and extend a minimum of six feet in all directions from the edge of stationary play equipment such as climbers and chin-up bars.**

The fall zone at the bottom or exit area of a slide should extend a minimum of six feet from the end of the slide for slides four feet or less in height. For slides higher than four feet, take the entrance height of the slide and add four feet to determine how far the surfacing should extend from the end of the slide.

Swings require a much greater area for the fall zone. **The fall zone should extend two times the height of the pivot or swing hanger in front of and behind the swing's seat. The fall zone should also extend six feet to the side of the support structure.**

3. Protrusion & Entanglement Hazards

A protrusion hazard is a component or piece of hardware that might be capable of impaling or cutting a child if a child should fall against the hazard. Some protrusions are also capable of catching drawstrings or items of clothing which might be worn around a child's neck. This type of entanglement is especially hazardous because it might result in strangulation. Special attention should be paid to the area at the top of slides and sliding devices. Look for:

- Bolt ends that extend more than two threads beyond the face of the nut.

- Hardware configurations that form a hook or leave a gap between components.

- Open "S" type hooks.

- Rungs or handholds that protrude outward from a support structure.

- Ropes that are not anchored securely at both ends that could form a loop or a noose.

4. Entrapment in Openings

Enclosed openings on playground equipment must be checked for head entrapment hazards. Children often enter openings feet first and attempt to slide through the opening. If the opening is not large enough it may allow the body to pass through the opening and entrap the head. **There should be no openings on playground equipment that measure between three and one half inches and nine inches.** Where the ground forms the lower boundary of the opening is not considered to be hazardous. Pay special attention to openings at the top of a slide, openings between platforms, and openings on climbers where the distance between rungs might be less than nine inches.

5. Insufficient Equipment Spacing

Improper spacing between pieces of play equipment can cause overcrowding of a play area which may create several hazards. Fall zones for equipment that is higher than twenty-four inches above the ground cannot overlap. **Therefore there should be a minimum of twelve feet in between two play structures.** This provides room for children to circulate and prevents the possibility of a child falling off of one structure and striking another structure. Swings and other pieces of moving equipment should be located in an area away from other structures.

6. Trip Hazards

Trip hazards are created by play structure components or items on the playground. Common trip hazards include:

- Exposed concrete footings
- Abrupt changes in surface elevations
- Containment borders
- Tree roots and tree stumps
- Rocks

7. Lack of Supervision:

The supervision of a playground environment directly relates to the overall safety of the environment. **A play area should be designed so that it is easy for a parent or caregiver to observe the children at play.** Young children are constantly challenging their own abilities, very often not being able to recognize potential hazards. It is estimated that over forty percent of all playground injuries are directly related to lack of supervision in some way. Parents must supervise their children in some way on the playground!

8. Age-Inappropriate Activities

Children's developmental needs vary greatly from age two to age twelve. In an effort to provide a challenging and safe play environment for all ages it is important to **make sure that the equipment in the playground setting is appropriate for the age of the intended user.** Areas for preschool age children should be separate from areas intended for school-age children.

9. Lack of Maintenance

Find out if your playground has a designated official who periodically inspects the playground. In order for playgrounds to remain in safe condition, a program of systematic, preventive maintenance must be present. Look for:

• Hardware that is loose or worn, or that has protrusions or projections.

• Exposed equipment footings.

• Scattered debris, litter, rocks, or tree roots.

• Wood, metal, or plastic that shows signs of fatigue or deterioration.

• Rust and chipped paint on metal components.

• Splinters, large cracks, and decayed wood components.

• Deterioration and corrosion on structural components that connect to the ground.

• Missing, damaged, or worn-out equipment components, such as handholds, guardrails, swing seats.

• Surfacing material that has not been maintained to the proper 12-inch depth.

• Signs of vandalism

the garden area. A parent with a special interest in plants and gardening could share this important talent with children in the outdoor classroom. Parent and community support can clearly strengthen the curriculum outdoors, just as in the classroom.

Committing to the Outdoor Environment

Playgrounds should be an extension of the indoor environment. D. Cohen (1994) suggests that play outdoors can stimulate all aspects of children's development if we plan for these many options.

If this perspective is to become a reality, teachers of young children must set aside much of the traditional thinking about playgrounds and begin viewing the outdoors differently. Although fixed equipment is useful outdoors, it should be considered secondary in importance to the movable options described throughout this chapter. Children learn best by physically manipulating the materials and equipment in their environment, and these options should be readily available to them outdoors.

This new way of thinking about playgrounds can be relatively easily and inexpensively implemented. Educators, with the help of parents and community members, can construct simple pieces of playground equipment from materials available in their local communities. Providing additional scrounged materials will encourage further creative play experiences. If educators think creatively about what is available to children indoors and bring those materials or similar ones outdoors, they will add diversity to the outdoor play options. Finally, the purchase of movable commercial equipment can support additional play options for children. When educators take these steps, children can have a play space outdoors that truly stimulates all aspects of child development (see Chapter 4) and provides children with a rich and varied playground experience.

But this rethinking of the outdoor space also must include a further commitment by teachers to planning and facilitating play in this setting. Teachers must plan each week for new and interesting play options outdoors. This means committing additional time to organizing and changing this play space regularly. Already-busy teachers must find the time needed to creatively prepare this space in addition to preparing the indoor setting. And teachers must also spend time outdoors with children, committing to the interactions needed to ensure that teachers facilitate outdoor play experiences in much the same way as indoor play.

This is by no means a small task. Teachers who decide to move in this direction must realize the commitment they are making in terms of time and energy. Yet, this is one area of the early childhood curriculum that has been significantly underestimated and has the potential for being a rich part of the lives of children. The benefits to children are great, and enriching outdoor play experiences will pay many dividends in terms of healthier, happier children.

Summary

Outdoor play is often devalued in early education. In this chapter, however, you learned of the importance of this activity and gained insights into planning quality playgrounds for young children. Children need different outdoor play spaces such as a transition area, manipulative/construction space, dramatic play, physical area, sand/water play, and a natural area. Teachers can design the playground to meet the developmental needs of infants/toddlers, preschool children, primary students, and children with special needs. The playground can incorporate commercial equipment, donated materials, and adult-made equipment. Regular change in the outdoor play environment is stimulating for children, and teachers should plan for these changes. Teachers and playground planners need to be aware of health and safety issues and must address these in the playground design. Finally, parent and community involvement can enrich playground activities; teachers are a vital force in educating parents and community members about the need for renewed commitment to outdoor activities for young children.

∾ For Discussion and Action

1. Is it worth all the effort required to make the outdoor play area more like the indoor classroom? Why or why not?

2. Visit a playground for young children, and look critically for the following: safety problems (surfacing, placement of equipment, developmentally inappropriate, etc.); fixed equipment (what is available and what condition is it in?); and movable equipment (describe).

3. Talk to a teacher of young children, and find out how much time children spend playing outdoors. What are the typical activities children get involved in? What problems does the teacher see associated with outdoor play?

4. Sketch a simple piece of equipment that could be built for use on the playground.

5. How do weather conditions influence outdoor play in your area? Can you think of ways to minimize the negative influences of weather for playground use?

6. Plan and actually put together a prop box that could be used to stimulate dramatic play outdoors.

∾ Building Your Personal Library

Frost, J. (1992). *Play and playscapes.* Albany, NY: Delmar Publishers. This book provides an in-depth discussion of historical perspectives on playgrounds, clear guidelines for playground development, key points on playground safety issues, and important information on adult roles on the playground.

10. Pinch, Crush, Shearing, and Sharp Edge Hazards

Components in the play environment should be inspected to make sure that there are no sharp edges or points that could cut skin. There should be no dangerous pieces of hardware, such as protruding bolt ends and narrow gaps in metal connections. Exposed hardware can cut children and puncture skin.

Moving components should be checked to make sure that there are no moving parts or mechanisms that might crush or pinch a child's finger. These mechanisms can be found on suspension bridges, track rides, merry-go-rounds, seesaws, and some swings.

11. Platforms with No Guardrails

Elevated surfaces such as platforms, ramps, and bridgeways should have guardrails that would prevent accidental falls. Preschool-age children are more at risk from falls. **Equipment intended for preschool-age children should have guardrails on elevated surfaces higher than twenty inches. Equipment intended for school-age children should have guardrails on elevated surfaces higher than thirty inches.**

12. Equipment Not Recommended for Public Playgrounds

Accidents associated with the following types of equipment have resulted in the Consumer Product Safety Commission recommending that they **not be** used on public playgrounds:

• Heavy swings such as animal figure swings or multiple occupancy/glider type swings.

• Free swinging ropes that may fray or form a loop.

• Swinging exercise rings or trapeze bars; they are considered athletic equipment and **not** recommended for public playgrounds. (Overhead hanging rings that have a short amount of chain and are intended for use as a ring trek—generally four to eight rings—are allowed on public playground equipment.)

[Adapted from information in the public domain provided by the Consumer Product Safety Commission, Office of Information and Public Affairs, Washington, D.C. 20207. http://www.cpsc.gov/cpscpub/pubs/playtips.html]

As a teacher and caregiver, you will be responsible for providing safe play opportunities for children. Go to your local school or community playground, and use this checklist and the information above to inspect the facilities and environment. How does it compare to the safety guidelines issued by the CPSC and NPSI? Mark the checklist below with an X in the left column if the playground has any one of the hazards discussed previously. Briefly describe the hazard in the column on the right.

X	Type of Playground Hazard	Description of Hazard
	1. Improper Protective Surfacing	
	2. Inadequate Fall Zone	
	3. Protrusion & Entanglement Hazards	
	4. Entrapment in Openings Hazards	
	5. Insufficient Equipment Spacing	
	6. Trip Hazards	
	7. Lack of Supervision	
	8. Age-Inappropriate Activities	
	9. Lack of Maintenance	
	10. Pinch, Crush, Shearing, and Sharp Edge Hazards	
	11. Platforms with No Guardrails	
	12. Equipment Not Recommended for Public Playgrounds	

If you marked any items with an "X," what would be the next appropriate action to take? Which school or park official could you notify to make sure the appropriate maintenance or repair work is completed?

Guddemi, M., & Jambor, T. (Eds.). (1993). *A right to play*. Little Rock, AR: Southern Early Childhood Association. The articles in this edited book make a strong case for allowing children creative play experiences both indoors and on the playground. Many suggestions are provided on preparing the outdoor setting and ways in which adults can support the play opportunities there.

Hewes, J. (1975). *Build your own playground*. Boston: Houghton Mifflin. Describes the procedures necessary for getting parents and community members organized and involved in constructing inexpensive playground equipment. Presents many drawings and pictures of possible projects.

Marston, L. (1984). *Playground equipment*. Jefferson, NC: McFarland and Company. This book is full of sketches of playground structures that adults can build inexpensively and with average construction skills. The ideas are adaptable to a variety of ages within the early childhood range.

Rivkin, M. (1995). *The great outdoors: Restoring children's right to play outside*. Washington, DC: National Association for the Education of Young Children. This little book is a must-read for those who are not yet convinced of the importance of outdoor play. Rivkin makes an impassioned plea for the child's right to quality outdoor play experiences and gives many good resources to help the interested reader get started.

In this chapter you will

- Study the components of developmentally appropriate curriculum.
- Understand the importance of observations in planning and assessment activities.
- Learn about activity and lesson planning.
- Identify elements of an integrated curriculum and the project approach.
- Read about scheduling issues and the curriculum.
- Clarify the important elements of assessment in the early childhood classroom.

Mary Beth's mother just finished talking to you following the Open House. She is concerned about allowing children time to play in the second-grade classroom. The curriculum has so many required components that taking major blocks of time to play just doesn't seem right to her. This conversation is no surprise to you as the classroom teacher. Having recently modified your activities to provide a more developmentally appropriate curriculum, you expected this response from some of your parents. The letter you sent home before the school year began emphasized this shift and encouraged parents to come in to see the learning that was taking place. Although several did drop in, others still need to be convinced. Tonight's discussion on developmentally appropriate practice seemed to help others understand as well. Time and more positive communications appear to be needed before this issue can be fully resolved.

Creating a more play-oriented, developmentally appropriate curriculum will probably generate the kind of response just described. Parents, other teachers, and administrators often need to be convinced that an approach to teaching and learning that includes freedom of choice, manipulation of real-world materials, and child-directed learning is appropriate for young children. This is particularly true at the primary level. When the more traditional curriculum is balanced with one that actively engages children in learning through hands-on manipulation of materials in their environment, adults unfamiliar with this approach must learn more before they can accept it as valuable for young children.

Creating a Developmentally Appropriate Curriculum

Although preparing a play-oriented, developmentally appropriate curriculum may appear rather simple, it is actually a challenging task requiring clear understandings of children and their development. Earlier chapters in this text have outlined important components in this process. Understanding child development and learning (Chapter 4), the importance of play (Chapter 5), and working with parents (Chapter 7) are all essential to the developmentally appropriate curriculum.

Guidelines for the Developmentally Appropriate Curriculum

The National Association for the Education of Young Children (NAEYC) has identified nine guidelines for a developmentally appropriate curriculum:

- It provides for all aspects of the child's development (physical, social, emotional, and cognitive).
- The curriculum for young children is intellectually interesting and meaningful to them.
- New knowledge is built upon already existing understandings and abilities.
- Much of the time, traditional subject matter areas are integrated, rather than taught separately, to help children make more meaningful connections and develop richer concepts.
- Although learning concepts and skills is important, the early childhood curriculum should also emphasize the development of problem-solving skills and an interest in lifelong learning.
- An age-appropriate curriculum for early childhood education also has intellectual integrity. It challenges children to use the concepts and tools of the different disciplines.
- While supporting the child's home culture and language, a quality curriculum also strengthens the ability to participate in the shared culture.
- Goals for the curriculum are reasonable and attainable for most children.
- Technology used in the early childhood classroom is physically and philosophically integrated into the classroom curriculum (Bredekamp & Copple, 1997).

Due to the unique makeup of each child and the diverse mix of children found in every early childhood classroom, it is not possible to simply pick up a teacher's guide and begin teaching. The developmentally appropriate curriculum must be tailored to the needs and interests of the children involved. Although this is a more difficult way to teach, the end result is a classroom in which active, excited learners are growing to their fullest potential.

Developmental Considerations

In addition to the preceding guidelines, early childhood teachers must base their planning on specific developmental characteristics of children. Activities and lessons will vary markedly between infant/toddler, preschool, and primary classrooms because of these developmental differences.

INTO PRACTICE . . .

Making National News Developmentally Appropriate

Young children encounter much information about the world around them that is difficult for them to understand. Much of the information parents view on television news programs or read in their local newspaper fits this category. Children are being either directly or indirectly exposed to news about earthquakes, tornadoes, floods, violence, and murder on a regular basis. Although young children will not understand these events in an adult way, it is often important to address these issues in interactions with them. McMath (1997) gives an example of this type and her response to the child:

> Recently, one child in a group of five said to me, "A lot of little kids got killed and bad mens blowed them up." "Yes," I replied, "some children did die, and I feel very sad. I'm glad that we are together and safe. All the grownups who know and love you are glad, too." (p. 82)

As may be evident from this example, children can learn of complex and frightening situations that require sensitive adults to support them in making sense of the information they have gathered. Developmentally appropriate responses include the following:

- Answer children's questions honestly and in terms they can understand.
- Take cues from children about how much or how little to tell them and what they are really interested in knowing (McMath, 1997).
- Tell students that caring adults in their lives will keep them safe and provide for their needs.
- Verbalize for children the fears and concerns that they appear to be having.
- Discuss issues with parents when children bring up news items they don't understand.

Caregivers at the infant/toddler level need to know, for example, that children are learning a great deal through the use of their senses. The environment should be richly furnished with materials that engage the child's sight, touch, hearing, taste, and smell. Colorful crib hangings, pictures of human faces, mirrors, and cheerful room furnishings all help create an exciting visual environment. Similarly, toys that infants and toddlers can shake, drop, squeeze, and push are effective tactile stimulants. By actively exploring these and other sensory materials, children are learning a great deal about their ever-expanding world.

Although developmental considerations are different during the preschool years, they are equally important in curriculum planning. For example, an understanding of emotional development at this age should influence the selection of books read to children. Reading and discussing books like *William's Doll* (Zolotow, 1985) and *Girls Can Be Anything* (Klein, 1973), for example, should be helpful to children as they struggle with stereotypic expectations.

During the early elementary years, curriculum planning is strongly influenced by local school district and state guidelines. At the same time, teachers at this level must develop lessons and use materials that match the developmental abilities and interests of these children. For example, primary children are developing the basic physical skills needed for games such as baseball and basketball. And while many children at this age show an interest in sports, they often become frustrated with the competitive element. The creative adult can teach the physical skills needed while encouraging children to play noncompetitive versions of these sports. Through an understanding of both the physical and emotional aspects of typical primary-aged children, the teacher can successfully introduce traditional sports activities.

Observation as a Curriculum Tool

Teachers who want to develop curricula based on student interests must find effective strategies for determining these preferences. Observing children as they work and play provides adults with many opportunities to gain these insights.

> As Maria and Angie play in the dress-up area in their preschool classroom, they are talking about Angie's mom, who is pregnant and expecting a new baby in a few months. After listening to their conversation for a few minutes, you realize that this issue is important to both these girls as well as several other children in the class. Raul has a new baby sister, and Maggie's mom just mentioned the other day that she was going in for a pregnancy test. Perhaps this topic could be part of the focus for the upcoming discussion on families.

Although teachers use many different types of observation techniques, the **anecdotal record** may be the most useful for curriculum planning. These brief written notes should include the date and time of the observation, who was observed, what the children were doing, and the words spoken. Despite the short time available for making good observations, the teacher should make every effort to provide as much detail as possible to clarify what was occurring. It is also important to separate what is actually seen and heard from your interpretation of events. One simple way to do this is to include insights that go beyond the actual behaviors in parentheses. These techniques require considerable effort to do well. Brief, specific notes should be made throughout the day to identify what children are learning:

> 8/29/97, 9:30 AM, Pat and Marcie (both age three), Block Area
> On the rug in the block area, Pat says: "Let's make a barn and pasture for our horses! Then we can play farm." (The class went on a field trip to a farm last week.) Marcie replies, "What about all the other animals? Where will the pigs and cows and chickens go?"

Taking time to make observations of children in your classroom is never an easy task. Preparing for each activity, assisting children who need your help, and teaching both large and small groups leaves little time for anything else. Yet, teachers frequently mention that observation is an essential element of the teaching/learning process. By carrying writing materials around throughout the school day and jotting brief but accurate notes about behaviors observed and comments made, teachers can develop a much clearer understanding of children's interests. This can ease curriculum planning and focus the curriculum on children's preferences.

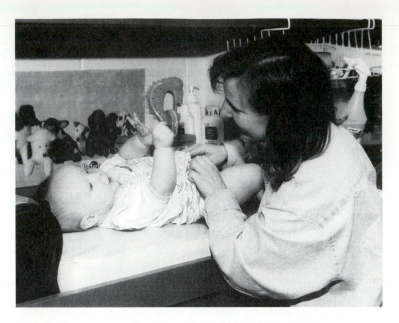

Diaper changing should be a rewarding and educational experience for the young child.

Curriculum Goals

In addition to knowing general guidelines for developmentally appropriate practice, creating a strong curriculum for young children requires a clear sense of what you are trying to accomplish. **Curriculum goals** are broad learning outcomes that identify the key results anticipated from the educational process. Goals are often created as part of a school-wide mission statement identifying the philosophy and values of the program. Because the goals are general, however, your personal interpretation of these goals may differ somewhat from those of other teachers with whom you work. It is important to stop and reflect on these broad learning outcomes and make decisions about how they can be implemented in your early childhood classroom.

In a developmentally appropriate program for young children, the curriculum goals should include all aspects of child development. The following are examples of common expectations in programs for young children:

- *Physical goals* (two-year-olds)
    1. Scribble using large crayons or other similar art materials.
    2. Develop ability to engage in running activities for short distances.

- *Social goals* (four-year-olds)
    1. Learn to control nonproductive impulses such as hitting and taking things without asking.

2. Listen when others are speaking, take turns talking, and use other conventions of communication.

- *Emotional goals* (five-year-olds)
  1. Use words to describe and deal with feelings experienced.
  2. Develop a sense of competence at school-related tasks.

- *Cognitive goals* (eight-year-olds)
  1. Use the scientific method to explore materials presented.
  2. Know and use the arithmetic operations of addition, subtraction, multiplication, and division.

Planning Activities and Lessons

The starting point for an effective early childhood curriculum is the physical setting itself. Developmentally appropriate activities require careful planning and preparation of the indoor and outdoor environments. Chapters 9 and 10 address these important topics.

Once these settings are prepared, however, much remains to be done in developing specific events for each day. The teacher should create **long-term plans** to give a sense of direction for several weeks, months, or even the entire school year. Because they are general plans, they provide a flexible framework for building a more specific curriculum as the year progresses. The teacher then prepares **short-term plans** weekly and daily to identify the activities children will be engaging in.

Whenever possible, the teacher should base these activities on children's interests.

Adam, a third-grade student, has just shared his rock collection during show and tell. Students were attentive and asked him many good questions about his specimens. You have decided to build several upcoming science activities around topics related to rocks and how they are formed.

After identifying student interests, the teacher must make decisions about procedures to be followed and materials needed. Hildebrand (1994) suggests that teachers begin by brainstorming possible pathways to investigate the topics selected. For example, an interest in the postal service by seven-year-olds could be studied in many different ways, including the following:

- Read written information about mail carriers and the postal service.
- Invite a postal employee into the classroom to talk about her work.
- Set up a post office in the classroom where children can create and send mail to one another.
- Visit a local post office to tour the facilities and see how mail is sorted and moved.
- Take a neighborhood walk to notice the different mailboxes that families use for their mail.

Activity planning should include some organized experiences indoors.

Once activities have been selected, the teacher must then plan times during the week when they can be implemented, organize the materials, schedule guests and field trips, and identify specific procedures for each activity. Experienced teachers accomplish this portion of their planning by making relatively brief notes to themselves. New teachers, however, may find that more detailed written plans are necessary for successful activities. The next two sections of this chapter describe options for creating effective activity and lesson plans.

Activity Planning.

✍ *Ryan and Amy are building together in the block area of their kindergarten classroom. Following a recent field trip to a local dairy farm, the play during center time has focused around this theme. Amy and Ryan are no exception. They are busily constructing a fenced pasture and barn for their dairy herd. It is clear from the conversation that much has been learned from the field trip, and the play theme is allowing them both to consolidate their understandings of this topic.*

Because play opportunities like those of Amy and Ryan are such an important part of the early childhood curriculum, planning for these experiences is a high

Figure 11–1   Mathematics Activity Plan

Purposes

1. Identify the geometric shapes of square, triangle, and parallelogram.
2. Use the tangram shapes to build a pattern matching those on accompanying cards.

Materials and Preparation

1. Tangram puzzle pieces (three sets). Each set consists of seven geometric shapes that fit together to form a square.
2. Pattern cards.
3. Select pattern cards of varying difficulties to challenge ability levels of different children.

Procedures

1. Discuss tangrams at group time, describing how they can be used to create patterns illustrated on accompanying cards.
2. Place tangram sets and pattern cards in the mathematics center for children to use during choice time.
3. Observe the mathematics center for tangram use, assisting children as needed.

Possible Variations

1. Encourage interested students to create their own pattern cards that others can use with the tangram sets.
2. Consider having some children work in pairs to solve puzzle patterns. Joint problem solving may be an important confidence booster for some students.

Evaluation

1. Observe students working with the tangram sets to see if they are enjoying the task and using effective problem-solving strategies as they work.
2. Discuss tangrams at group time to see if students use appropriate terminology for shapes and to determine if pattern cards are at an appropriate level of difficulty.

priority. It should be clear, however, that because play is open-ended and child-directed, the activity plans themselves must take into consideration this important element. Flexibility is a key component of these plans.

Teachers use many different formats for written activity plans, each of which has its own strengths and limitations. The essential elements, however, include purposes for the activity, materials and preparation needed, procedures to follow, variations that may be introduced, and an evaluation component. Figure 11–1 provides an example of a mathematics activity plan for a second-grade classroom.

Initially, developing detailed activity plans like the one in Figure 11–1 is necessary to ensure successful learning experiences for children. Every piece of play material found in the early childhood classroom should have a specific purpose, and the teacher should clearly understand procedures for effective use. With several centers and perhaps hundreds of options available to children, however, writing detailed plans for each experience is clearly overwhelming for the full-time teacher. Taking these planning steps while learning to be a teacher makes it possible to succeed with more mental planning later.

Lesson Planning.

> ◐   *Group time is the next scheduled event for your group of four-year-olds. Today, after singing two or three songs, a story is planned, followed by a movement activity, a discussion of growing plants, and more singing. A busy, but typical agenda.*

To make group times positive experiences, the teacher of young children must be well-organized and prepared. Lesson planning can help ensure success. Although similar to the activity plans described previously, lesson plans tend to be more specific in defining the teacher's procedures, questions, and comments. Although still flexible, lesson plans often focus more on specific learnings and predetermined procedures. A typical lesson plan includes objectives, introduction, content, methods and procedure, closure, resources and materials, and evaluation (Moore, 1995). A sample plan for the group time just described appears in Figure 11–2.

The Integrated Curriculum

> ◐   *Mariah and Amanda are working intently at the kitchen table in Mariah's home. These second-grade children recently returned from the local community's Fourth of July ceremonies. Intrigued by the concept of Independence Day, they researched the topic on the computer and became fascinated with the clothing from that period of American history. After making a list of interesting tidbits gleaned from the computer, they are now busy sketching out some articles of clothing they hope to make for their dolls. With some adult assistance, this interest could become a long-term project with considerable learning potential. Language, mathematics, and social studies are just a few of the naturally occurring curriculum elements built in to this experience. Mariah and Amanda are engaging in an integrated learning experience.*

Why Implement an Integrated Curriculum?

One important reason for using an integrated curriculum is evident from the preceding example: It is a natural way of learning that matches what children and adults do outside the classroom. Krogh (1995) describes an example of integrated adult learning in the real world: buying a car. Reading ads and brochures, computing payments, investigating fuel efficiency and engine power, considering the car's aesthetic appeal, and negotiating with the salesperson require language,

Figure 11–2 *Group-Time Lesson Plan for Four-Year-Olds*

Objectives

1. Students will participate in songs, listen to the story, and be involved in the movement activity.
2. Children will be able to identify the root system, stems, and leaves in three drawings of plants.

Introduction

1. "I brought a special living thing from my home today to share with the class. It is hidden in this brown grocery bag. It sits in my window sill at home. I water it once a week. Can anyone guess what it is?"
2. After giving children an opportunity to guess the bag's contents, remove the plant, and discuss its roots, stems, and leaves.
3. "Today at group time, we are going to spend time talking about plants and how they grow. Let's begin by singing a new song."

Content

1. Introduce new song about flower gardens. Sing two familiar songs.
2. Read a story about plants.
3. Movement activity to music.
4. Discussion of plants.
5. Concluding songs.

Methods and Procedure

1. Sing "Flower Garden" from *Piggyback Songs* and one or two other student choices for songs.
2. Read *In the Garden* by Eugene Booth.
3. Play "Over in the Meadow" by Raffi (*Baby Beluga* tape), and have children move to the music.
4. Use plant drawings to discuss the root system, stems, and leaves of plants.
5. Sing concluding songs chosen by children.

Closure

1. Put plant and drawings of plants out in the science area for children to use during free play time.
2. Have bean seeds, pots, and soil available outdoors for students interested in growing their own plants.

Resources and Materials

1. Plant from home, book, audiotape, and plant drawings described above.
2. Bean seeds, pots, and soil for planting activity.

Evaluation

1. As children discuss plant components during group time, are they able to accurately identify them?
2. Do children spend time observing the plant and drawings placed in the science center? Do they use appropriate terminology in describing what they observe?

mathematics, science, art, and social studies learnings. This is definitely an integrated (and complicated) real-world educational experience. Clearly, the lives of both children and adults are full of these naturally occurring integrated learning times.

Integrated learning makes the curriculum more relevant. Mathematics, for example, can be taught as a series of procedures and rote memorization tasks. Unfortunately, this approach fails to make mathematics meaningful and interesting to children. On the other hand, when adults demonstrate the usefulness of mathematics in real-life situations, such as computing the time it will take to save up allowances to buy a pair of roller blades, children can see the relevance of their learning and get excited about mathematics. Similarly, reading has little value until these skills can be applied to written topics that are of interest to children and that they want to know more about.

The integrated curriculum also takes advantage of the child's natural way of learning. That is, hands-on manipulation of materials is more likely in an integrated approach. Typically, this curriculum is organized around themes of interest to children. For example, a theme or unit on birds for a second-grade classroom could emphasize activities that include reading, mathematics, science, and social studies learnings, all of which involve children in reading, talking about, and manipulating materials.

A quality program based on integrated learning also allows for more in-depth study of the themes chosen. Because all content areas are considered in the planning of thematic units, longer blocks of time can be spent engaging in these learning activities. Rather than breaking the afternoon into half-hour segments for the study of mathematics, reading, social studies, and science, a first-grade teacher could plan and present an exciting thematic unit on community helpers using a larger block of time each day. Students could use graphing skills, for example, to chart the number of fires in the community within the last year. Children could read and discuss books on community helpers. A trip to the police station helps children learn more about their community. Letters of thanks to visiting community helpers provide opportunities for writing experiences. This type of integrated learning experience gives children more time to develop deeper and more relevant understandings of the concepts being learned.

Planning and Preparation

At first glance, the planning needed for integrated learning may seem easier and less complicated than for a more traditional curriculum. After all, it is a natural way for learning outside the classroom, and little preparation is needed for those experiences. Why can't we just gather some good materials together, and then just turn children loose with them and see what they come up with?

Unfortunately, planning an integrated curriculum is just not that simple. This approach is definitely more complicated and demanding for the classroom teacher than a more traditional curriculum. More planning and preparation are required, rather than less. For one thing, no how-to manuals clearly and specifically lay out a

Constance Kamii and Georgia DeClark (1985), a researcher and primary teacher, respectively, wrote a book describing the benefits of young children reinventing their mathematical understanding. Based on the theories of Jean Piaget, this book presents a detailed account of children constructing arithmetic understanding through play. The authors developed a complete first-grade mathematics curriculum based entirely on group games and activities that focus on everyday events in the lives of children. Some examples of activities and games of this type include the following:

Voting

In DeClark's first-grade classroom, she strongly encouraged voting on many issues throughout the day. This allowed children to use arithmetic skills in meaningful ways. For example, children had a chance to vote on the number of times they needed to practice writing letters in their journals. One child suggested six times on each line, and a second child thought nine times was more appropriate. Then children voted on which option they preferred, with twenty preferring six times, and five wanting the nine repetitions. On this occasion, after the votes were recorded, one child wanted to change his vote from nine repetitions to six. This allowed the class to discuss the results of

adding one vote to the first column and removing one from the second. Meaningful mathematics was being practiced.

Group Games

DeClark and Kamii used some common card games to promote additional arithmetic practice in more fun ways for first-grade children. The card game War is one example. Children use a deck of cards, and split them into equal piles (one for each child playing). Each child turns the top card up in her stack, and the child with the card having the highest numeral wins that set of cards. Tic-tac-toe is an example of a board game that DeClark encouraged as well. Although this activity doesn't build arithmetic skills, it helps children decenter (see things from another's perspective), which is important to growth in intellectual functioning.

1. *What do you see as the strengths and limitations of reinventing mathematics or any other curriculum area? Discuss your thoughts with classmates.*

2. *Why is play critical to this approach to learning? What is the role of play in the reinvention process?*

strong integrated curriculum for young children. Although good books are available (see, e.g., A. Mitchell & David, 1992) that provide effective guidance for the planning *process,* they are, of necessity, general in their focus. Because integrated learning should be based on student interests and abilities, themes selected and activities used will vary from one classroom to the next.

The starting point for planning an integrated curriculum is to **select appropriate themes.** The teacher should base the choice of topics primarily on the needs and interests of children, which will vary from one group of children to the next. Children in coastal Alaska, for example, would probably be interested in the life cycle of salmon, whereas those in Arizona would be more likely to find a study of cacti more relevant.

Although childhood needs and interests are the most important factors in selecting themes, it is also valuable to consider your own interests as a teacher. You will be spending large blocks of time and energy in preparing the materials and activities needed for the themes chosen. If the topic is something you can get excited about as an adult, the children are much more likely to do the same.

After selecting an appropriate theme, Dodge and Colker (1992) suggest the following steps in thematic planning:

- Learn about the topic selected.
- Find and organize materials related to the theme.
- Reflect on what you want the children to learn.
- Identify open-ended questions to encourage inquiry.
- Plan activities and lessons related to the theme.
- Invite parent participation.
- Determine a closing event or activity.
- Evaluate the theme and what children have learned.

To **learn about the chosen topic,** the teacher must become a student and read books and related written materials, explore field trip possibilities, talk to others who are more expert on the subject, and engage in some of the same activities that children may later explore. This process should be an exciting one—an opportunity to learn and grow as an adult while preparing for children's learning.

Finding and organizing materials is time-consuming but important in thematic planning. Because understanding during the early childhood years is best gained through hands-on manipulation of materials, finding objects that enhance learning about the chosen topics is essential. Books, puzzles, props for play, and pictures are all examples of materials that the teacher can collect and use for specific themes. Resource books such as Hamilton, Flemming, and Hicks (1990) are useful at this point in the planning process to help locate appropriate materials.

Reflecting on what you want children to learn brings focus to the thematic planning. What is it, specifically, that you want children to gain from the activities you are planning? Once this question has been answered, the activities themselves are more easily identified. Time should also be spent at this point identifying the relationships between this specific theme and the overarching goals and objectives for the school year. The objectives should clearly fit with your overall plan.

The process of **identifying open-ended questions for inquiry** often begins with the children themselves. Ask children what they already know about the upcoming theme. What do they need clarified? Are there questions they want answered?

Obviously, younger children will need more assistance with this discussion, but beginning in the preschool years, this planning step can provide much helpful information in developing the theme.

Planning lessons and activities for a chosen theme usually starts with a process called **webbing.** Basically, webbing is a brainstorming technique that provides a visual overview of the content to be emphasized in a unit. The teacher begins by writing the theme title in the middle of a page and drawing curriculum spokes for each area to be addressed. Typically, language, mathematics, science, art, music and movement, and social studies are each represented as a spoke (Krogh, 1995). For each of these areas, then, the teacher identifies as many activities as possible that address the separate curricular domains. Other teachers, resource books, and the Internet are all useful in adding items in this brainstorming effort. A major advantage of the webbing process is that it quickly identifies areas of the curriculum that are either over- or under-represented. At this point, it is easy to add or delete items to better balance the curriculum.

After creating the curriculum web, most teachers then develop a written overview of the thematic unit. This unit overview identifies the major activities planned for each week. If the classroom is set up in centers, this summary sheet briefly describes thematic activities found in each area. This overview usually includes group-time experiences, daily snacks, and outdoor activities as well.

Finally, the teacher creates lessons and activities using planning strategies discussed earlier in this chapter. New teachers generally find that they need more written planning for successful efforts, while more experienced instructors do more of this step mentally. In either case, having a clear understanding of the specific procedures and materials needed for productive learning experiences is a critical step.

It is also important to **invite parent participation** in the planning, preparation, and teaching of thematic activities. Collecting materials at home, helping organize a field trip, assisting in the classroom, and making suggestions for activities and events are all things that parents can do to help. Not only will parent participation make your job as teacher easier, but it increases the likelihood that what is learned in school will be reinforced at home. When parents are involved in some way in curriculum planning and teaching, children benefit.

Deciding on a **closing event or activity** brings a positive ending to the unit of study. For the theme of pets, for example, the teacher might plan a pet show as a closing event. Children and parents could bring pictures, videos, and pet accessories to share with the rest of the class. Besides being an enjoyable event, the closing activity allows children to summarize what they have learned and get ready to move on to the next theme. It brings closure to the unit activities.

The final step in planning for thematic learning, which should actually be ongoing throughout the teaching and learning activities, is to **evaluate the theme and what children have learned.** The teacher can collect written observations of children and samples of their work and use these to assess the successes and areas for improvement in the unit. The teacher can share these materials with parents and others to document the students' growth through thematic teaching.

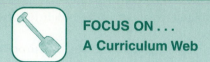
Your group of kindergarten children is interested in insects, so you decide to create a unit on this topic. The starting point for planning is a curriculum web:

1. What do you see as the benefits of curriculum webbing?

2. Choose a topic, and create a curriculum web for prekindergarten children.

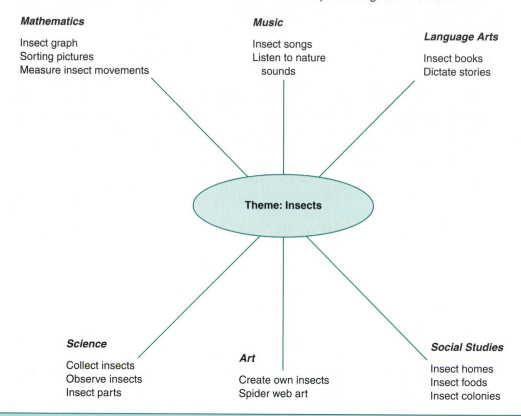

Mathematics

Insect graph
Sorting pictures
Measure insect movements

Music

Insect songs
Listen to nature
 sounds

Language Arts

Insect books
Dictate stories

Theme: Insects

Science

Collect insects
Observe insects
Insect parts

Art

Create own insects
Spider web art

Social Studies

Insect homes
Insect foods
Insect colonies

The Project Approach

Over the last several years, many teachers of young children have become interested in involving children in group projects. This trend has been strongly influenced by the impressive results of project work done by young children in prekindergarten programs in Reggio Emilia, Italy, described in Chapter 3 (see also

Computers with Internet access provide a wealth of information for project work.

C. Edwards, Gandini, & Forman, 1993). Although this approach to teaching is not new, it is receiving considerable attention by many educators.

A project can be described as an in-depth study of a topic of interest to children (Katz & Chard, 1989). Typically, a group of children within a class undertakes a project that springs from a desire to find answers to questions about the topic. The following situation is an example of how children become interested in a subject, which can then lead to an in-depth investigation:

> One day after a rainstorm five-year-old children noticed a large puddle in the schoolyard and asked to go outside to play. As they explored the puddle, stamping their boots, floating leaves, and making circles by casting pebbles, they noticed that their reflections were upside down. This discovery surprised them and led them to pose many questions and hypotheses. (C. Edwards & Springate, 1993, p. 9)

Edwards and Springate (1993) describe how teachers took advantage of the interests of these children to create a project that led in many different directions. Children wondered what would happen if everything in the world was upside down. This concept was discussed and explored. The rainy day also got students thinking about where water goes after the storm. They began a study of the underground areas of city streets. Each new insight led to further questions and new areas for investigation as the project continued to expand, grow, and change. At all times, the students' interests and questions provided direction for the project, while teachers helped focus their efforts and suggested materials and activities to explore the issues raised.

Katz and Chard (1989) describe three phases of a project. Phase one is called **getting started** and is the time when children and teacher spend several discussion periods selecting and refining the topic to be investigated. Phase two, **field work,** is the direct study of the project selected and may include field trips, activities, careful observations, drawings, models of the concept being studied, and discussions of findings. The final phase, **culminating and debriefing events,** consists of concluding activities that help children summarize their new learnings.

It should be clear from this discussion that project learning parallels the thematic approach described earlier. The major difference is that in project learning, the activities chosen and new directions taken are not clearly defined before beginning the study but, rather, are based on questions children pose along the way. Careful planning is still needed, but it is done daily and weekly to keep pace with children's changing interests and needs.

Scheduling Issues

In addition to carefully planning lessons and activities for young children, it is important to think about how all these events fit together to form a daily schedule. Teachers should consider several important issues as a schedule is created:

- **Length of the school day.** As the school day lengthens, teachers must plan rest/nap times, snacks/meals, outdoor options, and play times to accommodate the longer time span.

- **Large blocks of time.** When teachers plan a play-oriented, theme-based curriculum, children need large blocks of time. Thirty- to sixty-minute periods both indoors and outside make quality experiences possible.

- **A balance of active/quiet times.** Schedule planning must also take into consideration the need to have periods of both high physical activity and calmer, quieter times. These should be mixed throughout the program day.

- **Meeting children's needs.** The physical needs of young children require scheduled times as well. Teachers must consider time for snacks and meals, planned toileting opportunities, and rest/nap/quiet times.

- **Smooth transitions.** Younger children often struggle with transitions. Planning consistent times during the day for transitions helps make these times less stressful. The schedule should include times for arrival, departure, and cleanup after play.

- **Consistent sequence of events.** During the early childhood years children are just beginning to understand time; so, beginning centers activities each day at 9:15 is less important for this age than the fact that this experience follows group time. When activities follow a consistent sequence, children are more secure and content with the day. This deemphasis on rigid starting and ending points for activities provides additional flexibility to the day and enhances hands-on learning.

The sequence of events for an early childhood classroom varies from one room to the next, but sample schedules for full-day programs at both the prekindergarten and primary level follow:

	Four-Year-Old Program		Second-Grade Classroom
7:00 AM	Arrival, breakfast, limited centers	8:45 AM	Arrival, greetings
8:30 AM	Opening group	9:00 AM	Opening group time
8:45 AM	Indoor centers	9:15 AM	Learning centers
10:00 AM	Toileting, snack	10:30 AM	Outdoor play
10:30 AM	Outdoor time	11:00 AM	Reading
11:30 AM	Lunch	11:45 AM	Lunch/outdoors
Noon	Group time story	12:30 AM	Story time
12:30 PM	Quiet time	1:00 AM	Mathematics
2:00 PM	Center time	1:45 PM	Library/music/physical education
3:00 PM	Snack	2:30 PM	Silent, sustained reading
3:30 PM	Physical education/ outdoors	2:50 PM	Closing group
4:15 PM	Limited centers	3:15 PM	Departure
5:00 PM	Departure		

Assessment

The play-oriented, theme-based approach to the curriculum described here does not lend itself to the more traditional forms of evaluation commonly found in school settings. For instance, no tests assess the learning that is taking place in pretend play. Other, more appropriate, techniques must be used to appraise most aspects of student progress in the early childhood classroom. Observations of children have proven effective in both assessment and curriculum development. Portfolios (which often include observations) are the other major tool for evaluation in the early childhood classroom.

The Role of Observation in Assessment

As mentioned earlier, observation is an important tool in determining student needs and interests for curriculum planning. It is an equally valuable technique for assessment purposes. Because the physical space plays such an important role in early childhood education, observations of how children use their environment are an important aspect of evaluation. Do children avoid some areas or use other areas too often? Can children move easily from one center to the next? Which materials are children using? These are questions that need to be answered through careful observations of the environment.

Taking time to observe children as they work and play can pay big dividends.

An emphasis on developing the whole child provides an additional rationale for using observations of children in assessment. Identifying physical skill development, listening to oral language children are using as they play, and studying social interactions are all examples of important evaluation strategies that teachers can implement. Observations are often the best techniques to use in assessing these aspects of the child's development.

> ∾ *Raylynn is a cheerful first grader who is having difficulty learning to read. She tries hard, seems interested in books, and comes from a home that emphasizes the importance of school. Yet, her progress is agonizingly slow and difficult. Some careful observation may be needed to help determine the problems she faces. After several observations in the book corner, the teacher has decided to refer Raylynn for a vision test. She seems to have difficulty clearly seeing the printed letters and words.*

Early childhood classrooms have many children like Raylynn. They struggle with some aspect of learning or development, but the specific cause is not easily determined. Observations can again be useful in identifying the root problems and helping guide the teacher in choosing effective strategies for intervention.

A major reason we engage in evaluation experiences is to document the progress children are making in our programs. Parents, other teachers, administrators, and community members all want to know what skills children are learning through their efforts and ours. When children engage in hands-on learning, observation is again one of the best choices for assessing this progress. When observations are objective and detailed, they provide excellent records of what children have accomplished.

The **anecdotal record** described earlier in this chapter is one of the best observation tools to use for assessment purposes. A good anecdotal record should

- Include necessary identifying information (names of children observed, date and location of observation).
- Provide a continuous, detailed description of student behavior.
- Record only observed behavior during the observation time.
- Provide interpretation later than, and separate from, what was actually observed (Gallagher, 1998).

Read the box entitled, "Focus On . . . Making Good Observations." See if you are up to the challenge of refining a less effective anecdotal record.

If you stopped to rework those anecdotal records, you probably discovered that making good observations is a skill that requires considerable practice. Often, early attempts at observation are very general and not useful for planning purposes. Another common problem is that observers have difficulty distinguishing between what is actually being observed and their interpretation of the events taking place. Observations require time, energy, and practice to accomplish effectively.

A second observational technique that provides many insights is the **checklist.** Although published checklists are available for teacher use, many times, teachers need to develop an appropriate form. Wortham (1995) identifies four steps in creating a checklist:

1. Identify the skills to be included.
2. List separately the behaviors to be observed.
3. Sequence the checklist in order of complexity or difficulty.
4. Develop a simple system of record keeping.

After developing the checklist, the teacher merely places a check beside the items observed during the program day. When used consistently, the checklist can be an effective method of monitoring specific behaviors or equipment use.

The Portfolio and Its Use

"A portfolio is a way of compiling, organizing, and making sense of a wide variety of information about a child" (McAfee & Leong, 1994, p. 111). Although the use of portfolios in education is a relatively new assessment technique, the concept has been around for a long time. Artists and photographers, for example, have long

FOCUS ON . . .
Making Good Observations

Good observations force the adult to notice details in human behavior, record accurately what is seen, and separate interpretations from what was observed. This process is far from simple and requires considerable practice. The following two anecdotal record observations provide first, a good example, then one that needs considerable work.

Good Observation

 1/9/98 9:15 AM, Third Grade, Roosevelt Elementary

Emilio and Sharon are working together in the math center, using Cuisenaire Rods to solve multiples of ten mathematics problems. The current problem is 9×10. Emilio frowns as he looks at the problem card and says, "We don't have enough orange rods (ten-unit rod) to this one." Sharon pauses for a moment and then states, "That's okay, Emilio. We can use other rods that add up to ten. Two yellows equal ten, or a blue and white rod are the same as orange." (Strong problem-solving strategy.)

Weak Observation

2/10/98 2:45 PM, Kindergarten, Mountain View Elementary

Kerrie and Matt are <u>building with blocks</u> during free play time. They are <u>fighting over</u> who can use some of the blocks. <u>Matt took the materials he wanted</u> without asking and simply continued building his structure. <u>He needs to learn to use words to communicate his needs to others</u>.

1. Can you identify the elements that make the first observation a good one?
2. What could be done to improve the second observation? The underlined portions are the key problem areas. Can you rewrite these sections to make this a stronger observation?

used collections of their best work to demonstrate their abilities to others. DeFina (1992) presents seven assumptions about portfolios:

- *They represent a systematic effort to collect meaningful student works.* Selecting and updating the best materials for a portfolio require considerable planning and preparation by both the student and teacher.

- *Students should be actively involved in selecting pieces to include in the portfolio.* Because students create many of the materials found in their portfolios, they need to be major participants in choosing items to include.

- *Portfolios can contain materials from teachers, parents, peers, and school administrators.* Including items from a variety of sources adds important dimensions to this assessment tool.

- *Portfolios should reflect the actual daily learning activities of children.* Portfolios should measure what students have accomplished in day-to-day experiences.

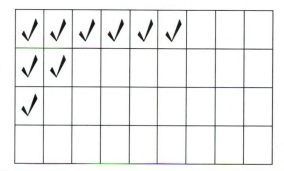

Figure 11–4 *Observation Checklist*

Teachers can develop checklists to record occurrences of nearly any type of child behavior. Infant/toddler caregivers could use the following example to record observations of oral language development.

Child's Name ___Meghan___   **Parent(s)** ___Anita Smith___
Observer ___Adrienne___   **Birth date** ___9/10/98___

Directions: Mark the appropriate category each time you observe one of the following verbalizations from the targeted child.

Vocalization	✓	✓	✓	✓	✓	✓			
Single-word utterance	✓	✓							
Two-word sentence	✓								
Three or more words									

- *Portfolios demonstrate the students' progress over time.* Growth is best documented over a longer period. Ideally, portfolios should follow students from one year to the next.

- *Portfolios may have subcomponents.* Some students may want to separate finished projects from works that are still in progress. Having sections for notes about items in the portfolio, activities in progress, and best works may help the organization of the portfolio.

- *A variety of media can be used.* Written work, art projects, audiotapes, and videotapes are examples of the different media that may be found in portfolios.

Involving Parents

Involving parents in curriculum planning and assessment makes good sense. When parents understand and support the curriculum, they can be important allies. Families are valuable resources for finding and collecting materials, planning and preparing activities, assisting in the classroom, and extending learning options at home. For a unit on friends, for example, parents could collect and organize pictures from home that include friends, tape-record an oral story about a close friend, help their child write a letter to a friend, and assist in the classroom with planned activities on friendships.

INTO PRACTICE . . .
Organizing Portfolios

To be useful as an assessment instrument, portfolios need to be systematic and organized. Wortham (1995) suggests organizing portfolios by developmental category. By dividing the portfolio into separate sections for motor development, social and emotional development, language development, and cognitive development, the teacher and student can collect and organize works that represent the child's abilities in all areas. Some examples of materials that may be assembled for two aspects of development for a six-year-old child follow:

Cognitive Development (Mathematics, Science, and Social Studies)

- Photographs of child building with blocks.
- Child's record of mathematics games played.
- Work samples demonstrating number concept understanding.

- Child-developed graphs summarizing observations of plant growth.
- Written account of community helpers project.
- Teacher observations of child's activity during math and science time.
- Taped interview documenting problem-solving strategies with child-initiated problem.
- Computer-generated listing of time spent and activities on the computer.

Personal and Social Development

- Teacher observations that document interactions between children in classroom settings and on the playground.
- Child response to questionnaire on friendships in the classroom.
- Child's story about family life.
- Notes from meetings with parents.

When parents are left out of the planning process, difficulties are sure to follow. Parents often misunderstand the use of learning centers and play-oriented activities. Parents' experiences in school settings were frequently quite different, causing many misinterpretations. If parents haven't been involved in creating the curriculum, they are much more likely to question this approach. You can educate parents regarding these issues by helping them to get involved. Then they will see firsthand the importance and value of these tasks.

Summary

Several general guidelines can help teachers begin the process of creating a developmentally appropriate curriculum. Teachers must also understand the roles of child development, observation, curriculum goals, and planning in creating a developmentally appropriate program for young children. Early childhood practitioners rely on an integrated curriculum and the project approach as they work with young children. Scheduling issues are important in curriculum planning. Observations and portfolio development are important assessment alternatives. Teachers should involve parents in curriculum planning and assessment issues.

For Discussion and Action

1. Spend some time observing in an early childhood classroom. Look for some indicators of student interests. Could any of these interests be developed into a thematic unit?

2. Practice making anecdotal record observations. For variety, try observing children in a nonschool setting such as a public park, a soccer game, in a friend's home, or at the local grocery store.

3. Create a checklist for use in observing an aspect of child development. Try it out with a group of children.

4. Create a curriculum web for a theme of your choice. Use the subject areas of mathematics, language, art, music, movement, science, and social studies for the spokes of the web.

5. Talk with your classmates about the strengths and limitations of projects when compared with the thematic approach to planning the curriculum.

Building Your Personal Library

Bredekamp, S., & Copple, C. (Eds.). (1997). *Developmentally appropriate practice in early childhood programs* (rev. ed.). Washington, DC: National Association for the Education of Young Children. This revised book is the definitive statement on developmentally appropriate practice from the largest, most influential professional organization in the early childhood arena. The book contains sections describing foundational principles and separate discussions of developmentally appropriate practice for infant/toddlers, preschoolers, and primary children.

Krogh, S. (1995). *The integrated early childhood curriculum* (2nd ed.). New York: McGraw-Hill. This text provides a strong rationale for using an integrated curriculum. It then presents practical ideas for developing this approach for the early childhood classroom. Included is a clear description of curriculum webbing.

McAfee, O., & Leong, D. (1994). *Assessing and guiding young children's development and learning.* Boston: Allyn & Bacon. McAfee and Leong present a strong framework for effective assessment in the early childhood classroom. They provide good discussions of making and using observations in assessment and the portfolio process.

Wortham, S. (1996). *The integrated classroom: The assessment–curriculum link in early childhood education.* Upper Saddle River, NJ: Merrill/Prentice Hall. As the title implies, this book emphasizes the importance of integrating assessment and curriculum in the planning and teaching of young children. Included is an important chapter on screening and assessment in early childhood programs.

IV

The Curriculum

❧ *12*
Enhancing Physical Development

❧ *13*
Supporting Social and Emotional Development

❧ *14*
Mathematics, Science, and Social Studies Learning

❧ *15*
Language and Literacy Learning

❧ *16*
Using the Creative Arts to Support Development and Learning

❧ *17*
Using Technology to Support Development and Learning

In this chapter you will

- Learn about the components of physical development.

- Study the role of the teacher in facilitating children's physical development.

- Understand the role of toys and play in enhancing gross and fine motor skills.

- Gain insight regarding the importance of outdoor activities in physical development.

- Read about health and safety issues in early childhood.

Friday afternoon, at last. It has been a busy, exciting week in your first-grade classroom. The cool, crisp weather of fall seems to be reflected in the active behaviors of the children. As you sit down to plan for the coming week, you are reminded of the difficulties children had in staying on task this past week—too much sitting and listening for many of your students. To make the classroom day more manageable and enjoyable for children, you decide to add more active class involvement. This will also help provide new opportunities for building physical development activities into your curriculum. Several ideas come to mind. Perhaps it is time to bring out the math manipulatives. In addition to their usefulness in teaching mathematical concepts, the Cuisenaire Rods and Unifix cubes give children opportunities to develop fine motor skills. Another option is to add art materials to the academic tasks when children have finished other projects. The easel and art activity table will give students additional play options that also enhance small muscle development. Songs like "Head, and Shoulders, Knees, and Toes" can add some spice to your group-time activities. An obstacle course in the gym for rainy day play can supplement the outdoor play that is so important to the development of large muscle skills.

It certainly makes a difference when plans for the next week include fun, active participation. Combining learning and physical activity makes good sense.

Throughout the early childhood years, children need to spend much of their classroom days moving and doing. Not only is this a major way of learning about the world at this age, it is also important as a vehicle for breaking up the necessary times of sitting and listening that young children experience in the school setting. Furthermore, movement activities promote the child's physical development. Although many teachers often overlook careful planning for motor skills, it is an important component of the early childhood curriculum.

The Importance of Motor Skills

From the first days of life, children begin using their bodies to learn about the world around them. Piaget (1950) suggests that sensory and motor experiences are the basis for all intellectual functioning for approximately the first two years of life. As children continue to mature, their reliance on physical interactions with people and objects remains strong. Motor skills are an essential component of development for all children. Gallahue (1993b) puts it this way:

> Movement is at the very center of young children's lives. It is an important facet of all aspects of their development, whether in the motor, cognitive, or affective domains of human behavior. To deny children the opportunity to reap the many benefits of regular, vigorous physical activity is to deny them the opportunity to experience the joy of efficient movement, the health effects of movement, and a lifetime as confident, competent movers. (p. 24)

Social Skills and Physical Development

Movement activities are especially well-suited to helping children develop social skills (Altman, 1992). As children participate in group tasks that require movement, they learn that their efforts are critical to the success of the group. Coordinating the movements of the group in parachute play, for example, allows children to create a dome overhead and sit inside at the same time. Simple games like this for young children also require cooperation and positive social skills.

Motor Activities and Emotions

Physical activity has long been viewed as a positive way to release the pent-up energy generated from strong emotions. Vigorous physical activity such as running outdoors is generally considered an acceptable way to get rid of angry feelings. Such activities are far more positive than aggressive interactions with other children.

More subtle, perhaps, is the use of art materials for emotional release. Children painting at the easel or molding with play dough or clay may well be playing out their feelings in a socially acceptable way. This behavior, which Freud labeled **sublimation** (Thomas, 1985), provides children with positive ways to work through emotions using physical activity.

Bunker (1991) reminds us that children acquire self-confidence and self-esteem in part through successful physical activities. As children master and refine basic motor skills, they see themselves as more competent and capable. The preschool child who has mastered the monkey bars and exclaims for all the world to hear "Hey, look at me!" is feeling good about himself and his accomplishment.

Connections to Cognitive Development

Early childhood education is rooted in the notion that learning through doing is fundamental for young children. Infants learning to crawl are working hard to master a physical skill that will enable them to explore more fully the home or school environment. Toddlers have even greater opportunities for touching, manipulating, and creating with the objects around them. The mobility of toddlers

Movement and music make a wonderful combination for learning and development.

opens up many new learning situations. Building with a set of blocks in the preschool classroom allows young children to learn about such mathematical concepts as proportionality and number. The refinement of fine motor skills in play makes it possible for children to succeed with writing tasks in the primary classroom. Physical competence is fundamental to cognitive development during early childhood.

Montessori (1967) stated that, for learning to reach its full potential, it must be directly connected to physical movement for the young child. This **unity of mental and physical activity** is at the heart of the Montessori method of education. When the motor skill is directly related to the task being learned, children can understand concepts more completely and quickly. For example, a Montessori item called the Pink Tower is a collection of pink blocks that are stacked from largest on the bottom to the smallest on top. As children practice this physical task, they learn about seriation (ordering from largest to smallest), which is essential to later mathematical understanding.

Foundation for Physical Fitness

Although educators of young children traditionally haven't thought of physical fitness as a major concern, mounting evidence indicates that teachers should encourage their young students to be more active. Poest, Williams, Witt, and

Atwood (1990) identify the following issues as a rationale for engaging young children in fitness activities:

- The first signs of arteriosclerosis (hardening of the arteries) are appearing as early as age five.
- Young children are not engaging in the intense physical activity needed to increase cardiovascular fitness.
- Of every hundred children, at least sixteen are obese.
- Over the last thirty years, obesity has increased significantly.

Little research has been done in the area of early childhood fitness. One early study of motor development in preschool children found that free play wasn't as effective as planned motor activities in improving large muscle development (S. Miller, 1978). This indicates that more structured motor activities are needed to overcome the problems in the preceding list (Gallahue, 1993a). With careful planning, these motor activities can effectively complement the natural movement that is a part of children's free play.

The Components of Physical Development

> Katie, age five, has just lost her first tooth.
> Armondo, age three, needs your help cutting paper.
> Keneesha, at seven, can dribble and pass a soccer ball.
> George, age four, is learning to move to music at group time without bumping into other children.
> Lee, at eight, has shown interest in running for fitness and fun. He can run several laps around the school track without stopping.

Each of these very different scenarios exemplifies an aspect of physical development that is important to understand. Physical growth, gross and fine motor skills, and perceptual-motor development are all important to the early childhood teacher. An understanding of each will provide a foundation for physical education at these ages.

Physical Growth

Knowing how children develop physically can give the teacher many important insights for teaching in the early childhood classroom. Child development experts (Anselmo & Franz, 1995) suggest the following generalizations about physical growth:

- Early childhood is the period of most rapid growth.
- Development proceeds in spurts, rather than at an even pace.

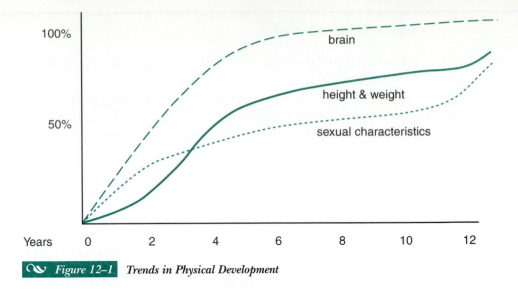

Figure 12–1   *Trends in Physical Development*

- Large muscles develop before smaller ones.
- Both heredity and environment play important roles in physical development.
- Physical development proceeds in a sequence from the top of the child's head to the toes. This is referred to as **cephalocaudal development.**
- A second sequence seen in physical growth is the development from the center of the body outward to the extremities. This is called **proximodistal development.**

Different components of the child's physical self develop at varying rates during childhood. Figure 12–1 describes these patterns for brain, height and weight, and sexual growth. As these growth curves emphasize, the early years are a time of rapid development. It is important for teachers to be aware of these trends and use them in planning appropriate experiences for the early childhood classroom.

Physical development influences the ways in which adults interact with children. As toddlers become more mobile, adults generally give them more freedom of movement and greater opportunities to explore their world. When a young child stands five inches taller than any of her classmates, adults unconsciously think of the child as being older and may treat the child as though she is more emotionally or intellectually mature. A physically attractive child will probably receive better treatment from his teachers than would an unattractive peer. In these examples, physical characteristics of children affect the adult–child relationship.

Gross Motor Development

Gross motor activities involve moving the entire body or the large muscles of the arms and legs. Because large muscles develop first, the youngest children begin

Have you ever noticed how you just seem to be more comfortable around some children than others? Several factors probably contribute to those feelings, not the least of which is physical attractiveness. Although we don't often admit it, cleanliness, good health, and appearance influence our ability to relate to children. Dopyera and Dopyera (1987) state

> Can you care as much about a hollow-cheeked, sallow-skinned child with decaying teeth and large protruding ears as you can about a cute, freckle-faced redhead with an engaging smile and a stylish haircut? (p. 53)

If we truly want to relate positively to all children in our classrooms, we must

- Be aware of our natural tendencies in terms of physical attractiveness.

- Understand our own tolerances of differences.
- Make a conscious effort to have positive interactions with children we are not attracted to.
- Work to involve all children in activities and discussions, regardless of their physical attributes.

1. Think about what you find attractive or unattractive in children. How might your own preferences influence the way you teach?

2. Many times, we are not aware of our own likes and dislikes regarding physical attractiveness. Think of some specific things you might do to discover these preferences.

refining their use. Starting with walking, infants and toddlers become increasingly able to manipulate their leg muscle movements and move from unsteady toddling, to confident walking, to more complex tasks such as running, hopping, skipping, and jumping. Coordination and use of arm muscles follow a similar pattern of refinement. By the end of the early childhood years, children have mastered basic gross motor skills.

Benelli and Yongue (1995) suggest that during the early childhood years, children master basic movements needed for later, more complex physical activities. **Fundamental movement skills** are those needed for basic locomotion, manipulative or ball skills, and balancing. Examples for each category (Poest et al., 1990) follow:

Basic Locomotion	*Ball Skills*	*Balancing*
Walking	Throwing	Bending
Running	Kicking	Stretching
Jumping	Striking	Twisting
Hopping	Bouncing	Swinging

Well-developed fine motor skills are needed to tie a shoe.

Fine Motor Skills

Fine motor development involves the small muscles of the body, primarily the hands and feet. The educator's main concern is for development of the hand muscles necessary for such skills as eating, dressing, writing, and making artwork. Beginning in infancy and following the development of larger muscles, the young child refines use of these small muscles. This process continues well beyond the early childhood years.

Using small muscles in the hands allows children to gradually develop skill in the use of a variety of tools. Infants learning to grasp are practicing an early fine motor skill that will allow them to use a simple tool such as a rattle to make a noise. During the preschool years, children are refining small muscle control and can use such cooking utensils as potato mashers and spoons in food preparation. In the primary grades, students can use pencils and crayons as tools to write and communicate with others.

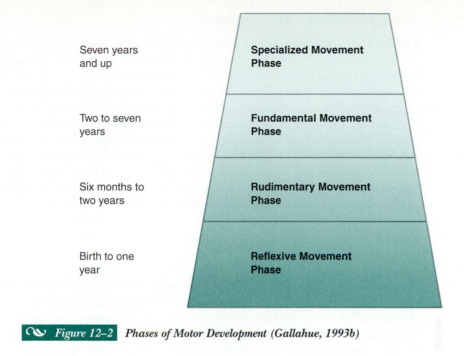

Seven years and up	**Specialized Movement Phase**
Two to seven years	**Fundamental Movement Phase**
Six months to two years	**Rudimentary Movement Phase**
Birth to one year	**Reflexive Movement Phase**

Figure 12–2 **Phases of Motor Development (Gallahue, 1993b)**

Phases of Motor Development

Gallahue (1993b) suggests that children move through phases in their gross and fine motor development, much like they do in cognitive and social/emotional development. He has identified four specific phases of motor development, summarized in Figure 12–2.

During the **reflexive movement phase,** children in the first year of life gradually replace reflexive movements such as the sucking and rooting reflex with more voluntary muscle movements. The **rudimentary movement phase**—when grasping, sitting, standing, and walking become possible for the young child—begins during the first year of life and predominates during the second year. From approximately two to seven years of age, children are in the **fundamental movement phase.** Children are mastering basic skills such as jumping, running, throwing, catching, and kicking. During the **specialized movement phase,** starting at approximately age seven, children begin to combine fundamental movements with other skills to develop specialized movements such as the layup shot in basketball.

Teachers during the early childhood years need to be aware of these developmental phases and assist children in developing the fundamental movements defined here. Although many children need little direct instruction, others will benefit from adult guidance. If children do not master these skills during their early years, it will be more difficult for them to do so later (Gallahue, 1993b).

Perceptual-Motor Development

Children also learn to take in information from the environment, process it, and respond motorically. Perceptual-motor development is generally thought to include body, time, spatial, directional, visual, and auditory awareness (Gabbard, 1992). **Body awareness** is the child's ability to locate, name, and correctly describe body part functions. Moving to a steady beat, making coordinated movements, and increasing or decreasing rates of movement are aspects of **time awareness.** A child's ability to control his body as it moves through space exemplifies **spatial awareness. Directional awareness** includes the child's capacity to understand relational concepts such as *up, down, in, out, over,* and *under.* Skill in seeing and copying demonstrated movements is referred to as **visual awareness.** Finally, a child's capacity to focus on verbal directions and distinguish between different sounds is called **auditory awareness.**

Teaching Physical Development

Although children rather naturally engage in physical activity, it is necessary for the teacher to plan for and periodically teach the skills needed for healthy motor development. By planning for and encouraging physical skills during play, and by teaching developmentally appropriate motor activities, the early childhood teacher can assist children in an important aspect of their development.

Basic Considerations

Regardless of the skill being learned or the ability levels of individual children, teachers of young children can use several general guidelines to promote physical development:

- Create time in the daily schedule for children to engage in both play-oriented and teacher-directed movement activities.
- Plan for physical pursuits both indoors and outdoors.
- Make sure all children get involved in a variety of motor activities.
- Evaluate your responses to both boys and girls to ensure equitable opportunities for physical movement.
- Identify your expectations for children's motor development. Consider these goals as you plan your curriculum.
- Establish clear rules for children as they engage in movement activities. Two basics: Respect one another's personal space; keep noise to a minimum.
- Identify for children the boundaries for physical activities. Where are they allowed to play the game, toss the ball, move to music?
- Integrate physical development activities into all aspects of the curriculum. Mathematics, science, art, and music are just some of the possibilities for integration.

Instructional Strategies for Physical Education

Pica (1995) describes three teaching methods for early childhood physical education. The direct approach, guided discovery, and exploration are all effective in different situations for teaching motor skills.

The Direct Approach

Some physical activities are best taught through direct instruction. The Hokey Pokey is a traditional dance activity that young children thoroughly enjoy. Through description, modeling, and imitating the necessary steps, children can readily learn this task. This approach has the advantage of allowing the teacher to quickly discover if any children are having trouble following the directions or producing the desired movement.

Guided Discovery

Guided discovery is a child-centered approach that allows for inventiveness and experimenta-

tion as the teacher guides children toward an appropriate solution to a problem. For example, the teacher can use a series of questions to lead children to discover the skills needed for a forward roll. Guided discovery gives children an important role in learning the physical skill being taught.

Exploration

Also referred to as *divergent problem-solving,* the exploration approach should be used as much as possible. When children explore, they produce a variety of responses to each challenge. For example, asking children to balance on two body parts should result in many different responses from a group of students. Extending and refining children's initial responses to a specific challenge give them many opportunities for practicing skills.

- Careful observation of children as they engage in physical activity is essential in determining strengths and areas for improvement. It should also form the basis for future planning.

- The materials and equipment for physical development should be developmentally appropriate and meet the diverse needs and abilities of children.

- Remember that children need repeated opportunities for practice as they learn new skills.

Physical Development and Play

Play is critical to the overall development of the child. Childhood play enhances every aspect of growth, including physical development. As the teacher plans for motor development, it is essential to consider ways in which play can be used to encourage movement skills. Careful planning of the indoor and outdoor environments (see Chapters 9 and 10) and the teacher's comments and questions are both important.

Teachers should select play equipment to stimulate gross and fine motor development and perceptual-motor skills. Toys and equipment that could be used include the following:

Gross Motor	Fine Motor	Perceptual-Motor
Climber	Water play	Rhythm instruments
Digging area	Blocks	Dance scarves
Balls	Crayons	Pattern blocks
Wheeled toys	Legos	Body part puzzles
Tumbling mats	Sand play	Sound cylinders

When quality toys and equipment are available to young children, they will use these materials in play to naturally develop motor abilities.

During free play time, the teacher's primary role is to serve as facilitator. By asking the right questions, making appropriate comments, and redirecting children to more positive options, early educators assist in overall development. When the focus becomes physical development, teachers help facilitate these skills in children:

- "Suzanna, where should you put your hands so that you can reach the next level on the climber?"
- "Adrianne, your handwriting has improved so much lately! You have learned how to make *b*'s and *d*'s correctly and are printing so much clearer now. Congratulations!"
- "Eddie, let me show you how I use a saw to cut a board. Watch how I push and pull the saw blade across the wood."

By actively facilitating physical skills during play, the teacher can help emphasize these important abilities throughout the school day.

Organized Physical Activities

Although infants and toddlers benefit most from play-oriented activities for the development of motor skills, teachers can productively introduce more teacher-directed tasks during the preschool and primary years. These activities should be fun for children, should include specific guidance on how to perform various skills, and should also allow for many opportunities to practice newly learned movements (Benelli & Yongue, 1995).

- *Throwing activities.* Children can learn to step forward with the opposite foot when throwing. Use of a target, such as a decorated sheet, helps ensure success. Beanbags and smaller soft balls are better for throwing tasks. Verbal cues help the child learn appropriate motions.
- *Catching activities.* A bright, colorful ball helps the younger child follow it visually. Yarn balls, balloons, and beach balls are good beginning items for catching. If the person throwing can toss at a consistent speed and height, children will have more success in catching.

Organized physical activity can help children develop more complex movement skills.

- *Striking activities.* As in throwing, children will be more successful in striking an object when they step forward with the leg closest to the target. A soft ball, placed on a batting tee at waist level, creates an easier target for preschool and early primary children. A bat made from a plastic 2-liter bottle and a dowel rod is helpful for many young children.

- *Kicking skills.* Targets help children improve their kicking skills. A large sheet or plastic 2-liter bottles set up like bowling pins make good targets. Children should be told to step beside the ball as they kick it with their dominant leg. Watching the ball also helps improve success rates with kicking.

- *Balancing tasks.* These activities can initially be practiced on the floor. Walking forward and backward on a line drawn on the floor, and then using an uneven surface such as a rope or hoop will help children develop skills to walk on a balance beam.

- *Jumping activities.* Jumping off low platforms is an enjoyable event for most young children. Providing safe, stable alternatives for jumping is a good beginning here. This can be followed by having children practice jumping vertically and horizontally.

- *Spatial awareness.* Children need to practice moving, dodging, balancing, and stopping without invading the personal space of others. Music and movement activities provide many opportunities for spatial awareness.

- *Fitness activities.* Although young children tire easily from vigorous activity, it is important to encourage walking, running, and jumping for fitness. Make sure to have fun, and downplay the competitive element. The important thing is to get children engaged in aerobic movement.

Enhancing Physical Development Indoors

As teachers of young children plan for organized physical activities indoors, they need to balance the many different categories listed previously. By identifying key curriculum resources (see, e.g., Pica, 1995) and building ideas for involvement around student needs and interests, teachers can implement a strong motor skills program. The following is a sampling of more specific tasks that may be adapted for use in the early childhood classroom.

Organized Games and Activities: Indoors

Magical Marching.   Having children march to music, swinging their arms and raising their knees, can be a fun fitness activity. A variety of musical recordings are available that encourage a range of marching speeds. Accompanying the music with a drumbeat can be helpful for younger children. Either pretending to play a musical instrument as children march or actually including simple rhythm instruments can add variety and interest to this task. Allowing children to assume special pretend roles such as drum major, baton twirler, and flag bearer add further opportunities for playfulness.

The Bunny Hop.   Children love to pretend, and animals are a favorite theme. Why not combine these interests with physical movement? Children can pretend to be rabbits and hop across the rug. Remind students to avoid leaping into another child's path. Then consider other hopping creatures. Frogs and kangaroos are two other possibilities. Keep students actively involved yet under control for some exciting hopping experiences. Other animals may be the starting point for additional movement possibilities (horses? crabs? others?).

Quick, Freeze!   Movement and music go together very well in early childhood. Play an instrumental piece of music, and ask children to move any way they like until the music stops. Then they must quick, freeze in the position they were in when the music stops. Use a variety of musical styles and rhythms to encourage different movements and to add interest to the activity. Make sure to stop the music at unexpected times so that children must be careful listeners as well as creative movers. Props such as scarves and streamers help self-conscious students focus more on the prop and move more productively to the music.

Hit the Bull's-Eye.   Beanbags make great initial throwing instruments for young children. They are easy to grasp, weighted for good distance, and soft enough to be safe when the toss is off target. Decorate an old donated sheet with a large bull's-eye and a hole for the center, attach it securely to the ceiling, and have children practice tossing the beanbags at the target. Tape on the floor at varying distances from the target can add further challenges for children as they become more accurate in their tosses.

Finger Frolics.   Young children love to engage in activities that involve their fingers and hands. A variety of fingerplays and action songs are available (see Chapter 16 for more specifics) that allow children to practice fine and gross motor skills. "Five Little Speckled Frogs," "The Eensy Weensy Spider," and "Head, and Shoulders, Knees, and Toes" are well-known examples of fine and gross motor activities combined with games and singing. Make sure to repeat them often, because children enjoy them even more with practice.

Catch Me If You Can.   The eye–hand coordination needed for a young child to catch a ball or other object is higher than might first be expected. Begin by having children catch their own bounced ball. Next, try having an adult who is an accurate tosser throw a beach ball or other large, soft object for catching. Mastering tossing an object into the air and catching it is yet another step in the process.

Catching tends to be more difficult than tossing activities for many children. They may be afraid of being hit by whatever is being tossed. Be sensitive to this as you introduce the activity.

Balancing Circus.   Balance activities can follow a sequence from fairly simple to more complex. A good beginning for young children is to have children pretend to be circus high-wire performers and walk on a line taped to the floor. Next, they can walk on a small rope secured to the floor. Have children walk forward, placing one foot in front of the other. Later, they can practice moving sideways along the rope and then backward. Older children can use the same procedures with a low balance beam as they gain skill and confidence in moving and balancing.

Enhancing Physical Development Outdoors

The outdoor environment provides children with many opportunities for motor skill development. The wide-open spaces and fewer restrictions beckon children to move. Free play activities outdoors are full of large and small muscle movement. The classroom teacher organizes events to encourage additional practice in movement.

Rough-and-Tumble Play

Bobbie and D.J. are two very active first-grade students. On the playground, they love to wrestle and chase each other across the grass. This type of vigorous activity is referred to as rough-and-tumble play (Pelligrini & Perlmutter, 1988). Wrestling, play fighting, chasing, and fleeing behaviors are common when children engage in this play. Although at first glance, this activity may seem to lead to more aggressive behavior, research (Pelligrini, 1987) indicates that rough-and-tumble play has positive educational and developmental value, especially for boys, and should be encouraged.

This play type is clearly valuable in getting children to engage in high-energy activity that stimulates cardiovascular fitness and large muscle use. As such, it is an important element in physical development activities in the early childhood classroom. Teachers need to carefully observe as children engage in rough-and-tumble play to make sure the activity remains positive. Teachers may need to intervene to redirect the play in new ways.

Organized Games and Activities: Outdoors

The outdoor setting is an ideal place for teachers to lead children in organized physical development activities. The wide-open spaces and reduced noise restrictions make the outdoors valuable for the development of motor skills. Many good resources for children's games and activities can be effectively used with young children outdoors (see, e.g., Kamii & DeVries, 1980; Kirchner,

1991; Orlick, 1978). With careful selection and planning, these games and activities will be popular with children and provide many opportunities for growth. Good games for young children should have simple rules, include all children who want to be involved, and be noncompetitive (Isenberg & Jalongo, 1997).

> ∾ *The children in your second-grade classroom have been struggling at recess to implement a game of kickball. They are arguing over how to choose teams, and they have hurt feelings regarding winning and losing. Rather than discourage their obvious interest in this active game, you decide to plan for this activity later in the week. After discussing the problems with competition at group time, you take children out to recess, arbitrarily assign students to teams, and then show them how they can play the game and de-emphasize the competitive element. The next week, you notice that several children have spontaneously chosen your modified game and are actively and happily involved during recess.*

This example highlights one of the biggest problems with organized games for young children: competition. Piaget (1965) suggests that until about seven or eight years of age, children are often not cognitively or emotionally ready for games with rules, many of which contain significant amounts of competition. Losing is difficult for young children and should be downplayed in games (Rivkin, 1995). With creativity and thought, teachers can modify most games so that competition is reduced or eliminated. Orlick (1978) identifies many new noncompetitive game options and describes traditional competitive games that have been made more cooperative. An example of each follows:

- *Fish Gobbler.* In a large grassy area with enough space for all the children to spread out, the caller (known as the Fish Gobbler) says, "Ship," and children run to a designated spot on the playground. When the caller announces, "Shore," children run to a second location. The direction "Fish Gobbler" requires children to drop quickly to the grass. While laying on their stomachs, students link arms, legs, or bodies together so that the Fish Gobbler can't come by and gobble them up. Later, the teacher can add other directions such as "Sardines" or "Crabs," and children can respond with appropriate motions.

- *Nonelimination Musical Chairs.* Even though chairs are removed when the music is stopped, as in the traditional version, the object of this game is to keep everyone involved. Children simply come up with creative ways to share the remaining chairs. They must work together to make sure the game can continue.

- *Tug of Peace.* Rather than playing the traditional game of tug of war, where children compete in teams and pull against each other, introduce children to the tug of peace. In this game, children cooperate by working together with a rope to meet a specific objective. For example, in small groups, children can create a geometric pattern such as a triangle or rectangle. Or they can create different letters of the alphabet as another cooperative task. Small groups can then be combined to form larger groups for more complex tasks.

Gardening is a wonderful outdoor experience that combines physical activity with many learning opportunities.

Although many of the ideas presented earlier for indoor use can be effective on the playground, the additional options presented here provide a larger sample of appropriate activities for children during the early childhood years:

The Road Runner.   After discussing the "Road Runner" cartoon and how fast he runs, encourage children to practice being road runners on the playground. A poster mounted in the classroom with the designated trail and decorated with individual road runners who have made the trip may encourage others to try it as well. Praise individuals (avoid comparing children to downplay competition), and have students challenge themselves to run longer distances as the year progresses.

The Bumble Bee.   Children enjoy pretending and can creatively move to music or a drumbeat. Combine these interests into a playground movement activity. Talk about how a bumble bee travels through the air and what body parts children could move to imitate the bee. Question them about what body parts they can move slowly or quickly. Give students plenty of room, and have them pretend to be bumble bees. This activity can be expanded by asking children to suggest other things they could imitate. They will probably come up with a long list. Discuss the movements required, and then have children practice different rates of speed by pretending to be the creatures they have suggested.

Mountain Climbing.   Using an obstacle course is a fun way for children to develop their physical skills outdoors. A combination of movable climbers, ladders, boards, wooden boxes, tires, cable spools, and barrels can challenge children to climb over, crawl under, and step through the skills course. Encourage pretending by discussing mountain climbing/hiking at group time and suggesting that the obstacle course is actually a mountain trail that the children can explore. After several days of exploring the trail, change the trail and give it a new name (the jungle, etc.).

La Piñata.   A favorite multicultural celebration can also be a good introductory striking experience for young children. A piñata attached to a rope and hung from a stationary piece of outdoor equipment makes a large target for this age. Depending on children's abilities, the piñata can remain at a fixed height for younger children, or it can be raised and lowered to increase the challenge for older students. The bat should be light enough for children to easily swing and wide at the striking end to ensure success in hitting the target. Choose a piñata that can be broken by children, fill it with healthy treats, and give each child a chance to strike away.

Traffic Jam.   Wheeled toys like tricycles and wagons help young children develop leg muscle coordination. Pretend city streets laid out by adults on the playground can be a fun way to encourage children to pedal and steer in and around various obstacles. Stop signs, turn indicators, a simple ramp to drive over, traffic cones, and a pretend gas pump can stimulate good exercise that children will enjoy for many days. Changing the traffic patterns every few days will help maintain interest in this activity.

Parachute Play.   Group activities with a parachute can help promote cooperation and allow for both large and small muscle use. Begin by demonstrating how to grip the chute: either palms down, palms up, or alternating. Children can use the parachute to create waves, using different large arm movements to make it go up and down. Experiment with different positions (sitting, kneeling, standing) and a variety of motions as children gain confidence in manipulating the parachute. For a more advanced activity, place a lightweight ball on the parachute and have children keep it bouncing.

Although physical skills may present many challenges to children with special needs, the benefits of involvement include

- Better coordination
- Improved listening skills
- Enhanced expressive abilities

Although these are important arguments for including children with special needs, perhaps the most significant reason is improved self-concept (Gallahue, 1993a). Many disabilities make it harder for children to participate in physical tasks, or when they do get involved, the outcome is different from that of other children. This can lead to a distorted body image. Involving children with special needs in successful movement activities can help them feel good about themselves.

Some planning considerations for including children with special needs (Pica, 1995):

- Make sure that all children can succeed with the tasks you include.
- You may need to modify movement activities or materials to make them positive experiences.
- Music is an important component that can help improve response, motivation, and enjoyment.
- Consult with parents and special educators for other insights in planning for physical activities.

1. Take a look at playground equipment for young children. What adaptations would be needed (or were made) to make them accessible to children with physical handicaps?

2. Talk to a physical education teacher, and find out the strengths and problems of involving children with special needs in movement activities.

Teaching Children to Care for Their Bodies

Helping children develop motor skills is an important part of physical development during the early childhood years. In addition, it is important for educators to promote an understanding of health-related issues and safety concerns. Young children develop patterns of behavior during these years that may last a lifetime. Teaching respect and care for one's body is an essential element of the early childhood curriculum.

Health Education

The soaring costs of medical care and a growing realization that it is easier to avoid problems than to cure them has led to positive changes in the health care professions (Marotz, Cross, & Rush, 1993). The focus is now on preventive health. For young children, issues that can be addressed include

- Good dietary habits
- Physical fitness
- The importance of medical and dental care
- Personal hygiene
- Stress reduction

Nutritional status clearly influences the young child's behavior. A good **diet** helps children be more alert, attentive, and active in the early childhood classroom. Poor nutrition will generally have the opposite effects and may contribute to the child's resistance to illnesses. Overeating and malnutrition also contribute to many problems in childhood, and early childhood educators need to address these issues.

Educators can teach good dietary habits through modeling them in the early childhood classroom. Teachers should carefully plan snacks and meals, with an emphasis on balanced nutrition. Discussion of what makes a good diet can then occur naturally as children eat the foods prepared for them. Cooking experiences are another common and fun project for young children that can help teach good nutrition. For example, a fruit salad is easy and fun for young children to prepare and provides a healthy alternative to high sugar or fatty cooking projects.

The issue of **physical fitness** is growing in importance for the early childhood years. As increasing numbers of young children are classified as obese (Poest et al., 1990) and their activity levels decrease, teachers must work to counter this trend. Although it is essential to downplay competition and remember that short periods of vigorous activity are best, young children can benefit from simple fitness activities (National Association for Sport and Physical Education, 1998). For example, teachers can encourage running and walking in playful ways to increase cardiovascular health.

Although good **medical and dental care** are normal in many households, other children don't have adequate health care. Low-income families and those without medical and dental insurance may be unable to afford these services. Many schools for young children therefore provide information about the importance of good care and referrals to low-cost alternatives.

Educators must also be alert to health problems that could lead to later difficulties for children. Providing for vision, hearing, and speech screening is a common first step that schools can take to help identify potential health problems. Careful observation by the teacher can also be helpful in discovering other concerns.

     You have overheard Rachel complaining of headaches for the last several days in your third-grade classroom. With the school's annual standardized tests scheduled for tomorrow, Rachel's headaches may be related to stress. You decide to call her parents to discuss the problem further.

A final component of health education during the early childhood years is an emphasis on **personal hygiene.** When teachers integrate good health habits into the classroom activities, young children can learn and practice these important routines. Hand washing before eating and after toileting activities are examples of this emphasis. Hair care, brushing teeth, and caring for a runny nose are other aspects of good personal hygiene.

Safety Issues

Amelia, a four-year-old, knows that she can explore the materials on the shelves in her preschool classroom. She is encouraged to take the blocks and build with them or create art projects from the many options available in that center. But what about under the sink near the snack area? As she opens the cupboards to investigate, she finds two different cleaning agents among the sponges and rags. Luckily, her teacher notices Amelia's inquisitiveness and redirects her to more appropriate areas. Furthermore, Mrs. Abbot decides to bring up the issue of storing cleaners in a more secure area at the next staff meeting.

Young children are naturally interested in everything around them and work hard to learn through hands-on exploration of their environment. Adults need to prepare the indoor and outdoor settings (see Chapters 9 and 10) so that harmful materials are out of reach and potential accidents and injuries are minimized. As much as possible, children should be able to unleash their curiosities in environments that are free from unnecessary hazards. For example, the classroom should not include toys and equipment that break easily or are hard to clean. In addition, small objects that infants and toddlers can put in their mouths are hazardous. With common sense and an understanding of child development, the teacher of young children can create an atmosphere that is supportive of the child's natural ways of learning.

Working with Parents and Families

Parents can be major contributors to every aspect of their child's growth, including physical skills. Teachers can assist in this process by providing families with information and activities that support motor development. This parent education effort should be built on the positive things parents are already doing and take minimal effort for families to implement.

Understanding Physical Growth

Parents know a great deal about their individual children but often know little about how typical they are. "Is it normal for Aletha to be so clumsy at age seven?" "Mike's first-grade writing assignments are so hard to read. How does he compare to other children his age?" Parents benefit from information that describes clearly how children develop large and small muscle skills. Teachers can informally share this information with parents as issues arise or include it in written materials such as newsletters. Some parent groups may be interested in an evening meeting at which physical skill development is discussed.

Importance of Active Play

Although early childhood educators view childhood play as critical to development, most parents see play as a fun, but trivial, part of children's lives. To counter this widely held perspective, teachers should give parents many opportunities to learn about the importance of play for all aspects of child development. This includes information about its role in physical development. Teachers can share brochures, videos, and articles in early childhood journals to help parents understand the impact of play on learning, fine and gross motor skills, and childhood fitness.

Nutrition Information

With very few exceptions, parents want the best for their children. In many instances, however, they need guidance in knowing what can be done to encourage healthy development. Without putting parents on the defensive or making them feel like they are failures, teachers need to help them learn about good nutrition and diet for young children. While many families do well in this area, others eat foods high in fat, sugar, salt, and preservatives. Providing resources (see, e.g., Wanamaker, Hearn, & Richarz, 1979) for simple, nutritious alternatives to fast foods and communicating with parents about the importance of healthy diets will make a difference in overall physical development of young children.

Competitive Sports

Elkind (1981b) reminds us that most children during the early childhood years are not ready for highly competitive sports and games. He suggests that parents who push their children into early competitive sports activities are hurrying them to grow up too quickly and adding extra stress to their lives. Underwood (1981) puts it this way:

> To visit on small heads the pressure to win, the pressure to be "just like mean Joe Green" is indecent. To dress children up like pros in costly outfits is ridiculous. In so doing, we take away many of the qualities that competitive sports are designed to give to the growing process. (p. 73)

Many well-meaning parents create unnecessary structure in their children's lives by introducing them to early competitive sports. Although organized sports for young children are improving, with more appropriate coaching and fewer fanatical parents shouting from the sidelines, most children are better off throughout the early childhood years engaging in unstructured, vigorous play activities. Parents need to hear this message repeatedly from a variety of experts so that this concern can be effectively addressed.

Summary

Motor skills have a significant influence on the development of social, emotional, and cognitive skills. Therefore, teachers must emphasize motor development during the early years. It is important to understand the components of physical development and create plans for teaching physical skills. Many activities are available for enhancing motor skills both indoors and on the playground. Health and safety issues are additional components of the physical development curriculum. Working with parents and families is an important step in enhancing children's physical development.

❧ For Discussion and Action

1. Survey a parent concerning his child's television viewing during an average week. Try to get the parent to be as accurate as possible. Compare your findings with others doing the same task, and then discuss the impact of television on childhood fitness.

2. Read about motor skills in a book on child development, and then discuss with a small group the roles of heredity and environment in physical development.

3. Using a beanbag or a large, soft ball, play a game of catch with a preschool child. Do the same thing with a primary-aged child. Describe the differences in physical abilities of the two children.

4. Talk with a teacher about his strategies for encouraging physical development. Discuss your findings with classmates.

5. Watch a competitive sport for young children. Observe the children's reactions to the game, the coaches' interactions with players, and the communications between parents and children.

❧ Building Your Personal Library

Graham, G., Holt-Hale, S., & Parker, M. (1993). *Children moving: A reflective approach to teaching physical education* (3rd ed.). Mountain View, CA: Mayfield Publishing. Although this book focuses more on the elementary grades, it does provide a strong discussion of developmentally appropriate practice for physical education. It is a good overview of physical education for younger children.

Marotz, L., Cross, M., & Rush, J. (1993). *Health, safety and nutrition for the young child* (3rd ed.). Albany, NY: Delmar. As the title implies, this book provides an overview of health, safety, and nutrition issues for young children. It gives practical advice about disease control, accident prevention, and providing nutritious meals.

National Center for Education in Maternal and Child Health. (1992). *National health and safety performance standards: Guidelines for out-of-home child care programs.* Arlington, VA: Author. This large three-ring binder provides definitive information on health and safety guidelines for early childhood classrooms. It makes specific recommendations for both the indoor and outdoor settings.

Pica, R. (1995). *Experiences in movement: With music, activities, and theory.* Albany, NY: Delmar. An excellent book with a balance of movement activities and theory regarding teaching physical development. It addresses the entire early childhood range, giving many good tips and ideas for classroom teachers.

13 Supporting Social and Emotional Development

In this chapter you will

- Study the social development curriculum.

- Gain understanding in helping children deal with their feelings.

- Recognize the impact of stress on social and emotional development.

- Focus on developmental issues and their relationships to growth in these areas.

- Address the importance of working with parents and families to enhance social and emotional development.

Andrea has changed over the past few weeks from an excited, busy five-year-old in your kindergarten classroom to a withdrawn and anxious child. Her life was turned upside down recently with the sudden death of her father. It is affecting her ability to relate to other children and has led to a short attention span and lackluster play experiences.

Some other children in the group, although not experiencing the same dramatic loss, live in single-parent homes and have limited contact with their fathers. They are wrestling with their own related problems.

You have decided that you should provide materials and activities in your classroom to assist children in working through these stressors. Many excellent children's books are available that deal with living in single-parent homes, and you can add some to the library corner. A family of puppets is another good possibility for the dramatic play area. In addition, now may be the time for that unit on families that you have been planning to introduce. ◗

The problems of separation and loss just described are only two of many issues that young children and their families face today. Combine these stressors with the more normal challenges of social and emotional development, and it becomes clear that the curriculum of the early childhood classroom must address these important topics. A quality program for young children recognizes the value of guiding the growth of social skills, emotional development, and the coping strategies necessary to deal with stress.

Toward Social Competence

The process of **socialization** begins at birth and continues throughout childhood. It includes learning to relate to a variety of people in many different circumstances (McClellan & Katz, 1997). For example, relating to parents is different from interacting with teachers, grocery clerks, strangers on the street, and peers. Children also must learn that different environments call for varying social skills. It is generally okay to shout, run, and get dirty outdoors; the classroom tends to be a somewhat quieter environment. Similarly, churches, drug stores, and swimming pools each have their own environmental requirements for social interactions.

Historically, early educators have placed a heavy emphasis on encouraging positive social development (Braun & Edwards, 1972). More recent research helps substantiate the value of this emphasis. Hartup (1992) states:

> Indeed, the single best childhood predictor of adult adaptation is *not* IQ, *not* school grades, and *not* classroom behavior, but, rather the adequacy with which the child gets along with other children. Children who are generally disliked, who are aggressive and disruptive, who are unable to sustain close relationships with other children, and who cannot establish a place for themselves in the peer culture are seriously "at risk." (p. 2)

Given the importance of quality social skills, it is helpful to have a list of positive attributes to encourage in the early childhood classroom. McClellan and Katz (1993) provide a checklist of social skills as a guide for teachers:

- Approaches others positively
- Expresses wishes and preferences clearly
- Asserts personal rights and needs appropriately
- Is not easily intimidated by bullies
- Expresses frustrations and anger in positive ways
- Easily joins others in work or play
- Participates in discussions and makes contributions to activities
- Able to take turns
- Shows an interest in others
- Can negotiate and compromise in interactions with others
- Accepts and enjoys people of ethnic groups other than their own
- Uses appropriate nonverbal communication such as smiles and waves

Building a Sense of Self

Social and emotional development strongly influence one another in childhood. One example of this is the relationship between a child's self-concept and social development. **Self-concept** can be defined as how people feel about themselves and is generally considered a component of emotional development. It has three dimensions (Kostelnik, Stein, Whiren, & Soderman, 1993):

- *Competence*—the belief that you can accomplish tasks and achieve goals.
- *Worth*—a person's sense of being valued by others.
- *Control*—the degree to which people feel they can influence events around them.

Self-concept is seen as a significant factor in emotional development, but it also plays a role in the socialization process (Kostelnik et al., 1993). Children with a strong self-concept think of themselves as competent and likable. They

INTO PRACTICE . . .
Enhancing Self-Concept

Teachers can strengthen students' self-concepts in two major ways. The first is through their daily interactions with children. Dreikurs, Grunwald, and Pepper (1982) call this **encouragement**; it is the teacher's efforts to let children know she trusts and believes in them. The second method of building self-concept is through **planned activities.** Examples of each type follow:

Encouragement

Although every child reacts differently to adult interactions, children often view these behaviors as encouraging:

- Smiling, pat on the shoulder, a hug
- Spending time finding out about a child's weekend
- Praise for work well done
- Pointing out a child's strengths
- Displaying a child's work
- Attending an after-school sports event

Planned Activities

Planning events may appear contrived but are still very productive in helping children feel good about themselves. The titles for these activities are meant to be playful descriptors of their intent.

- *I Like . . .* Choose one member of the class each day, and have students share things they like about that person. With younger children, come prepared with several things you like about the targeted child so that many examples can be presented. Make sure that every student eventually has a chance to be the center of attention for this activity.

- *V.I.P. (Very Important Person) of the Week* Give every child in the class a week when they are the V.I.P. for that week. Special privileges can be granted, such as leading the flag salute or being first in line for music. A bulletin board created by family members and the child can focus on pictures and other highlights. The teacher can also invite family members to the classroom.

look forward to the challenges of social interactions, expecting to do well. Individuals with a low self-concept, on the other hand, often feel inadequate in social situations and fear rejection.

Obviously, we want to promote positive self-concepts in the classroom and need to engage children in activities and interactions that enhance conceptions of themselves. Canfield and Wells (1994) suggest the following principles for building self-concepts:

- Teachers can either positively or negatively influence self-concept. Learn and use the positive strategies.
- Building a strong self-concept isn't easy. It takes time and considerable energy.
- Although they are harder to change, try to influence central beliefs, such as feelings about academic ability, social skills, or attractiveness.
- Relate the successes and strengths you observe in children to one another. This enhances those central beliefs.
- All the little things you do—such as calling students by their names and complimenting them for positive interactions—help build strong self-concepts.

Building Teacher–Student Relationships

When teachers focus on strengthening students' self-concepts, relationships are also enhanced. Jones and Jones (1998) present the following guidelines for building effective relationships:

- *Engage in an open, appropriate dialogue.* Honest and open communication about the lives of students and the teacher can create a climate where caring relationships develop. Without getting overly involved in students' lives, the teacher must demonstrate a willingness to talk about and help with much more than just academics.

- *Maintain a high ratio of positive to negative statements.* Although it is necessary to deal with inappropriate words or actions of children, teachers must commit to interacting much more often with students when they engage in positive behaviors.

- *Communicate high expectations.* When adults have high expectations for children, children feel better about themselves and know that the adults care about them. Teacher–student relationships are strengthened.

- *Take time for personal communications.* Showing an interest in students' activities, eating lunch occasionally with children, joining in childhood play from time to time, and sending students a birthday card are some examples of this type of personal communication.

Teacher–Student Relationships

Teachers in the early childhood classroom are a very important factor in the development of children's social skills. Teachers' efforts to relate effectively with students, the classroom climate that teachers create, and teachers' intervention strategies are all significant in this process.

Without question, teachers are **models** of behavior that young children imitate (Bandura, 1989). Children listen to the words that teachers use to communicate with others and then try them out in their own speech. Students use polite comments like "please" and "thank you" far more often in classrooms where teachers use them regularly. Children imitate smiles, eye contact, and physical touch when they see adults using these nonverbal skills. And children also observe and imitate the techniques adults use to resolve problems with children and other adults.

The **classroom climate** that the teacher creates is another important factor influencing children's developing social skills. Glasser (1990) calls this **building a friendly workplace** and identifies several strategies that are helpful to teachers in this process:

- Avoid becoming adversarial in relationships with students.
- Create an atmosphere where courtesy prevails.
- Show an interest in students' lives, and share some information about yourself as a person.
- Ask students for advice and help whenever you can.
- Develop close, caring, work relationships with students.

The way a teacher organizes and decorates the physical environment also influences the overall classroom climate. For example, a comfortable child-sized couch or several throw pillows create an inviting space for reading or other quiet activities. Decorating the walls with children's artwork and creative writing also delivers an important message that this work is valued by those who work and play there. Careful attention to these details in the beginning of the school year can pay big dividends later.

The **intervention strategies** that the teacher uses to deal with socialization problems that come up throughout the day also strongly influence the skills children develop.

> ∾ *Margaret is an active, busy four-year-old in your day care program. She is a natural leader, and others in the group often follow her direction. Margaret is playing in the block center and decides that she wants to use the dump truck Deforrest is filling with blocks. She says, "Deforrest, if you let me use the truck, I'll play with you later." New to the group and naturally shy, he reluctantly agrees rather than cause conflict.*

How should the teacher intervene in this situation to help both children learn better strategies for interacting? Deforrest needs to develop positive ways to stand up for himself while at the same time becoming more a part of the group. Margaret has to learn she can't always have her own way and to channel her leadership abilities in more positive directions. One possible response is, "Margaret, Deforrest is using the truck right now. When he is finished, I hope you will ask him again to play with you." The intervention strategies the teacher uses to deal with this situation and others will help determine how effectively both children learn to relate in social settings.

Peer Interactions

Relationships with teachers and other adults help children develop social skills; interactions with peers are the proving ground for these unfolding abilities. Developing peer relationships is an important step for children and one that is difficult to accomplish. Infants and toddlers spend most of their time interacting with adults and only gradually move toward the more challenging task of socializing with peers.

One of the reasons children struggle with peer relationships is their level of cognitive development. Piaget suggests that young children are **egocentric** (Flavell, 1963). They have difficulty seeing issues from the perspective of others. Recent research (see, e.g., Newcombe & Huttenlocher, 1992) suggests that children may be less rigid in their perspective taking than Piaget originally believed; however, it is only gradually, and through repeated interactions with peers in play and work situations that children consistently recognize that others may have opinions, attitudes, and needs that are separate from their own.

Play, both indoors and on the playground, is one of the best settings for the development of social skills (Van Hoorn, Nourot, Scales, & Alward, 1993). Most

VIDEO CASE STUDY:
Wild About Learning

Watch the ABC News video segment "Wild About Learning" and consider these excerpts:

"Kids having to stand in line way too long, teachers doing things for kids that they don't need to do for them. Kids not excited. There's no zest or passion. We have enough color-by-number people. We want people who can think, because those kids are going to write the new computer programs, those are the kids who are going to solve the environmental issues, those are the kids who are always going to look for a different way to do something."

— Bev Bos, Preschool Teacher

"There is a perception, when you walk into a classroom where children are active, that it may be chaotic, but I think what's important is that what we see is child choice and child-initiated activity. . . When children are playing, they are learning. In fact, they are doing some of the most important learning that they will ever do in their lives."

— Dr. Sue Bredekamp, Past President of NAEYC

"We should have never have started to call it preschool. What we did was set ourselves up for criticism, because we said we're getting them ready for school. But let me tell you, you can't get kids ready for school. You've got to get schools ready for children."

— Bev Bos, Preschool Teacher

"There's been a trend nationwide for the last 10 years that has been toward what we call a push-down curriculum, so that what used to be taught in first grade is now taught in kindergarten, and what used to be taught in kindergarten then gets pushed down to preschool and even earlier. Education is not a race. It's not who gets to the finish line first. It's who stays with it the longest."

— Dr. Sue Bredekamp, Past President of NAEYC

"We need to take everything we do at an early childhood level and move it up into the public schools and into all schools, where the kids walk in the door and they're excited and they're passionate and they have a zest for learning. Then we're going to have to qualify education. It is possible. And above all, life ought to be fun. All life ought to be fun for kids."

— Bev Bos, Preschool Teacher

Now that you have seen the ABC News video segment, consider what it means for teachers and caregivers to interact with children in ways that are developmentally appropriate. According to Kostelnik et al. (1993), the guidelines for developmentally appropriate practice (DAP) issued by the National Association for the Education of Young Children (NAEYC) are based on these three principles:

1. Developmentally appropriate means taking into account what is known about how young children develop and learn and matching that to the content and strategies they encounter in early childhood programs. We must first think about what children are like and then develop activities, routines, and expectations that accommodate and complement those characteristics.

2. Developmentally appropriate means approaching children as individuals, not as a cohort group. We must know more than a few descriptive facts about a child, such as birthdate and gender, to design meaningful educational programs. We have to look at children within the context of their family, culture, community, and past experience to create age-appropriate as well as individually appropriate living and learning environments.

3. Developmentally appropriate means treating children with respect-- understanding children's changing capacities and having faith in children's continuing capacity to change. We must recognize the unique ways in which children are children and not simply miniature adults. Experiences and outcomes planned for the child should reflect the notion that childhood is a time of life qualitatively different from adulthood.

As a teacher and caregiver, you will be responsible for providing children with developmentally appropriate activities and lessons, and interacting with them in ways that meet their needs as they develop and learn.

Visit a local early childhood classroom or care center, and observe the classroom environment, the teachers and caregivers, and the children. In order to determine whether or not the teachers there are encouraging children's development and learning within the context of developmentally appropriate practice, use the checklist below, based on the NAEYC guidelines for developmentally appropriate practice in the area of teaching (Bredekamp & Copple, 1997). Circle the Y in the left-hand column if the teacher's practices are developmentally appropriate, or the N if they are not.

Is Practice Developmentally Appropriate?	NAEYC Guideline for Developmentally Appropriate Practice	What You Might Observe a Teacher Doing if Practice is Developmentally Appropriate
Y / N	Teachers respect, value and accept children	• teachers treat children with dignity at all times
Y / N	Teachers make it a priority to know each child well	• teachers have positive, personal relationships with children • teachers listen to children and adapt their responses to the individual child • teachers observe children's spontaneous play • teachers have relationships with families • teachers are alert to signs of undue stress • teachers supervise children at all times
Y / N	Teachers create an intellectually engaging, responsive environment	• teachers organize the environment and plan curricula based on knowledge of children • teachers provide a rich variety of experiences • teachers provide children the opportunity to make meaningful choices • teachers organize the schedule to provide extended blocks of time for play and projects
Y / N	Teachers make plans to enable children to reach curriculum goals	• teachers provide experiences that accommodate children's differences • teachers bring each child's home culture and language into the school culture • teachers are prepared to meet the special needs of individual children
Y / N	Teachers foster children's collaboration	• teachers foster collaboration without "taking over" • teachers use flexible grouping of children
Y / N	Teachers develop, refine, and use a wide repertoire of teaching strategies	• teachers help children develop initiative • teachers stimulate children's thinking by posing problems and asking questions • teachers present novel experiences and introduce stimulating ideas • teachers use a range of strategies to sustain a child's effort or engagement • teachers coach and/or directly guide students as needed • teachers calibrate the complexity of activities to suit children's level of skill and knowledge • teachers "scaffold" children's learning • teachers provide experiences that strengthen children's confidence • teachers encourage children to be reflective
Y / N	Teachers facilitate the development of responsibility and self-regulation in children	• teachers set clear, consistent, and fair limits for children's behavior • teachers hold children accountable to standards of acceptable behavior • teachers redirect children to more acceptable behavior • teachers acknowledge children's feelings • teachers guide children to resolve conflicts and solve problems independently

If you see that a teacher's actions do not conform to these guidelines for developmentally appropriate practice, how could those practices be adjusted to better serve the children?

Developing friendships and learning to interact with peers is an important element of early learning.

play sequences include several children and require effective communication, compromise, leaders, and followers in order to be successful. Children have many opportunities to practice all aspects of their developing social skills as they engage in play themes. Jambor (1994b) suggests that, unfortunately for school-age children, recess time on the playground is one of the few opportunities they have to engage in meaningful social experiences.

As children engage in play activities and other interactions with peers, they develop important social skills:

- *Making friends.* The essentials of friendship are commitment and reciprocity between two persons who are fairly equal in power. Early friendships often set the stage for making and keeping friends later in life (Hartup & Moore, 1990).

- *Sharing and helping.* Taking turns with toys, helping with a puzzle, and sharing food at snack time are examples of behaviors that children engage in regularly when encouraged to do so. Practicing these skills helps develop caring adults who support and encourage one another.

- *Cooperation.* When children willingly and without coercion by an authority figure support and assist one another, they are engaging in cooperative activity. Play provides many opportunities for cooperation.

- *Respecting rules.* Rules or conventions for appropriate conduct are an important part of all social interactions. Listening when another is speaking is just one of these rules that children must learn to follow if they want to participate effectively in social interactions.

Through kindergarten, most children have many opportunities for socializing with their peers in the early childhood classroom. As they engage in play activities in various centers, children have time to talk to and interact with others. Beginning in the first grade, however, the opportunities for extended socialization are often limited. Time on the playground is one of the few chances primary children have to interact with their peers. The following quotations are designed to get you thinking about the potential benefits of this time outdoors:

> Recess encourages all areas of children's development. As children interact, they use language and nonverbal communications: they make decisions and solve problems, and they deal with the emotional trials and tribulations of their interactions. (Jambor, 1994b)

> Recess is one of the few times during the school day when children are free to exhibit a wide range of social competencies—sharing, cooperation, negative and passive language—in the context that they see meaningful. Only at recess does the playground become one of the few places where children can actually define and enforce meaningful social interaction during the day. (Pelligrini & Glickman, 1989, p. 24)

With the low priority of recess in most elementary schools, Jambor (1994b) suggests several strategies for promoting this time:

- Educate administrators by providing them with articles about the importance of recess.
- Help parents and other teachers understand the importance of recess by describing the social and cognitive benefits.
- Provide in-class recesses to give students more time for outdoor play and socialization.
- Write letters and opinion pieces for the local newspaper, school board members, legislators, and others. Don't be afraid to speak out often for the importance of recess.

1. *Read an article about the importance of recess, and list the benefits cited.*
2. *Watch children at play on an elementary playground. Describe the kinds of social interactions you observed.*

- *Problem solving.* Social interactions often lead to disagreements that must be resolved. Children learn problem-solving strategies to deal with these conflicts.
- *Expressing feelings.* Although children often express their feelings in inappropriate ways with others (hitting, kicking, biting, name calling), they also quickly learn that these approaches get in the way of friendships and being part of a group. More appropriate ways of communicating feelings are needed.

The Social Development Curriculum

In many instances, the curriculum for developing social skills occurs spontaneously as children need assistance in dealing with peers or other adults. Quietly

Puppets are popular with preschool children, and teachers can use them to model appropriate social interactions.

assisting a child in problem-solving alternatives to hitting as an expression of anger is one such example. Yet, in addition to these teachable moments, many opportunities to plan for social skill development arise.

The Environment and Materials

The **physical setting** in which children interact is an important element in the socialization process. Careful planning of the space helps make positive interactions more likely. The following suggestions should be considered in organizing space:

- *Space to be social.* The physical space should invite children to interact with one another. Clusters of desks, several chairs for children's tables, large throw pillows, and open spaces for gathering are examples of this type.
- *Pictures that depict social activities.* When selecting pictures to decorate the walls in the different centers, try to find ones that show adults and children engaging in prosocial behaviors.

- *Materials that foster cooperation.* A mural for an art project, computer software that takes two or more to play, and noncompetitive board games are examples of materials that children can productively use to strengthen social skills.

- *Fewer options to encourage sharing.* Having just one piece of popular equipment (e.g., a special dump truck) for children may lead to major conflicts. Having too many pieces, however, eliminates the opportunity to practice sharing. The best option is to have fewer pieces than children would like so that some sharing is needed.

- *Books dealing with social skills.* A strong collection of children's books deals with socialization issues. One such example is *A Friend Is Someone Who Likes You* (Anglund, 1983). The teacher should rotate these books in and out of the library/book center throughout the school year.

The **daily schedule** of events also influences the development of social skills. When teachers provide adequate time for children to work and play in small groups or as a class, more productive interactions take place. It is critical to remember that short time blocks are seldom effective for socialization and may in fact be counterproductive. Children need time to warm up to the idea of working or playing with others, time to plan what they are going to do, additional opportunity to engage in the activity, and a cooling off period. Even for primary-aged children, these blocks of time are seldom productive if they are shorter than twenty or thirty minutes.

Activities and Themes

Planning the social curriculum should also include **activities** that promote the developmental skills emphasized in the early childhood program. Teachers can choose from a rich assortment of options. Some sample ideas for activities follow:

- *Songs.* Singing and music are wonderful learning tools for all areas of the curriculum. Social development is no exception. There are songs that are appropriate for every age within the early childhood range. Some examples that fit this category from a songbook by Warren (1983) titled *Piggyback Songs* include "Helping," "Friends," "Be My Friend," and "Here We Are Together."

- *Games.* Games for children this age should be noncompetitive because most young children find this element frustrating. Keeping this in mind, however, many excellent board games promote positive social interactions. For example, the ChildsWork ChildsPlay Corporation (800-962-1141) sells The Kindness Game and Sleeping Grump, both of which promote cooperation and kindness in young children.

- *Community workers.* An important aspect of social development is learning about and effectively relating to different people in the community. Having construction workers, firefighters, doctors, and others as guests in your classroom allows children opportunities to better understand and interact with these people.

CELEBRATING PLAY . . .
Games and Socialization

Sports and competitive games have long been viewed as valuable ways for people to develop abilities to work effectively with others. However, many suggest that, for the early childhood years, the emphasis should be on **cooperation** rather than competition. Games focusing on cooperative interactions develop stronger social skills and better prepare children for the competitive situations they will face later in life. A variety of good resources are available for those who are interested in using cooperative games:

Orlick, T. (1978). *The cooperative sports and games book: Challenge without competition.* New York: Pantheon. This is probably the best-known and most widely used book on cooperative games and sports. More than 100 options provide children of all ages with many enjoyable activities.

Orlick, T. (1982). *The second cooperative sports and games book.* New York: Pantheon. This

book presents an additional 200 games that can be used with children of all ages, including toddlers. The games emphasize imagination as well as cooperative skills.

Sobel, J. (1984). *Everybody wins: 393 noncompetitive games for young children.* New York: Walker and Company. The cooperative games in this book are specifically designed for children from three to ten years of age. The author also selected games that promote feelings of self-worth and confidence.

1. *Find one of the books described here, and locate a game that would be fun to play with young children. If you have a chance, try it out.*

2. *Why is competition so difficult for young children? Discuss this issue with a small group of peers.*

- *Discussions.* Reading a good book about social relationships or using a similar discussion starter can help generate a productive dialogue with children about social skills. When the discussion includes topics being experienced by children, meaningful communication can take place.

- *Cooperative learning.* For primary-aged children, the teacher can assign group projects that require children to work together to complete tasks. These cooperative learning experiences help build social skills and are quality educational opportunities (Ellis & Whalen, 1990).

Thematic teaching can also be used to stimulate social learning. The topic of cooperation is one example of a theme that teachers can productively use in the early childhood classroom to build social skills. The following examples of center materials and activities outline some of the content of a unit on cooperation:

- **Pictures** in centers showing adults and children cooperating help create the right atmosphere for the theme.

- **Cooperative block building** can be encouraged verbally and by providing a large map of a city that children can use as the foundation for creating their own city.
- **Difficult puzzles** in the manipulative center can be completed by two or more children.
- **Cooperative sand structures** can be part of the outdoor activities. Teachers can give pairs or small groups of children their own tools for building.
- **Mural art** projects allow children to work on a common art activity.
- **Group finger painting** is another art project that encourages children to work together.
- **Post office** props in the dramatic play area help children cooperate as they take different roles related to writing, sending, and receiving mail.
- **Books** on cooperation such as *Sharing* by Newman (1990).
- **Commercial music recordings** such as Fred Rogers's *Let's Be Together Today* or Marlo Thomas's *Free to Be You and Me* can be available in the music center.

Helping Children with Emotional Development

Emotional development in young children consists of a gradual growth in the ability to recognize, label, and appropriately respond to their feelings. Each of these steps is important to emotional health and must be learned through repeated interactions with others.

What Are Emotions?

Emotions are feelings that come in response to other people, experiences, or circumstances. Stimuli from the environment cause physiological responses in the body that lead to feelings such as anger, fear, sadness, or surprise (Kostelnik et al., 1993).

> *Seven-year-old Kimberly was severely bitten by a pit bull at age three and has since been fearful around dogs of all sorts. When she sees a dog, her heart rate goes up, and she literally begins to shake as she runs to her father for protection. Although not all emotional responses are as clearly defined as Kimberly's, we each have our own physical reactions to stimuli. These feelings are real and must be recognized and dealt with in positive ways.*

Researchers who have studied emotional development suggest that young children are genetically programmed with **core emotions** that include joy, anger, sadness, and fear (Plutchik, 1980). These intense, relatively pure emotions serve as the foundation for the later emergence of more **complex emotions** such as frustration, annoyance, jealousy, and boredom.

Children's emotions are often clearly observable in their facial expressions and body language.

Dealing with Feelings

Young children have much to learn about their feelings. Because it is very difficult to change our emotional responses to situations and people, it makes more sense to help children respond appropriately to their feelings.

Recognizing and Labeling Feelings. Before responding appropriately to emotions, children need to successfully recognize that they are having an emotional reaction and need to give that reaction a name. Through most of the early childhood years, teachers and other adults will need to help children with this task. When the adult sensitively recognizes the emotional signs and gives them a label, children gradually develop the ability to do the same.

> *Six-year-old Ara is playing with a car in the block corner, and he briefly leaves the area to get a drink of water. Upon his return, Ara sees that Adrienne has taken the car he was using. With a loud scream, Ara rushes into the center, grabs his vehicle, and violently kicks down the block structure Adrienne has constructed. The teacher enters the area, takes Ara by the hand, and leads him away to a quiet*

corner of the room. She gets down at the child's level and says, "I can tell by your scream and kicking that Adrienne made you very angry when she took the car you were using." The teacher needs to continue her discussion with both Ara and Adrienne, but even these initial comments make it clear that she has provided a label for Ara's feelings.

Accepting Feelings.   The emotions children experience can often be very powerful and seem almost overwhelming to them. Children need to know that it is normal to have strong feelings and that it is important to accept them as a natural part of life. Unfortunately, many adults have not learned this lesson and try to deny their own feelings or those of children. Often, they make comments to children such as: "You're okay. There is nothing to be afraid of!"

The words adults use in communicating with children about emotions help them accept their feelings. The teacher dealing with Ara in the preceding example could add the following to her initial comment: "It's okay to be angry. Everybody gets angry sometimes." This will help Ara accept the strong emotion he experienced.

Appropriate Responses to Emotions.   As children learn to recognize, label, and accept their feelings, they also need assistance in developing prosocial responses. Although hitting, kicking, crying, or withdrawal may be the natural reaction for many children, they must learn to use words to more effectively deal with emotions.

The teacher dealing with Ara in the preceding example could finish her discussion with him by saying:

ᵔ   *"Ara, even though you are angry, I can't let you scream or kick playthings in the classroom. Can you think of a better way to let Adrienne know that you are angry?" If the child is unable to come up with another option, the teacher can then suggest some other acceptable alternatives.*

Materials and Activities for Emotional Development

As the preceding example with Ara indicates, many teachable moments for emotional development are spontaneous and come from the lives of children themselves. In addition, however, teachers can use a variety of materials and activities in the early childhood classroom to help children learn about dealing with feelings. The following materials are effective in allowing children to express their feelings in positive ways:

• *Art materials.* Clay, play dough, paints, and finger painting are all examples of materials that many children use regularly to express their feelings. Playing with a lump of play dough or painting a picture can be a healthy release for many children.

FOCUS ON . . .
Playing Out Feelings

Aaron, age three, is playing in the dress-up corner. He is taking care of a doll, pretending it is a new baby. Aaron's mother came home from the hospital last week with a newborn baby girl. Sarah, age four, is in the center as well, pretending to be the mommy.

Aaron: There, there baby, don't cry. I'll take good care of you all day long.

(He rocks the doll lovingly in his arm, swinging it gently back and forth.)

Sarah: Aaron, Mommy has to go to the store for some groceries, so you take good care of the baby while I'm gone.

Aaron: Okay, Mom. Don't worry. I'll be fine. See you later.

(After Sarah leaves for the groceries, Aaron's attitude changes. He becomes more aggressive and rough with the doll.)

Aaron: Stop that crying! I'm sick and tired of it! If you don't stop, I'm going to spank you!

(Aaron proceeds to spank the doll roughly. He then hears some other boys playing in the block corner, drops the doll, and runs to join them.)

1. Most children feel both positively and negatively toward a new baby brother or sister. What do you think Aaron might be feeling about his new baby sister, based on this scenario?

2. How can play help Aaron deal with his conflicting feelings?

- *Dramatic play props.* Dolls, puppets, dress-up clothes, and housekeeping materials can also encourage children to act out the experiences that lead to strong emotions. By playing them out, they can understand their feelings better and gradually work them out.

- *Books.* Many excellent children's books are available that address children's emotional issues. The story lines of these books bring up difficult issues (e.g., divorce or death) or the more normal emotions we all experience and help children begin to deal with the feelings involved.

- *Sand and water activities.* Play with sand and water has a definite therapeutic value. When this play is combined with small figurines and dramatic play props, children can once again play out their emotional concerns. Some professional therapy techniques use sand to encourage disturbed youngsters to play out their severe emotional traumas (Yawkey & Pellegrini, 1984).

- *Music.* Records, tapes, and CDs are available that either provide a calming background for classroom activities or address specific emotional issues. An example of the latter is Rosey Greer's "It's All Right to Cry" (on the album by Marlo Thomas, *Free to Be You and Me*).

Stress as a Factor in Social and Emotional Development

When we think about stress, we generally associate it with adult life rather than child-hood. But over the last two decades or so, more and more people have been concerned about the levels of stress that even young children experience. David Elkind (1981b) has been the most visible and well-known spokesperson for this issue.

Stress has always been a part of childhood. Making friends, going to grandma's house, learning about the world around them, and living in a family are all examples of the normal stresses of growing up. But what Elkind and others are concerned about are the additional stressors children face today. Divorce, violence and sexual themes on television, and the increased pressures of schooling are examples.

This combination of both normal and extra stress is making it difficult for many children to successfully deal with aspects of their social/emotional development. At some time, almost every child reaches a point where stress becomes overwhelming and developmental progress suffers. For example, a common response from children of divorce is that they feel responsible for their parents' breakup (Elkind, 1981b). These feelings can then cause children to devalue themselves as individuals and may negatively affect not only their overall self-esteem but their social development as well.

Stress Factors

So, what are the major factors causing children stress? Some have been mentioned briefly here, but the following list helps clarify the most significant issues:

Family Circumstances. The most common stressor faced by today's children is divorce. But remarriage, two-career families, and gay parents are other examples of family situations that can cause children stress. For example, a young child in a two-career family may experience what Elkind (1981b) calls change overload from being shuttled between early morning care, school, and late afternoon supervision.

Early Pressure to Excel. Many well-meaning parents inadvertently put stress on their children through involving them in many special activities. For example, for over thirty years Glenn Doman (1961) has been encouraging parents to teach their infants and toddlers to read. Although it is possible to teach children to read at very early ages, no research indicates that this approach has any long-term value. In most cases, all that the parents accomplish is to stress children by pushing an activity they aren't really ready for. Similarly, while some young children benefit from early musical experiences, sports programs, and computer camps, more often these experiences add stress to their lives.

Media Stress. Television is often cited as the most stressful media children experience on a regular basis (see, e.g., Center for Communication Policy, 1995). Young children have difficulty separating fact from fantasy and therefore struggle to

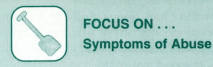

FOCUS ON . . .

Symptoms of Abuse

Child abuse is a serious issue that teachers must be prepared to deal with. As unpleasant as this topic is, child abuse affects many young children in American society (E. Blume, 1990). Teachers need to know the symptoms of abuse and report any suspected cases to the proper authorities. The following indicators are adapted from Bear, Schenk, and Buckner (1993):

	Physical Indicators	Behavioral Indicators
Physical abuse	Unexplained bruises	Self-destructive
	Unexplained burns	Behavioral extremes (withdrawn/aggressive)
	Unexplained fractures, lacerations, abrasions	Uncomfortable with physical contact
		Arrives at school early and stays late (afraid)
		Complains of soreness or moves uncomfortably
		Wears clothing to cover up body
Sexual abuse	Torn, stained, bloody underclothing	Withdrawn, chronic depression
	Pain, itching genitals	Hysteria, lack of emotional control
	Difficulty walking or sitting	Inappropriate sex play
	Bruises, bleeding in external genitalia	Threatened by physical contact, closeness
Emotional abuse	Speech disorders	Habit disorders (rocking)
	Delayed physical development	Neurotic traits (sleep disorders, inhibited play)
		Passive and aggressive behavioral extremes

1. Read more about child abuse and neglect. Report on your findings to a small group.

2. Talk to an early childhood teacher, and find out if she has had to deal with abuse. What were the reporting procedures? What were the results?

understand and cope with the violence and sexual themes. Television advertising has also been criticized because of the unhealthy foods and low-quality toys promoted (Notar, 1989). Movies, popular music, and even some children's books (e.g., see Carlsson-Paige & Levin, 1986) have also been cited for their stressful impact on children.

Child Abuse and Neglect. Parents and families under stress may react in very inappropriate ways to children. Physical abuse in the form of beatings, sexual relations between family members, and blatant neglect may result. Children want and need parental love; the added stresses of abuse and neglect are major barriers to healthy development.

Growing Up Too Quickly. Elkind (1981b) suggests that many children today are being pressured by society to grow into adulthood too quickly. He calls these children "hurried" and sees this push to grow up as a pervasive element in American society. Consider, for example, the clothing we now buy for our children. There is virtually no distinction between adults and children in the clothes we wear. When youngsters are dressed like adults, we expect them to engage in adult-like behavior. In many small ways like this, children are being hurried into adulthood.

Helping Children Cope

Clearly, children need adult assistance in working through both the normal stresses of development and the added complications of living in modern American society. Several good strategies are available to help children deal with stress (Elkind, 1981b; McCracken, 1986):

- *Be aware of the times we hurry children.* This recognition is the first step in helping children deal with their stress.
- *Analyze the distinctive effects of stress on each child.* The temperament, age, developmental level, and individual child's perception of the stress all influence the impact of stress. Some children seem to have an incredible ability to manage seemingly overwhelming circumstances; others struggle unsuccessfully to deal with much lower levels of stress.
- *Eliminate stressors whenever possible.* This is easy to say and much harder to do. But teachers and parents can work together to reduce stress by doing such things as making sure children eat right, get plenty of rest, slow down, have time to talk about issues and concerns, and avoid inappropriate television programming.
- *Take time to have fun with kids.* When teachers and other adults get to know children better by eating lunch with them occasionally or playing a game for fun, relationships are strengthened and children are fortified to better deal with the next stress to come their way.
- *Be respectful of children.* Elkind (1981b) suggests showing respect as a simple, direct way to let children know that we value them. Just knowing that adults care is a support to children under stress.

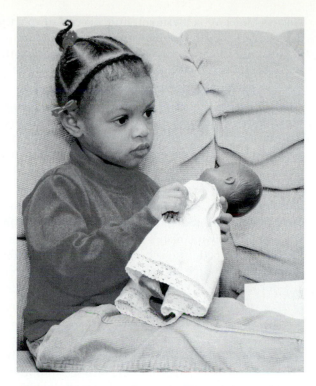

Children often play out the stresses they experience, using the toys and materials available to them.

- *Encourage childhood play.* Elkind states, "Basically, play is nature's way of dealing with stress for children as well as adults" (Elkind, 1981b, p. 197). When children can repeatedly play out the issues they are struggling to understand, they can make sense of them and gradually be able to set them aside. From the serious problems of a disturbed child (Axline, 1964) to the more mundane struggles of young children everywhere, childhood play is one of the best techniques available to work through stress (Henniger, 1994d).

Connecting with Parents and Families

Parents and families have major roles to play in the development of social and emotional competence. In addition to the effect of parents as models for their children, family life provides many opportunities for children to practice their developing skills in these areas. Teachers need to work cooperatively with the home to maximize the chances for consistency in both environments. This effort has three components:

1. *Parent education.* In many homes, parents and families need help in determining appropriate ways to assist children in their social/emotional development. A newsletter with a regular column on developing social skills, parent meetings to

discuss building self-esteem, and parent support groups are all examples of methods to provide families with the information they need to help their children in these areas. Parents who volunteer in the classroom also have the opportunity to observe the teacher's modeling of appropriate ways to encourage social and emotional development.

2. *Communication and cooperation.* By communicating goals for social and emotional development and the strategies the teacher will use for assisting children, parents can then work with the school in implementing this aspect of the curriculum. Similarly, when parents share their approaches with the teacher, home and school can cooperate in efforts to assist with the child's social and emotional development.

3. *The teacher as a resource.* In many instances, the issues faced by both children and their families are too complex to be managed by the teacher. For example, the stress of a family member's serious illness might lead to biting by a four-year-old. Help from outside the school may be needed. Teachers can assist parents by serving as a resource and guiding families to appropriate community agencies.

Summary

Teachers can enhance children's social competence by helping students develop a positive sense of self, by promoting strong student–teacher relationships, and by enabling effective peer interactions. Teachers need to be aware of the environment, materials, activities, and themes for a social development curriculum. Children experience a wide range of emotions; teachers can help children deal with their emotions, using materials and activities for the social development curriculum. Teachers can also help children cope with stress and can work with parents and families to facilitate the social and emotional development of young children.

∾ For Discussion and Action

1. Think about your own self-concept. What makes you feel good about yourself? Are there issues or events that cause you to feel less positive? Talk this over with others, and then apply your findings to working with children. How can this help you in building their self-concept?

2. Work with a small group of peers, and develop a list of specific ways in which teachers serve as models for young children in social relationships. Discuss the importance of being a good model.

3. Think back to your own childhood. Who was your first friend? What do you remember about this person? Discuss what you remember with others, and then talk about what this tells you about helping children build friendships.

4. In a small group, develop a list of positive ways of dealing with anger. Talk about how you could help a first-grade child use one or more of these strategies.

5. Spend some time in an early childhood classroom. Look especially for materials, books, and equipment that may help children with their social/emotional development. Talk to the teacher about how she specifically addresses this content in the curriculum.

∾ Building Your Personal Library

Canfield, J., & Wells, H. (1994). *100 ways to enhance self-concept in the classroom.* Boston: Allyn & Bacon. As the title suggests, this book is loaded with ideas for helping children develop healthy self-esteem. With modification in some instances, the ideas are useful in working with children throughout the early childhood range.

Elkind, D. (1981). *The hurried child: Growing up too fast too soon.* Reading, MA: Addison Wesley. This is a classic book describing the stresses children face today and the problems that come from pushing children to grow up too quickly. An excellent book for both parents and teachers.

Kostelnik, M., Stein, L., Whiren, A., & Soderman, A. (1993). *Guiding children's social development* (2nd ed.). Albany, NY: Delmar. Providing a strong developmental understanding of the social issues faced by young children, this book also gives much good advice about how to deal with the problems that arise.

McClellan, D., & Katz, L. (1997). *Fostering children's social competence: The teacher's role.* Washington, DC: National Association for the Education of Young Children. This book is designed to blend research and practice on the subject of strengthening young children's social skills. It is an important resource on the topic.

In this chapter you will

■ Study the goals for cognitive development in the early childhood classroom.

■ Develop an understanding of the constructivist approach to learning.

■ Address issues relating to mathematics instruction in early childhood.

■ Identify the science curriculum for young children.

■ Understand the importance of social studies in the early childhood classroom.

Michael and Eric are fascinated by their discoveries from morning recess. Using the bug catchers from the science center, they have managed to capture a ladybug, two spiders, and several ants. After creating separate homes for each of their bugs with leaves, sticks, and dirt, the boys are off to the computer to see if they can find out what their new friends like to eat. These second graders are learning to navigate the World Wide Web and soon will find some sites to explore.

During the afternoon recess, Michael and Eric scour the playground for food for their bug collection and additional materials for the habitats (a term they learned from the Web search). Following recess, they record what they have learned in the science center journal. The boys also make plans to describe their bug collection at tomorrow's sharing time. They talk with the teacher about what they want to do and how long it will take.

Eric decides to take home one of the books in the science center to help him prepare for tomorrow's presentation. Michael has agreed to spend some more time browsing the Web on his family's home computer to gather additional information for sharing time. Both boys leave school flushed with excitement and ready to continue learning about bugs.

In the situation just described, Michael and Eric are engaged in constructivist learning. As they study the living creatures found on the playground, both boys are developing mathematics, science, and language skills. They are engaged in the process of cognitive development.

The word *cognition* has its roots in the Latin word *cognoscere*, which means "to know." **Cognitive development** is the continuing process of learning about the world and all of its many components. Young children come to understand their environment best through manipulating real-world materials and discovering facts, concepts, and relationships. Although this intellectual growth is greatest during the early years, healthy people never stop learning.

Goals of the Cognitive Curriculum

A major role of the teaching profession is to facilitate students' intellectual understanding. The preparation for and teaching of mathematics, science, and social studies are central to education at all levels, including the early years. Therefore, teachers must clearly understand what should be taught in the early childhood classroom and how this instruction should take place.

FOCUS ON . . .
Brain Research—Blessing or Curse?

Research on brain development in young children has caught the imagination of the public. While the data have been accumulating for over twenty years, recent advances in technology have made it possible to gain even deeper insights into early brain functioning (Newberger, 1997).

The news confirms what early childhood educators have been promoting for many years: Young children learn a great deal during the first few years of life. The research makes it clear that

- Early brain stimulation is critical.
- Early deprivation can lead to permanent delays.
- Strong, caring relationships with adults are essential.

The good news is that this research reaffirms the importance of quality programs for young children. The brain's development is enhanced through early stimulation. Cognitive development should be an important part of the early childhood curriculum.

But, in the past, similar information has been misinterpreted by many adults and has led to childhood stress (Elkind, 1981a). When well-meaning parents or the uninformed public take this research to mean that children need early, more formalized learning experiences for development to proceed normally, children are poorly served. Most of the adults who misunderstand the current brain research assume that cognitive development is a structured, teacher-directed activity. Few realize that play, constructivist learning, and warm relationships with adults are the most important ways to stimulate the brain. Teachers need to educate parents and others about developmentally appropriate learning so that the public can interpret this important brain research appropriately.

1. Talk to a parent of an infant/toddler about the recent interest in brain research and its implications. Share your findings with others.

2. What would you suggest a parent of a preschool child do if she were concerned about helping stimulate brain development? Find a written source that supports your position.

Learning Facts

Think back to your elementary school years and the teaching of mathematics, science, and social studies. Unless your experience was very unusual, much of your time was spent on learning facts. Mathematics emphasized number facts such as the multiplication tables. Science probably included tasks like studying the parts of a flower. Social studies provided additional opportunities to memorize names and dates associated with important events or people.

How much of this information do you remember today? Most people find that they retain only a small portion of the facts they have learned. Although the instruction may have been both fun and intellectually stimulating at the time, the facts themselves are often forgotten. Does this tell you anything about the value of a cognitive curriculum that places heavy emphasis on the learning of facts?

Make no mistake: The learning of facts is often a very important task. Could you successfully balance your checkbook without ready recall of addition and subtraction facts? Isn't a basic knowledge of motor vehicle laws necessary every time you drive a car? There is much essential information that every adult needs to function as a productive member of society. However, when facts become the primary focus of the learning process, a child's development suffers.

In many instances, the factual information learned in early childhood settings is secondary to other more important goals. Take, for example, the science experiences of Michael and Eric described at the beginning of this chapter. As they explore the Internet, read books on bugs, and talk to others, they are learning facts. But it is the *process* of scientific learning that is most important and will lead to the greatest long-term benefits.

Critical Thinking

If the learning of facts should not be the primary focus of the cognitive curriculum in early childhood, what should? Educators have emphasized three goals: (1) Foster critical thinking, (2) encourage problem solving, and (3) promote lifelong learning (Bredekamp & Copple, 1997; National Center for Improving Science, 1989; National Council for Teachers of Mathematics, 1989).

Teachers in the early childhood classroom need to recognize the importance of promoting critical thinking in children. Today's citizens are bombarded with information from so many different sources that it is difficult even for adults to make sense of it all. Teachers need to help children develop the ability to critically examine data and determine what is useful in making specific decisions and what is not.

Piaget effectively describes the importance of critical thinking:

> [An essential] goal of education is to form minds which can be critical, can verify, and not accept everything they are offered. The great danger today is of slogans, collective opinions, ready-made trends of thought. We have to be able to resist individually, to criticize, to distinguish between what is proven and what is not. So we need pupils who are active, who learn early to find out by themselves, partly by their own spontaneous activity and partly through materials we set up for them. (quoted in Elkind, 1981a, p. 29)

Problem Solving

A second important goal for the cognitive curriculum is to help children become successful problem solvers. On a daily basis, each of us encounters situations that we must evaluate and deal with. Children need to develop skills in first recognizing, and then dealing with, the problems that come their way. The ability to confidently approach issues, identify possible strategies for dealing with them, and then successfully resolve problems requires considerable cognitive skill.

A major tool for encouraging problem solving in the early childhood classroom is the creative play experience. As children engage in play, they naturally encounter many problems to be resolved.

Shauntel and Blythe are playing in the sandbox outdoors. They are trying to create a tunnel connecting their two holes in the sand. Shauntel suggests trying to use sticks from the playground to strengthen the walls of their tunnel. Although the sticks help, both girls are disappointed in the results. Blythe adds a second option when she proposes they try digging their holes deeper and connecting farther down in the sandbox. This option, however, makes it difficult to make the bend needed to join the holes. After talking through their dilemma yet again, they decide to try moistening the sand with water so that it will remain firmer through the digging process. They have found a workable solution.

Because there are no right or wrong answers in play, children can feel free to experiment, explore, and problem solve as Shauntel and Blythe have done. Tegano, Sawyers, and Moran (1989) put it this way:

> When playing, young children openly and spontaneously express themselves because they are in a nonthreatening environment. The creative process—defining the problem, generating ideas and solutions, evaluating solutions, converting solutions into outcomes—is enhanced in an open, "psychologically safe" environment. (p. 93)

Lifelong Learning

A third important goal for the cognitive curriculum is to instill in children a love of learning that will help them continue growing intellectually throughout their lives. While young children tend to be naturally curious about the world around them, the schooling process has often been accused of dampening enthusiasm. Albert Einstein (1949) said this about education:

> It is in fact nothing short of a miracle that the modern methods of instruction have not yet entirely strangled the *holy curiosity of inquiry* [emphasis added]. . . . It is a very grave mistake to think that the enjoyment of seeing and searching can be promoted by means of coercion and a sense of duty. (p. 17)

Einstein is implying that, when instruction consists of hands-on learning through discovery, children are much more curious and are motivated to understand their world. This, again, reinforces the importance of play in the early childhood classroom. As children engage in center activities, they are spontaneously and naturally involved in cognitive development and are motivated to learn more. This playful way of knowing is essential in stimulating a positive attitude toward lifelong learning.

The Constructivist Approach

It should be clear from the preceding discussion that traditional educational methods in which the teacher dispenses knowledge to children who are passive recipients are not compatible with the goals described for the cognitive curriculum. A developmentally appropriate approach, which is much more effective, is referred to as **constructivist education.** Grounded in the developmental theories of Jean Piaget (Piaget, 1950), this approach to early education promotes the idea that children build or construct their own understanding of the world through activities based on personal interests. As they manipulate real-world objects, children create for themselves an understanding of the world around them.

Chaille and Britain (1997) have identified four characteristics of children that make the constructivist approach the best match for early learning:

1. *Young children are theory builders.* The constructivist position suggests that knowledge is built by children themselves as they make educated guesses about why things work the way they do and then test out their theories in the real world. Children do this naturally and without prompting by adults.

2. *Cognition requires a foundation of physical knowledge.* Children are naturally motivated to understand the physical world around them. This knowledge of how objects and materials such as balls and cubes work lays the foundation for the more abstract understandings that come later.

3. *Increasing autonomy and independence.* As young children mature, they gradually move from dependence on adults for meeting their needs to more independent functioning. Healthy youngsters have a strong need to experiment, explore, and discover on their own.

4. *Young children are social beings.* Children are naturally social and spend considerable effort planning and interacting with others. These interchanges are an important part of the learning process. Children construct many understandings through their social exchanges with adults and peers.

DeVries and Zan (1995) identify the following strategies for creating a constructivist classroom:

- *Cultivate an atmosphere of respect.* Children need to work and play in a classroom in which they are respected as individuals and encouraged to experiment and explore without fear of poor treatment by adults or peers. This atmosphere frees children to engage in constructing knowledge as they interact with people and things.

- *Allow children to be active learners.* The best learning occurs when children are allowed to pursue their own interests and physically manipulate the things in their environment. A child's mental functioning is enhanced when physical activity also takes place.

- *Foster social interactions.* When cognitive tasks allow for social interchange, childhood learning is enhanced. Sharing ideas with others helps clarify misunderstandings and provides additional perspectives that enrich the learning experiences.

- *Emphasize self-regulation and reflection.* As adults help children to take responsibility for their learning experiences, children become more independent and self-confident in seeking new knowledge. Encouraging reflection leads to an attitude of questioning that is at the heart of critical thinking.

Mathematics and Young Children

When many of us recall our own early mathematical experiences, memories of rote learning with little connection to real life often predominate. But mathematics is an exciting, interesting, relevant topic for investigation. With the constructivist approach, young children can learn a broad assortment of topics through manipulation and discovery and make mathematical connections to real issues in the world around them.

Classification

During early childhood, children develop cognitive understanding of many mathematical concepts that are essential to future growth in the discipline. One such concept is the ability to classify. Putting objects or ideas with similar characteristics into groups demonstrates **classification** competence.

Although this cognitive ability seems simple for us as adults, children require considerable practice and time to understand classification. For example, a three-year-old child given a set of colored blocks and asked to "put blocks together that are the same" may playfully organize and reorganize the blocks, not really using any logical thinking in creating his groupings.

Classification skills are fundamental to many mathematical concepts. For example, writing the numeral 43 requires an understanding of the "ten's place" and "one's place" as different groupings. In addition, the study of algebraic functions places a heavy emphasis on the ability to classify, for example, "Consider n to be the set of all integers greater than zero."

Teachers of young children can provide many opportunities for practicing an understanding of classification. Mary Baratta-Lorton (1976), in her classic book titled, *Mathematics Their Way,* provides many good ideas for simple materials that can be used for sorting and classifying tasks:

- People in the classroom
- Buttons for grouping
- Old bottle caps
- Natural materials for sorting such as acorns, leaves, rocks, shells
- Nuts and bolts
- Teacher-directed activities using geoboards (square board with twenty-five regularly spaced pegs over which rubber bands can be stretched)

Seriation

Ordering objects from smallest to largest is referred to as **seriation.** This sequencing can be based on height, weight, shades of color, or any other characteristic. This is another important cognitive task for young children to master. It is essential to an understanding of the number system.

Many opportunities to practice this skill are necessary for children to truly make sense of it. Although parts of this cognitive understanding are seen in many children at age three or four, full conceptual development is often reached at age eight or nine. Piaget spent considerable time studying the growth of this developmental task (Flavell, 1963).

Many excellent commercial materials are available to give children practice with seriation. One well-known example is Montessori's cylinder block. Each rectangular block has several wooden cylinders that fit into holes ordered from smallest to largest in the block. Children practice their sequencing skills by finding the right cylinder for each hole. Another set of materials that can be used for seriation activities are Cuisenaire Rods. These multicolored rods begin with a small cube as the basic unit and grow step by step to the longest rod, ten units in length.

Patterning

Being able to recognize and create visual, auditory, spatial, and numerical **patterns** is another important mathematical understanding. The discipline of mathematics is very logical and based on patterns of all sorts. The number system, for example, with groupings of ten has a clear pattern that children must recognize to truly understand its complexities. Students must also master patterns in arithmetic, algebra, and geometry.

Teachers can provide young children with many meaningful opportunities to engage in patterning activities. Some examples of appropriate materials and activities include

- Stringing beads in patterns
- Constructing designs with pattern blocks
- Repeating clapping patterns
- Listening to musical patterns
- Building with Unifix Cubes (plastic cubes that can be snapped together to form patterns)
- Playing with Cuisenaire Rods

Number Concepts

Children's understandings of number develop rapidly during the early childhood years. While a three-year-old often is just beginning to understand that one is a small number and others are larger, five-year-olds have typically mastered basic number concepts through nine (Murray & Mayer, 1988). During the primary years, children develop the ability to count forward and backward, skip count (counting by twos, fives, tens, etc.), and understand numbers into the hundreds (Wolfinger, 1994).

Patterning activities are an important element of the early childhood math curriculum.

Counting.   Much of the preschool child's understanding of number comes from repeated counting experiences. Many songs and finger plays (e.g., "Five Little Speckled Frogs" and "Ten Little Monkeys") are appropriate for teachers to use in order to give children rote counting experience. The day-to-day life of the classroom and home provide many other meaningful opportunities to count and understand number. Discussing the calendar at group time, counting crackers in the snack bowl, and finding out how many ladybugs were caught on the playground are examples of these natural opportunities for counting.

It is important to remember that primary children are often most comfortable in counting as they begin to add and subtract. Although this strategy eventually becomes cumbersome and slow, it does help many children make the transition to more mature arithmetic skills. The use of concrete materials in counting is still necessary for many primary children, and teachers should encourage it at this level.

Arithmetic Skills.   During the primary years, children develop the ability to understand addition, subtraction, and multiplication. However, part of the problem with the traditional approach to teaching these skills is that not all children are cognitively ready to begin when the teacher starts this instruction. Some may need more counting experience first, while others should spend additional time developing basic number concepts. When the teacher uses a constructivist approach and allows children to manipulate materials and discover arithmetic understandings as they work on real-world problems, children are much more able to set their own pace and conquer this task.

Preschool teacher: (Holding up a ball.) We're going to talk about shapes today. This ball is shaped like a *circle.*

Kindergarten teacher: (Writing on the chalkboard.) This is how we write the *number* five.

Second-grade teacher: (Demonstrating with manipulatives.) I have five Popsicle sticks in my right hand and seven in my left. Which hand is holding *less?*

In each of these situations, teachers have used inaccurate terms to describe mathematical situations. In the first, the preschool teacher has used a two-dimensional term to describe a three-dimensional object (sphere). The kindergarten teacher should have used the word *numeral* rather than *number* to describe her representation on the chalkboard. In the last situation, the more accurate term is *fewer,* rather than *less.*

These are common errors that many teachers make daily. They seem like pretty minor issues. Is it really worth the effort it would take to use more accurate terms?

Tracy (1994) makes a strong case for refining the language we use to teach mathematics.

Language directly influences the concepts we develop. Because mathematics is such a precise field of study, teachers need to use accurate language with children. Not only is it easier for children to understand precise language, but they enjoy using the more interesting terms. *Rhombus, ellipse, cube, rectangle,* and *numeral* are all words that children can learn and enjoy.

Teachers need to first recognize the terms they are using that may cause misunderstandings and then work to use more appropriate words to describe the mathematical concepts being presented. Although this is not an easy task, the benefits to children are worth the effort.

1. *In a small group, generate a list of inaccurate language that may cause mathematical misunderstandings in young children. What terms should be used in their place?*

2. *Is this issue really that important to overall cognitive development? Discuss this with a group of peers.*

Measurement

Another important mathematical understanding to be emphasized during the early years is the ability to quantify materials in the world. Finding the height, weight, volume, and dimensions of objects are examples of **measurement.** Piaget's work tells us that, until children have reached the stage of concrete operations (around age seven or eight), they have difficulty measuring using standardized units such as inches, pounds, and liters (Flavell, 1963). Younger children, however, can learn much when given the opportunity to measure with nonstandard units.

The preschool and kindergarten child can engage in the following types of informal measurement activities:

- Use blocks to measure tables, floor space, and other elements of the classroom environment.
- Find out how many plastic cups of sand or water it takes to fill containers in the sand or water play area.
- Use a balance beam to compare weights of different objects.
- Trace full-body silhouettes of children and have them compare heights.

Children in the primary grades can engage in many of these same activities but with the use of standardized units of measurement. Children this age can use and understand rulers, weight scales, and one-cup containers. Measurement activities should remain meaningful and relevant to the children's lives; to achieve this goal, consider weighing the class guinea pig, measuring the dimensions of playground equipment, and discovering how many liters of water are needed to fill the sink in the classroom.

Geometry

The study of two- and three-dimensional shapes and how they are related to one another is called **geometry.** Although this topic is often thought of as part of the high school mathematics curriculum, it is highly applicable in the early childhood classroom. The young child's world is filled with interesting shapes to explore and understand.

Young children develop geometric understandings from playing with materials such as unit blocks, pattern blocks, tangrams, and paper for origami. In addition, teachers can help children identify the many shapes that exist in the classroom and outdoors on the playground by casually pointing them out. Books like *My Very First Book of Shapes* (Carle, 1985) can be good discussion starters for this topic.

Problem Solving

The National Council for Teachers of Mathematics (NCTM) is working hard to reshape mathematics education at all levels. In a set of guidelines titled *Curriculum and Evaluation Standards for School Mathematics* (NCTM, 1989), this organization describes the need for mathematically literate workers for the coming century. No longer can mathematics be limited to rote learning of facts and procedures. Students must be encouraged to reason, analyze, and engage in effective problem solving.

As indicated earlier in this chapter, helping children become effective problem solvers is an important goal of the cognitive curriculum. Play experiences are wonderful opportunities for mathematical problem solving.

༄ *As Morgan and Blake play in the block area, they encounter a problem in building the last wall for their house. There aren't enough blocks of the appropriate size left to finish the construction. They discuss the possible options, including*

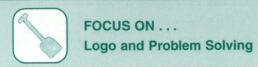
Seymour Papert, a professor at the Massachusetts Institute of Technology, developed a powerful computer programming language called Logo, which children can use to move the image of a turtle around the computer screen. Using a combination of basic commands such as forward, back, left, and right, young children can engage in high-level problem-solving tasks. In his groundbreaking book titled *Mindstorms: Children, Computers, and Powerful Ideas* (1980), Papert describes how this playing around with the turtle computer image has great potential for cognitive development:

> That all this would be fun needs no argument. But it is more than fun. Very powerful kinds of learning are taking place. Children working with an electronic sketchpad are learning a language for talking about shapes and fluxes of shapes, about velocities and rates of change, about processes and procedures. They are learning to speak mathematics, and acquiring a new image of themselves as mathematicians. (p. 13)

For many primary children, the Logo computer language can be a very powerful tool for problem solving and creative activity. Many curriculum tools have been developed so that teachers can assist children in using Logo in an open-ended, constructivist approach to learning. Although this program is one of the earliest attempts to create a playful computer environment for young children to explore, it is still one of the best options available (Clements, Nastasi, & Swaminathan, 1993) and should be included in the primary classroom.

1. Locate a copy of the Logo computer language, and spend some time finding out its properties. What are your impressions?

2. Are you aware of other computer programs that allow for open-ended exploration and quality problem-solving opportunities? Discuss this with a group of peers.

using twice as many blocks that are half as long as the others. When they try out their solution, it works. Blake and Morgan are gaining experience in mathematical problem solving.

Science Learning

Just as mathematical concepts are an important part of the early years, the science curriculum surrounds young children in their daily lives. What makes some things float and others sink at the water table? How does a flower grow? What does an ant eat? What makes a person grow? How do fish breathe? Why does a magnet pick up some things but not others? When teachers prepare an environment that allows children to manipulate and discover the answers to these important questions, the science curriculum will be a major success.

Scientific inquiry can be an exciting part of early learning.

Science consists of three main components: content, process, and attitudes (Wolfinger, 1994). **Content** is the actual body of knowledge developed over time by the scientific community. The **scientific process** consists of the methods that scientists use to gather information and solve problems. In this context, the term **attitudes** refers to the way a person approaches a scientific problem. Each of these components is described in the following sections.

Scientific Content

Conceptually, science content is often divided into the **physical sciences** (which include physics, chemistry, geology, and astronomy) and the **biological sciences** (biology, botany, and zoology). At first glance, these topics may seem more appropriate for the high school curriculum; however, teachers will find many opportunities to build developmentally appropriate science content into the early childhood classroom. The following examples should help clarify this point:

Early Physics Experiences. Physics can be defined as "the science of matter and energy and of interactions between the two" (Chaille & Britain, 1997, p. 76). When we provide children with opportunities to discover the physical properties of objects, they are learning physics concepts. Sprung (1996) provides three examples of appropriate physics activities:

- Ramp experiments provide materials that allow children to roll objects down ramps that they construct. Children learn about the properties of inclined planes.

- Water experiments provide materials that allow children to explore the properties of water. For example, funnels of different sizes allow children to experiment with the rate at which water moves through varying diameters.

- Tinkering experiments allow children to tinker with objects to see how they work. For example, children can take apart and put back together old appliances that adults have made safe.

Early Chemistry Experiences. Chemistry is defined as the study of substances and what happens when they are combined or come in contact with one another. Here are a few examples of chemistry activities for young children:

- *Cooking activities.* When mixing ingredients and cooking foods, teachers and children can observe and discuss the changes that are taking place in the materials used.

- *Mixing liquids of different viscosities.* Mix liquid corn oil and water, for example, and observe the results. To add an element of ecology, mix motor oil and water, and then try to figure out ways to separate the two liquids.

- *Engage in bubble-making activities.* The process of making bubble solutions can be a fun chemistry project. It often takes some effort to get the best solution. Using different items to blow bubbles adds an element of physics to the project.

Early Zoology Experiences. Zoology is the study of animals. Children love the opportunity to feed, hold, and learn more about all sorts of living creatures. Guinea pigs, rabbits, mice, hamsters, turtles, frogs, lizards, and gerbils are examples of animals that teachers can bring into the early childhood classroom for children to study as part of the zoology curriculum. Field trips to the zoo or a local farm can provide additional opportunities for learning about animals.

The examples presented here illustrate that scientific content does not have to be mysterious or foreign to young children. Teachers can develop similar appropriate methods for learning geology, astronomy, and botany concepts. Furthermore, strong early childhood programs have been presenting children with opportunities to study scientific content since the beginning of this century (Sprung, 1996).

Gardening with Young Children

Digging in the dirt is unquestionably a favorite activity for many young children. When combined with planting and growing vegetables, herbs, flowers, and other living things in a garden bed, young children have many wonderful opportunities for science learnings. Clemens (1996) describes four different types of gardens that teachers can effectively use with young children:

Container Gardens. By using small containers such as milk cartons or purchased pots, teachers can convert nearly any spot into a small garden area for children. Each container can hold a different type of plant, or each child can have her own container garden.

Square-Foot Gardens. Another option is to mark off a small area that can be considered the garden spot for a specific class. Because each garden is small, more classrooms can participate in the fun of gardening. It doesn't take much space to enjoy creative gardening activities.

Conventional Gardens. Having a somewhat larger space where vegetables and flowers can be planted in traditional rows can be another viable option. It requires more upkeep but is very workable if space is available.

Raised Gardens. A raised garden bed is created by using some sort of wood or rock border that builds the garden bed up several inches above the ground. This arrangement makes the bed easier to plant and weed and can allow for the addition of soil amendments to aid in growing. Additionally, the soil warms earlier in the spring for planting.

Gardening has great potential for helping children to learn science. Children can predict, experiment, draw conclusions, observe patterns, and understand interactions between plants, insects, and birds. They can learn about the growth process of plants and how it varies between species. Children can study and understand the effects of rain, drought, wind, and sun. The opportunities for constructivist learning are virtually unlimited.

The Scientific Process

The processes used to study science are even more important than the content. Early childhood specialists need to promote the same techniques that scientists themselves use in their inquiries. This process consists of the following steps:

1. *Identify a problem for investigation.* Scientists must first recognize that a situation needs to be studied. Teachers can help young children identify problems through the use of simple questions or statements like, "Abby, do you know what a spider eats?"

2. *Collect data.* Once a problem is identified, a scientist works to collect information that may be useful in solving the problem. For young children, practicing good observation techniques is a primary way to collect data.

3. *Generate possible solutions to problems.* Following the collection of data, scientists formulate several hypotheses or solutions for the problems they face. Play situations provide many opportunities for children to generate solutions to the problems they face.

4. *Test solutions.* Some potential solutions simply will not work, while others are only partially successful. The only way to work through a problem is to keep trying until success is achieved. Adults can help children know that it is normal to strike out many times before finding an option that works.

5. *Draw conclusions and share with others.* Once the testing has taken place, the scientist summarizes his findings and shares the results of his investigations with others.

Developing Scientific Attitudes

The scientist approaches problems with attitudes or ways of thinking that help her succeed. These approaches do not come easily to young children, and they will need assistance in using them. Teachers can model these attitudes while providing the guidance necessary to ensure that children use these approaches themselves. Wolfinger (1994) identifies five qualities that are essential to scientific investigations:

- *Objectivity.* This is perhaps the most difficult attitude to model and encourage in children. Basically, objectivity is the ability to look at all sides of an issue before making a decision. Many adults struggle with being objective. Children, because of their egocentrism during the early childhood years, also find this difficult. Adults must work hard to model appropriate objectivity as they work with children.

- *Willingness to suspend judgment.* A scientist waits until all of the evidence is in before making a decision. The adult must again be a good model by demonstrating a willingness to suspend judgment in problems encountered with children.

- *Skepticism.* Although this word often carries a negative connotation, the skeptic is one who questions all things. Rather than simply accepting the first idea that comes to mind, the scientist questions, searches for additional information, and critically evaluates the available data. The teacher can guide children through this process as they approach science activities.

- *Respect for the environment.* Scientific inquiry should never be damaging to any part of the natural environment. Taking fallen leaves on a nature walk rather than stripping live ones from a tree, keeping insects alive for observation and study rather than killing them, and using organic methods for controlling insects in a garden bed are all examples of environmentally friendly approaches to science activities.

- *Positive approach to failure.* When students make predictions for solutions to a problem, many will prove to be wrong. But, often in scientific work, much is learned from failure. It helps refine an understanding of the problem and may lead to a future solution. Adults need to work hard to let children know that it is perfectly acceptable to make predictions that are wrong and need to help children learn from their misperceptions.

Because of the importance of mathematics and science in today's world, all children must have the opportunity to succeed in these fields. Unfortunately, however, statistics indicate that this currently is not the case. For example, although women represent 45 percent of the total work force, only 13 percent are scientists and engineers (Shaw & Blake, 1998). In mathematics performance, white students have consistently achieved higher than their black or Hispanic peers, and Asian American students perform higher than whites (Shaw & Blake, 1998).

What can be done to improve this situation? Although attitudes change slowly, and it will be difficult to improve conditions quickly, the following two ideas can be important first steps:

Equal Opportunities to Participate

Most teachers intuitively feel that they encourage boys, girls, all cultures, and all socioeconomic groups to participate at the same level in science and math activities. However, research suggests this is not the case. For example, consider the way teachers usually set up a block center. The accessories are typically those that interest boys: trucks, airplanes, zoo animals, and so on. When the block center includes materials more attractive to girls, both sexes will use it to learn important math and science concepts. Teachers also need to become more aware of how effectively they are verbally encouraging children to engage in science and math activities. Either videotaping or audiotaping a portion of the day can help in discovering problem spots.

Get the Support of Parents

Parents play a significant role in all of child development. They make a big difference in how children perceive the importance of science and mathematics. If parents support the value of these subjects, assist with simple learning experiences around the home, and encourage play and reading activities to replace unregulated television viewing, children will be much more successful in mathematics and science. Unfortunately, this role is often hard for many parents who were themselves unsuccessful in these subjects in their own childhood. Thoughtful parent education and involvement are needed to correct this difficult situation.

1. *Spend some time working with a young child who is struggling in science or math. Try to find ways to make the child feel she can succeed.*

2. *Talk to a teacher about ways she tries to encourage children to engage in math and science activities.*

Young Children and the Social Studies

Social studies help children understand relationships between people and environmental factors influencing their lives. In the adult world, this very broad topic includes the disciplines of history, psychology, economics, sociology, anthropology, geography, and political science. Young children are constantly engaged in the process of learning about human relationships and the factors that influence them.

Developmentally, children begin their lives learning to relate to their primary caregivers. Crying, smiling, touching, staring, and vocalizing are early attempts to understand and communicate with parents and significant others. Gradually, children begin to expand their sphere of learning about people, relationships, and the environment. Developing an understanding of self and family, relating to friends and relatives, and developing relationships in school are all examples of this growing interest in broader social studies learnings.

Urie Bronfenbrenner (1979) created an influential theory of human development called the **ecological model** to describe the many different systems that contribute to the overall development of the child. He proposes four major systems that influence children's growth (see Figure 14–1):

- *Microsystem.* This includes close relationships within the home, school, neighborhood, and church. These are the earliest and some of the strongest influences on the young child's development.

- *Mesosystem.* Surrounding the microsystem, these factors include the interactions and relationships between home, school, neighborhood, and church. For example, the communications and interactions between parents and teachers have an impact on the child's development.

- *Exosystem.* The exosystem consists of local governmental agencies, the parents' workplace, mass media, and local industry. Although the influences of these elements are less direct, it should be clear that they all impact the overall development of children.

- *Macrosystem.* Encompassing all of the other systems is the macrosystem, which includes the dominant beliefs and ideologies of the culture. These beliefs also influence the child's development.

Bronfenbrenner's model is helpful in describing the systems that influence child development; it also identifies the general direction of learning in the social studies. Young children focus most of their efforts on learning about people and relationships in the microsystem. Gradually, during the elementary years, children begin to take an interest in learning about the mesosystem and exosystem. Although even very young children experience the influence of the macrosystem, a conscious understanding of this system will likely come after the early childhood years.

Understanding Self

The young child's social studies interests begin with an understanding of self. Although this is a lifelong process for each of us, it is during the early childhood years that children become aware of their physical, emotional, and intellectual selves and begin to understand how they are similar to and different from others.

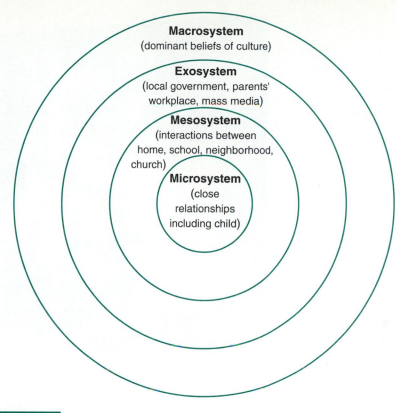

Macrosystem
(dominant beliefs of culture)

Exosystem
(local government, parents'
workplace, mass media)

Mesosystem
(interactions between
home, school, neighborhood,
church)

Microsystem
(close
relationships
including child)

❧ *Figure 14–1*   *Bronfenbrenner's Ecology of Human Development*

Much of this learning about self is informal and comes from interactions with parents, teachers, and others. At the same time, more structured experiences help children learn about themselves. Hamilton, Flemming, and Hicks (1990) suggest the following categories for this study of self:

My body.

I belong to someone.

My family is special.

I can change by growing.

I can change by learning.

I can change by dressing differently.

I can change by getting sick/well.

I can change by acting differently.

Some things I cannot change.

An understanding of self begins during the first year of life.

A closer look at one of these categories may help clarify the kinds of planned events that help children develop a sense of self. A study of children's physical selves (the first category mentioned) might include the following activities:

- *Body art.* In the art center, children can create their own handprints and footprints and can have an adult trace their bodies on large sheets of paper for decoration.

- *Polaroid photos.* Take photographs of children in the class, discuss similarities and differences at group time, and then mount the pictures on a bulletin board so that children can study them in more detail.

- *Read stories.* Collect several books that talk about children's physical selves, and read them at group time. Two examples are Berry (1986), *Teach Me about Series: My Body,* and Brenner (1970), *Bodies.* Have the books available during center time for children to browse.

- *Sing songs.* Many songs help children understand their physical selves. Some examples include "Head, and Shoulders, Knees, and Toes," "You Are Special" (Mr. Rogers), and "Getting to Know Myself" (Hap Palmer).

Understanding Others

Throughout the early years, children are expanding their knowledge of human relationships as they interact with parents, teachers, peers, and others. Understanding **relationships within the family** are important starting points for this growing knowledge base. Families influence almost every aspect of the young child's early development and generate much interest as a topic of discussion in the classroom. Some ideas for the study of families include

- *Family of the week.* Make sure each family in your classroom has a special week when they can share with others elements of their lives at home. Invite parents/caregivers and siblings into the classroom; have the family create a bulletin board, family scrapbook, or videotape that helps others know about them; encourage parents/caregivers to share occupations, hobbies, and family traditions.

- *Holiday celebrations.* Every family is shaped by their cultural roots, and this can be celebrated through the sharing of special holiday traditions. Take advantage of the diversity of families within the classroom to learn about similarities and differences between cultures.

- *Family volunteers.* Encouraging parents, relatives, and older siblings to spend time helping out in the classroom can be an effective way for children to learn about family differences through casual interactions.

- *Family foods.* Have families sign up to provide special snack foods that are popular in the home. Food is a great socializer and can be another way to initiate conversations about similarities and differences among families.

- *Family jobs.* Parents/caregivers can share with the class their work responsibilities. A photo essay, videotape, field trip, or personal sharing time (with appropriate work props) can be a productive way to learn more about families.

A second important component of understanding others is the study of **community relationships.** A frequent starting point for this discussion is to learn about community helpers. What does a police officer do? How does a firefighter control a burning building? Why does the doctor listen to my chest with her stethoscope? Children are fascinated by these issues and many more. Taking a field trip to these community work sites or inviting these workers into the classroom makes for exciting social studies learning.

Many aspects of community relationships remain hidden to children unless we take the time to point them out. Where does the garbage go once the truck picks it up? How do grocery stores work? Who fixes the city street when it needs repair? Children are curious about these issues and more. Adults should make sure that the early childhood program has many opportunities to address the complexities of community relationships.

Constructivist Social Studies

One important way to involve children in valuable social studies experiences is to build on the current events in their daily lives. Using these experiences as a starting point, children can construct deeper understandings of the world around them. Suskind (1993) describes one example of this approach used with preschool children. During the Persian Gulf war of 1990, children in an army preschool whose parents were being sent to participate in Operation Desert Shield encountered the following materials in their classroom:

We converted a corner of the classroom into a small version of Saudi Arabia. We hung camouflage netting over an army cot covered with a drab-green sleeping bag. We put camouflage clothing, mock Arab headdresses, and an army helmet in a locker. A "communication board" with holes for two sets of headphones sat on a table,

along with black-painted papercups and cardboard telephones. We taped a stuffed paper camel to the wall. On a table sat a small plastic sandbox and four basins. Children drove their toy jeeps and cars through the sand and later washed them, learning about the desert's effect on vehicles. (pp. 43–44)

Their teachers provided these young children with an environment where the children could construct their knowledge of a foreign place. The children were able to work through an initially frightening experience in play.

While creating a war zone in the classroom may seem a bit bizarre, for these children, it was an important part of their lives and led to fine learning experiences. Similar opportunities to build on current events can lead to quality constructivist social studies.

Integrating Cognitive Learnings throughout the Curriculum

It should be obvious at this point that cognitive development occurs throughout the day as children interact with adults, peers, and materials in their environment. Intellectual understanding is not limited to specific topics taught at set times. Rather, all that the child does, hears, and sees provides the raw material for cognitive growth.

Every center within the early childhood classroom, as well as the outdoor environment, encourages intellectual development. Playing with blocks, painting in the art center, digging in the garden, and reading books in the library center are all examples of activities that can lead to cognitive growth. As the teacher prepares each of these centers, she needs to plan for developmentally appropriate materials and activities that enhance learning opportunities for young children. These preparations will vary with the ages and developmental abilities of the children in the program.

Infant/Toddler Materials and Activities

Piaget (Ginsburg & Opper, 1969) describes the infant/toddler's cognitive functioning as sensorimotor intelligence. By this he means that children at this age are learning about their world through sensory and motor exploration. Sights, sounds, tastes, and physical manipulation provide many opportunities for intellectual growth.

To integrate cognitive learning throughout the infant/toddler environment, caregivers need to provide materials and activities that children can experience through sensory/motor activity. Some examples follow:

- Mobiles in cribs, pictures of human faces around the room, and picture books to stimulate visual exploration
- Blocks, stacking toys, and push–pull toys for physical manipulation
- Balls made of different materials, texture sheets, water play activities; corn meal, rice, or dried peas in a dishpan; food experiences that include a variety of textures for tactile stimulation
- Talking to and holding children to develop relationships and communicate caring
- Music-making materials, sound discrimination toys for auditory stimulation, and music to listen to

Children Three through Five

As discussed in Chapters 9 and 10, most preschool and kindergarten classrooms are organized into centers with schedules that allow children to spend large blocks of time playfully exploring the indoor environment and playground. Teachers should provide materials for each center that enhance children's cognitive understandings. Examples for each center follow:

Block Center.   Unit blocks are one of the best materials in the early childhood classroom for cognitive learning. Counting, shape recognition, understanding stability and balance, and developing beginning mapping skills are just a few of the many learnings possible (Hirsch, 1974). In addition, the accessories added can help facilitate other learning. For example, the teacher can place multicultural family figures in the center to help children realize that families are diverse. With the assistance of the teacher, children can begin to discuss and understand these diversity issues.

Art Center.   Providing paints of different textures and colors and a variety of brushes and applicators allows children to explore the properties of the art materials and how they can be used to create different paintings. Conceptually, children learn to recognize patterns, identify colors and shapes, and develop an understanding of symmetry as they playfully explore these materials (Schirrmacher, 1998).

Manipulative Center.   Legos, Bristle Blocks, Tinker Toys, puzzles, simple matching games, and most of the typical materials found in the manipulative area help children develop concepts of color, size, and shape. Children practice patterning, one-to-one correspondence, and counting skills as they work with manipulatives as well.

Book Center. The pictures and text in any good children's book have great potential for stimulating conceptual growth. Understanding relationships, specific information on science and mathematics topics (e.g., different types of birds), and books addressing feelings are just a few of the possibilities for learning. Providing a variety of books that focus on specific themes and are changed regularly will stimulate many learning opportunities.

Dramatic Play/Housekeeping Center. As children play out themes in these centers, they learn properties of real-world materials through the use of toys (e.g., a toy stethoscope), grow in their understanding of roles (doctor, nurses, etc.), and gain information from other players ("Hey, doctors don't do it that way, they . . . ").

Music Center. Play with musical instruments can be useful in building conceptual knowledge as well. Strumming a xylophone, for example, and then discussing what causes the sound can be an excellent learning opportunity. Many songs (e.g., "Five Little Speckled Frogs") also contain conceptual information that children learn as they sing.

Discovery Center. The science materials in this center have clear potential for stimulating cognitive development. Examining, classifying, and reading about different rocks is one example. Measuring a plant's growth and charting it on a graph are other possible learning activities for this center.

The Primary Grades

Although interest in other options is growing, the traditional elementary school curriculum tends to teach cognitive subjects in isolation from one another. That is, mathematics, science, and social studies each have a distinct time for teaching. This more segmented approach is in direct conflict with the constructivist approach. The child in the constructivist classroom learns through manipulation and discovery, which is much more open-ended in terms of outcomes. Any given task generally provides opportunities for cognitive growth in many different areas.

One highly appropriate technique that engages children in constructivist learning is called the **project approach.** Children who have decided to pursue a particular subject in more depth form a small group to take on a project (see Chapters 3 and 11 for more detailed descriptions). Katz (1994) describes a project involving investigation of an everyday object—balls:

A kindergarten teacher asked the children to collect from home, friends, relatives, and others as many old balls as they could. She developed a study web by asking what the children might like to know about the balls. The children collected thirty-one different kinds of balls, including a gumball, a cotton ball, a globe of the earth, and an American football (which led to a discussion of the concepts of sphere, hemisphere, and cone).

Project learning allows children to study topics in depth and learn from their peers.

The children then formed subgroups to examine specific questions. One group studied the surface texture of each ball, and made rubbings to represent their findings; another measured the circumference of each ball with pieces of string; and a third tried to determine what each ball was made of.

As children engaged in their study of balls, new questions arose, groups shared information, and the children learned concepts of science, mathematics, and social studies. Excited children learned rapidly from this project.

Although not all experiences in the primary classroom can be organized around projects, clearly this option works well and leads to important conceptual growth.

Parental Roles in Cognitive Development

Parents are children's first and best teachers. They play crucial roles in cognitive development. Parents need to support the importance of intellectual growth, assist in classroom learning, and engage children at home in cognitive tasks.

Supporting the Importance of Cognitive Development

Parents, teachers, and community members generally agree about the importance of learning mathematics, science, and social studies concepts and readily concede the values of cognitive development. Achievement in these areas is a major factor needed for success in work and life.

The content and process of this learning, however, are less often agreed upon. Many of these differences of opinion come from the parents' experiences as children. If social studies learning, for example, focused on the memorization of names, dates, and significant historical events, this is what many parents feel is appropriate for their own children. "It worked for me," they think, "so why shouldn't it work for my kids?"

The past approaches focusing on rote learning, however, have proven to be ineffective for many children. The constructivist approach described earlier in this chapter is a much more positive technique for encouraging cognitive development (DeVries & Kohlberg, 1987; Kamii & DeVries, 1978). But because it is new to many parents, teachers need to spend time helping parents understand this approach. As they see constructivist learning in action, discuss the approach with others, read about its benefits, and observe the results of these efforts, parents can become strong advocates of this alternative to rote learning.

Assisting with Classroom Learning

Parents who can spend time helping out in the classroom are assisting with cognitive development. Reading to children, helping individual children with mathematics projects, and going on class field trips are examples of this support. More mundane tasks like preparing materials for an art project or constructing a game help free up the teacher's time for more direct assistance in cognitive learning. The parents' presence in the classroom also sends children the message that their own work is important and motivates them to do their best.

Parents who are unavailable during the school day can help out at home by gathering the ingredients for the upcoming science project, saving materials for mathematics manipulatives, or making telephone calls for the field trip next week. These kinds of tasks give parents important roles to play when they can't come into the classroom.

Home Learning Tasks

Parents have many unique opportunities to promote cognitive understanding outside the school environment. Often, however, parents don't take advantage of these opportunities because parents fail to recognize the value of their many informal experiences with children. Setting the table for dinner, for example, gives young children the chance to count and practice one-to-one correspondence (one fork, spoon, and knife for each person) as they assist with a household chore. Or a trip to the grocery store can be a great time to practice money concepts and discuss the rationale for buying some foods but not others.

Many teachers send parents lists of simple activities that parents can build into daily life and that promote cognitive development. These home learning tasks should be easy to prepare for and fun to do. Berger (1995) suggests many good ideas for activities to do at home, including

- *Cooking activities.* Have children help with cooking. It can teach number concepts, fractions, measurement, and much more.
- *Backyard science.* Encourage exploration outdoors for insects, leaves, and rocks. Plant seeds and bulbs in the garden. Children engaged in these kinds of activities are classifying, observing, and experimenting with variables as they play with the materials outdoors.
- *Play games with children.* Children, for example, can learn to discriminate between size, shape, and color as they play simple card-matching games. Parents often need suggestions for taking competitive games and making them more cooperative.
- *Visit museums.* Take time to explore the resources within the community, including museums of interest to children. When these experiences include things children can touch and manipulate, the interest will be greater. While providing many opportunities for learning, museums are wonderful opportunities for children to have meaningful experiences learning about history.

Summary

The goals of the mathematics, science, and social studies curricula are important beginning points in understanding these components of early education. Teaching the cognitive curriculum requires an emphasis on critical thinking, problem solving, and lifelong learning rather than overemphasizing the learning of facts. The constructivist approach to mathematics, science, and social studies learning is emphasized in the early childhood classroom. Mathematics learning for young children includes classification, seriation, patterning, number concepts, measurement, geometry, and problem-solving experiences. An understanding of scientific content, process, and attitudes is essential to the science curriculum. Understanding self and others are the two key elements of the early childhood social studies curriculum. It is important to integrate cognitive learnings with other components of the early childhood curriculum at the infant/toddler, preschool, and primary levels. Parents play important roles in cognitive development during the early childhood years.

For Discussion and Action

1. Take a second look at the goals for cognitive development presented in this chapter. How well do you think you have met these goals in your own life? Will your experiences influence the way you teach conceptual knowledge?

2. Many adults are math or science anxious, meaning they had poor experiences while studying one or both of these subjects and have come to see themselves as failures in these areas. How can you help avoid these phobias in the children you teach?

3. The learning of facts does have a place in the early childhood classroom. What should that place be? Make a case for learning some facts (names, dates, events) in the primary social studies curriculum.

4. Compare and contrast constructivist learning and play. How are they similar and different?

5. Choose an age within the early childhood range, and brainstorm a list of home learning tasks that parents could do easily and that would be fun for both the child and the parent.

Building Your Personal Library

Chaille, C., & Britain, L. (1997). *The young child as scientist: A constructivist approach to early childhood science education* (2nd ed.). New York: Longman. The authors promote the idea that children naturally engage in strategies for learning that are much like those used by scientists. They present many good ideas for promoting this constructivist approach in science education.

DeVries, R., & Kohlberg, L. (1987). *Constructivist early education: Overview and comparison with other programs.* Washington, DC: National Association for the Education of Young Children. A comprehensive description of the constructivist approach to early education by two key promoters.

Shaw, J., & Blake, S. (1998). *Mathematics for young children.* Upper Saddle River, NJ: Merrill/Prentice Hall. This book presents many good ideas for developing a mathematics curriculum for young children that goes beyond the rote learning so typical of this subject.

Wolfinger, D. (1994). *Science and mathematics in early childhood education.* New York: HarperCollins. This book presents numerous developmental characteristics of children during the early childhood years and then describes appropriate activities in mathematics and science.

15 *Language and Literacy Learning*

In this chapter you will

- Investigate the development of language in young children.

- Differentiate among the many linguistic systems children must master to understand language.

- Study techniques for facilitating language learning.

- Develop an understanding of the young child's emerging reading and writing skills.

- Review effective techniques and materials for language and literacy learning.

Your class of four-year-olds is playing during their free choice time indoors. For the moment, children are productively interacting with peers and play materials, so you have time to step back and observe what is taking place. With a notepad in hand, you focus your attention on the play themes unfolding around you.

Blake and Abby are in the art center, involved in the fingerpainting activity there. "Ooo, ooo, ooo. Goo, goo, goo!" chimes Blake as he smears the shaving cream mix in large circular motions on his tray. "Boo, hoo, hoo. You're full of moo!" responds Abby as she looks up from her painting. Both children giggle and then return to their art project.

Terrance and Stuart pretend to be shopper and grocery clerk in the store set up in the dramatic play area. As Terrance brings his groceries up to Stuart for bagging, he says "Say, you got any peanut butter? Ah love my peanut butter!" "Sorry," replies Stuart, "We're out. How about some beans?" "Nah, beans and me don't get along too well," responds Terrance. "I'll buy what I've got." They continue to dramatize their play theme while chatting.

Tina is in the book corner with a parent volunteer where the two are absorbed in reading the book Mike Mulligan and His Steam Shovel *(Burton, 1939)*. They have read the story once and are just beginning a second reading at Tina's request. This time, she stops the parent periodically to ask questions about the steam shovel and Mike Mulligan. Tina is fascinated by the story. ᘯ

The children in the class just described are engaged in language and literacy learning. No direct instruction is taking place, but as they play and communicate, children are intuitively learning how language works, practicing its many nuances, and gaining insights into the meanings of written language.

Language and literacy competence are at the heart of the human experience. The ability to communicate with others enables us to learn and grow, while enriching our lives. Adults working with children during the early childhood years need considerable knowledge about language and literacy learning so that they can facilitate these important experiences.

Language and literacy learning, though clearly related, are generally thought of as complementary processes. **Language** can be defined as either oral or hand-signed communication between humans. Each culture arbitrarily assigns meaning to sounds. Then people use combinations of these basic units to create words and sentences that communicate messages to others. Rules govern the ways we use sounds to form words and how we then combine those words to form sentences. Speakers of the language intuitively (but usually not consciously) understand these rules.

Literacy concerns language in written form. Literate people are those who can read and write the language of their culture. Cultures arbitrarily assign meaning to written symbols and construct systems to organize these symbols on the written page. Literacy is the ability to interpret the intended message of these symbols (reading) and to use them to communicate information to others (writing).

Language Learning

The process of learning language may appear effortless, but in reality it is a major undertaking for young children. Those who study language acquisition have considerable difficulty even explaining it. This section should help you understand how children learn language and the strategies adults can use to assist in the process.

Theoretical Perspectives

Theorists have proposed three different views of how children learn language. **Behaviorists** argue that children acquire language through the same stimulus–response connections that influence learning in all areas (Skinner, 1957). Children hear language spoken by parents and others, imitate that speech, and are rewarded for their efforts. This positive reinforcement encourages them to communicate more.

While behaviorist theory helps explain some aspects of language learning, other perspectives add further insight into how children develop linguistic competence. The **maturationist** theory suggests that every child, regardless of culture, intellectual ability, or socioeconomic status, inherits the genetic capability for language. When children are exposed to language, this innate ability, or **language acquisition device (LAD)** allows them to gradually make sense of the rules for oral communication (Chomsky, 1965).

A third view of language learning is the **interactionist** approach. Proponents of this theory suggest that language acquisition combines an innate ability with environmental influences. Both factors interact in complex ways as children learn language. The writings of both Piaget (1959) and Vygotsky (1962) support the interactionist view.

Language Development

Children vary in the rate at which they learn language, but eventually almost every child masters the complex linguistic system in which she is immersed. This process begins in infancy and continues throughout the early childhood years.

Infancy. Even newborn infants work to communicate with others and are beginning to learn about their linguistic system (Kuhl, 1993). Crying is the earliest form of infant communication, and parents quickly learn the many different messages children can send with this simple tool: "I'm wet. Feed me! I'm sleepy."

At the same time, infants are attending to the oral language of caregivers and others. They notice changes in sounds, rhythm, and intonation. At about three or four months of age, children start to coo and babble. Gradually, infants start to recognize and babble the sounds of the specific language they must eventually master (Kuhl, 1993).

Near the end of the first year of life, children begin to speak words. To the great thrill of their parents, "mama" or "dadda" are often the earliest words spoken. Many infants have expanded their initial vocabulary to about a dozen words by their first birthday.

Toddlerhood.   Toddlers proceed rapidly in their acquisition of language. By the end of the second year of life, children have expanded their vocabularies up to as many as fifty words. Many of these words carry much more meaning than the adult equivalent. This is referred to as **holophrasic speech.** For example: "More!" may well mean: "Give me more milk right now! I'm still hungry!"

As toddlers mature, they begin the process of stringing two words together to form simple sentences. A toddler, for example, who wants to go in the car with Daddy may say, "Me go!" Often referred to as **telegraphic speech** because of limited word usage, these two-word sentences are a major step forward in the young child's expression of language.

The Preschool Years.   The language understanding of children during the preschool years continues to expand rapidly. Vocabulary increases at an amazing rate, with new words added almost daily. Sentences move quickly beyond the two-word stage to more complex combinations. These young children are refining their understanding of the rules of communication and becoming more proficient at holding a conversation with others.

The Primary Grades.   Growth in vocabulary and sentence complexity continues throughout the primary grades. By this time, children have mastered most of the grammar needed for oral language communication. They are adding the finer nuances of linguistics: learning about humor, multiple meanings for words and phrases, and the importance of intonation in communications.

Linguistic Systems

When adults study language, it is generally divided into five main elements or systems. Children must master each of these systems to become competent in communicating with others. Without any direct instruction, youngsters learn about phonology, morphology, syntax, semantics, and pragmatics.

Phonology is the system of sounds used to make up words in a specific language. Cultures assign arbitrary meaning to these sounds, and speakers use consistent rules

FOCUS ON . . .

Chomsky on Language Development

Noam Chomsky (1965) has strongly influenced how linguists view language acquisition. He emphasized the idea that children inherit the innate abilities necessary to learn language. Chomsky called these capacities a *language acquisition device (LAD)*. Without formal training, the child uses this LAD to understand the rules governing oral communications. For example, when children begin learning to use past tense, they often overgeneralize the rules they are acquiring. After learning that the past tense of *help* is *helped* and *kicked* is the past tense of *kick*, young children often say *goed* instead of *went* and *hitted* instead of *hit*. Rather than simply imitating what they hear adults saying, young children are unconsciously working to understand the rules that underlie their linguistic system.

Another famous example of this effort to learn the rules of language comes from a nonsense sentence that Chomsky used with children. "Colorless green ideas sleep furiously." As young children learn the rules of syntax, they can develop a certain sense of meaning from

even this nonsense sentence. If asked, "What slept furiously?" (ideas) or "What kinds of ideas were sleeping?" (colorless green ideas), young children can answer appropriately. An intuitive understanding of the rules of syntax allows the child to make some sense from this nonsense.

So, as children hear verbal communications in the world around them, they gradually are able to internalize the patterns and learn the rules that govern their linguistic system. They can't verbalize these rules but have developed understandings of them, nonetheless.

1. *Make up your own nonsense sentence, and try it out on others with appropriate questions. If possible, use your sentence on a young child. Share your findings with classmates.*

2. *Assuming children do have a LAD, what are the implications for adults who want to encourage language learning?*

to combine these sounds into words. Phonology also includes an understanding of the intonations used to add meanings to combinations of sounds.

A second linguistic system is referred to as **morphology.** Language learners must understand the rules for combining sounds to form words within a specific language. The rules for creating plurals (*apples*) and tense (*went* for past tense; *will go* for future tense) are examples of morphology. This system is complex and varies within a single language, as well as from one language to the next.

The **semantics** of language is a third system children must master. This involves the meanings given to words. For some words like *hat*, this is a relatively simple task; other words vary in meaning depending on the context. How many different meanings, for example, exist for the word *nurse*? Because of the literalness of young children, many words or phrases are difficult to comprehend. "I've got a frog in my throat" may actually be a frightening concept to a three-year-old struggling to understand the semantics of this statement.

A fourth linguistic system is called **syntax** and refers to the procedures for combining words into phrases and sentences. Even nonsense words acquire some meaning when placed in phrases and sentences. "The crog slagged zuppily across the waggor" contains many nonsense words, but even young children can find meaning in this sentence because of the syntax, or placement of the words.

The final linguistic system is **pragmatics**; it consists of the understandings necessary for adapting language to different social situations. A five-year-old learns that talking to a baby is different from interacting with peers, for example. Recognizing that "please" and "thank you" are expected in many social interactions is another aspect of pragmatics. Children gradually learn that certain words, phrases, and styles of communication are appropriate in some situations and not in others.

Facilitating Language Learning

Maria Montessori (Lillard, 1972) promoted the idea of **sensitive periods** in the child's life. During these blocks of time, children have a keen interest in certain aspects of their development. The early childhood years are generally considered the sensitive period for language; therefore, adults should do all they can to assist children in the development of linguistic competence.

Infants and Toddlers.   Beginning very early in their lives, infants and toddlers spend much of their time making sense of the language that surrounds them. A quality early childhood program should provide children with many opportunities to have positive oral language experiences with caring adults. Some suggestions for integrating oral language at this level follow:

- *Build language into routines.* Toileting, eating, and sleeping activities are significant components of the day for very young children. Adults should take advantage of these times to talk positively with the child as they assist in meeting the child's needs. For example, talking to the child, singing a song, or playing "This Little Piggy" while changing a diaper make this event more interesting and fun for both the child and the adult and give natural opportunities for language learning during the day.

- *Provide experiences that encourage language.* When children experience textures, smells, tastes, and sounds that interest them, they want to tell others. The infant's rapid movements and vocalizations on seeing an interesting mobile, although not officially language, are attempts to communicate. Such efforts will eventually lead to more adult-like verbalizations.

- *Model appropriate language.* Adults can communicate with young children using appropriate terms and sentences as they interact with materials in the classroom. "One, two, three. You are stacking those blocks very well, Michael!" Gradually, after hearing repeated verbalizations from the adults around them, infants and toddlers make sense of these combinations of sounds and learn to use them in their own communications.

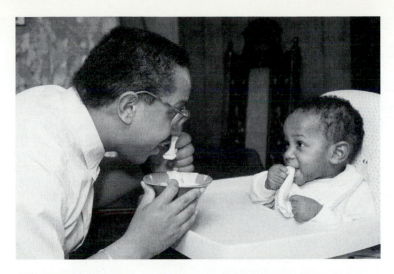

Playful language and interactions make routines more enjoyable for both the adult and child.

Informal Conversations.   During the preschool and primary years, one important way for adults to help children develop communicative competence is through informal conversations. These interchanges don't need to be long or carefully planned ahead of time, but when teachers use opportunities to engage in casual interactions, children can learn a great deal about language and the world around them. Some suggestions for making these conversations more productive follow:

- *Show interest* by listening carefully to what the child has to say. Give the child your full attention as she speaks. This will encourage further discussion by the child.

- *Use questions* to get the child to elaborate on what has already been said. In response to "Grammy's in Vermont," you could say, "That sounds like fun. What is she doing there?"

- *Model good communication* by speaking courteously and using good grammar and proper word choice. Make sure both the verbal and nonverbal messages you send do not contradict one another.

- *Build on the child's interests* as you communicate. This will help make conversation attractive to the child. For example, a simple response to a child interested in insects might be, "Janet, I found a new book on insects yesterday in the school library. Would you like to look at it during silent reading?"

- *Expand vocabulary* by using words that children may not know but that are relevant to their lives. Labeling the emotions children express, using precise terms for science concepts they experience, and identifying occupations within the community are examples.

- *Be sensitive* to children. Listen when that is needed; lead the conversation when it is appropriate to do so; and try to avoid interrupting productive play time or interactions with peers to engage in conversation.

When playful physical activities are combined with language training, young children benefit. Conner-Kuntz and Dummer (1996) studied children four to six years of age in special education, Head Start, and typical preschool classes. They provided some of these students with guided physical activities and gave the rest both the physical activities and additional language skills training.

They gave children in the latter group natural opportunities to learn language concepts related to their physical activities such as

- Around
- Over and under
- Front and behind
- Above and below
- Distance
- Height
- Shape

Children receiving these additional language experiences, including those with impaired cognitive and language abilities, showed improvements in their language skills. Furthermore, these children showed equivalent gains in their motor skills to those receiving the physical training alone.

1. Which of the theories presented in this book would support the results of this study? Review Chapters 2 and 3, and then discuss this with your classmates.

2. Do the results of this study make sense to you? Why should playful physical activities combined with adult language enrichment lead to improved language skills? Discuss this with others.

Play. Childhood play provides numerous opportunities for language learning. Garvey (1990) describes how children engage in **playing with language.** As they vocalize, children explore how to combine sounds, learn about syntax, and experiment with fantasy and nonsense. Garvey shares the following example of two five-year-olds playing with language:

> Girl 1: *Mommy, Mommy, I got new friends called Dool, Sol, Ta.*
>
> Girl 2: *Dool, Sue, and Ta? (both girls laugh)*
>
> Girl 1: *Those are funny names, aren't they?*
>
> Girl 2: *No, its Poopi, Daigi, and Dia. . . Diarrhea. (both laugh again) (Garvey, 1990, p. 71)*

Language is also an important part of the play experience itself. Children have many opportunities to practice using language as they engage in play. Children use **metacommunication** statements to structure and organize the play. Designating the make-believe properties of an object ("Let's pretend this stick is a fishing pole."), assigning roles ("You be the daddy, I'll be the baby."), and planning the story line ("First, we'll cook dinner, and then we'll sit down and eat.") are all examples of metacommunication statements for enacting play sequences.

The **language used in play** provides additional opportunities for developing linguistic competence. The conversation necessary to engage in pretend play is one good example of this language usage: "Hush baby! Mommy is on the telephone." Children must communicate in other types of play as well. Two boys constructing a block tower, for example, use language to discuss their intent and rationale for placement of blocks, ask each other for feedback as they proceed, and discuss alternatives while they build.

Language-Rich Experiences.   The motivation to expand vocabulary and communicate with others is greatly enhanced when children have adventures that excite them in some way. Teachers can provide children with a diversity of experiences to assist in language development. **Good books** can be that kind of opportunity for many children. By touching on issues that are meaningful or interesting to children, books become a starting point for further investigation and communication.

Field trips also have the potential to spark children's interests in a topic. Traveling to a nearby pond to collect tadpoles, insects, and underwater plant life could be an excellent starting point for a science unit and a great way to generate individual and group discussion on these topics. Every community has many potentially beneficial sites for field trips.

Taking advantage of **people and events in the community** may be yet another language-rich experience for young children. For example, a retired volunteer who is good at storytelling could come into the classroom and talk about his experiences as a child. Participating in a community-sponsored musical concert or going to see a play or puppet show for young children can provide other experiences that children can talk about at home or in the classroom.

Language Learning Materials

Virtually every toy and piece of equipment in the early childhood classroom can lead to language experiences; some options are particularly important in stimulating linguistic exploration. One such material is the **flannelboard story.** For younger children, having figures that relate to popular books helps them to retell familiar story lines. Older children can benefit from a collection of flannel pieces that they can use to tell their own stories. Teachers can either make or purchase commercial flannel pieces to use in the classroom.

Another material closely related to the flannelboard is the **magnetic board.** As the name implies, pieces stick to a metal board rather than flannel. Using magnetic strips, adults can create figures that children can manipulate to tell familiar or invented stories.

Puppets are another versatile material that children use for extensive language experiences. Handmade and commercial puppets stimulate increased verbal interactions in the classroom. Many quiet children are much more verbal with a puppet on their hand.

INTO PRACTICE . . .
A Trip to the Post Office

Mrs. Riley's first-grade classroom is off for their field trip to the community post office. With the help of several parent volunteers, they arrive safely at mid-morning and are greeted by postal workers who have prepared a tour of the facilities. Children see where the mail arrives in big trucks and how it is unloaded, sorted, and prepared for delivery. They also see how mail on its way to other cities is prepared for shipping. Students watch postal workers dealing with customers who need stamps and packages mailed. It is a busy morning.

Upon returning to the classroom, children spend time as a large group talking with Mrs. Riley about what they saw. She records their comments on the overhead projector. Later, she will combine this written record with student illustrations to construct the monthly newsletter for parents.

Mrs. Riley has set up the dramatic play center as a post office with pretend stamps, envelopes, paper, writing instruments, and mailboxes for each member of the class. Children can spend free time writing, sending, and reading their mail. The center is buzzing with activity throughout the day.

The library corner has three new books with mail-related themes: *What's It Like to be a Postal Worker?* (Matthews, 1990); *The Postman's Palace* (Henri, 1990); and *Here Comes the Mail* (Skurzynski, 1992). Mrs. Riley introduced these books at group time, and children are eagerly browsing through them with the parent volunteer. They recognize many of the procedures that they saw earlier at the post office.

Book making is the theme of the writing center, and several children spend time there working on tales about the trip to the post office. They draw pictures of remembered events and then dictate stories to the parent volunteer. Children add their finished books to the library corner and read them to other interested children.

Dramatic play props create additional opportunities for language development. Some examples include

- Restaurant props
- Camping materials
- Doctor's office
- Grocery store
- Barber/beauty shop

Literacy Learning

As stated earlier, language and literacy learning are related but not identical processes. Although almost all children learn oral language, many find reading and writing more difficult. Illiteracy is unfortunately a burden that some adults carry with them throughout their lives. The impact on self-esteem and job status is very strong.

As with oral language development, the early childhood years are pivotal times for learning to read and write. Children who have good literacy experiences during these years are much more likely to become literate adults. Teachers need to understand the theory behind these aspects of development and work to prepare materials and activities that facilitate growth in reading and writing.

Literacy Development

As with the development of speech, literacy awareness and learning begin in infancy. The eight-month-old child who cuddles up on her father's lap to look at a picture book is developing early literacy understandings. The eighteen-month-old scribbling on a piece of paper is preparing for writing in later childhood. Young children slowly learn concepts such as beginning in the front of the book and moving sequentially to the back, reading from left to right, making marks on paper that others can understand, and being aware that print has meaning.

Traditional View. The idea that even infants are engaged in meaningful literacy learning is relatively new. The more traditional view has been that language and literacy development are different (Christie, Enz, & Vukelich, 1997). This approach is based on the premise that reading and writing instruction should begin around age six, when children have developed the mental and physical maturity needed for these tasks. Furthermore, this traditional view promotes the idea that children be taught reading and writing through the use of basal readers, worksheets, and handwriting practice.

Emergent Literacy. The idea that learning to read and write has much in common with oral language development is called **emergent literacy** (Sulzby & Teale, 1991). This approach promotes the idea that children begin learning about reading and writing in infancy. With appropriate materials and supportive adults, young children construct knowledge about print and gradually become literate. By immersing the child in a print-rich environment and providing guidance during the discovery process, adults help children grow into readers and writers.

Learning to Read and Write

The emergent literacy perspective means that early childhood educators working with prekindergarten children need to get involved in providing experiences that lead to learning about reading and writing. It also changes the approaches that primary teachers should use with this age range. Teachers need to find alternatives to the traditional basal readers, worksheets, and handwriting exercises.

Print-Rich Environments. Teachers at all levels within the early childhood range need to provide children with meaningful written materials that they can learn from. The most obvious of these are books. Beginning in infant/toddler

Reading to infants and toddlers should not be confused with teaching babies to read. The latter, although promising many rewards (Doman, 1961), probably does more harm than good. But taking the time to read appropriate books to infants and toddlers can be a very rewarding experience for both the child and the adult. Benefits often cited include

- Building infant–adult relationships.
- Enhancing verbal communications between children and adults.
- Creating interest in printed communications.
- Strengthening early abilities to imagine and pretend.
- Gaining fundamental understandings of reading (start at the front of a book and proceed to the back, read from the top of the page to the bottom, and from left to right, etc.).

Although very young infants have limited speaking vocabularies, they understand more than they can say. The pleasant interactions that take place when an adult takes the time to snuggle up with a young child and a book help add new words to a rapidly expanding vocabulary and create a basis for future interest in reading and writing.

When timed right, this experience is generally very rewarding for the adult as well. Allowing the infant or toddler to set the pace, help turn pages, and point to pictures of interest helps maintain interest and enthusiasm. The physical closeness, combined with an interested child, makes for fond memories for both the infant/toddler and adult.

1. Volunteer some time to work with infants and toddlers. Read a book to a young child, and discuss the experience with your peers.

2. Browse through the infant/toddler books section of a larger book store. What reactions do you have to the selections they offer?

programs (Kupetz & Green, 1997), adults should provide children with access to a wide variety of books and should read to individual children or small groups.

Christie et al. (1997) describe several key elements of a print-rich environment:

- *A variety of materials for reading.* In addition to books, classrooms should have many types of print that serve real-life functions (labels on food items, restaurant menus, road signs, etc.).

- *Diverse writing materials.* A well-equipped writing center should be the focus of these activities, with materials available throughout the classroom that encourage children (or adults) to record important written communications (title of artwork, description of block structure, story to accompany flannelboard figures, etc.).

- *Displays of children's written products.* Teachers help children see the importance of writing by displaying their stories, books, and letters to friends and families.

- *Integrated printed materials.* Written materials should be connected with ongoing activities in the classroom. Gardening activities outdoors could be connected to

Making connections between oral and written language is an important step in the literacy process.

teacher-recorded stories of children's gardening experiences, labeling of plant rows, recordings of plant growth, and books in the library center about aspects of gardening.

• *Literacy as part of routines.* Literacy activities can be highlighted during the routines of the school day. The attendance charts, hot and cold lunch counts, daily schedule, pledge of allegiance, and weather chart can be used for meaningful reading and writing experiences.

Making the Oral and Written Language Connection.   Young children need meaningful opportunities to grasp the connections between oral and written language. Understanding that what is said can be written down and understanding that printed information can be spoken orally are important steps during the early childhood years.

An important technique that many early childhood teachers use in order to help children make these connections is the **language experience** approach. Children dictate information about personal experiences while an adult writes them down. The adult can then read the story back to children and encourage them to practice reading their dictated work. Christie et al. (1997) describe three language experience options:

• *Group experience stories.* Following a shared group experience such as a field trip to the bakery, the class can discuss the highlights of the event and together create a story about the activity. As the class dictates the story, the teacher writes it down. This can be followed by the teacher rereading the completed story and then asking children to join in choral reading.

- *Individual experience stories.* These stories come from individual children, who dictate them to the teacher. An example of this type is a child creating a picture book of her family's trip to the zoo with space at the bottom of each page for the dictated story.
- *Classroom newspaper.* First, children share interesting things that have happened to them. Then the teacher records these experiences and compiles them into a newspaper to share with parents. Teachers who have an overabundance of news items may limit the number of students sharing, making sure that all the children eventually have a chance to have their stories recorded.

Literacy Learning through Play.   Many different play types can be effective in stimulating literacy understandings. Dramatic play, for example, can lead to early reading and writing experiences.

> ❧ *Liam, Jerome, and Erika are playing in their preschool classroom's restaurant. Liam is the cook, Jerome is the waiter, and Erika is the customer. Erika pretends to read the menu and gives her order to Jerome, who writes it down and takes it to the cook. As these children engage in dramatic play, they are dealing with many beginning literacy concepts.*

Construction play in the block area can also lead to reading and writing opportunities.

> ❧ *Chad and Marshall, two third graders, have just completed building a castle based loosely on a book they recently read in the library center. Now they are interested in writing their own story about medieval times and life in a castle. They plan to spend time on the Internet collecting more information about castles before engaging in their literary efforts.*

Each center in the early childhood classroom can be equipped with literacy-related materials that children can use in their play. Pencils and paper for writing, signs, magazines, and an old typewriter are examples (Rybczynski & Troy, 1995). Parents and children can help collect these print-rich materials to encourage literacy learning.

Reading to Children.   Many experts consider reading books to young children to be the most important way to develop early literacy skills in young children. The Commission on Reading (Anderson, Hiebert, Scott, & Wilkinson, 1985) states, "The single most important activity for building the knowledge required for eventual success in reading is reading aloud to children" (p. 23). This process should begin in infancy and continue throughout the early childhood years, both at home and in school.

Kupetz and Green (1997) provide the following guidelines for reading to children:

- Read to children when they are in the mood for it.
- Choose a book appropriate to the age of the children.

- Read stories that are of interest to you as well.
- Have special reading times as part of the routine of the day.
- Allow the children to assist you in the reading process.
- Use your voice to show interest and help tell the story.

Preparing a comfortable center where children can go to read with others is an essential component of the early childhood classroom. In addition to displaying plenty of reading options, this area should invite children to participate in the wonder of books. You should provide children with a cozy pillow to lie on, comfortable chairs, and good lighting. Take extra special care in preparing this corner of the classroom.

Children's Books

Every early childhood classroom should have an excellent collection of books to entice children into the library corner. Fractor, Woodruff, Martinez, and Teale (1993) suggest that a classroom library for elementary children should have five to eight books for every child. Some of these books can remain in the center throughout the year, but most books should be rotated in and out of the classroom on a regular basis.

Over the course of the school year, early childhood teachers may literally need hundreds of children's books for their library centers. Although teachers of course can check books out from school and public libraries, collecting your own books also makes good sense. Christie et al. (1997) suggest the following resources for building your own classroom library:

- Commercial publishers (expensive but important resources)
- Used bookstores
- Garage sales
- Public library sales
- Parent donations

Selecting Books. Machado (1995) provides several criteria for selecting books for young children. First, does the book match the **attention span, maturity, and interests** of the children with whom it is to be used? These characteristics vary widely across the early childhood range. Even within a homogeneous age group, attention spans, for example, vary greatly. Books chosen should reflect this diversity.

Adults working with young children should also select books that help develop **broad literary and artistic tastes.** Texts from each of the categories presented here, books by a variety of authors, and ethnically and culturally diverse writers and illustrators encourage breadth in children's literature.

Is the author's **writing style** interesting to young children? The vocabulary and story sequence should be appropriate for the targeted children. Repetition of

Children's Literature on the Web

Although there are many different ways to locate good children's literature, one relatively new option is to browse the World Wide Web. The Children's Literature Web Guide (http://www.ucalgary.ca/~dkbrown/index.html) is one excellent site for those who have Internet access.

Created by David K. Brown at the University of Calgary, this Web site features many avenues for reviewing and using children's literature:

- Book and resource lists
- Teaching ideas
- Discussion groups
- Links to other Web sites

One example of how this Web site can be used is to locate children's books available on specific themes. A link for one of the book lists provides subject bibliographies. By clicking on Native American Books, for example, the interested reader can find bibliographies of children's books on this topic.

Primary children should find this site of interest as well. By clicking on Authors on the Web, they can go to specific sites created by or about children's book authors. Children can find out more about their favorite writers or even e-mail them.

words, actions, or rhymes makes the book more enjoyable to young children. Humor that children can understand and silliness can add to the attractiveness of an author's writing.

Books can be selected in part based on their **educational value.** Does the content of the book add to the child's knowledge of the world? Books that add new vocabulary to areas of childhood interest should be considered. Are the issues faced by characters in the books the same ones that children and their families encounter? Are the solutions presented workable ones for real-world problems?

Books for Infants and Toddlers.   It is never too early to integrate literacy experiences into the lives of young children. Adults can share books with infants and toddlers so that the wonder and excitement of print communications can be a part of their lives. Kupetz and Green (1997) describe five types of books that are appropriate for this age:

- *Rhythmical language books.* Books with rhymes and lullabies (e.g., *Mother Goose*) are some of the first to interest very young children.

- *Point-and-say books.* Containing pictures or photographs of familiar animals, toys, family members, and the like, these books allow the adult to point to pictures and say their names. Eventually, children can do the pointing and become more involved in the reading.

- *Touch-and-smell books.* Children are presented with different textures to touch and/or a variety of smells to get them actively involved in exploring these books.

- *Board books.* These durable books are made of board-like materials that withstand the banging and chewing of young children. Children can thus spend more time independently exploring these books.

- *Early picture storybooks.* Many toddlers are ready for books with simple story lines and clear illustrations that help tell the story.

Books for Preschool and Primary Children. Neuman and Roskos (1993) suggest the following categories of books for preschool and primary children:

- *Action books.* These books contain mostly pictures and have pop-ups, pull-tabs, and other movable parts to encourage active child participation.

- *Informational books.* Books that share through words and pictures specific content on topics of interest to young children fit this category. A story about how milk is produced (Carrick, 1985) or the life of a squirrel (Lane, 1981) are examples.

- *Picture books.* Books of this type contain mostly pictures and have limited print. Young children can learn many of the conventions of reading books (e.g., reading each page from left to right and top to bottom) while enjoying the pictures.

- *Predictable books.* These books have repetitive patterns that make it easy for children to predict what comes next. Many of the Dr. Seuss books (see, e.g., Seuss, 1960) fit this category.

- *Story books.* Although containing pictures on most pages, these books also provide children with an interesting story line to follow. *Leo the Late Bloomer* (Kraus, 1971) is an example of this type.

- *Wordless books.* Children can use the pictures in these books to tell their own stories. An example is Mayer (1974) *Frog Goes to Dinner.*

- *Beginning chapter books.* These books are more adult-like and have limited pictures, complex plots, and are organized into chapters. Parents or teachers often read these books to primary children. Judy Blume's (1970) book *Freckle Juice* is a popular example of this type.

Writing Tools

Just as children's books are important tools for emerging readers, certain materials are particularly helpful in fostering early writing experiences. The following items provide playful ways for children to experiment with producing written language:

- *Magnetic boards.* When used with a set of magnetic letters, the magnetic board provides children with unlimited ways to combine letters into words. Without actually needing to draw letters with their own hand, children can experiment with writing.

- *Paper and writing instruments.* Teachers should stock each center with paper and writing materials of all types for children to use. Children can effectively use

Selecting good books for children is a difficult task. Hundreds of quality books have been published since the 1940s. Furthermore, each year approximately 500 new books for children are published, many of which are excellent additions to the literature base. But busy parents, teachers, and librarians have limited time to spend in reading through new books.

Since 1975, the Children's Book Council and the International Reading Association have helped make this selection process easier by publishing a list of books that children enjoy reading. Every fall, children's most popular choices are published in *The Reading Teacher* with a brief summary of each book's content.

The Children's Choice Awards list books that are appropriate for the following categories:

All ages

Beginning independent reading

Younger readers (approximately five to eight years)

Middle grades (ages eight to ten)

Older readers (approximately ten to thirteen)

Approximately 10,000 children participate in the selection process each year, helping ensure that the books chosen will have wide appeal. These awards, although not the only source for book ideas, help make it easier for adults to select good literature for children to read.

Two other ways to recognize quality children's literature are through the Newbery and Caldecott awards. The Newbery is for the year's most distinguished new book for children. The Caldecott is awarded for the best illustrated book of the year.

_____

1. *Review a recent Children's Choice Awards list, and then browse through several recommended books. What do you think of this list as a selection tool?*

2. *Discuss with your classmates other awards that you are familiar with for children's literature. Talk about both the strengths and limitations of each award.*

lined paper, unlined paper, recycled paper, note pads, notebooks, pencils, pens, marking pens, crayons, and so on for writing activities.

- *Child-sized chalkboards.* The unique feel, shape, and smell of chalk make it an inviting writing instrument. Child-sized chalkboards allow children to sit comfortably and work on their own writing tasks. Plus, chalk is easy to erase, allowing children to change their writing.

- *Tracing materials.* Montessori (Lillard, 1972) developed a set of shapes that children can trace around with a writing instrument. These and similar materials help develop the fine motor skills necessary for writing.

- *Typewriter.* Young children are fascinated with how things work. An old manual or electric typewriter not only gives them a chance to see a machine at work but

Language and literacy skills can be enhanced with the use of quality word processing software.

also encourages children to write something—or pretend to write something. Preschool children can particularly benefit from this option.

• *Computer.* A major use for computers is word processing. This has led several software designers to create some excellent programs to help primary children write. In addition, younger children can benefit from just having a computer in the classroom to create letters and words on the screen.

Encouraging Parent Involvement

While parents play significant roles in all aspects of the young child's development, none are more critical to academic success than the promotion of language and literacy learning. Parents who create an environment in the home that stimulates positive communications and demonstrates the importance of written language provide their children with an invaluable asset that is difficult to duplicate.

For many parents, one of the most difficult hurdles to overcome is not believing that what they do in the home really does make a difference in language and literacy development. Parents need to be educated about the importance of their role. Articles from professional journals, workshops for parents on language and

INTO PRACTICE . . .

Getting Children to Write

Do you remember how you were taught to write? For many students, the teacher assigned the topics that were used to practice writing skills. At the beginning of the school year, a popular tactic was to ask children to write about events that occurred over summer vacation. Or perhaps you remember story starters like, "The sun was going down over the dusty plains. Exhausted from the day's travels, the riders dismounted from their horses and. . . ." While children can learn from these experiences, it is much better to teach writing (Harwayne, 1992) and to allow children to choose their own topics.

Christie et al. (1997) and many others are now promoting teaching the **behaviors of good writers.** Good writers think about what they want to write (prewrite); read and reread what they are drafting; revise their drafts through adding, deleting, and reorganizing; and edit for spelling, grammar, and punctuation problems. This process is often referred to as teaching the writing work-

shop way. This relatively new approach includes the following:

- Children need to choose their own topics for writing.
- Writing should be done for real audiences (peers, parents, and others) rather than imaginary audiences.
- Initially, writing should focus on what the writer wants to tell others. Once that is achieved, the writer should polish the grammar, spelling, and punctuation.
- Children should have the opportunity to do many drafts so that they can create a quality piece of writing.
- In addition to having plenty of time, children need the chance to talk to the teacher and peers about their writing.
- Teachers should provide opportunities to engage in a variety of writing categories (narrative, persuasive, informative).

literacy learning, and informal discussions with individual parents are some potential ideas that teachers can use to help promote this concept.

Taking Advantage of Daily Living

At the same time that parents are being convinced of their important role in language and literacy development, many need specific ideas about how they can assist in this process. Numerous activities that parents and children engage in daily are excellent opportunities for encouraging oral and written language understandings. Machado (1995) gives examples of these natural learning opportunities:

- Spend some time each day giving individual attention to each child in the family. Talk about your life or what is happening in the child's day; make it a pleasant time of sharing.
- Try to extend the child's vocabulary by adding new and interesting words to your communications.
- Take time to point out meaningful print in the child's world such as names on food containers and road signs.

Parents and teachers need to take advantage of the many opportunities for meaningful print experiences.

- Make trips to the grocery store (and similar chores) learning opportunities by talking about the things being purchased, pointing out and discussing labels and brand names.
- Become a skilled questioner to promote thinking and effective communication.
- Be a good conversationalist. Listen carefully to what the child has to say, and try to build on his comments in your responses.
- Model the importance of reading by taking time to read yourself. Share what you read about with your child.

Simple Home Learning Tasks

The natural opportunities for language and literacy learning just described make a big difference, but other more specific tasks are also very valuable. These should be easy to prepare for and require a limited time commitment by the parent. The following examples highlight the diversity of these simple home learning tasks:

- Read, read, and read some more to your child. These times should be enjoyable for both the parent and child. Reading one or more books before bed each night is an excellent habit to develop.
- Construct a writing center in the home with paper and writing instruments that the child can use to create her own stories and books.

- Make books with young children. If needed, the parent can write down the child's story and then the child can illustrate it.
- Do things together as a family: visit the zoo, browse through museums, spend time at the public library, attend musical concerts. Spend time talking and writing about these special events after returning.
- Encourage children to write thank you cards, birthday messages, and letters to friends and relatives. Make sure children see you doing the same.

Summary

Language and literacy development in young children include oral language learning, reading, and writing tasks. To assist with oral language development, educators need to understand different theoretical perspectives, the developmental patterns associated with growth in verbal communications, the adult's role in facilitating language learning, and appropriate materials for language learning. Supporting literacy learning requires an understanding of literacy development, the importance of print-rich environments in learning to read and write, recognizing the role of play in literacy learning, and the critical importance of reading to children. It is important to select quality books for young children that match their interests and developmental abilities. Teachers need to include materials in the classroom that support children's early writing efforts. Parents need to be educated about their critical roles in language and literacy learning.

∾ For Discussion and Action

1. Spend some time in a public place such as a playground, grocery store, or restaurant, and observe how parents and children talk to each other. Share what you find with classmates.
2. Observe children interacting in a preschool classroom. Focus on how children communicate verbally with each other. Share your findings with your peers.
3. Observe primary children at play. What kinds of language interactions did you see? Share this information with your classmates.
4. Choose and read a book to a young child. Describe your reactions and those of the child to reading the story.
5. Browse through a collection of books for children. See if you can find one or two that you remember as a child. What made those books memorable to you?

❧ Building Your Personal Library

Christie, J., Enz, B., & Vukelich, C. (1997). *Teaching language and literacy: Preschool through the elementary grades.* New York: Longman. This book provides a nice blend of theory and practical ideas that are useful in helping children develop language and literacy skills.

Cullinan, B., & Galda, L. (1994). *Literature and the child* (3rd ed.). Orlando, FL: Harcourt Brace. This book overviews the topic of children's literature and describes how to select and use books with young children.

Halliday, M. (1975). *Learning how to mean: Explorations in the development of language.* London: Edward Arnold. This book is an excellent overview of the interactionalist perspective on language development.

Sulzby, E., & Teale, W. (1991). Emergent literacy. In R. Barr, M. Kamil, P. Mosenthal, & P. Pearson (Eds.), *Handbook of reading research* (Vol. 2, pp. 210–223). New York: Longman. This scholarly chapter provides a valuable overview of the early development of reading and writing skills.

In this chapter you will

- Define creativity as it applies to young children in the early childhood classroom.

- Clarify the importance of art and music in child development and learning.

- Understand the teacher's role in facilitating the creative arts.

- Identify creative art and music activities for children from birth to age eight.

- Discover parents' roles in the creative arts.

Your kindergarten classroom has just begun its morning schedule. Children gather at circle time for opening activities, two or three familiar songs, and a discussion of the activities available in the classroom centers. You explain that a fingerpainting activity will be available in the art center, in addition to the regular art supplies.

As children wander off after group time, you watch as Jaylani and Amanda head straight to the art corner for the fingerpainting activity. They are tentative at first in getting their hands covered with the gooey paint and shaving cream mix. Soon, however, they are happily weaving intricate patterns on the table top. They spend nearly twenty minutes exploring this activity before moving on to another center.

Matt and Karen have discovered some new materials in the music center and are busily exploring the music-making potential of these new instruments. The shallow drum and home-made stringed instrument are the main attraction. As they pluck and tap, they sing their newly created song about the Eensy Weensy Tadpole.

This is just a small sampling of the musical and artistic activities that your students regularly experience. Each day many new activities are available for children to explore.

Quality early childhood programs are full of opportunities for creative expression. Like the children in the class just described, young people want and need a wide variety of outlets for their creativity. When they are given the right materials and allowed the freedom to explore in their own special ways, children delight in art and musical experiences.

The Association for Childhood Education International (ACEI) believes that all children should be able to express themselves through the arts. They have developed a position paper in which they affirm the following:

- Every child should have many opportunities for creative expression.
- When we stimulate the child's imagination, we are helping prepare her to become a life-long learner.
- The key to equity and multicultural understanding is an educated imagination.
- The creative process in childhood is different from that of an adult.
- The arts should be woven into the entire curriculum.

- Excellence in teaching and learning is fostered through the development of imagination.
- Schools of the twenty-first century must be refashioned to include a stronger emphasis on the creative arts (Jalongo, 1990).

What Is Creativity?

Before looking specifically at art and music, a discussion of the concept of creativity itself is necessary. Creative expression takes place throughout the day in the early childhood classroom. E. Paul Torrance, a leader in this area, suggests the following as a rather whimsical description of creative activity:

Creativity is digging deeper.

Creativity is looking twice.

Creativity is crossing out mistakes.

Creativity is talking/listening to a cat.

Creativity is getting in deep water.

Creativity is getting out from behind locked doors.

Creativity is plugging in the sun.

Creativity is wanting to know.

Creativity is having a ball.

Creativity is building sand castles.

Creativity is singing in your own way.

Creativity is shaking hands with the future. (quoted in L. Edwards, 1997, p. 27)

Defining Creativity

Clearly, the activities that Torrance (cited in L. Edwards, 1997) includes under the broad umbrella of creativity are many and varied. Defining the term therefore is difficult. In general, however, definitions of creative activity have two common criteria: novelty and appropriateness (Starko, 1995).

To be creative, an idea or product must be new, or **novel.** The key question that must be asked, however, is novel to whom? Does the idea or product need to be new to humankind? If so, very, very few of us are creative. Creative acts would be limited to the Mozarts and Einsteins of the world. On the other hand, if ideas or products are new to the person who produced them, then most people engage in creative activity. This latter description makes the most sense when working with children.

The second criterion for judging an act as creative is **appropriateness.** For adults, this means that activities are creative when they are acceptable and useful by some set of criteria. These criteria vary from one culture to the next and between groups of adults. Whereas some might view an adult's photo essay of migrant farm workers as creative, others could see it as meaningless and therefore not appropriate.

Once again, the lines blur as we apply the criterion of appropriateness to children. Using adult standards of appropriateness to evaluate children's artwork or musical productions, for example, makes little sense. We can't expect beginning artists and musicians to produce creative materials rivaling those of adults. Rather, when children's efforts are meaningful to them, they are appropriate.

Take, for example, seven-year-old Lisa. She has just spent the past thirty minutes in the art center painting at the easel. Lisa has been intently creating a picture of her home and front yard. She has chosen colors carefully and has created a good representation of that environment. Are her efforts novel and appropriate as defined earlier? From Lisa's perspective, it is a new activity that she finds meaningful and useful. Her efforts should be viewed by adults as a creative activity.

Characteristics of Creative Individuals

The list of characteristics associated with creative individuals is lengthy and varies from one researcher to the next. Torrance (1962) describes the following seven characteristics of highly creative young children:

- *Curiosity.* Creative children have a healthy curiosity; they consistently ask meaningful questions and manipulate materials in the environment.
- *Flexibility.* Creative children are flexible. When one approach to a problem doesn't work, they simply try something else.
- *Sensitivity to problems.* Creative children are able to sense missing elements and quickly identify problem situations.
- *Originality.* Creative children commonly have unusual ideas and create original products.
- *Independence.* Creative children are comfortable in working alone as they play with ideas or materials. Creative individuals often work with others, but they can accomplish much on their own.
- *Redefinition.* Creative children combine ideas or materials in new and unusual ways.
- *Penetration.* Creative children gain much insight from spending time thinking deeply about ideas and problems.

Assisting with the Creative Process

It is counterproductive to think about formally teaching children to be creative, but teachers and parents have important roles to play in facilitating creativity. Several key ingredients are needed for children to be creative individuals. One such element is to **value creativity.** Children need to know that the creative process is very important in the adult world and that creativity enriches each of our lives. In addition to the unquestioned value of the ideas and products of highly creative

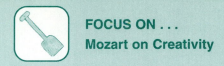

FOCUS ON . . .
Mozart on Creativity

The following is an excerpt from a letter written by Wolfgang Amadeus Mozart, discussing his musical creativity:

> When I am, as it were, completely myself, entirely alone and of good cheer—say, travelling in a carriage, or walking after a good meal, or during the night when I cannot sleep; it is on such occasions that my ideas flow best and most abundantly. Whence and how they come, I know not; nor can I force them. Those ideas that please me I retain in memory, and am accustomed, as I have been told, to hum them to myself. If I continue in this way, it soon occurs to me how I may turn this or that morsel to account, so as to make a good dish of it, that is to say, agreeably to the rules of counterpoint, to the peculiarities of the various instruments, etc.
>
> All this fires my soul, and, provided I am not disturbed, my subject enlarges itself, becomes methodised and defined, and the whole, though it be long, stands almost complete and finished in my mind, so that I can survey it, like a fine picture or a beautiful statue, at a glance. (Ghiselin, 1952, pp. 44–45)

What an amazingly creative man. To be able to think about, and create such beautiful music in its entirety in his head is truly an extraordinary gift. Very, very few are gifted in this way.

Unfortunately, however, when many of us assess our own creative potential, we try to measure ourselves against the truly great achievements of the past and find we are sorely lacking. This leads many to believe that they are uncreative, and this attitude carries over to their interactions with children.

If we can overlook the final outcome of Mozart's work, however, and address the *process* he used, perhaps we can learn from what Mozart writes.

1. *What does Mozart's message say to you about creativity?*
2. *Can you apply this information to children and their creative activities?*

---

adults, new solutions to the everyday problems faced by adults also help make life more enjoyable and pleasant. By valuing originality with our words and actions, we can help children grow into more creative adults.

Teachers can promote creative activity by establishing **low-risk classroom environments.** As children solve problems, explore, and experiment, they need to know that failure is acceptable and normal. Wasserman (1992) puts it this way: "Inventions of the new do not come from duplicating what is already there. They come from minds that are unafraid to take risks to try" (p. 135). Creativity is only possible when teachers encourage children to experiment with ideas that may not work. They learn from these failures and come back with even better, more creative solutions.

Teachers also need to create an environment in which children have the **freedom to explore.** Children need large blocks of time for exploration and experimentation if creativity is to take place. Children must also be free to choose the activities that interest them and to mess around with materials in their own unique

Scarves and streamers do wonders in helping little feet move creatively to music.

ways. Although these activities are often noisy and messy, this freedom to explore will pay big dividends in terms of creative activity.

A rich assortment of **open-ended materials** provides children with increased opportunities for creative expression. Interesting art materials, such as colorful paints and a variety of paper textures, help children produce imaginative works that express their unique personalities and developmental abilities.

Creativity and Play

> ❧ *During group time today, your four-year-olds requested "The Eensy Weensy Spider" once again for music. Then Adam suggested a variation he called "The Eensy Weensy Caterpillar." It was a big hit. Following group time, Adam and Marika stayed on the rug and spent another ten minutes creating their own playful modifications to "The Eensy Weensy Spider." They developed words and hand movements for "The Eensy Weensy Frog" and "The Eensy Weensy Bird."*

Perhaps you have noticed already that many of the concepts discussed earlier about childhood play (Chapter 5) also apply to creativity. In fact, play and creativity are closely linked. Although it is possible to play and not be creative, or for creativity to occur outside of the play experience, the two often take place together.

Highly creative adults, for example, often describe their creative acts as playing around with ideas or materials. Goertzel and Goertzel (1962) describe the lives of famous people such as the Wright brothers, Frank Lloyd Wright, Thomas Edison, and others as filled with playful explorations and discoveries.

Wasserman (1992) quotes Richard Feynman, a Nobel Prize winner in physics, as saying this about his playfulness:

> Why did I enjoy doing it [physics]? I used to play with it. I used to do whatever I felt like doing. It didn't have to do with whether it was important for the development of nuclear physics, but instead whether it was interesting and amusing for me to play with. (p. 139)

This ability to simply play around with physics concepts eventually led to a discovery that won Mr. Feynman the Nobel Prize.

Play probably won't lead most of us to this level of creativity, but clearly, lives are enriched when children and adults alike engage in quality play experiences. Albert Einstein (1954), considered one of the greatest thinkers of the twentieth century, felt that play was necessary for creative thinking: "Play seems to be the essential feature in productive thought" (p. 26).

The Young Artist

Art and music aren't the only ways for young children to express their creative talents; however, they are important options in the early childhood classroom. The foundation laid in these early years often determines whether or not individuals enjoy the creative arts throughout their lives.

Why Include Art?

Historically, most Americans have viewed the creative arts as less important than the teaching of more academic subjects. Consequently, at all levels of public education, when budgets or time became tight, the art and music programs were often the first to be cut or deemphasized. This attitude has influenced many parents and teachers at the prekindergarten level as well.

However, recently, the creative arts are being recognized as central to the curriculum for the twenty-first century. The National Education Goals Panel (1991), for example, identified the arts as essential components of the subject matter that students must master in public school if they are to succeed in later life. Richard Riley, Secretary of Education, stated it this way:

> The arts in education is an absolute necessity. If, in this day and time, we do not tap into the creative side of a young person's brain in every possible way, then we are not going to have the innovation and the economic and cultural growth experience that this country must have. (Getty Center for Education in the Arts, 1994, p. 7)

Ernest Boyer (1987) has identified three main reasons for including the creative arts as significant parts of the curriculum:

• The arts help children express feelings and ideas that are very difficult to share using words.

- Teachers can integrate the generally splintered academic world of students through the arts. Seeing connections and finding patterns across disciplines can be accomplished through the arts.
- The arts provide the child with a universal language that is very useful in communicating with others.

The Association for Childhood Education International (Jalongo, 1990) describes four major benefits associated with the expressive arts:

- They foster authentic learning that changes behavior and encourages reflection.
- They enhance the child's ability to interpret symbols, which are the foundation on which everything distinctly human develops.
- They are associated with growth in all areas of development, including academics.
- While engaged in creative arts activities, the child is a meaning maker, a constructor, and a discoverer rather than a passive recipient of someone else's answers.

Developmental Trends in Art

Rhonda, at eighteen months, is a very busy young girl. At her day care center, she is particularly interested in playing with paper and pencils. Rhonda has been fascinated with her older sister's pictures and stories and spends several minutes each day creating her own artful scribbles. To the untrained eye, they appear to be simply scratch marks on paper. But to Rhonda, they are important first steps in communicating with others.

As children mature both physically and mentally, they progress from the rather random scribbles during the infant/toddler years, described here, to more recognizable art during the primary years. Many researchers, including Rhoda Kellogg (1969), have carefully studied these developmental trends. Kellogg's collection of children's paintings and drawings from the United States and other countries around the world totals over a million samples. Schirrmacher (1993) summarizes the research of Kellogg and others and identifies the following stages in children's art:

- *Scribbling and mark-making stage (birth to about age two).* Kellogg (cited in Schirrmacher, 1993) identified twenty basic scribbles that young children refine as the foundation for future art activities. These move from simple dots and lines to the more complex motions needed to create an imperfect circle. Children begin by making random marks and gradually move to more controlled and purposeful scribbling.
- *Very personal symbol and design stage (approximately two to four years of age).* During this period, children make scribbles and marks in specific areas on their paper to create personal symbols and designs. For example, a large imperfect circle

Jalongo (1995) suggests that many people have misconceptions about art, and educators need to take action to counteract them. She identifies five misconceptions that we should actively work to overcome:

- *Art is a nonessential element of the curriculum.* This misconception is widespread and needs to be carefully addressed by teachers. First of all, communicating to others through the medium of art is an essential element of our humanity and cannot be taken lightly. Second, children practice considerable higher-level thinking skills as they engage in art activities. Art needs to be considered an essential component of education rather than an unnecessary frill.

- *Discovering talent is the goal.* Our job as teachers of young children is *not* to discover the next Picasso or Monet. Every child should be encouraged to participate in art. Teachers should emphasize the process, not the product.

- *Teachers must have performance skills in art to teach it.* It is most important to share with children an enthusiasm for art and its production. This doesn't require strong performance skills. When teachers communicate excitement,

provide materials for creative art experiences, and facilitate children's efforts, a rich curriculum in art is ensured.

- *Creative teaching is teacher-centered.* Although it is possible to assist children in their creative efforts (see information on Reggio Emilia in this chapter), the process of creative thinking and expression must come from within the child. Making an art pattern for children to cut out and decorate is not helpful in stimulating creativity.

- *The teacher is uninvolved.* While the teacher cannot directly teach creative art, much can be done to ensure quality experiences. In addition to providing quality materials, the teacher needs to ask appropriate questions, make helpful comments, and guide the creative efforts of young children.

1. *Are you guilty of believing any of the preceding misconceptions about art?*

2. *How can you help parents and others who believe in one or more of these misconceptions to see a better way?*

with four lines protruding at odd angles might become an early symbol for the human figure. The young child includes whatever features he views as important and omits those elements that he considers insignificant.

- *Attempts at public representation (approximately four to seven years).* At this point, children modify their personal symbols and gradually produce art that is more recognizable to others. They include more details, and accurate representation becomes increasingly important to children. For example, if a child is drawing her mother, who has brown hair and blue eyes, the drawing will contain these details.

Time and appropriate materials lead to creative art experiences for young children.

- *Realism stage (late primary years and up).* Children at this point strive hard to include even the smallest of realistic details as they create their artwork. This attempted photographic realism emphasizes size, placement, proportion, and other elements in attempts at reproducing replicas of people, places, and things the child has experienced.

The Early Childhood Art Curriculum

The content of the art program for young children may appear straightforward; however, many experts suggest that it is more than just the production of art using a variety of media. Opportunities for making art are only one part of the larger curriculum children need to explore. Schirrmacher (1993) identifies four central elements in a strong art program:

- *Sensing and experiencing.* When children use their senses and engage in meaningful experiences, these experiences form the foundation for creative expression. Art is an expression of these events to others.
- *Making art.* Children need to express themselves by making art with diverse art media.

- *Learning about art, artists, and their styles.* The natural interest of young children in learning about community helpers can be extended to include artists. Local artists using a variety of styles and media can tell their stories and share works with children.
- *Aesthetics.* Aesthetics is the study of beauty in color, form, and design. With assistance, children can come to appreciate beauty in different artworks and in the natural world around them.

Another recent approach to the art curriculum in early childhood education is referred to as **discipline-based art education.** The Getty Center for Education in the Arts (Kaagan, 1990) has been a major proponent of this approach. Designed for children in the primary grades and beyond, this perspective promotes developing the technical skills needed in art production, plus the teaching of four disciplines that help children create, understand, and appreciate art:

- Art production
- Art history
- Art criticism
- Aesthetics

The Adult Role in Art Experiences

Teachers can facilitate creative art experiences in the early childhood classroom in many ways. An important first step is **providing a variety of appropriate materials** for children to explore. Tempera paints, watercolors, chalk, and clay are all examples of diverse art materials that children can use productively during the preschool and primary years. By rotating exciting materials in and out of the art center, teachers provide children with experiences using different materials, which maintains a high level of interest in making art. Chapter 9 describes additional materials for the art center.

Another teacher task is to **value creativity** in art. Unfortunately, many well-meaning adults can permanently damage the creative abilities of young children with their comments and interactions. Rather than shutting down the creative expressiveness of young children, we need to let children know, both through our words and actions, that we value their unique uses of art materials. That kind of emotional climate will keep children motivated to engage in art activities.

> *During center time, Mrs. Duncan's first-grade students are engaged in a variety of activities, including art. Aletha is using the colorful cloth scraps to create an intricate design on her paper. Mrs. Duncan takes a moment to carefully observe Aletha at work and then says, "Aletha, I'm impressed with the variety of colors you are using and the wonderful designs being created. Very interesting!" Mrs. Duncan is showing Aletha that she values her creative efforts in art.*

The model preschool program known as Reggio Emilia is well-known for its artwork. Seefeldt (1995) describes it as having rather amazing results:

> Stunning displays of art surround you. Brightly colored drawings and paintings, surrealistic in appearance and depicting all kinds of animals—giraffes, zebras, horses, lions, and tigers—decorate the walls. A mural of children playing in a field of red poppies hangs from the ceiling. Shelves and pedestals hold sculptures. (p. 39)

This is not a description of what most preschool teachers in the United States regularly experience. What makes the artwork of children in the Reggio Emilia approach so astonishing? The maturity and complexity of the productions are truly amazing. Certainly, the children are no different from those in preschool programs in the United States. So, where do the differences come from?

Seefeldt (1995) argues that in Reggio Emilia teachers consider art *serious work*. They organize the art program around three principles:

• **Understand cognitive theories of art.** A basic premise of cognitive theories is that art is an important form of communicating ideas and feelings to others. Art becomes a language of expressing cognitive understandings to others.

• **Motivate children to produce art.** Children who are provided with quality experiences can be motivated to express their learnings to others through art. Deeply meaningful experiences can lead to amazing art.

• **Carefully select teaching strategies.** Teachers in the Reggio Emilia program are actively involved in teaching young children the skills they need to succeed in art. This is done individually as the child demonstrates a need for instruction. Modeling appropriate techniques, physically assisting the young child from time to time, and providing specific verbal feedback are all used to teach art to young children.

1. *Are there benefits and potential drawbacks to viewing art as serious business in the early childhood classroom?*

2. *Read Seefeldt (1995) or another article about Reggio Emilia, and talk to classmates about your findings regarding artwork and its implications for American preschools.*

Children also benefit when adults **describe and/or demonstrate appropriate uses for art tools and materials.** When an early childhood teacher casually describes how positioning a paint brush allows the artist to make different strokes, she is providing young children with valuable art instruction. And because children learn in different ways, some will find it more helpful to watch the teacher demonstrate how to use some materials rather than listening to a verbal description. In both instances, children can benefit from this one-on-one assistance in using art tools and materials.

It is critical, however, that these demonstration efforts **avoid the use of models.** Models that the teacher constructs have no place in the early childhood classroom. They send children the message that their art is of poor quality because it can never look as good as the teacher's example. Models also say to children that there is a right way to use these materials. When adult interactions say to children that there is a correct way to paint or construct with art items, their creativity and motivation are diminished.

Teachers of young children also need to **emphasize the process** of art, rather than the product. Creative acts occur when children have plenty of opportunities to explore and experiment. This means that many of the products will be the result of messing around with materials. Although it is important to teach children specific art techniques, an emphasis on the product makes it less likely that the much-needed experimentation will take place. L. Edwards (1997) suggests that teachers of young children:

- Put away patterns, ditto masters, and premarked papers.
- Throw out coloring books.
- Avoid cookbook art activities.
- Enjoy the freedom that basic materials provide.

Talking about art with children is yet another important way in which teachers can guide the developing artist's work. The wrong questions and comments can be very damaging to children. Although well-meaning, questions such as "What is it?" may be difficult to answer and emphasize the product rather that the process of art.

Making appropriate comments and asking the right questions require thoughtfulness and insight. Engel (1996) suggests that adults must learn to look more carefully at children's art so that they can respond in positive ways. She identifies six questions that teachers can ask themselves as they prepare to talk with children about art:

- What is it made of (size, tools, medium)?
- What does the adult see (lines, angles, shapes, symmetry, colors, overlaps)?
- What does it represent (design, story, scene, symbol)?
- How is it organized (perspective, composition, action, view, completion)?
- What is it about, what is the nature of involvement (violence, peace, love, sadness, persuasion, information)?
- Where does the idea come from (imagination, observation, literature, imitation, TV, messing around)?

When teachers respond enthusiastically and with these kinds of questions, children get excited about producing art that is meaningful to them.

Finally, teachers need to **display children's art** in the classroom. The message adults must convey is that art is a means of expression for all; not just something for a select few who demonstrate special talent. Displaying artwork from each child helps both parents and children value the creative activities of each classmate. The teacher should place art at the child's eye level and rotate it regularly to make sure children fully appreciate the artwork of their peers.

Music and the Young Child

Just as art provides many opportunities for young children to express themselves, music draws others into creative activities in the early childhood classroom. When adults carefully prepare the environment with appropriate materials and encourage musical experiences, children become willing participants in a variety of musical activities.

The Importance of Music in Early Childhood

The technical quality of musical productions at this age shows that children are just beginning to develop their skills. However, most children are genuinely interested in, and enjoy musical experiences. And, just as with the child's developing art abilities, the foundations for later musical production and enjoyment are built during the early childhood years. Ball (1995) cites longitudinal research that reveals that musical aptitude (the potential to learn music) becomes stabilized by age nine. The clear implication is that if we want to help children develop the basic skills necessary for musical expression later in life, they need many opportunities to experience music during the early childhood years.

Numerous reasons support including music in the curriculum. Isenberg and Jalongo (1997) have identified the following roles of music in child development:

- *Psychomotor skills.* As children strum the xylophone, tap their rhythm sticks, beat a drum, or move to music, they are refining their control over large and small muscle movements.

- *Perceptual skills.* Recognizing a familiar tune and imitating it or tapping out a rhythmic pattern are examples of how music allows children opportunities to develop perceptual abilities.

- *Affective development.* Music naturally leads to emotional responses and provides many children with important and appropriate ways to express their feelings.

- *Cognitive growth.* Viadero (1996) describes two recent studies that suggest that musical experiences have been found to enhance the reasoning abilities of young children. Children develop higher-level thinking skills and memory through musical activities.

- *Social skills.* Many musical experiences encourage participation, sharing, and cooperation. These important social skills need constant reinforcement in the early childhood classroom in natural and meaningful ways.

- *Cultural understandings.* Multicultural musical experiences help familiarize children with an important aspect of different cultures. This can lead to meaningful discussions of the similarities and differences between cultures. Children also identify with music from their own culture and react positively when teachers include this music in the classroom.

Musical Development

> 〰 *John and Astra are sitting on the circle time rug and singing along with their favorite music tape by Raffi. These busy three-year-olds then decide to add some music making of their own to the activity. John takes a drum off the shelf, while Astra locates a triangle to use for her rhythm instrument. They restart the tape, and sing along while keeping a reasonably accurate beat with their instruments. John and Astra are progressing normally in their musical development.*

Researchers who have studied the development of musical abilities in young children (e.g., Bayless & Ramsey, 1991) generally describe their results in terms of typical performance at different ages rather than identifying stages of development. The following abilities are milestones in musical development:

- *Infants* respond to the loudness and softness of sounds; react to the human voice, particularly the primary caregiver's; and express lively reactions to action songs and more subdued responses to lullabies.

- *Toddlers* discriminate among sounds and may try to approximate; listen to music, enthusiastically responding to certain songs, repeating repetitive phrases; enjoy making sounds with musical instruments or common household items; may sing or hum casually as they play.

- *Three-year-olds* develop better voice control and can master simple songs; many have favorite tunes they recognize; they can play rhythm instruments with a basic understanding of beat.

- *Four-year-olds* can learn basic musical concepts such as pitch, duration, tempo, and loudness; are able to classify musical instruments by sound, shape, size, and pitch; sing complete songs from memory with improving rhythm and pitch; have an average singing range of five notes.

- *Five-year-olds* have a maturing sense of pitch, rhythm, and melody; like longer songs with predictable elements; reproduce a melody in an echo song; extend their singing range to six notes.

- *Six-, seven-, and eight-year-olds* have singing voices that approach maturity; can sing in tune with up to ten notes; are beginning to develop a sense of harmony; enjoy silliness and word play in songs; have a greater awareness of printed music and its role; often have well-established musical preferences; may show an interest in playing a musical instrument.

The Music Curriculum for Young Children

The early childhood music curriculum has four components (Bayless & Ramsey, 1987; L. Edwards, 1997). **Listening to music** is the first of these elements. The teacher could lead a group activity in which she plays recordings of different musical styles, instruments, or old favorites and helps children listen more carefully to the elements of the music. Individual children can put on headphones and listen to taped music during free time. Finally, some teachers play music at different times

Many songs for young children also include hand and body movements.

during the day to create a pleasant atmosphere in the classroom. In all these instances, children are refining their musical listening skills in an enjoyable setting.

A second element of the early childhood music curriculum is **responding to music through movement.** Young children have an almost irresistible urge to move to the music they hear. Adults can encourage this through modeling, group activities, and providing materials and space for movement. Many songs for young children also include hand motions; adults can teach these, and children can use them when singing. Teachers can also create a marching band with musical instruments and a lively recording. Children can use scarves and streamers in the music corner as they move to music during free play.

A third important component of the music curriculum is that children must have many opportunities to **make music.** Singing enjoyable songs is one way to have fun making music. Many excellent songbooks and recordings (see Hamilton, Flemming, & Hicks, 1990, for examples) can provide children with a variety of singing experiences. Playing different musical and rhythmic instruments gives great pleasure to young children as well. Rotating these options in and out of the classroom adds further interest to this aspect of music making. Making music is an important way for children to engage in creative expression; teachers should encourage them to create new verses for familiar songs and develop their own musical and rhythmic expressions.

Music for the Nonmusician

Does all this discussion about music make you nervous? Would you consider yourself below average in musical abilities? If you haven't had any musical training, the thought of encouraging young children to engage in these activities may seem daunting. The good news is that you really don't need to be highly proficient musically to have a strong program for young children. Jalongo (1996) suggests five ways the nonmusician can use recorded music to create quality experiences for young children:

- *Choose music that is at a comfortable pitch.* Young children's voices are still maturing, and music that has a high pitch is harder to sing. Singers such as Raffi and Ella Jenkins have many recordings that are easy for children (and adults) to sing along with because of the lower pitch.

- *Expand your musical repertoire.* Try to avoid sticking to what you are familiar with. Borrow some recorded music from the library or other teachers, and work on expanding your musical

horizons. This helps ensure that students are getting richer musical experiences.

- *Become familiar with the best music available for young children.* Several musical awards are presented regularly for children's music, such as the Parent's Choice Seal of Approval. Professional journals also review recordings, and these can be helpful in selecting quality options. Talking to other teachers and music specialists provides additional insight for selection.

- *Provide a wide range of musical styles, including ethnic music.* Recordings of songs sung in different languages and others that use culture-specific instruments can be excellent additions to the early childhood classroom.

- *Arrange many opportunities for quiet listening.* Teachers can set up a cassette player with headphones and a basket of tapes for listening times. Background music at different times during the day can provide another productive listening experience.

The final element of the early childhood music curriculum is to help children begin to **understand music and music making.** For example, children need to acquire a vocabulary that helps them describe musical experiences. Children can learn and use musical terms such as *pitch, duration, tempo,* and *loudness* to help them describe both their own and others' musical experiences. Teachers can also present the appropriate names for musical instruments and simple explanations for how each makes music. Learning that music communicates feelings and helping children to identify the emotions generated by specific pieces is yet another way to begin developing a cognitive understanding of music.

Facilitating Musical Experiences

Adults play important roles in facilitating quality musical experiences. Having positive attitudes about music and taking the time needed for adequate planning and preparation can help ensure exciting adventures in this aspect of the curriculum. The following guidelines identify specific strategies that teachers can use:

- *Prepare the classroom environment.* Careful planning and preparation are the essential starting points for good musical experiences. Thoughtful selection of songs to sing, music to play, and instruments available for children to use will strengthen the music curriculum. While children love to repeat favorite songs and enjoy the opportunity to thoroughly explore musical instruments, it is also very important to have new materials and songs to maintain interest.

- *Encourage creative expression.* Teachers need to allow young children the freedom to experiment and explore with music. When adults value creative musical expression, children's performances blossom. As they make up songs or new verses to familiar tunes and create their own rhythmic expressions, children are truly making music in very meaningful ways.

- *Emphasize enjoyment.* The quality of musical expression should *not* be the focus of the early childhood music curriculum. Children have yet to develop the skills needed for quality performance. Rather, the emphasis should be on enjoying a variety of musical experiences. Developing a love of music during the early years can help maintain interest and involvement in later life.

- *Make music fun.* Teachers have a major role to play in making musical experiences fun for young children. It is important, for example, to demonstrate to children your own excitement. If the teacher is animated and involved, children will be, too. Active participation in musical experiences increases the likelihood that children will find them fun. Adding props to songs, selecting motivating music, and providing quality musical instruments also help make these activities more fun for children.

- *Carefully observe.* Observations serve several purposes in the early childhood music curriculum. They allow teachers to determine which music materials are being used and when change is needed. Observations help adults recognize who is participating and what can be done to get others involved. Children's musical understandings can also be assessed through observation and activities planned to meet deficits.

Activities in Art and Music

Many idea books are available to assist teachers of young children in planning creative art and music activities. Hamilton et al. (1990) and Herr and Libby (1995) are two good examples of resource guides that are useful in planning for art and music. Teachers should take care to adapt the suggestions of these or other idea books to meet the needs and interests of specific children. Similarly, the ideas that follow may need modifications to succeed with children you know.

Activities for Infant/Toddlers

Programs for infant/toddlers spend much time and effort dealing with the routines of young children's lives (Bassett, 1995). Toileting, bathing, eating, and sleeping activities consume much of the day. An art and music curriculum at this age

INTO PRACTICE . . .

Singing Songs with Young Children

Singing should be an integral part of the curriculum in early childhood. Songs can strengthen conceptual understandings, to make the more routine activities such as cleanup time more pleasant, and simply as an enjoyable addition to the day. If you enjoy singing, so will young children. You can even make up songs that can be sung to familiar music and create your own music curriculum.

Singing to Strengthen Conceptual Understanding

Many songs allow children to learn while they sing. The following is an example for mathematics:

Four Little Horses

Four little horses, galloping through town
Two are white and two are brown
Two gallop up and two gallop down
Four little horses galloping through town.

You can create your own tune for this song and, using fingers for horses, merrily sing about four, six, eight, or even five little horses.

Singing during Routines

Songs are a good way to alert children to the start of routine times like snack, cleanup, and outdoor time. An example of this type is:

Brushing Teeth
(Sing to the tune of "Mulberry Bush")

This is the way we brush our teeth,
    brush our teeth, brush our teeth.
This is the way we brush our teeth
    so early in the morning

(Herr & Libby, 1995, p. 187)

Singing for Fun

Songs with hand motions or full-body involvement are often popular with young children and are frequently requested. "The Eensy Weensy Spider" and "Head, and Shoulders, Knees, and Toes" are two traditional favorites.

---

should be integrated with these activities whenever possible. Some possibilities include the following:

- Adults can place artwork within the view of infants and toddlers as they participate in various routines.
- Adults can playfully sing to young children while diapering, feeding, or preparing them for naps.
- Playing background music during the routines of the day introduces infants and toddlers to pleasant musical experiences.
- Adults can place rattles and other noisemakers within reach of young children for playful exploration during diaper-changing times.

During the rest of the day, adults can give infants and toddlers additional opportunities to explore art and music. Infants and toddlers can use simple (and safe) drawing materials for scribble art, for example. Teachers can encourage toddlers to move to music by providing a space and some lively music. Edible play dough is another enjoyable alternative for this age.

Art often includes sensory experiences as part of the process.

Art and Music for Preschoolers

The preschool child's blossoming skills allow for a much-expanded art and music curriculum. Teachers should provide for old favorites like crayons and easel painting for art and classic songs like "The Eensy Weensy Spider"; children also need the chance to experience new creative arts activities.

Art Ideas. The following are selected examples of creative art experiences for preschool children:

- *Mural painting.* This can be a fun outdoor activity for young children. Tape a large sheet of butcher paper to any exterior wall, and let children collectively paint to their hearts' content. Or provide children with buckets of water and paint brushes of different sizes and encourage them to paint the walls and other structures with water.
- *Straw painting.* Provide children with glossy paper and straws. Children put small amounts of fairly runny paint on the paper and then blow through the straws to create interesting images and mixing of paints. Be sure to instruct younger preschoolers to blow out, rather than suck up through their straws.
- *Crayon rubbings.* Using items with a definite texture, such as leaves, coins, or sandpaper, place a piece of newsprint on top, and have children rub the flat side

of the crayon over the paper. Let children experiment with objects of their own choosing for making rubbings.

- *Working with clay.* Although clay is more difficult for young children to work than the more traditional play dough, it can be an enjoyable experience with careful preparation. And although it may be possible to create finished fired pottery, products aren't necessary for children to have a meaningful experience with clay.

Music Ideas.   Many different types of musical experiences can be valuable for preschool children. The following suggestions provide a beginning point for this level:

- *Scarves.* Collect silky scarves from parents, and use these to help young children move to music. Have the scarves available in the group time area with music to fit the mood you want to encourage. Help children realize that they need to avoid collisions with others, and simply turn them loose. A favorite activity for many children.
- *"I Know an Old Lady."* This classic song about an old lady who swallows a fly (and much more) is often sung with primary children. But with props for the flannel-board, this song has considerable appeal for younger students. The catchy tune, combined with much repetition, makes it a hit.
- *Marching band.* With a good collection of rhythm instruments—such as cymbals, bells, and drums—children can practice making music by marching around the classroom (or outdoors) in time to a good piece of music with a clear beat. The addition of hats and a band leader (the teacher initially) makes the activity even more attractive to young children.
- *Music appreciation.* Choose several pieces of music that create different moods for you as an adult. Have children close their eyes and listen to each piece, imagining that they are doing something as they listen. Talk about what children imagined and how the music created that mood. Add your own insights.

The Primary Years

The continued development of motor skills and cognitive understanding makes it possible for teachers to plan and implement increasingly complex art and music activities for primary-aged children. The following examples are designed to get you thinking about the possibilities for this level.

Art Suggestions.   Schirrmacher (1998) has many good suggestions for primary children. He reminds us that the young artist at this age is still eager to simply mess around with materials, exploring their properties and enjoying the process of art. Providing plenty of paper, glue, scissors, crayons, and paint for basic exploration is still important. Adding new materials like **chalk and pastels** is also useful.

Teachers can productively use a diverse collection of multicultural musical instruments in the early childhood classroom. Although it is important to avoid being stereotypic, presenting traditional instruments can open up a productive dialogue about the similarities and differences between cultures. In addition, the musical experiences can be very rewarding for children. Here are a few examples of instruments that you may want to consider as part of the music curriculum:

- *Rain stick.* This instrument comes from Chile and is made from a long, cylindrical, dried cactus, with the spines pounded inward and sealed with small pebbles inside. Tipping the stick allows the stones to bounce off the cactus spines and create a very pleasant tinkling sound.

- *Ocarina.* This instrument is also called a *vessel flute* and originated in South America. Made from clay, it has a small built-in mouthpiece and several holes for making different musical notes. More appropriate for primary children, this instrument needs careful handling and cleaning between players.

- *Drums.* No one culture holds a monopoly on drums. They seem to come from many different places and make a wide range of sounds.

African, Chinese, Brazilian, and Native American cultures all have diverse drums for use in the early childhood classroom. Children enjoy trying out the many different varieties and talking about similarities and differences.

- *Guiro.* This traditional rhythm instrument originated in Mexico and is a favorite for all ages. Shaped somewhat like a shortened, hollow, baseball bat with grooves running horizontally around the instrument, the player taps or rubs a short stick over the grooves on the exterior of the guiro to keep time with the music.

- *Shakeree.* This rhythm instrument comes from Africa and consists of a large gourd with seeds strung over its exterior in an intricate pattern. Shaking the gourd causes the seeds to make a rattling sound similar to maracas.

1. *Locate a musical instrument from another culture, and try it out with children. What were their reactions?*

2. *Find a resource in your community for multicultural musical instruments (parents, business, etc.).*

Although messy, these give children the opportunity to blend colors in beautiful combinations. Light chalk on dark paper, wet chalk, and pastels on heavy paper are possibilities.

Using **crayon shavings** to make art projects is another option for this age. The teacher can scrape old broken crayons with a dull knife to create the shavings needed for the project. To create attractive designs, the children place the shavings on a piece of waxed paper and put another sheet of waxed paper on top. The teacher presses these with a warm iron, through a protective sheet of plain paper.

Before adding the second piece of waxed paper, children can include other items, such as glitter, bits of ribbon, or tissue paper, to individualize their creations.

Some children at the primary level begin to show an interest in drawing or **sketching.** Simple sketches of each other, objects in the room, or things at home may be attractive activities for many primary children. Brookes (1986) provides excellent ideas for helping children develop their creative drawing abilities.

Making **stars and snowflakes** is another fun activity for winter-time art. Coffee filters (flat-bottomed rather than conical) are just the right shape, size, and thickness for creating individually designed stars or snowflakes. By folding the filters into quarters, snipping off small pieces, and carefully unfolding the paper, children can easily construct and then display on classroom windows their efforts.

Music Activities.   The musical experiences of primary children should include many different ways to make music. Children this age can productively use **more complex instruments.** The autoharp is an excellent example that both teachers and children can use. When the autoharp has clear markings for chords, children who have learned songs the teacher has previously played can re-create the appropriate chords by reading a song card. Orff instruments, designed by the German composer Carl Orff, are other examples of more complex instruments that produce beautiful musical tones. The metallophone, for example, is like the traditional xylophone, but produces rich alto and bass tones on bars of thick metal.

Primary children can enjoy listening to, and discussing **classical music.** L. Edwards (1997) suggests the following for young children: Mozart, Symphony no. 39 in E Flat and Symphony no. 41 in C; Chopin, Sonata no. 3, op. 58; Beethoven, String Quartet no. 3 in D Major and String Quartet no. 4 in C; and Bach, Brandenburg Concerto no. 106.

Singing songs remains a high priority for children at this age. With increasing musical abilities, children can enjoy singing songs in rounds. A classic example is "Row, Row, Row Your Boat." Silly songs with child-oriented humor are also very popular. Take, for example, "Fried Ham":

> Fried ham, fried ham
> Cheese and bologna
> After the macaroni
> We'll have more fried ham, fried ham, fried ham!

Children enjoy singing this silly song using a variety of unusual voices, such as under water, robot, and baby. It is great fun and provides many opportunities for creative expression.

Summary

An understanding of the creative process is important to the teaching of art and music. Studying definitions of creativity, the characteristics of creative individuals, how adults can assist with the creative process, and the relationships between play and creativity provides the foundation needed to understand this complex process. Although some consider art education less important, there is a strong rationale for including art in the early childhood classroom. Understanding developmental trends in art, the content of the early childhood art curriculum, and the adult's role in art experiences allows teachers to create appropriate and interesting art experiences for young children. Music is another important element of the early childhood curriculum. When teachers understand the developmental patterns children follow in their musical growth, appropriate content for the music curriculum, ways in which adults can facilitate musical experiences, and appropriate materials and activities for young children, they can implement exciting musical experiences in the classroom.

∾ For Discussion and Action

1. What do you like to do when you are being creative? Discuss this with a small group, and then talk about what this tells you about creativity.

2. As you were growing up, do you remember an adult who either positively or negatively influenced how you felt about your creative talents in art or music? What did that person say or do?

3. Observe children participating in an early childhood art experience. What did they do? Was it creative? Why or why not?

4. Plan a simple music activity for young children. Locate a song to sing, a musical instrument to play, or some other musical experience, and try it out with children. Describe the results.

5. Look for a creative art experience to do with young children, collect all the materials needed, and try it out. How did children respond? Would you do things differently another time?

∾ Building Your Personal Library

Brookes, M. (1986). *Drawing with children: A creative teaching and learning method that works for adults, too.* New York: G.T. Putnam's Sons. This book describes a nonthreatening process for teaching children techniques for improving drawing. The emphasis is on enhancing creativity, not on the end product of the drawing process.

Edwards, L. (1997). *The creative arts: A process approach for teachers and children.* Upper Saddle River, NJ: Prentice Hall. This book begins with a good description of the creative process and has strong chapters on musical and artistic experiences for young children. It also includes some excellent resources for the creative arts.

Isenberg, J., & Jalongo, M. (1997). *Creative expression and play in early childhood* (2nd ed.). Upper Saddle River, NJ: Prentice Hall. These well-respected authors make a strong case for the connections between play and creative activities. They address both music and art activities and present many good ideas for making them a playful part of the early childhood classroom.

Schirrmacher, R. (1998). *Art and creative development for young children* (3rd ed.). Albany, NY: Delmar. This book focuses on art for young children and provides an in-depth look at creativity, developmental aspects of art, the adult's roles, and setting up a creative art center.

In this chapter you will

- Learn about the relationships between technology and play.
- Study the impact of television on young children.
- Investigate characteristics of developmentally appropriate software for the early childhood classroom.
- Identify the teacher's role in technology use.
- Clarify strategies for communicating with parents about technology.

Navin and Mark are playing at the computer in their preschool classroom. Like the rest of their classmates, these four-year-old children fearlessly experiment with the computer as they navigate through the art program they are using. As they draw and paint on the computer screen, Mark and Navin talk about their creation. "Let's try the stamps" insists Navin as they change the background color from white to green. "Okay, I want butterflies in our picture, and they have some in the stamp part," states Mark. The two children continue negotiating elements of their project as play proceeds over the next fifteen minutes. Once the picture is complete, they print it out, show it to two interested classmates, and then take off for the block corner to engage in additional play.

The scene just described is becoming more and more common in the early childhood classroom. Teachers and parents are beginning to see the value of computer use for young children, and opportunities to use computers on a regular basis are expanding. Children are enthusiastically using the computer as an effective tool for exploration, learning, and play.

Until fairly recently, however, many adults have questioned the value of computers in the early childhood classroom. During the 1980s, as computers became more accessible to children in pre-K–12 education, some educators voiced concerns about developmental readiness (Barnes & Hill, 1983), lack of social interactions (Heller & Martin, 1982), and the move away from concrete, real-world materials (Cuffaro, 1984) associated with computer use by young children.

More recent writing and research have generally been supportive of computer use by young children. Socialization issues (Baron, 1991), concerns over software options (Shade, 1992), and developmental appropriateness (Clements & Nastasi, 1992) have been addressed to the satisfaction of many early educators.

This chapter demonstrates the appropriateness of computers and other forms of technology as learning tools in the early childhood classroom. Although this equipment can be misused, with careful selection and operation, activities involving technology can be a significant complement to other more traditional activities of young children.

Television and Young Children

Television is one form of technology that has been available to parents and teachers for many years. Much has been written about the problems associated with this technology and young children. Time spent viewing, the content of programming, and advertising issues have all been concerns related to television viewing. Despite these valid criticisms, limited television viewing in the early childhood classroom may be useful. In this section, we will look at both the limitations and potential for effective television viewing.

Time Spent Viewing

One major concern voiced about television use is the large amount of time spent viewing. Miller (1997) indicates that children in the United States watch an average of three to five hours of television daily. By the time young adults graduate from high school, they have spent more time watching television than doing any other activity except sleeping (S. Cohen, 1994). Even if all the programming being watched were excellent, this large block of time in front of the television significantly decreases the child's opportunities for other valuable activities. For children during the early childhood years, the activity that television most probably replaces is play. Let's create a typical day in the life of a five-year-old child to see the potential impact of an average level of television viewing:

7:00 AM	Wake up, dress, breakfast, television
8:30 AM	Leave for kindergarten
2:30 PM	After-school care
5:00 PM	Home, television, dinner
6:30 PM	Television
8:30 PM	Prepare for bed

It doesn't take much imagination to see that this child has little time for anything other than the regular routine and about three hours of television viewing. The TV has crowded out most of the opportunities for socializing with others, being read to, or playing.

Sex, Violence, and Advertising

A careful analysis of television programming during prime time also shows considerable content that is inappropriate for young children. **Sexual themes** and

Parents and early childhood educators are concerned about the sexual themes and acts of violence that children are viewing on television. Many cite a recent increase in violent play among young children and express concern that children are more violent in their interactions with others (Silva, 1996). Others worry about the impact of the sexual themes on young children (Hughes, 1993). Consider the following information about sex and violence on television:

- Children see approximately thirty-two acts of violence per hour on Saturday morning cartoons (Silva, 1996).

- Prime-time television broadcasting had a total of forty-five sexual scenes in one week of viewing. Of this number, twenty-three involved unmarried heterosexual partners, and sixteen depicted adulterous relationships (Hughes, 1993).

- By the end of the elementary school years, children will have viewed approximately 8,000 murders and 100,000 acts of violence (Silva, 1996).

- Those who initiate violence go unpunished in 73 percent of all scenes depicted on television (NAEYC, 1996e).

1. *Do you think the results described here are accurate? Discuss the implications of this information on the development of young children.*

2. *Do your own study of television programming, focusing on shows designed for young children. Consider watching one educational program and one cartoon show. What did you discover?*

acts of violence are often cited as problem areas (Lawton, 1995; National Association for the Education of Young Children, 1996e). Children are viewing a variety of adult-oriented sexual situations and many different acts of violence on a daily basis. Their ability to make sense of these situations is limited, at best, and leads to considerable confusion and misunderstanding among children. If something is on television, does that mean it is acceptable in the real world? Young children are struggling to define the borders between reality and fantasy. Unfortunately, television often blurs this already unclear distinction. The results are painfully evident in the inappropriate behaviors of young children.

Another problem area associated with television viewing is the **advertising** that children are exposed to. It is estimated that the average child sees approximately 20,000 commercials a year, many of them specifically targeting children as consumers (Clearinghouse on Elementary and Early Childhood Education, 1990). The majority of food advertising for children is for highly sugared products, rather than more healthy alternatives. Similarly, the toys being promoted tend to be less creative and playful than other products available to young children. Many parent–child conflicts over what toys to buy can be traced to the advertising seen on television.

Too much television and inappropriate programming can cause problems for young children.

Redeeming Aspects?

The preceding discussion suggests that television viewing has a strong negative impact on the lives of young children. Although good evidence validates this perspective, other evidence indicates that all is not lost when children spend time watching TV. **Educational programs** like *Sesame Street* are receiving good reports in terms of their impact on preparing children for school. Regular viewing of these programs was statistically significant in improving letter–word recognition, enhancing mathematics skills, and increasing children's vocabularies (Wright & Huston, 1995). So, although many television shows have limited or no value, educational programming may be a valuable experience for young children.

Guidelines for Parents

Perhaps the most universal piece of technology found in American homes is the television. Very few are without at least one, and most have two or three. Many families provide little guidance and supervision for young children's viewing. The following ideas may help parents deal more effectively with the television:

• *Collect articles* from the professional literature that provide information about the problems and benefits of television viewing. The National Association for the Education of Young Children (1996e) and Wright and Huston (1995) are examples of articles for your collection.

- *Encourage parents to limit television viewing* by suggesting alternatives that are healthier for the child's overall development. When provided with specific suggestions for simple play experiences, parents can take the difficult step to turn off the television for part of the child's free time.

- *Suggest that parents discuss* what the children are watching. Whenever possible, parents can view programming along with children and talk about the negative aspects that are being presented. This can help children be better consumers of the shows they watch.

- *Move the television* to a room not in the center of family life. This will help encourage other more valuable activities when members gather.

The Video Game Dilemma

> *Matt and Alan rush home from their second-grade classroom and head straight to the video game shelf. They select a favorite game, plug it in, and spend the next forty-five minutes deeply engrossed in manipulating their joysticks. Their animated conversation and intense focus show that Matt and Alan are definitely excited about the game.*

Many children like Matt and Alan find video games highly motivating. And the number of homes with these games continues to grow. In a recent study of low-income families, approximately 75 percent of the homes had **video games** for young children (Wright & Huston, 1995).

The Debate over Value

Although on average, children spend considerably less time playing video games than watching television, many adults are concerned about video game use. Fantasy, violence, and autonomous action rather than cooperation are frequently cited as problem areas (Funk, 1993). For some children, another issue is the large amount of time spent playing these games. Again, this leaves little time to engage in other more important activities such as vigorous physical activity and creative play.

Some adults feel that video games offer benefits over television viewing, however. While TV is a passive activity, video games may increase a child's eye–hand coordination and improve attention to detail. Others suggest that these games can be a nonthreatening way to introduce children to computers. Finally, many children also gain a sense of accomplishment from playing (Cesarone, 1994).

One other influential thinker suggests that video games give insight into the potential power of computers to transform the way children learn. Seymour Papert (1993) states that parents and teachers should try to understand why video games captivate children. "Any adult who thinks one of these games is easy need only sit down and try to master one. Most are hard, with complex information—as well as technique—to be mastered" (p. 4). Video games allow children to explore and experiment in situations with predetermined rules and to learn a great deal from these experiences. Papert wants computers to provide similar types of playful interactions for children.

Parental Roles

Many of the issues facing parents in relation to video games are similar to those for television viewing. One major concern is the amount of time some children spend playing video games. Parents should be encouraged to help their children find other activities when children spend too much time manipulating a joystick. Another significant issue is the concern over the level of violence portrayed in many video games. Many children are drawn to this aspect of these activities (Funk, 1993). Parents should be made aware of the impact of violence on young children (National Association for the Education of Young Children, 1997):

- Children who view violence tend to see it as an acceptable way of resolving conflict.
- They become less sensitive to the suffering of others.
- Anxieties may increase in some children. They may be more fearful of the world around them.

Selection of video games should be carefully made after thorough review of the games themselves.

Can Computer Use Be Developmentally Appropriate?

When the National Association for the Education of Young Children (NAEYC) first published its description of developmentally appropriate practice in 1987, it did not mention computers (Bredekamp, 1987). At that time, fewer computers were being used by young children, and there was considerable disagreement among leaders in the field (Mageau, 1993) regarding their appropriateness. After much discussion, however, the NAEYC approved and published a position statement describing effective technology use in the early childhood classroom (NAEYC, 1996c). This document emphasizes the following points:

1. The teacher must exercise professional judgment to ensure that each opportunity for computer use is age appropriate, individually appropriate, and sensitive to cultural diversity.
2. When implemented properly, technology can stimulate children's cognitive and social skills.
3. Computers should be integrated into the classroom environment and used by children as simply another learning option.
4. All children should have equitable access to the computers in the school.

5. Software selected for use should avoid stereotyping any group of people and shun the use of violence as a problem-solving strategy.

6. Teachers and parents should work cooperatively to advocate for quality hardware and software options for young children.

7. Early childhood educators need training in appropriate computer use, including its implementation as a tool for working with other professionals.

Computers and Play

As discussed in Chapter 5, a key element of developmentally appropriate practice is playful interaction with materials found in the environment. Play is a primary means for learning in the early childhood classroom. If the computer is to become an important option for young children, it must also encourage playful behaviors.

The software available to children is the key ingredient to playful computer use. When it is designed to be used creatively by children, the potential for playful interactions is greatly enhanced. Many companies produce software for the early childhood age range. Some, however, have been more actively involved in creating valuable products for young children. Figure 17–1 lists a selection of these companies as a starting point for educators seeking quality software for young children. The figure includes addresses, telephone numbers, and samples of software titles produced.

By reviewing characteristics of play and discussing them in relation to computers, we can evaluate the usefulness of technology for young children (Henniger, 1994b):

- *Play is active.* Rather than being a passive event, play is generally associated with physical activity. Yet, the level of physicalness varies from one play event to the next. Puzzles, for example, require small muscle movements similar to those needed for manipulating the mouse and keyboard of a computer.

- *Play is child selected.* Good play experiences are chosen by the child from a variety of available options. When teachers place computers in the classroom and make them available to children during choice time, playfulness is enhanced.

- *Play is child directed.* Children can engage in quality play events with limited adult intervention. Independent use of the computer requires careful software selection, because much of the software currently available requires considerable adult assistance.

- *Play is process oriented.* In play, the process is more important than any product the child may create. Computers should allow children to enjoy the process of exploring and experimenting without emphasizing an end product.

- *Play stimulates imagination and creativity.* Many play experiences allow children to use their imaginations and be creative in their interactions with people and things. Drill-and-practice software (discussed later in this chapter, in the section entitled, "Selecting Computer Software") discourages these important characteristics. More creative software is limited in availability.

> **Figure 17–1** Software Companies

Broderbund Software
500 Redwood Boulevard
Novato, CA 94948-6121
(800) 521-6263
Produces KidPix, The Playroom, The Print Shop

Davidson and Associates, Inc.
19840 Pioneer Avenue
Torrance, CA 90503
(800) 523-2983
Produces Kid Works 2, Math Blaster Plus

Edmark Corporation
6727 185th Avenue N.E.
Redmond, WA 98052
(800) 426-0856
Produces Millie's Math House, Thinkin Things, Sammy's Science House, Bailey's Book House

Lawrence Productions, Inc.
1800 South 35th Street
Galesburg, MI 49053
(800) 421-4157
Produces Katie's Farm, McGee at the Fun Fair

The Learning Company
6493 Kaiser Drive
Fremont, CA 94555
(800) 852-2255
Produces Children's Writing and Publishing Center, Math Rabbit, Reader Rabbit

Minnesota Ed. Comp Corp.
6160 Summit Drive North
Minneapolis, MN 55430
(800) 685-6322
Produces Storybook Weaver, Number Munchers

William K. Bradford Publishers
310 School Street
Acton, MA 01720
(800) 421-2009
Produces Explore-a-Story Titles: Princess and the Pea, Stone Soup, Three Little Pigs

Sunburst Communications
1600 Green Hills Road
Scotts Valley, CA 95067
(800) 321-7511
Produces Storybook Theatre, Winker's World of Patterns

• *Play is a low-risk activity.* Play provides an opportunity for children to experiment and explore with little risk of failure. Software that is difficult for children to use independently or that requires specific responses is less playful. Drill-and-practice software again receives low marks in this category.

As the preceding discussion indicates, the key ingredient in developmentally appropriate computer use is the software selected. Excellent software is available. But much of the software offered has limited play value. Teachers need to examine software carefully to ensure that young children have quality computer experiences.

Social Interactions

An early concern about computers was that they would isolate children, thus **discouraging the social experiences** that are so important to development. And when

With proper preparation, computer use can be a social activity.

we think about how adults use this technology, this fear seems justified. To accomplish tasks on the computer, most adults need to shut out other distractions and focus their energies on manipulating the keyboard and mouse. It becomes a very solitary activity.

Yet, with children, this problem can be easily overcome. When teachers encourage socialization as children use the computer, the response is very positive. By simply putting more than one chair out at each available computer and encouraging children to help each other as they work their way through various software programs, teachers can significantly enhance social exchanges. Research indicates that in at least some instances, computer use can be more social than other more traditional activities for young children (Clements, Nastasi, & Swaminathan, 1993).

Developmental Abilities

Another frequently cited concern related to young children using computers is the issue of **developmental readiness.** Do children have the cognitive skills needed to understand and manipulate the computer? Early detractors suggested they do not. Barnes and Hill (1983) argued that developmentally, children need to be in Piaget's stage of concrete operations (approximately age eight) before they are ready to use the computer. At that point, they suggest, children can more effectively manage the symbol world of the computer. Similarly, Cuffaro (1984) was concerned that preschool children should use concrete, real-world materials rather than the abstract, symbol-oriented computer.

Although young children need many opportunities to manipulate objects in the real world, they can use symbols in their play at an early age. Consider the following situation:

> ❧ *Aletha and Selena (both age four) are playing in the dress-up area of their preschool classroom. Following their recent trip to the fire station, they have decided to dress up as firefighters and pretend to put out a fire. Aletha describes the scene: "Let's say the wall is the apartment building on fire. It has three stories, and there are people hollering for us to quick, put out the fire! You hold the hose, and I'll get the water started!"*

Clearly, these two girls are using a wealth of symbols in their pretend play. They are envisioning complex situations that are not physically present, and they are manipulating these symbols successfully in play.

Young children can manage the symbol world of the computer, although it is one step removed from real objects and interactions (Clements & Nastasi, 1992; Clements et al., 1993). When computers are one of many choices, they can provide quality experiences that expand, rather than detract from, the young child's learning opportunities.

The Child with Special Needs

Computers and technology are potentially powerful tools for assisting children with special needs. For example, computers help some children with attention deficits focus more effectively on their learning tasks; children with autistic tendencies may improve their interactions with peers as they use the computer together (Haugland & Wright, 1997). Teachers can consult experts in the field to locate software and hardware that meet the needs of children with special needs.

Some children need specialized hardware to take advantage of the computer. Touch screens, trackballs, and simplified keyboards are just a few of the options that are available to make the computer more accessible to children with special needs. When teachers combine this hardware with appropriate software, children can move from dependent to more independent learners (Snider & Badgett, 1995).

Selecting Computers and Software

One of the major challenges facing early educators who want to use computer technology in their classrooms is to choose appropriate hardware and software. Numerous options are available, and new products are being developed regularly, so that it is difficult for even the experts to keep up with all the choices. A variety

CELEBRATING DIVERSITY . . .
Assistive Technology

Public Law 100-407, The Technology-Related Assistance for Individuals with Disabilities Act, was passed in 1988 to ensure that children with special needs and their families have access to technology resources. These children benefit significantly from having this technology in their early childhood classrooms. Roblyer, Edwards, and Havriluk (1997) have identified two major benefits:

- *Improved motivation and self-concept.* Children with special needs spend more time on instructional tasks and have improved self-confidence when provided with assistive technology.

- *Enhanced communication and interaction with others.* Technology also helps children with special needs express themselves more effectively in their communications with others.

Recently, many tools have been designed to make technology more useful to children with special needs. Some examples follow:

- *Alternate-input devices.* Some students with physical disabilities find it difficult to use the keyboard and mouse to enter information into the computer. Touch screens, alternative keyboards, and voice-controlled devices are examples of some of the hardware available to help these students.

- *Substitute output devices.* Children with visual impairments need devices such as enlarged computer images, speech devices that tell what the program is doing, or printers that produce Braille to assist them in productively using a computer.

- *Equipment to assist deaf learners.* Captioned video that provides subtitles for television and other video presentations is one example of this type.

1. *Visit an early childhood program that includes children with special needs. Review the assistive technology available for use.*

2. *Observe a child with special needs using technology. What benefits can you see from your observation? Discuss this with others.*

of monitors, hard drives, multimedia options, CD-ROM drives, printers, and hundreds of software options make selections mind-boggling for many. Although each of these decisions is personal, some guidelines may help make the process more manageable.

Hardware Options

First, the latest hardware isn't always necessary for effective computer experiences. Young preschool children can benefit from even the oldest computer with a monochrome monitor and little software. Just becoming comfortable with the technology and being able to type and print are valuable experiences for this age. Donations of this older hardware by either parents or community members are common and can be an easy way to get started using technology in the classroom.

Having said this, however, if you are serious about computer use, it makes sense to consider having the following basic hardware for your classroom:

- **Color monitor.** Color makes most software programs come to life and will motivate young children to explore.
- **Hard drive.** A hard drive allows the computer to be used without handling floppy disks. It is a simpler, quicker way for children to access software.
- **Sound capabilities.** Although sound can be a distracting feature (see section on software selection), it does add another dimension to computer use and should be included. External speakers may offer better sound quality than those built into most computers. The sound option can be turned off when it is too distracting.
- **CD-ROM drive.** This option greatly expands the software options available. Many of the new programs run most effectively from the CD-ROM drive.
- **Color printer.** The costs of color printers have dropped significantly over the last few years. This is now an affordable option that increases the ability of children to create pictures and stories on the computer and then print them out.

The preceding options generally require an IBM-compatible computer with a minimum of 8 megabytes of random access memory (RAM), an 80-megabyte hard drive, and a 486 microprocessor. Macintosh users should plan for equivalent capabilities.

Selecting Computer Software

Many software options are available for young children, and their numbers are growing rapidly. Approximately 300 new titles are released each year (Buckleitner, 1994). Although many programs provide children with positive experiences, numerous others are inappropriate and should be avoided. The teacher's most important task, therefore, is to select the best software from the hundreds available.

The following characteristics should be evident in the software before teachers consider it for use in the early childhood classroom (Henniger, 1994d):

- *Minimal adult instruction and interaction.* Materials in a good early childhood classroom have a significant characteristic in common: They can all be used with little or no adult instruction or assistance. Good software should have this same quality. It should be simple enough to use that the teacher can install the software on the hard drive and turn children loose to explore its possibilities.
- *Easy to enter and exit.* Quality programs should also allow children to enter the software and later exit without assistance. This seemingly small characteristic can make a big difference in the child's confidence level in approaching and using the computer. When software is user friendly, children will be more likely to try it out and have greater success along the way.

The best way to evaluate computer software is to spend time reviewing its capabilities in use.

- *Verbal instructions.* Because most children in the early childhood years are either nonreaders or beginning readers, the instructions that are necessary for software use should be verbal or pictorial rather than written.

- *Child manipulated.* Good software allows children to experiment, explore, and manipulate the program as they see fit. The child then takes control and uses the software in ways that are interesting and developmentally appropriate. Children will spend more time with these options and learn more along the way.

- *Stimulates imagination and creativity.* When children play, they frequently use their imaginations and creativity as they work through roles and situations. Quality software should also encourage these important qualities.

- *Simple in design, complex in use.* The best play materials for children are simple in design, yet can be used in virtually unlimited ways. Blocks are a good example of this concept. Without overwhelming the young child with too many choices, a good software program should allow the child to manipulate and explore for long periods of time. Imaginative, creative experiences are often the result.

INTO PRACTICE . . .
Drill and Practice Software

Estimates indicate that nearly three-fourths of all software being produced for young children is drill and practice. The computer prompts the user to respond in a specific, predesigned way to problems it poses. Although this makes for more limited uses by young children, some drill and practice software programs do make rote learning experiences more interesting. As long as this drill and practice is not the primary type of software available, teachers can productively use some drill and practice software programs in the early childhood classroom. The following examples highlight some effective uses of this software type:

• *Learning arithmetic/number facts.* Most of us can remember the traditional flash cards used to teach basic arithmetic facts. This approach, although effective in many ways, is not very exciting. Several software companies have produced much more motivating ways to learn these basic facts. Number Munchers by MECC and Math Blaster Plus by Davidson are good examples.

• *Spelling.* Another rather routine task faced by children in the primary grades is the learning of appropriate spelling of words. The Spell It software options from Davidson present more interesting activities for children.

• *Prereading and reading activities.* Letter recognition and phonics activities can be effective supplements to the whole language approach to reading. Sunburst, MECC, and The Learning Company all produce software that help with these tasks.

Much of the software available for young children does not meet these criteria. Haugland and Shade (1994) estimate that approximately 70 percent of the software developed for young children has limited value. One category of programs that fits this undesirable category is **drill and practice software.** This type of software requires children to respond with one right answer to closed-ended questions and leaves little opportunity for independent, creative manipulation. Although some drill and practice software has value in teaching early math and reading skills, this option should comprise only a small portion of the programs in the early childhood classroom.

Good software can be organized into several categories. Although not all programs in these areas are developmentally appropriate, they tend to be the better options for young children. These categories include the following:

• *Storyboard software.* Shade (1995) states that these programs allow children to build a story by first picking a background and then adding their own choices of objects and people, much like the more traditional flannelboard stories children create.

• *Draw/paint programs.* Some software programs allow children to use the computer much like an electronic easel. Children can draw pictures, paint, use electronic stamps, and a variety of other options to create an art project on the computer screen.

Effective computer use in the early childhood classroom depends heavily on selecting quality software. With hundreds of titles available, it is difficult for most teachers to find the time to adequately review software in preparation for purchase. Fortunately, several good resources can help narrow the list of options down to a manageable size:

- *Children's Software Review.* This bimonthly newsletter reviews children's software. Edited by Warren Buckleitner, this publication evaluates over 100 software titles in each issue. Call (800) 993-9499 for more information.

- *High/Scope Buyer's Guide to Children's Software.* The High/Scope Foundation regularly publishes a book that evaluates new software for young children. This book provides much good basic information on new software options, rating each on a variety of characteristics. Call (313) 485-2000 for ordering information.

- *Parent's Guide to Children's Software.* Available on CD-ROM and as a paperback book, this product reviews new software that has received the "Editors' Choice" award from the editors of *Newsweek Magazine.* For ordering information, call (800) 634-3002.

1. Take a look at one of these review options. What do you like about it? Do you have any problems or questions? Discuss these issues with classmates.

2. Find a piece of software reviewed by one of these resources. Try it out, and then compare your findings with those from the expert. What did you find?

- *Electronic books.* With the growth of CD-ROM software, many stories have been computerized, with excellent graphics and sound capabilities that allow the computer to read to the child.

- *Writing/publishing software.* Several good programs are available for children to write and publish their own stories. They are designed for children in the primary grades and above and often allow children to illustrate their creations as well.

Helping Parents to Select Software

With the hundreds of software titles being sold for young children, it is difficult for parents to choose the software that will best meet their children's needs and interests. Perhaps the most useful assistance that teachers can provide is to share with parents resources for rating software quality. The accompanying box, "Focus On . . . Software Reviews," presents several of these resources, which can be shared with interested parents. Having some of the best options available in the classroom and letting parents see and try out these programs are also helpful. Identifying the

Charland (1998) presents an exciting technology option for communicating with parents and community members. She suggests creating a homepage on the Internet to inform parents and others about the activities in your classroom. This electronic bulletin board could be used for many things, including

- Sharing discipline procedures
- Identifying homework and grading policies
- Discussing home learning tasks (see Chapter 7)
- Asking for assistance in the classroom or at home

- Providing parenting information
- Sharing the calendar of classroom events for the week or month
- Opening a dialogue with parents on a variety of topics relevant to the classroom, for example, issues surrounding television viewing

Creating a homepage sounds like a difficult task, but newer software makes the project very manageable for those with average computer skills. Charland (1998) also suggests that getting students involved can help make the experience educational for them as well.

limitations of drill and practice software is also beneficial for parents. Finally, differentiating between quality **playful software** and those that are just entertaining may provide parents with additional insights for software selection.

Computers in the Classroom

If children are to use computers in developmentally appropriate ways, teachers need to physically incorporate computers into the classroom space. When technology becomes readily accessible on a daily basis, it becomes just another tool that students can use to further their knowledge about the world. Computers become integrated into the learning experiences that take place. This natural connection helps make technology developmentally appropriate for young children (NAEYC, 1996c).

To effectively integrate computers into the early childhood classroom, teachers should consider the following:

- Set up a computer center, with open access during designated times during the school day.
- Place the screen and keyboard at appropriate heights for the children using them.
- Organize each computer with at least two chairs to encourage more than one child to use the computer at a time.
- Make sure that the teacher can easily observe children working at the computer so that she can help as needed.
- Develop activities and lessons that make it more likely that children will use the computer as a regular part of their school day.

The Internet is an international network of computers that allows people around the world to share information. As more people gain access to the Internet, greater numbers of resources are available for adults interested in information related to children and families. The following is a sampling of Internet addresses that may be of interest to you.

Electronic Discussion Groups

The Internet provides many opportunities for communicating with other people around the world interested in the same issues. Here are a few examples and an e-mail address to write for more information. Contact: ERIC/EECE (e-mail: ericeece@ux1.cso.uiuc.edu):

- REGGIO-L: This discussion group deals with issues related to the Reggio Emilia approach to early education.
- ECENET-L: The development, education, and care of children birth through age eight is the focus of this group.
- PARENTING-L: Parents and others interested in sharing concerns and questions about the challenges of family life are using this discussion site.

World Wide Web Sites

The following are examples of the diversity of information sources available for early childhood educators:

- ERIC/EECE information:
  http://ericps.ed.uiuc.edu/ericeece.html
- U.S. Department of Education Publications:
  http://www.ed.gov
- National Child Care Information Center:
  http://ericps.ed.uiuc.edu/nccic/nccichome.html
- How to buy educational software:
  http://www.microweb.com/pepsite/index.html

1. *Find a computer with Internet access, and see what you can find. Try out one or more of these addresses, and spend some time discovering what is there.*

2. *As you were browsing the Internet, did you find sites that would be inappropriate for children to view? What could you do to prevent children from viewing inappropriate content?*

Interacting with Children Using Computers

Davis and Shade (1994) suggest three key roles for teachers as they interact with children using computers:

1. *Teacher as instructor.* When the computer is brought into the early childhood classroom, the teacher will need to help children learn how to use the technology.

2. *Teacher as coach.* As children become more comfortable with the computer, the teacher becomes more of a facilitator by providing assistance as needed and guiding children into appropriate use of the technology.

Teachers play an important role in effective computer use.

3. *Teacher as model.* Children should see the teacher using the computer as well. Recording children's oral stories, creating charts and signs for use in the classroom, and incorporating computers into small-group activities are some examples of this type of teacher modeling.

In addition to making good decisions about the software available to children, teachers must also be prepared to **restrict access to inappropriate Internet sites.** Unfortunately, many World Wide Web sites contain materials that are harmful to children. Teachers and parents need to monitor student use of the Internet to make sure children are making appropriate choices of web sites.

Summary

Television has a significant impact on young children's lives. They spend a large amount of time viewing TV, often watching programs with sexual themes, violence, and misleading advertising. Parents play an important role in helping children make sense of what they see on television.

Both strengths and weaknesses are associated with children's use of video games. Again, parents can assist young children in their use of these games.

The use of computers in the early childhood classroom has been a controversial issue, especially at the prekindergarten level. Educators have expressed concerns about the developmental appropriateness of computers and problems associated with solitary computer use. With the selection of playful computer software and careful organization of the computer in the early childhood classroom, these problems can be overcome. It is important to select hardware and software carefully and to provide options for children with special needs. The teacher has an important role to play in facilitating technology use in the early childhood classroom.

∾ For Discussion and Action

1. Find an early childhood classroom that has a computer in the room. Review the software, and critique it using the selection criteria listed in this chapter.
2. Survey your classmates regarding televisions in the home. Find out how many televisions each person has at home. What does this tell you about this form of technology in American homes?
3. Review an hour of television broadcasting between 7:00 and 8:00 PM, critically analyzing the acts of violence, sexual situations, and advertising presented. Think about and discuss the potential impact of this content on young children.
4. Play a video game designed for young children. Describe its strengths and weaknesses.
5. Watch an educational television program (like *Sesame Street*) designed especially for young children. Talk about its strengths and limitations.

∾ Building Your Personal Library

Haugland, S., & Wright, J. (1997). *Young children and technology: A world of discovery.* Boston: Allyn & Bacon. This book provides much practical information about the appropriateness of computers in the early childhood classroom, guidelines on selecting good software, and integrating the computer into the classroom. Approximately 130 software titles are reviewed as well.

Liebert, R., & Sprafkin, J. (1988). *The early window: Effects of television on children and youth* (3rd ed.). New York: Pergamon Press. This book chronicles the impact of television viewing on children. It describes how, for many American families, the television has become an integral part of family life, consuming more free time than any other activity.

Papert, S. (1993). *The children's machine: Rethinking school in the age of the computer.* New York: Basic Books. Papert gained fame through the development of a computer language called Logo, which allows children to program the computer. In this book, he describes how computers and software like Logo can potentially transform the way in which schools operate—a thought-provoking book.

References

Aboud, F. (1988). *Children and prejudice.* London: Basil Blackwell.

Ainsworth, M. (1973). The development of infant and mother attachment. In B. Caldwell & H. Ricciuti (Eds.), *Review of child development research* (Vol. 3, pp. 121–143). Chicago: University of Chicago Press.

Altman, R. (1992). Movement in early childhood. In A. Mitchell & J. David (Eds.), *Explorations with young children: A curriculum guide from the Bank Street College of Education* (pp. 229–240). Mt. Rainier, MD: Gryphon House.

American Association for Gifted Children. (1998). *A special guide for parents* [On-line]. Available http://www.jayi.com/jayi/aagc/gifted.html

Anderson, R., Hiebert, E., Scott, J., & Wilkinson, I. (1985). *Becoming a nation of readers: The report of the Commission on Reading.* Washington, DC: National Academy of Education.

Anglund, J. (1983). *A friend is someone who likes you.* San Diego: Harcourt Brace Jovanovich.

Annie E. Casey Foundation. (1996). *Kids count data book.* Baltimore, MD: Annie E. Casey Foundation.

Anselmo, S., & Franz, W. (1995). *Early childhood development: Prenatal through age eight* (2nd ed.). Upper Saddle River, NJ: Merrill/Prentice Hall.

Archer, J. (1996, March 27). Surge in Hispanic student enrollment predicted. *Education Week,* p. 3.

Aries, P. (1962). *Centuries of childhood.* New York: Vintage Books.

Association of Teacher Educators & National Association for the Education of Young Children. (1991). Early childhood teacher certification. *Young Children, 47*(1), 16–21.

Atlas, J., & Lapidus, L. (1987). Patterns of symbolic expression in subgroups of the childhood psychoses. *Journal of Clinical Psychology, 43,* 177–188.

Axline, V. (1947). *Play therapy.* Boston: Houghton Mifflin.

Axline, V. (1964). *DIBS: In search of self.* Boston: Houghton Mifflin.

Baker, K. (1966). *Let's play outdoors.* Washington, DC: National Association for the Education of Young Children.

Ball, W. (1995). Nurturing musical aptitude in children. *Dimensions of Early Childhood, 23*(4), 19–24.

Bandura, A. (1989). Social cognitive theory. *Annals of Child Development, 6,* 1–60.

Banks, J. (1993). Multicultural education for young children: Racial and ethnic attitudes and their modification. In Spodek, B. (Ed.), *Handbook of research on the education of young children* (pp. 236–250). Upper Saddle River, NJ: Prentice Hall.

Baratta-Lorton, M. (1976). *Mathematics their way.* Menlo Park, CA: Addison-Wesley.

Barbour, C., & Barbour, N. (1997). *Families, schools, and communities: Building partnerships for educating children.* Upper Saddle River, NJ: Merrill/Prentice Hall.

Barnes, B., & Hill, S. (1983). Should young children work with microcomputers—Logo before Lego? *The Computing Teacher, 10*(9), 11–14.

Baron, L. (1991). Peer tutoring, microcomputer learning and young children. *Journal of Computing in Childhood Education, 2*(4), 27–40.

Bassett, M. (1995). *Infant and child care skills.* Albany, NY: Delmar.

Bayless, K., & Ramsey, M. (1987). *Music: A way of life for the young child*. Upper Saddle River, NJ: Merrill/Prentice Hall.

Bayless, K., & Ramsey, M. (1991). *Music: A way of life for the young child* (4th ed.). Upper Saddle River, NJ: Prentice Hall.

Bear, T., Schenk, S., & Buckner, L. (1993). Supporting victims of child abuse. *Educational Leadership, 50*(4), 42–47.

Beaty, J. (1995). *Converting conflicts in preschool*. Ft. Worth, TX: Harcourt Brace.

Bee, H. (1995). *The developing child*. Cambridge, MA: HarperCollins.

Bell, D., & Low, R. (1977). *Observing and recording children's behavior*. Richland, WA: Performance Associates.

Benelli, C., & Yongue, B. (1995). Supporting young children's motor skill development. *Childhood Education, 71*(4), 217–220.

Berger, E. H. (1995). *Parents as partners in education* (4th ed.). Upper Saddle River, NJ: Prentice Hall.

Berk, L. (1994). Vygotsky's theory: The importance of make-believe play. *Young Children, 50*(1), 30–39.

Berry, J. (1986). *Teach me about series: My body*. Danbury, CT: Grolier.

Betz, C. (1994). Beyond time-out: Tips from a teacher. *Young Children, 49*(3), 10–14.

Blume, E. (1990). *Secret survivors*. New York: Free Press.

Blume, J. (1970). *Freckle juice*. Scarsdale, NY: Bradbury.

Boutte, G., & McCormick, C. (1992). Authentic multicultural activities. *Childhood Education, 68*(3), 140–144.

Bowlby, J. (1969). *Attachment and loss. Vol. I: Attachment*. New York: Basic Books.

Bowman, B. (1994). The challenge of diversity. *Phi Delta Kappan, 76*(3), 218–224.

Boyer, E. (1987, January). Keynote address to the National Invitational Conference sponsored by the Getty Center for Education in the Arts, Los Angeles.

Brand, S. (1996). Making parent involvement a reality: Helping teachers develop partnerships with parents. *Young Children, 51*(2), 76–81.

Braun, S., & Edwards, E. (1972). *History and theory of early childhood education*. Belmont, CA: Wadsworth Publishing.

Bredekamp, S. (Ed.). (1987). *Developmentally appropriate practice in early childhood programs serving children from birth through age 8*. Washington, DC: National Association for the Education of Young Children.

Bredekamp, S. (1993). Reflections on Reggio Emilia. *Young Children, 49*(1), 13–17.

Bredekamp, S. (1996). 25 years of educating young children: The High/Scope approach to preschool education. *Young Children, 51*(4), 57–61.

Bredekamp, S., & Copple, C. (Eds.). (1997). *Developmentally appropriate practice in early childhood programs* (rev. ed.). Washington, DC: National Association for the Education of Young Children.

Bredekamp, S., & Glowacki, S. (1996). The first decade of NAEYC accreditation: Growth and impact on the field. *Young Children, 51*(3), 38–44.

Bredekamp, S., & Willer, B. (1993). Professionalizing the field of early childhood education: Pros and cons. *Young Children, 48*(3), 82–84.

Bredekamp, S., & Willer, B. (1996). (Eds.). *NAEYC accreditation: A decade of learning and the years ahead*. Washington, DC: National Association for the Education of Young Children.

Brenner, B. (1970). *Bodies*. New York: Dutton.

Bronfenbrenner, U. (1974). *Is early intervention effective?* (Vols. 1 & 2). Washington, DC: U.S. Government Printing Office.

Bronfenbrenner, U. (1979). *The ecology of human development*. Cambridge, MA: Harvard University Press.

Brookes, M. (1986). *Drawing with children: A creative teaching and learning method that works for adults, too*. New York: G. P. Putnam's Sons.

Brown, N., Curry, N., & Tittnich, E. (1971). How groups of children deal with commom stress through play. In N. Curry & S. Arnaud (Eds.), *Play: The child strives toward self-realization* (pp. 26–38). Washington, DC: National Association for the Education of Young Children.

Brown, T. (1991). *Someone special, just like you*. New York: Holt, Rinehart & Winston.

Bruner, J. (1966). *Toward a theory of instruction*. Cambridge, MA: Harvard University Press.

Bruner, J. (1972). The nature and uses of immaturity. *American Psychologist, 27,* 687–708.

Buckleitner, W. (1994). Hardware news: 1994 in review. *Children's Software Review, 2*(6), 12.

Bunker, L. (1991). The role of play and motor skill development in building children's self-confidence and self-esteem. *The Elementary School Journal, 91*(5), 467–471.

Burton, V. (1939). *Mike Mulligan and his steam shovel.* Boston: Houghton Mifflin.

Caldwell, B. (1987). Advocacy is everybody's business. *Child Care Information Exchange, 54,* 29–32.

Campbell, B. (1992). Multiple intelligences in action. *Childhood Education, 68*(4), 197–201.

Canfield, J., & Wells, H. (1994). *100 ways to enhance self-concept in the classroom* (2nd ed.). Boston: Allyn & Bacon.

Carle, E. (1985). *My very first book of shapes.* New York: Harper & Row.

Carlsson-Paige, N., & Levin, D. (1986). The butter battle book: Uses and abuses with young children. *Young Children, 41*(3), 37–42.

Carrick, D. (1985). *Milk.* New York: Greenwillow.

Castle, K. (1990). Children's invented games. *Childhood Education, 67,* 82–85.

Center for Communication Policy. (1995). *The UCLA television violence monitoring report.* Los Angeles, CA: The University of California at Los Angeles.

Center for the Future of Children. (1995). *The future of children. Long-term outcomes of early childhood programs* (Vol. 5, No. 3). Los Altos, CA: Author.

Cesarone, B. (1994, January). Video games and children. *ERIC Digest,* EDO-PS-94-3. Urbana, IL: ERIC Clearinghouse on Elementary and Early Childhood Education.

Chaille, C., & Britain, L. (1997). *The young child as scientist: A constructivist approach to early childhood science education* (2nd ed.). New York: Longman.

Chaille, C., & Silvern, S. (1996). Understanding through play. *Childhood Education, 72*(5), 274–277.

Charland, T. (1998). Classroom homepage connections. *T.H.E. Journal, 25*(9), 62–64.

Charlesworth, R. (1996). *Understanding child development* (4th ed.). Albany, New York: Delmar.

Chattin-McNichols, J. (1992). Montessori programs in public schools. *ERIC Digest,* EDO-PS-92-7. Urbana, IL: ERIC Clearinghouse on Elementary and Early Childhood Education.

Children's Defense Fund. (1997). *The state of America's children: Yearbook 1997.* Washington, DC: Children's Defense Fund.

Chomsky, N. (1965). *Aspects of a theory of syntax.* Cambridge, MA: MIT Press.

Christie, J., Enz, B., & Vukelich, C. (1997). *Teaching language and literacy—Preschool through the elementary grades.* New York: Longman.

Clark, R. (1995). Violence, young children and the healing power of play. *Dimensions of Early Childhood, 23*(3), 28–30, 39.

Clearinghouse on Elementary and Early Childhood Education. (1990). Guidelines for family television viewing. *ERIC Digest,* EDO-PS-90-3. Urbana, IL: ERIC Clearinghouse on Elementary and Early Childhood Education.

Clemens, J. (1996). Gardening with children. *Young Children, 51*(4), 22–27.

Clements, D., & Nastasi, B. (1992). Computers and early childhood education. In M. Gettinger, S. Eliot, & T. Kratochwill (Eds.), *Preschool and early childhood treatment directions* (pp. 178–192). Hillsdale, NJ: Lawrence Erlbaum.

Clements, D., Nastasi, B., & Swaminathan, S. (1993). Young children and computers: Crossroads and directions from research. *Young Children, 48*(2), 56–64.

Cohen, D. (1994). Building the better playground. *Education Week, 13*(21), 33–35.

Cohen, S. (1994). Television in the lives of children and their families. *Childhood Education, 70*(2), 103–104.

Coleman, J. (1966). *Equality of educational opportunity.* Washington, DC: U.S. Government Printing Office.

Coleman, M. (1991). Planning for the changing nature of family life in schools for young children. *Young Children, 46*(4), 15–20.

Comenius, J. (1896). *School of infancy.* Boston: Heath.

Community Playthings. (1990). *Criteria for play equipment.* Rifton, NY: Community Playthings, Inc.

Connor-Kuntz, F., & Dummer, G. (1996). Teaching across the curriculum: Language-enriched physical education for preschool children. *Adapted Physical Activity Quarterly, 13*(3), 302–315.

Consumer Product Safety Commission. (1990). *Handbook for public playground safety.* Washington, DC: Consumer Product Safety Commission.

Coopersmith, S. (1967). *The antecedents of self-esteem.* San Francisco: W. H. Freeman.

Copple, C. (1991). *Quality matters—Improving the professional development of the early childhood work force.* Washington, DC: National Institute for Early Childhood Professional Development.

Crain, W. (1985). *Theories of development: Concepts and applications* (2nd ed.). Upper Saddle River, NJ: Prentice Hall.

Cuffaro, H. (1984). Microcomputers in education: Why is earlier better? *Teacher's College Record, 85,* 559–567.

Dainton, M. (1993). The myth and misconceptions of stepmother identity. *Family Relations, 42*(1), 93–98.

Damon, W. (1983). *Social and personality development: Infancy through adolescence.* New York: W. W. Norton.

Davis, B., & Shade, D. (1994, December). Integrate, don't isolate! Computers in the early childhood curriculum. *ERIC Digest,* EDO-PS-94-17. Urbana, IL: ERIC Clearinghouse on Elementary and Early Childhood Education.

DeFina, A. (1992). *Portfolio assessment.* New York: Scholastic Professional Books.

Deiner, P. (1993). *Resources for teaching children with diverse abilities* (2nd ed.). New York: Harcourt Brace.

Delisle, J. (1994, September 21). Reach out—But don't touch. *Education Week,* p. 33.

Derman-Sparks, L. (1989). *Anti-bias curriculum: Tools for empowering young children.* Washington, DC: National Association for the Education of Young Children.

Derman-Sparks, L. (1993). Revisiting multicultural education. What children need to live in a diverse society. *Dimensions of Early Childhood, 21*(2), 6–10.

Derman-Sparks, L. (1994). Empowering children to create a caring culture in a world of differences. *Childhood Education, 70*(2), 66–71.

DeVries, R., & Kohlberg, L. (1987). *Constructivist early education: Overview and comparison with other programs.* Washington, DC: National Association for the Education of Young Children.

DeVries, R., & Zan, B. (1995). Creating a constructivist classroom atmosphere. *Young Children, 51*(1), 4–13.

Dewey, J. (1929). *Democracy and education.* New York: Macmillan.

Dinwiddie, S. (1993). Playing in the gutters: Enhancing childen's cognitive and social play. *Young Children, 48*(6), 70–73.

Dodge, D., & Colker, L. (1992). *The creative curriculum for early childhood* (3rd ed.). Washington, DC: Teaching Strategies, Inc.

Dolan, K. (1996). *Communication—A practical guide to school and community relations.* Belmont, CA: Wadsworth.

Doman, G. (1961). *Teach your baby to read.* London: Jonathan Cape.

Dopyera, M., & Dopyera, J. (1987). *Becoming a teacher of young children* (3rd ed.). Lexington, MA: Heath.

Dreikurs, R., Grunwald, B., & Pepper, F. (1982). *Maintaining sanity in the classroom* (2nd ed.). New York: Harper & Row.

Early, P. (1994). *Goals 2000: Educate America Act: Implications for teacher educators.* Washington, DC: American Association of Colleges for Teacher Education.

Edwards, C., Gandini, L., & Forman, G. (Eds.). (1993). *The hundred languages of children: The Reggio Emilia approach to early childhood education.* Norwood, NJ: Ablex.

Edwards, C., & Springate, K. (1993). Inviting children into project work. *Dimensions of Early Childhood, 22*(1), 9–12, 40.

Edwards, L. (1997). *The creative arts: A process approach for teachers and children* (2nd ed.). Upper Saddle River, NJ: Merrill/Prentice Hall.

Ehly, S., & Dustin, D. (1994, May 4). Surviving parent–teacher involvement. *Education Week,* pp. 33–34.

Einstein, A. (1949). Autobiographical notes. In P. A. Schilpp (Ed.), *Albert Einstein: Philosopher and scientist.* Evanston, IL: The Library of Living Philosophers.

Einstein, A. (1954). *Ideas and opinions.* New York: Crown Publishers.

Eisenberg, L. (1990). *What's happening to the American family?* PS 019 149. Paper presented at the annual meeting of the American Academy of Pediatrics, Boston. (ERIC Document Reproduction Service No. ED 325 222).

Elkind, D. (1981a). *Children and adolescents* (3rd ed.). New York: Oxford University Press.

Elkind, D. (1981b). *The hurried child: Growing up too fast too soon.* Reading, MA: Addison-Wesley.

Ellis, M. (1973). *Why people play.* Upper Saddle River, NJ: Prentice Hall.

Ellis, S., & Whalen, S. (1990). *Cooperative learning: Getting started.* New York: Scholastic Professional Books.

Engel, B. (1996). Learning to look: Appreciating child art. *Young Children, 51*(3), 74–79.

Epstein, J. (1995). School/family/community partnerships: Caring for the children we share. *Phi Delta Kappan, 76*(9), 701–712.

Erikson, E. (1963). *Childhood and society* (2nd ed.). New York: W. W. Norton.

Esbensen, S. (1987). *An outdoor classroom.* Ypsilanti, MI: High/Scope Press.

Family portrait. (1995, October 25). *Education Week*, p. 4.

Fields, M., & Boesser, C. (1998). *Constructive guidance and discipline: Preschool and primary education* (2nd ed.). Upper Saddle River, NJ: Merrill/Prentice Hall.

Flavell, J. (1963). *The developmental psychology of Jean Piaget.* New York: D. Van Nostrand.

Foster, S. M. (1994). Successful parent meetings. *Young Children, 50*(1), 78–81.

Fractor, J., Woodruff, M., Martinez, M., & Teale, W. (1993). Let's not miss opportunities to promote voluntary reading: Classroom libraries in the elementary school. *The Reading Teacher, 46*, 476–484.

Freud, S. (1938). *An outline of psychoanalysis.* London: Hogarth.

Froebel, F. (1886). *Education of man* (J. Jarvis, Trans.). New York: Appleton-Century-Crofts.

Froebel, F. (1906). *Mother-play and nursery songs.* New York: Lothrop, Lee, & Shepard.

Fromberg, D. (1990). An agenda for research on play in early childhood education. In E. Klugman & S. Smilansky (Eds.), *Children's play and learning: Perspectives and policy implications* (pp. 63–87). New York: Teachers College Press.

Frost, J. (1992). *Play and playscapes.* Albany, NY: Delmar Publishers.

Frost, J. (1994, May/June). Making the most of outdoor play. *Scholastic Early Childhood Today*, pp. 47–54.

Frost, J., Bowers, L., & Wortham, S. (1990). The state of American preschool playgrounds. *Journal of Physical Education, Recreation, and Dance, 61*(8), 18–23.

Frost, J., & Henniger, M. (1979). Making playgrounds safe for children and children safe for playgrounds. *Young Children, 34*(5), 23–30.

Frost, J., & Jacobs, P. (1995). Play deprivation: A factor in juvenile violence. *Dimensions of Early Childhood, 23*(3), 14–20, 39.

Frost, J., & Wortham, S. (1988). The evolution of American playgrounds. *Young Children, 43*(5), 19–28.

Fuller, M., & Olsen, G. (1998). *Home–school relations: Working successfully with parents and families.* Boston: Allyn & Bacon.

Funk, J. (1993). Reevaluating the impact of video games. *Clinical Pediatrics, 32*, 86–90.

Furman, R. (1995). Helping children cope with stress and deal with feelings. *Young Children, 50*(2), 33–41.

Gabbard, C. (1992). *Lifelong motor development.* Dubuque, IA: William C. Brown.

Gallagher, J. (1998). *Classroom assessment for teachers.* Upper Saddle River, NJ: Merrill/Prentice Hall.

Gallahue, D. (1982). *Understanding motor development in children.* New York: Wiley.

Gallahue, D. (1993a). *Developmental physical education for today's children.* Dubuque, IA: Brown & Benchmark.

Gallahue, D. (1993b). Motor development and movement skill acquisition in early childhood education. In B. Spodek (Ed.), *Handbook of research on the education of young children* (pp. 24–41). Upper Saddle River, NJ: Prentice Hall.

Gandini, L. (1993). Fundamentals of the Reggio Emilia approach to early childhood education. *Young Children, 49*(1), 4–8.

Gardner, H. (1983). *Frames of mind: The theory of multiple intelligences.* New York: Basic Books.

Gardner, H. (1993). *Multiple intelligences: The theory in practice.* New York: Basic Books.

Garvey, C. (1990). *Play* (enlarged ed.). Cambridge, MA: Harvard University Press.

Gesell, A., & Ilg, F. (1943). *Infant and child in the culture of today.* New York: Harper & Brothers.

Gesell, A., & Ilg, F. (1949). *Child development: An introduction to the study of human growth.* New York: Harper & Brothers.

Gestwicki, C. (1995). *Developmentally appropriate practice: Curriculum and development in early education.* Albany, NY: Delmar.

Gestwicki, C. (1996). *Home, school and community relations* (3rd ed.). Albany, NY: Delmar.

Getty Center for Education in the Arts. (1994, Winter). *Newsletter*, p. 7.

Ghiselin, B. (1952). *The creative process.* New York: Penguin Books.

Ginott, H. (1972). *Teacher and child.* New York: Macmillan.

Ginsburg, H., & Opper, S. (1969). *Piaget's theory of intellectual development.* Upper Saddle River, NJ: Prentice Hall.

Glasser, W. (1969). *Schools without failure.* New York: Harper & Row.

Glasser, W. (1990). *The quality school.* New York: Harper & Row.

Goertzel, M., & Goertzel, R. (1962). *Cradles of eminence.* Boston: Little, Brown.

Goffin, S., & Lombardi, J. (1988). *Speaking out: Early childhood advocacy.* Washington, DC: National Association for the Education of Young Children.

Gordon, T. (1974). *Teacher effectiveness training.* New York: Wyden.

Greenman, J. (1988). *Caring spaces, learning places: Children's environments that work.* Redmond, WA: Exchange Press.

Greenspan, S. (1997). *The growth of the mind and the endangered origins of intelligence.* Reading, MA: Addison-Wesley.

Guddemi, M., & Eriksen, A. (1992). Designing outdoor learning environments for and with children. *Dimensions of Early Childhood, 20*(4), 15–18, 23–24, 40.

Guimps, R. (1890). *Pestalozzi: His life and work* (J. Russell, Trans.). New York: Appleton.

Hallahan, D., & Kauffman, J. (1994). *Exceptional children: Introduction to special education* (6th ed.). Boston: Allyn & Bacon.

Hamilton, D., Flemming, B., & Hicks, J. (1990). *Resources for creative teaching in early childhood education* (2nd ed.). San Diego, CA: Harcourt, Brace, Jovanovich.

Harris, T. (1994). The snack shop: Block play in a primary classroom. *Dimensions of Early Childhood, 22*(4), 22–23.

Hatcher, B., Nicosia, T., & Pape, D. (1994). *Interested in inviting and sustaining play behaviors? Prop boxes offer promise!* Paper presented at the Annual Conference of the Association for Childhood Education International, New Orleans, LA.

Hatcher, B., Pape, D., & Nicosia, T. (1988). Group games for global awareness. *Childhood Education, 65*(1), 8–13.

Harms, T., & Clifford, R. (1980). *Early childhood environment rating scale.* New York: Teachers College Press.

Harms, T., Clifford, R., & Cryer, D. (1998). *Early childhood environment rating scale (ECRS)* (rev. ed.). New York: Teachers College Press.

Hartup, W. (1992). Having friends, making friends, and keeping friends: Relationships as educational contexts. *ERIC Digest,* EDO-PS-92-4. Urbana, IL: ERIC Clearinghouse on Elementary and Early Childhood Education. (ERIC Document Reproduction Service No. ED 345 854)

Hartup, W., & Moore, S. (1990). Early peer relations: Developmental significance and prognostic implications. *Early Childhood Research Quarterly, 5*(1), 1–18.

Harwayne, S. (1992). *Lasting impressions.* Portsmouth, NH: Heinemann.

Haugland, S., & Shade, D. (1994). Software evaluation for young children. In J. Wright & D. Shade (Eds.), *Young children: Active learners in a technological age* (pp. 17–24). Washington, DC: National Association for the Education of Young Children.

Haugland, S., & Wright, J. (1997). *Young children and technology.* Needham Heights, MA: Allyn & Bacon.

Head Start star. (1995, April 26). *Education Week,* p. 4.

Heller, R., & Martin, C. (1982). *Bits 'n bytes about computing.* Rockville, MD: Computer Science Press.

Hendrick, J. (1994). *Total learning: Developmental curriculum for the young child* (4th ed.). Upper Saddle River, NJ: Merrill/Prentice Hall.

Hendrick, J. (Ed.). (1997). *First steps toward teaching the Reggio way.* Upper Saddle River, NJ: Merrill/Prentice Hall.

Henniger, M. (1982). *The telephone and parent/teacher communication* (Report No. PS-012-590). Washington, DC: Department of Health, Education, and Welfare, National Institute of Education. (ERIC Document Reproduction Service No. ED 211 215)

Henniger, M. (1984). Involving parents through written communication. *Dimensions, 12*(4), 12–14.

Henniger, M. (1985). Preschool children's play behaviors in an indoor and outdoor environment. In J. L. Frost & S. Sunderlin (Eds.), *When children play* (pp. 145–149). Wheaton, MD: Association for Childhood Education International.

Henniger, M. (1994a). Adult perceptions of favorite play experiences. *Early Child Development and Care, 99,* 23–30.

Henniger, M. (1994b). Computers and preschool children's play: Are they compatible? *Journal of Computing in Childhood Education, 5*(3/4), 231–239.

Henniger, M. (1994c). Planning for outdoor play. *Young Children, 49*(4), 10–15.

Henniger, M. (1994d). Play: Antidote for childhood stress. *Early Child Development and Care, 105,* 7–12.

Henniger, M. (1994e). Software for the early childhood classroom: What should it look like? *Journal of Computing in Childhood Education, 5*(2), 167–175.

Henniger, M. (1995). Supporting multicultural awareness at learning centers. *Dimensions of Early Childhood, 23*(4), 20–23.

Henri, A. (1990). *The postman's palace.* New York: Macmillan Children's Book Group.

Hernandez, D. (1995). Changing demographics: Past and future demands for early childhood programs. *The Future of Children* (Vol. 5, No. 3). Los Altos, CA: The Center for the Future of Children.

Herr, J., & Libby, Y. (1995). *Creative resources for the early childhood classroom* (2nd ed.). Albany, NY: Delmar.

Hewes, J. (1975). *Build your own playground.* Boston: Houghton Mifflin.

Hildebrand, V. (1994). *Guiding young children* (5th ed.). Upper Saddle River, NJ: Merrill/Prentice Hall.

Hill, D. (1996, September 11). Odd man out. *Education Week,* p. 28.

Hirsch, E. (Ed.). (1974). *The block book.* Washington, DC: National Association for the Education of Young Children.

Hodgins, D. (1996, January/February). What children can't do . . . yet. *Early Childhood News* [Online]. Available: http://www.earlychildhoodnews.com/cantdo.htm

Hohmann, C. (1996). *Foundations in elementary education: Overview.* Ypsilanti, MI: High/Scope Press.

Hohmann, M., Banet, B., & Weikart, D. (1979). *Young children in action.* Ypsilanti, MI: High/Scope Press.

Hohmann, M., & Weikart, D. (1995). *Educating young children: Active learning practices for preschool and child care programs.* Ypsilanti, MI: High/Scope Press.

Hughes, F. (1995). *Children, play, and development* (2nd ed.). Boston: Allyn & Bacon.

Hughes, M. (1993, July 8). Restraining TV violence sure to take time. *The Bellingham Herald,* p. C1.

Hymes, J. (1978). *Living history interviews.* Carmel, CA: Hacienda Press.

Isenberg, J., & Jalongo, M. (1997). *Creative expression and play in early childhood.* Upper Saddle River, NJ: Merrill/Prentice Hall.

Itard, J. (1962). *Wild boy of Aveyron.* New York: Appleton-Century-Crofts.

Jacobson, L. (1997, February 12). Full funding of New Hampshire kindergarten sought. *Education Week,* p. 21.

Jalongo, M. (1990). The child's right to the expressive arts: Nurturing the imagination as well as the intellect. *Childhood Education, 66*(4), 195–202.

Jalongo, M. (1995). Awaken to the artistry within young children! *Dimensions of Early Childhood, 23*(4), 8–14.

Jalongo, M. (1996). Using recorded music with young children: A guide for nonmusicians. *Young Children, 51*(5), 6–14.

Jalongo, M., & Isenberg, J. (1994). *Teachers' stories: From personal narrative to professional insight.* San Francisco: Jossey-Bass.

Jambor, T. (1994a). A playground raising: Context for intergenerational relationships. *Dimensions of Early Childhood, 22*(2), 31–36.

Jambor, T. (1994b). School recess and social development. *Dimensions of Early Childhood, 23*(1), 17–20.

Jelks, P., & Dukes, L. (1985). Promising props for outdoor play. *Day Care and Early Education, 13*(1), 18–20.

Johnson, J., Christie, J., & Yawkey, T. (1987). *Play and early childhood development.* Glenview, IL: Scott, Foresman.

Jones, V., & Jones, L. (1998). *Comprehensive classroom management: Creating communities of support and solving problems.* Boston: Allyn & Bacon.

Kaagan, S. (1990). *Aesthetic persuasion: Pressing the cause of arts education in American schools.* Santa Monica, CA: Getty Center for Education in the Arts.

Kameenui, E., & Darch, C. (1995). *Instructional classroom management.* White Plains, NY: Longman.

Kamii, C., & DeClark, G. (1985). *Young children reinvent arithmetic: Implications of Piaget's theory.* New York: Teachers College Press.

Kamii, C., & DeVries, R. (1978). *Physical knowledge in preschool education.* Upper Saddle River, NJ: Merrill/Prentice Hall.

Kamii, C., & DeVries, R. (1980). Group games in early education. Washington, DC: National Association for the Education of Young Children.

Kamii, C., & Ewing, J. (1996). Basing teaching on Piaget's constructivism. *Childhood Education, 72*(5), 260–264.

Karnes, M. (1994, May/June). Outdoor play for children with special needs. *Scholastic Early Childhood Today,* p. 55.

Kasting, A. (1994). Respect, responsibility and reciprocity: The three Rs of parent involvement. *Childhood Education, 70*(3), 146–150.

Katz, L. (1993). The nature of professions: Where is early childhood education? *Montessori Life, 5*(2), 31–35.

Katz, L. (1994). The project approach. *ERIC Digest.* EDO-PS-94-6. Urbana, IL: ERIC Clearinghouse on Elementary and Early Childhood Education.

Katz, L., & Chard, S. (1989). *Engaging children's minds: The project approach.* New York: Ablex.

Kellogg, R. (1969). *Analyzing children's art.* Palo Alto, CA: Mayfield Publishing.

Kirchner, G. (1991). *Children's games from around the world.* Dubuque, IA: William C. Brown.

Klein, N. (1973). *Girls can be anything.* New York: Dutton.

Kostelnik, M., Soderman, A., & Whiren, A. (1993). *Developmentally appropriate programs in early childhood education.* Upper Saddle River, NJ: Merrill/Prentice Hall.

Kostelnik, M., Stein, L., Whiren, A., & Soderman, A. (1993). *Guiding children's social development* (2nd ed.). Albany, NY: Delmar.

Kraus, R. (1971). *Leo the late bloomer.* New York: Windmill.

Kritchevsky, S., & Prescott, E. (1969). *Planning environments for young children: Physical space.* Washington, DC: National Association for the Education of Young Children.

Krogh, S. (1995). *The integrated early childhood curriculum* (2nd ed.). New York: McGraw-Hill.

Kuhl, P. (1993). *Life language.* Seattle, WA: University of Washington.

Kupetz, B., & Green, E. (1997). Sharing books with infants and toddlers: Facing the challenges. *Young Children, 52*(2), 22–27.

Lally, R. (1995). The impact of child care policies and practices on infant/toddler identity formation. *Young Children, 51*(1), 58–67.

Landau, S., & McAninch, C. (1993). Young children with attention deficits. *Young Children, 48*(4), 49–58.

Lane, M. (1981). *The squirrel.* New York: Dial.

Latimer, D. J. (1994). Involving grandparents and other older adults in the preschool classroom. *Dimensions of Early Childhood, 22*(2).

Lawler, S. D. (1991). *Parent–teacher conferencing in early childhood education.* Washington, DC: National Education Association.

Lawton, M. (1995, September 27). Children's tv still too violent, report says. *Education Week,* p. 9.

Lewis, R. (1994, March 16). Hands-on nurturing. Teaching children how to care. *Education Week,* p. 46.

Lillard, P. (1972). *Montessori—A modern approach.* New York: Schocken Books.

Lillard, P. (1996). *Montessori today: A comprehensive approach to education from birth to adulthood.* New York: Schocken Books.

Machado, J. (1995). *Early childhood experiences in language arts* (5th ed.). New York: Delmar.

Mageau, T. (Ed.). (1993). Early childhood and school success. *Electronic Learning, 12*(5), 23.

Marion, M. (1995). *Guidance of young children* (4th ed.). Upper Saddle River, NJ: Merrill/Prentice Hall.

Marland, S. (1972). *Education of the gifted and talented.* Washington, DC: U.S. Government Printing Office.

Marotz, L., Cross, M., & Rush, J. (1993). *Health, safety and nutrition for the young child* (3rd ed.). Albany, NY: Delmar.

Marston, L. (1984). *Playground equipment.* Jefferson, NC: McFarland.

Maslow, A. (1968). *Toward a psychology of being.* Princeton, NJ: Van Nostrand Reinhold.

Matthews, M. (1990). *What's it like to be a postal worker?* Mahwah, NJ: Troll Associates.

Mayer, M. (1974). *Frog goes to dinner.* New York: Dial.

McAfee, O., & Leong, D. (1994). *Assessing and guiding young children's development and learning.* Boston: Allyn & Bacon.

McClellan, D., & Katz, L. (1993). Young children's social development: A checklist. *ERIC Digest,* EDO-PS-93-6. Urbana, IL: ERIC Clearinghouse on Elementary and Early Childhood Education.

McClellan, D., & Katz, L. (1997). *Fostering children's social competence: The teacher's role.* Washington, DC: National Association for the Education of Young Children.

McCracken, J. (Ed.). (1986). *Reducing stress in young children's lives.* Washington, DC: National Association for the Education of Young Children.

McMath, J. (1997). Young children, national tragedy, and picture books. *Young Children, 52*(3), 82–84.

Miller, D. (1996). *Positive child guidance* (2nd ed.). Albany, NY: Delmar.

Miller, S. (1978). *The facilitation of fundamental motor skill learning in young children.* Unpublished doctoral dissertation, Michigan State University, East Lansing.

Miller, S. (1997). Family television viewing—How to gain control. *Childhood Education, 74*(1), 38–41.

Mitchell, A., & David, J. (Eds.). (1992). *Explorations with young children.* Mt. Rainier, MD: Gryphon House.

Mitchell, E., & Mason, B. (1948). *The theory of play.* New York: Barnes.

Montagu, A. (1978). *Touching: The human significance of the skin* (2nd ed.). New York: Harper & Row.

Montessori, M. (1936). *The secret of childhood.* Bombay: Orient Longmans.

Montessori, M. (1965). *Dr. Montessori's own handbook.* New York: Schocken Books.

Montessori, M. (1967). *The absorbent mind.* New York: Dell Publishing. (Original work published 1949).

Moore, K. (1995). *Classroom teaching skills* (3rd ed.). New York: McGraw-Hill.

Murray, P., & Mayer, R. (1988). Preschool children's judgements of number magnitude. *Journal of Educational Psychology, 80,* 206–209.

Myhre, S. (1993). Enhancing your dramatic-play area through the use of prop boxes. *Young Children, 48*(5), 6–11.

Nash, A., & Fraleigh, K. (1993, March). *The influence of older siblings on the sex-typed toy play of young children.* Paper presented at the Biennial Conference of the Society for Research in Child Development, New Orleans.

National Asssociation for the Education of Young Children. (1984). NAEYC position statement on nomenclature, salaries, benefits, and the status of the early childhood profession. *Young Children, 40*(1), 52–55.

National Association for the Education of Young Children. (1991). *Accreditation criteria and procedures of the National Academy of Early Childhood Programs* (rev. ed.). Washington, DC: National Association for the Education of Young Children.

National Association for the Education of Young Children. (1993). Enriching classroom diversity with books for children, in-depth discussion of them, and story-extension activities. *Young Children, 48*(3), 10–12.

National Association for the Education of Young Children. (1994). NAEYC position statement: A conceptual framework for early childhood professional development. *Young Children, 49*(3), 68–77.

National Association for the Education of Young Children. (1996a). Be a children's champion. *Young Children, 51*(2), 58–60.

National Association for the Education of Young Children. (1996b). Celebrating holidays in early childhood programs. In *Early years are learning years* (release No. 18). Washington, DC: National Association for the Education of Young Children.

National Association for the Education of Young Children. (1996c). NAEYC position statement: Technology and young children—Ages three through eight. *Young Children, 51*(6), 11–16.

National Association for the Education of Young Children. (1996d). NAEYC's code of ethical conduct: Guidelines for responsible behavior in early childhood education. *Young Children, 51*(3), 57–60.

National Association for the Education of Young Children. (1996e). The national television violence study: Key findings and recommendations. *Young Children, 51*(3), 54–55.

National Association for the Education of Young Children. (1997). Media violence and young children. In *Early years are learning years* (release No. 97/5). Washington, DC: National Association for the Education of Young Children.

National Association for Sport and Physical Education. (1998). *Physical activity for children: A statement of guidelines.* Reston, VA: Author.

National Center for Education in Maternal and Child Health. (1992). *National health and safety performance standards: Guidelines for out-of-home child care programs.* Arlington, VA: Author.

National Center for Improving Science. (1989). *Science and technology education for the elementary years: Frameworks for curriculum and instruction.* Andover, MA: Author.

National Center for the Early Childhood Work Force. (1995). Child care listed as lowest-paid occupation in the U.S. *Worthy Wage News, 2*(2), 2.

National Commission on Children. (1991). *Beyond rhetoric: A new American agenda for children and families.* Washington, DC: National Commission on Children.

National Council for Teachers of Mathematics. (1989). *Curriculum and evaluation standards for school mathematics.* Reston, VA: Author.

National Education Goals Panel. (1991). *National education goals report: Building a nation of learners.* Washington, DC: Author.

Neuman, S., & Roskos, K. (1993). *Language and literacy learning in the early years.* Ft. Worth, TX: Harcourt Brace Jovanovich.

New, R. (1990). Excellent early education: A city in Italy has it. *Young Children, 45*(6), 4–10.

Newberger, J. (1997). New brain development research—A wonderful window of opportunity to build public support for early childhood education! *Young Children, 52*(4), 4–9.

Newcombe, N., & Huttenlocher, J. (1992). Children's early ability to solve perspective-taking problems. *Developmental Psychology, 28*(4), 635–643.

Newman, N. (1990). *Sharing.* New York: Doubleday.

Notar, E. (1989). Children and TV commercials: Wave after wave of exploitation. *Childhood Education, 66,* 66–67.

Nourot, P., & Van Hoorn, J. (1991). Symbolic play in preschool and primary settings. *Young Children, 46*(6), 40–50.

Orlick, T. (1978). *The cooperative sports and games book.* New York: Pantheon.

Papert, S. (1980). *Mindstorms: Children, computers, and powerful ideas.* New York: Basic Books.

Papert, S. (1993). *The children's machine. Rethinking school in the age of the computer.* New York: Basic Books.

Parten, M. (1933). Social play among preschool children. *Journal of Abnormal and Social Psychology, 28,* 136–147.

Pelligrini, A. (1987). Elementary school children's rough-and-tumble play. *Monographs of the Institute for Behavioral Research.* Athens: University of Georgia.

Pelligrini, A., & Glickman, C. (1989). The educational benefits of recess. *Principal, 62*(5), 23–24.

Pelligrini, A., & Perlmutter, J. (1988). Rough-and-tumble play on the elementary school playground. *Young Children, 43*(2), 14–17.

Pepler, D., & Ross, H. (1981). The effects of play on convergent and divergent problem solving. *Child Development, 52,* 1202–1210.

Phillips, C. (1990). The Child Development Associate program: Entering a new era. *Young Children, 45*(3), 24–27.

Piaget, J. (1950). *The psychology of intelligence* (M. Piercy & D. Berlyne, Trans.). New York: Harcourt, Brace.

Piaget, J. (1959). *The language and thought of the child* (3rd ed.) (M. Gabain, Trans.). London: Routledge & Kegan Paul.

Piaget, J. (1962). *Play, dreams, and imitation in childhood* (C. Gattegno & F. Hodgson, Trans.). New York: W. W. Norton.

Piaget, J. (1965). *The moral judgement of the child* (M. Gabain, Trans.). New York: Free Press.

Piaget, J., & Inhelder, B. (1969). *The psychology of the child* (H. Weaver, Trans.). New York: Basic Books.

Pica, R. (1995). *Experiences in movement: With music, activities, and theory.* Albany, NY: Delmar.

Piirto, J. (1994). *Talented children and adults: Their development and education.* Upper Saddle River, NJ: Merrill/Prentice Hall.

Plutchik, R. (1980). *Emotion: A psychoevolutionary synthesis.* New York: Harper & Row.

Poest, C., Williams, J., Witt, D., & Atwood, M. (1990). Challenge me to move: Large muscle development in young children. *Young Children, 45*(5), 4–10.

Raikes, H. (1993). Relationship duration in infant care: Time with a high ability teacher and infant–teacher attachment. *Early Childhood Research Quarterly, 8,* 309–325.

Raikes, H. (1996). A secure base for babies: Applying attachment concepts to the infant care setting. *Young Children, 51*(5), 59–67.

Readdick, C. (1993). Solitary pursuits: Supporting children's privacy needs in early childhood settings. *Young Children, 49*(1), 60–64.

Reynolds, E. (1996). *Guiding young children. A child-centered approach* (2nd ed.). Mountain View, CA: Mayfield Publishing.

Rivkin, M. (1990). Outdoor play—What happens here? In S. Wortham & J. Frost (Eds.), *Playgrounds for young children: National survey and perspectives* (pp. 191–214). Reston, VA: American Alliance for Health, Physical Education, Recreation and Dance.

Rivkin, M. (1995). *The great outdoors: Restoring children's right to play outside.* Washington, DC: National Association for the Education of Young Children.

Roblyer, M., Edwards, J., & Havriluk, M. (1997). *Integrating educational technology into teaching.* Upper Saddle River, NJ: Prentice Hall.

Rockwell, R. E., Andre, L. C., & Hawley, M. K. (1996). *Parents and teachers as partners.* Fort Worth, TX: Harcourt Brace.

Roopnarine, J., & Johnson, J. (1993). *Approaches to early childhood education* (2nd ed.). Upper Saddle River, NJ: Merrill/Prentice Hall.

Rothenberg, D. (1995). Full-day kindergarten programs. *ERIC Digest,* EDO-PS-95-4. Urbana, IL: ERIC Clearinghouse on Elementary and Early Childhood Education.

Rousseau, J. (1979). *Emile* (A. Bloom, Trans.). New York: Basic Books. (Original work published 1762).

Rybczynski, M., & Troy, A. (1995). Literacy-enriched play centers: Trying them out in "the real world." *Childhood Education, 72*(1), 7–12.

Saracho, O., & Spodek, B. (1993). Professionalism and the preparation of early childhood education practitioners. *Early Child Development and Care, 89,* 1–17.

Schickedanz, J., Schickedanz, D., Forsyth, P., & Forsyth, G. (1998). *Understanding children and adolescents* (3rd ed.). Needham Heights, MA: Allyn & Bacon.

Schirrmacher, R. (1998). *Art and creative development for young children* (3rd ed.). Albany, NY: Delmar.

Schweinhart, L. (1993). Observing young children in action: The key to early childhood assessment. *Young Children, 48*(5), 29–33.

Schweinhart, L., & Weikart, D. (1993). Success by empowerment: The High/Scope Perry Preschool Study through age 27. *Young Children, 49*(1), 54–58.

Schweinhart, L. (1993). Observing young children in action: The key to early childhood assessment. *Young Children, 48*(5), 29–33.

Schweinhart, L., & Weikart, D. (1993). Success by empowerment: The High/Scope Perry Preschool Study through age 27. *Young Children, 49*(1), 54–58.

Seagoe, M. (1970). An instrument for the analysis of children's play as an index of socialization. *Journal of School Psychology, 8,* 139–144.

Seefeldt, C. (Ed.). (1990). *Continuing issues in early childhood education.* Upper Saddle River, NJ: Merrill/Prentice Hall.

Seefeldt, C. (1995). Art—A serious work. *Young Children, 50*(3), 39–45.

Seguin, E. (1907). *Idiocy and its treatment.* Albany, NY: Press of Brandow Printing Co.

Seidel, J. (1992). Children with HIV-related developmental difficulties. *Phi Delta Kappan, 74,* 38–40, 56.

Seuss, Dr. (1960). *Green eggs and ham.* New York: Random House.

Shade, D. (1992). Computers and young children: Software with the appeal of blocks. *Day Care and Early Education, 19*(3), 41–43.

Shade, D. (1995). Storyboard software: Flannel boards in the computer age. *Day Care and Early Education, 22*(3), 45–46.

Shartrand, A., Weiss, H., Kreider, H., & Lopez, M. (1997). *New skills for new schools: Preparing teachers in family involvement.* Cambridge, MA: Harvard Family Research Project.

Shaw, J., & Blake, S. (1998). *Mathematics for young children.* Upper Saddle River, NJ: Merrill/Prentice Hall.

Shellenbarger, S. (1994, July 22). Companies help solve day-care problems. *Wall Street Journal,* pp. B1, B10.

Shepherd, T. R., & Shepherd, W. L. (1984). Living with a child with autistic tendencies. In M. Henniger & L. Nesselroad (Eds.), *Working with parents of handicapped children* (pp. 85–106). Lanham, MD: University Press of America.

Shores, E. (1995). Howard Gardner on the eighth intelligence: Seeing the natural world. *Dimensions of Early Childhood, 23*(4), 5–7.

Singer, D., & Singer, J. (1990). *The house of make-believe.* Cambridge, MA: Harvard University Press.

Skeels, H. (1966). Adult status of children with constrasting early life experience. *Monographs of the Society for Research in Child Development, 31*(3, Serial No. 105).

Skinner, B. (1957). *Verbal behavior.* New York: Appleton-Century-Crofts.

Skinner, B. (1974). *About behaviorism.* New York: Knopf.

Skurzynski, G. (1992). *Here comes the mail.* New York: Macmillan Children's Book Group.

Silva, D. (1996). Moving young children's play away from TV violence. Baltimore, MD: Ready at Five Partnership. (ERIC Document Reproduction Service No. ED 400 052)

Smilansky, S. (1968). *The effects of sociodramatic play on disadvantaged preschool children.* New York: Wiley.

Smilansky, S., & Shefatya, L. (1990). *Facilitating play: A medium for promoting cognitive, socio-emotional and academic development in young children.* Gaithersburg, MD: Psychosocial and Educational Publications.

Smith, S. (1990). The riskiness of the playground. *The Journal of Educational Thought, 24*(2), 71–87.

Snider, S., & Badgett, T. (1995). I have this computer, what do I do now? Using technology to enhance every child's learning. *Early Childhood Education Journal, 23*(2), 101–105.

Spodek, B., & Saracho, O. (1994). *Dealing with individual differences in the early childhood classroom.* New York: Longman.

Spodek, B., Saracho, O., & Peters, D. (Eds.). (1988). *Professionalism and the early childhood practitioner.* New York: Teachers College Press.

Sprung, B. (1996). Physics is fun, physics is important, and physics belongs in the early childhood curriculum. *Young Children, 51*(5), 29–33.

Standing, E. (1962). *Maria Montessori: Her life and work.* Fresno, CA: Academy Guild Press.

Starko, A. (1995). *Creativity in the classroom: Schools of curious delight.* White Plains, NY: Longman.

Steiner, G. (1976). *The children's cause.* Washington, DC: Brookings Institution.

Stephens, K. (1994, September/October). Aiding families with referrals. *First Teacher,* pp. 34–35.

Stipek, D., Rosenblatt, L., & DiRocco, L. (1994). Making parents your allies. *Young Children, 49*(3), 4–9.

Stone, S. (1995). Wanted: Advocates for play in the primary grades. *Young Children, 50*(6), 45–54.

Sulzby, E., & Teale, W. (1991). Emergent literacy. In R. Barr, M. Kamil, P. Mosentahl, & P. Pearson (Eds.), *Handbook of reading research* (Vol. 2, pp. 82–97). New York: Longman.

Suskind, D. (1993). Project Desert Shield—Preschool style. *Young Children, 48*(2), 43–45.

Sutton-Smith, B., & Roberts, J. (1981). Play, games, and sports. In H. C. Triandis & A. Heron (Eds.), *Handbook of cross-cultural psychology. Vol. 4. Developmental psychology* (pp. 223–241). Boston: Allyn & Bacon.

Swick, K., Boutte, G., & van Scoy, I. (1995, March). Family involvement in early multicultural learning. *ERIC Digest,* EDO-PS-95-2. Urbana, IL: ERIC Clearinghouse on Elementary and Early Childhood Education.

Swiniarski, L. (1991). Toys: Universals for teaching global education. *Childhood Education, 67*(3), 161–163.

Tegano, D., Sawyers, J., & Moran, J. (1989). Problem-finding and solving in play: The teacher's role. *Childhood Education, 66*(2), 92–97.

Thomas, R. (1985). *Comparing theories of child development* (2nd ed.). Belmont, CA: Wadsworth.

Torrance, E. (1962). *Guiding creative talent.* Upper Saddle River, NJ: Prentice Hall.

Tracy, D. (1994). Using mathematical language to enhance mathematical conceptualization. *Childhood Education, 70*(4), 221–224.

Trawick-Smith, J. (1994). *Interactions in the classroom: Facilitating play in the early years.* Upper Saddle River, NJ: Merrill/Prentice Hall.

Trawick-Smith, J. (1997). *Early childhood development: A multicultural perspective.* Upper Saddle River, NJ: Merrill/Prentice Hall.

Tucker, D. (1997, April 29). NCAA gender equity study shows gains by women. *The Bellingham Herald,* p. B1.

Underwood, J. (1981, February 23). A game plan for America. *Sports Illustrated,* pp. 64–80.

U.S. Department of Education. (1996). *To assure the free appropriate public education of all children with disabilities: Eighteenth annual report to Congress in the implementation of the Individuals with Disabilities Education Act.* Washington, DC: Author.

U.S. Department of Health and Human Services. (1984). *Head Start performance standards.* Washington, DC: Author.

U.S. Department of Health and Human Services. (1990). *Head Start: A child development program.* Washington, DC: Author.

Van Hoorn, J., Nourot, P., Scales, B., & Alward, K. (1993). *Play at the center of the curriculum.* Upper Saddle River, NJ: Merrill/Prentice Hall.

Vandenberg, B. (1980). Play, problem-solving and creativity. *New Directions for Child Development, 9,* 49–68.

Viadero, D. (1996, May 8). Mixed blessings. *Education Week,* pp. 31–33.

Vukelich, C. (1990). Where's the paper? Literacy during dramatic play. *Childhood Education, 66*(4), 205–209.

Vygotsky, L. (1962). *Thought and language.* Cambridge, MA: M.I.T. Press.

Vygotsky, L. (1978). *Mind in society: The development of higher psychological processes.* Cambridge, MA: Harvard University Press.

Waelder, R. (1933). The psychoanalytic theory of play. *Psychoanalytic Quarterly, 2,* 208–224.

Wallis, C. (1994, July 18). Life in overdrive. *Time,* pp. 43–50.

Wanamaker, N., Hearn, K., & Richarz, S. (1979). *More than graham crackers: Nutrition education and food preparation with young children.* Washington, DC: National Association for the Education of Young Children.

Ward, C. (1996). Adult intervention: Appropriate strategies for enriching the quality of children's play. *Young Children, 51*(3), 20–25.

Warren, J. (1983). *Piggyback songs.* Everett, WA: Warren Publishing.

Wash, D., & Brand, L. (1990). Child day care services. An industry at a crossroads. *Monthly Labor Review, 113*(12), 17–24.

Wassermann, S. (1990). *Serious players in the primary classroom. Empowering children through active learning experiences.* New York: Teachers College Press.

Wasserman, S. (1992). Serious play in the classroom—How messing around can win you the Nobel prize. *Childhood Education, 68*(3), 133–139.

Watson, J. (1924). *Behaviorism.* New York: W. W. Norton.

Waxman, S. (1976a). *What is a boy?* Los Angeles: Peace Press.

Waxman, S. (1976b). *What is a girl?* Los Angeles: Peace Press.

Weber, E. (1984). *Ideas influencing early childhood education.* New York: Teachers College Press.

Weikart, D., Rogers, L., Adcock, C., & McClelland, D. (1971). *The cognitively oriented curriculum.* Washington, DC: National Association for the Education of Young Children.

Whitebook, M. (1995). *Salary improvements in Head Start. Lessons for the early care and education field.* Washington, DC: National Center for the Early Childhood Work Force.

Williams, D. L., & Chavkin, N. F. (1989, October). Essential elements of strong parent involvement programs. *Educational Leadership,* pp. 18–20.

Winter, S. (1985). Toddler play behaviors and equipment choices in an outdoor playground. In J. Frost & S. Sunderlin (Eds.), *When children play* (pp. 129–138). Wheaton, MD: Association for Childhood Education International.

Winter, S., Bell, M., & Dempsey, J. (1994). Creating play environments for children with special needs. *Childhood Education, 71*(1), 28–32.

Wolery, M., & Wilbers, J. (Eds.). (1994). *Including children with special needs in early childhood programs.* Washington, DC: National Association for the Education of Young Children.

Wolfinger, D. (1994). *Science and mathematics in early childhood education.* New York: Harper-Collins.

Wortham, S. (1989, Summer). Outdoor play environments for infants and toddlers. *Day Care and Early Education,* pp. 28–30.

Wortham, S. (1995). *Measurement and evaluation in early childhood education* (2nd ed.). Upper Saddle River, NJ: Merrill/Prentice Hall.

Wright, J., & Huston, A. (1995). *Effects of educational tv viewing of lower income preschoolers on academic skills, school readiness, and school adjustment one to three years later.* Lawrence, KS: Center for Research on the Influences of Television on Children.

Yawkey, T., & Pellegrini, A. (Eds.). (1984). *Child's play and play therapy.* Lancaster, PA: Technomic Publishing.

Yokota, J. (1993). Issues in selecting multicultural children's literature. *Language Arts, 70,* 43–50.

Zolotow, C. (1985). *William's doll.* New York: Harper & Row.

Index

Aboud, F., 192
Absorbent minds, 87
Abstract symbolism. *See* Symbolism
Abuse, 345, 346
Academic Montessori materials, 57
Academic skills. *See* Cognitive development
Accelerated education, 68
Accessibility, 202, 205, 237, 367
Accident prevention, 240–241
Accommodation, 89, 91, 118
Accreditation, 454
ACEI. *See* Association for Childhood Education International
Acquired immune deficiency syndrome (AIDS), 240
Action books, 397
Active centers, 215–216
Active learning, 42, 61, 81, 91, 356
   Comenius on, 33
   and group guidance, 158–159
   in Montessori theory, 86
   and play, 113
Active listening, 143
Active play. *See* Physical development; Play; Playgrounds
Activities
   and children with special needs, 237–238
   creative arts, 422–427
   for emotional development, 332, 342–343
   and group guidance, 158–159
   multicultural, 114, 198, 201–202, 260, 321
   organized physical, 314–316
      indoor, 316–318
      outdoor, 318–321
   planning, 281–284
   for social development, 338–340
   solitary, 121, 217, 251
Adcock, C., 59
ADHD. *See* Attention-deficit/hyperactivity disorder
Administrative support, for parent involvement, 181
Adult-made equipment, 235–237, 263–265

Adult-movable playground equipment, 264, 266–267
Adult needs, and classroom environment, 217, 219, 229, 241
Adventure Playgrounds, 250
Advertising, television, 434
Advocacy, 19–20
Aesthetics, 415
Affection, 84
Affective development. *See* Emotional development
African-American students and families, 104, 189, 367
After-school care, 11
Age appropriateness, 81
AIDS. *See* Acquired immune deficiency syndrome
Ainsworth, Mary, 82
Alternate-input devices, 422
Altman, R., 305
Alward, K., 132, 133, 334
American Association for Gifted Children, 105
American Federation of Teachers, 45
American Montessori Society, 27, 58
Americans with Disabilities Act (P.L. 101–336), 190
Anderson, R., 394
Andre, L. C., 177
Anecdotal records, 279, 295, 296
Anglund, J., 338
Annie E. Casey Foundation, 104, 165, 167, 168
Anselmo, S., 102, 103, 108, 307
Antelope in the Net, 198
Antibias curriculum, 196. *See also* Diversity
Anxiety, 82, 83, 437
Appropriateness. *See also* Developmentally appropriate curriculum
   age and individual, 81
   and creativity, 407–408
Archer, J., 166
Aries, P., 43
Arithmetic skills, 359, 445. *See also* Mathematics

Arousal seeking, play as, 118
Arrival, 149
Art, 38, 305, 340, 342, 411–415. *See also* Creative arts
   activities, 422–427
   adult role in, 413, 415–418
Art centers, 219–220, 373
Artifacts, multicultural, 200
Artist apprentice, teacher as, 131, 132
Asia for Kids, 195, 235
Asian American students and families, 169, 367
Assessment, 40, 72–73
   environmental, 218–219
   observation, 63, 64, 293–295, 296, 297
   of parent involvement, 181
   portfolios, 295–297, 298
   of thematic units, 289
Assimilation, 89, 91, 118
Associate degree programs, 25
Association for Childhood Education International (ACEI), 26, 406, 412
Association Montessori Internationale, 58
Association of Teacher Educators, 26
Associative play, 121
Atelier, 71, 72
Atelierista, 72
Atlas, J., 189
At-risk children, 103, 104
Attachment, 82–83, 93
Attempts at public representation stage, 413
Attention-deficit/hyperactivity disorder (ADHD), 101, 102–103
Attractiveness, physical, 308, 309
Atwood, M., 307
Auditory awareness, 312
Authentic measures, 40
Autoharps, 427
Autonomy, 89, 356
Axline, V., 118, 347

Bach, Johann Sebastian, 427
Badgett, T., 441
Baker, K., 249
Balancing, 309, 315
Balancing Circus, 318
Ball, W., 418
Balls, 309, 374–375
Bandura, A., 333
Banks, C., 209
Banks, J., 81, 189, 209
Bank Street College of Education, 42, 44, 64
Bank Street model, 53, 64–69
Baratta-Lorton, Mary, 357
Barbour, C., 165, 169, 176, 177, 178, 183, 185, 189
Barbour, N., 165, 169, 176, 177, 178, 183, 185, 189
Barnes, B., 432, 440
Baron, L., 432
Basic locomotion, 309
Bassett, M., 422
Bayless, K., 419
Bear, T., 345
Beaty, J., 138, 160
Bee, H., 92, 103
Beethoven, Ludwig van, 427
Before- and after-school care, 11
Beginning chapter books, 397
Behavior
    and Bank Street model, 67
    modeling, 333
    and play, 39
Behaviorism, 66, 146–147, 383
Bell, M., 237
Belongingness, 84
Benelli, C., 309, 314
Berger, E. H., 167, 171, 175, 180, 377
Berk, L., 39, 87, 108
Berry, J., 370
Betz, C., 147
Big Toys, 264
Biological sciences, 363
Blake, S., 367, 378
Blended families, 166–167
Block centers, 221–223, 373
Blocks, 54, 205, 340, 358, 394
Blume, E., 345
Blume, Judy, 397
Board books, 397
Bodily kinesthetic intelligence, 85
Body art, 370
Body awareness, 312
Body language, 143, 173, 175
Boesser, C., 138, 152
Bonding, 82–83

Book centers, 221, 374, 395
Books, 395–397. See also Literacy
    awards, 398
    for diversity education, 199–200
    electronic, 446
    for emotional development, 278, 343
    and language development, 389
    making, 402
    and print-rich environments, 392
    on self, 370
    on social skills, 338, 340
Boutte, G., 194, 195, 207
Bowers, L., 248
Bowlby, John, 82
Bowman, B., 192
Boyer, Ernest, 411
Brain research, 353
Brand, S., 14
Braun, E., 331
Braun, S., 33, 34, 36, 41, 44, 46, 48, 254
Bredekamp, S., 45, 58, 69, 81, 113, 247, 277, 299, 354, 437
Brenner, B., 370
Britain, L., 356, 364, 378
Broderbund Software, 439
Bronfenbrenner, Urie, 177, 368
Brookes, M., 427, 428
Brown, David K., 396
Brown, N., 118
Brown, T., 199
Bruner, Jerome, 113, 115, 123
"Brushing Teeth" (song), 423
Bubble-making, 364
Buckleitner, Warren, 443, 446
Buckner, L., 345
Bulletin boards, 177
Bumble Bee, 321
Bunker, L., 305
Bunny Hop, 317
Bureau of Educational Experiments, 42, 44. See also Bank Street College of Education
Business meetings, 179
Buttoning frames, 54
Buzzell, J. B., 185

Caldecott award, 398
Campbell, B., 85
Canfield, J., 332, 349
Career awareness, 183–184, 371
Carle, Eric, 361
Carlsson-Paige, N., 346
Carrick, D., 397
Casa dei Bambini, 37
Castle, K., 120

Catching, 314, 317–318
Catch Me If You Can (game), 317–318
CDA. See Child Development Associate program
CD-ROM, 443, 446
Center for Communications Policy, 344
Center for the Future of Children, 166
Centers, 14, 226–227, 229–230, 232
    art, 219–220, 373
    block, 221–223, 373
    book/quiet, 221, 374, 395
    discovery, 225, 374
    dramatic play, 223–224, 374
    dry vs. wet, 216
    housekeeping, 223, 374
    manipulative, 220–221, 373
    music, 224–225, 374
    and noise levels, 215–216
Cephalocaudal development, 308
Cesarone, B., 436
Chaille, C., 113, 205, 356, 364, 378
Chalk, 425
Chalkboards, child-sized, 398
Chapter I, 15
Chard, S., 291, 292
Charland, T., 447
Charlesworth, R., 38, 91
Chattin-McNichols, J., 58
Chavkin, N. F., 180
Checklists, 295, 297
Chemistry, 364
Child abuse, 345, 346
Child care. See Day care
Child development. See also Cognitive development; Developmentally appropriate curriculum; Emotional development; Language development; Physical development; Social development; Theorists of early childhood
    and Bank Street model, 53, 65, 66–67
    of children with special needs, 103–106, 238
    children with disabilities, 100–103, 188, 322
    and Child Study movement, 43
    and computers, 432–433, 437–441
    and creative arts, 412–414, 418–419
    and gender, 188
    and literacy, 391
    and outdoor play, 247, 255–260, 262
    and portfolio organization, 298

Child development, *continued*
similarities and differences, 91–92
understanding, 5, 106–107
Child Development Associate (CDA) program, 24–25
Child-movable playground equipment, 267
Child neglect, 345, 346
Child Observational Record (COR), 63, 64
Children
ethical responsibilities to, 21
interacting with, 22
parent involvement benefits to, 171–172
Children at risk, 103, 104
Children's Book Council, 398
Children's Choice Awards, 398
Children's Defense Fund, 165, 166
Children's House (Casa dei Bambini), 37
Children's literature. *See also* Books
awards, 398
in classroom library, 221
for diversity education, 199–200
on the Web, 396
Children with special needs. *See also* Diversity
at-risk children, 103, 104
and attention deficit/hyperactivity disorder, 101, 102–103
attitudes toward, 190–192
children's literature regarding, 199
classroom environment for, 202, 237–238
development of, 103–106, 238
and disabilities, 100–103, 188, 322
families of, 181–182
gifted, 57, 68, 103–106
guidance for, 159, 189
and learning disabilities, 101–102
multidisciplinary collaboration regarding, 203–204
physical activities for, 322
and playgrounds, 260, 262
programs for, 11–12, 15
social interactions with, 202–203
technology resources for, 441, 442
Child-sized equipment, 55
Child Study movement, 43
ChildsWork ChildsPlay Corporation, 338
Chipman, M., 209
Choices, 143–144
and logical consequences, 146
and play, 113

Chomsky, Noam, 383, 385
Chopin, Frederic, 427
Christie, J., 131, 226, 391, 392, 393, 400, 403
Circle time, 36, 63, 156, 158, 216
Civil Rights Act of 1964, 189
Clark, R., 128
Classical music, 427
Classification, 61, 357
Classroom centers. *See* Centers
Classroom climate, 333
Classroom environment, 22, 214–218. *See also* Centers
age-related considerations, 227–232
assessment of, 218–219
and Bank Street model, 68
changing, 238–239
for children with special needs, 202, 237–238
equipment and materials selection, 234–237
and guidance, 140, 141, 156–157
and health and safety, 239–241
in High/Scope curriculum, 63–64
infant/toddler, 227–229, 230, 278
low-risk, 409
Montessori, 55–57
and music, 224–225, 421–422
parent space, 241
preschool and kindergarten, 229–232
primary school, 232, 233
in Reggio Emilia program, 70–71
and social development, 219, 337–338
and teacher-student relationships, 334
Classroom newspaper, 394
Classroom schedules. *See* Schedules
Clay, 425
Cleanliness, 227
Cleanup, 63, 144
Clear-cut attachment phase, 83
Clearinghouse on Elementary and Early Childhood Education, 434
Clemens, J., 365
Clements, D., 362, 432, 440, 441
Clifford, R., 219
Climbers, 248–249
Clinton, Bill, 164
Closing events, 289
Cognitive development. *See also* Mathematics
and art, 416
and Bank Street model, 65

centers for, 232
and computers, 437
and constructivist approach, 91, 352, 355–356, 372, 374
curriculum goals, 281, 352–355
infant/toddler, 90, 93, 94, 119, 229, 372–373
integrated across curriculum, 372–375
and music, 418
parental roles in, 375–377
and peer interactions, 334
and physical development, 304–306
and play, 118–120, 123–124
portfolios, 298
preschoolers, 90–91, 95–97, 98, 120, 373–374
in primary grades, 91, 98, 99, 100, 120, 260
and project approach, 374–375
science learning, 362–367, 377
social studies learning, 367–372
stages of, 39, 89–91, 118–120, 124, 229, 372
Cohen, D., 271
Cohen, S., 433
Coleman, J., 47
Coleman, M., 165
Colker, L., 158, 220, 242, 288
Collaborative learning, 40
Colleagues
interacting with, 21, 22, 141–142
multidisciplinary collaboration among, 203–204
Collectibles, 221
College-supported programs, 18
Columbia University Teachers College, 42, 44
Comenius, John Amos, 33–34
Commercial equipment and materials, 234–235, 263
Communication. *See also* Language
parent-teacher, 69, 106–107, 173–175, 348
methods, 175–180
and special needs technology, 442
and teacher-student relationships, 64, 333
Community colleges, 25
Community Playthings, 234
Community-school relationships, 7–8, 21, 182–184, 338
and language-rich experiences, 389
playground construction, 269–271
and social studies, 371

Compensatory education programs, 47–48
Competence, 65, 137, 331
Competition, 319, 325–326
Complex emotions, 340
Computer centers, 227
Computers, 220, 399
    appropriateness of, 432–433, 437–441
    incorporating, 447
    selecting, 441–443
Computer software, 362, 399, 438, 439
    selecting, 443–447
Concept development, in Montessori education, 55
Conclusions, drawing, 366
Concrete operations stage, 91, 120, 260, 360, 440–441
Conflict, and Bank Street model, 67
Conner-Kuntz, F., 388
Consequences, natural and logical, 145, 146
Conservation, 90, 91
Consistency, 230, 232, 238, 292
Construction areas, playground, 252
Construction play, 119, 251, 394
Constructive Playthings, 234, 235, 264
Constructivism, 39, 40, 59, 91, 352, 355–356. See also Developmentally appropriate curriculum; High/Scope model; Piaget, Jean
    and project approach, 374
    and social studies, 372
Consumer Product Safety Commission (CPSC), 267–268
Container gardens, 365
Content, scientific, 363–364
Continuing education. See Professional development
Control, 137, 331
Conventional gardens, 365
Conversation, 387, 401
Cooking, 364, 377
Cooks, teachers as, 19
Cooperation
    with parents and families, 348
    and play, 114, 120, 121
    and social development, 335, 338, 339–340
Cooperative-competitive play, 122
Cooperative games, 221, 319, 339
Cooperative learning, 232, 339
Cooperative programs, 14–15
Co-playing, 132
Copple, C., 113, 247, 277, 299, 354

COR. See Child Observational Record
Core emotions, 340
Corporal punishment, 147
Corporate day care, 16–17
Council for Exceptional Children, 27, 200
Counselors, teachers as, 19
Counting, 359
CPSC. See Consumer Product Safety Commission
Crain, W., 82, 89
Crayon rubbings, 424–425
Crayon shavings, 426–427
Creative activities, space for, 219
Creative arts, 407–410. See also Art; Music
    activities, 422–427
    importance of, 406–407, 411–412, 413
    and play, 410–411
Creative Educational Surplus, 235
Creativity
    and computer software, 444
    defining, 407–408
    and play, 115, 129, 410–411, 438
    process of, 408–410
    valuing, 415, 422
Crib toys, 230
Critical thinking, 354, 356
Cross, M., 239, 240, 242, 322, 327
Cross-disciplinary activities, 40
Cruz-Janzen, M., 209
Cryer, D., 219
Cuffaro, H., 432, 441
Cuisenaire Company of America, 235
Cullinan, B., 403
Culminating events, 292
Cultural and artistic Montessori materials, 57
Cultural diversity. See also Diversity; Multicultural education
    attitudes toward, 189–190, 193
    family differences, 166, 168–169, 189
Curiosity, 408
Current events, 278, 372
Curriculum. See also Developmentally appropriate curriculum; Integrated curruculum; specific developmental areas
    community involvement in, 183
Curry, N., 118
Cylinder blocks, 54, 358

Daily living Montessori materials, 56
Daily schedule. See Schedules

Dainton, M., 167
Darch, C., 146
Data collection, 365
David, J., 65, 67, 68, 69, 75, 157, 242, 287
Davidson and Associates, Inc., 439
Davis, B., 448
Day care, 11, 166
    on-site, 16–17, 46
Deaf learners, 101, 442
Debriefing events, 292
Decision making. See also Problem solving
    community involvement in, 184
    guidance for, 144
DeClark, Georgia, 287
Deficiency needs, 83
DeFina, A., 296
Deiner, P., 105
Delisle, J., 142
Dempsey, J., 237
Departure, 149
Derman-Sparks, Louise, 193, 194, 196, 209
Descartes, René, 86
Developmental interactionist model, 65. See also Bank Street model
Developmentally appropriate curriculum, 80–81, 276–277. See also Child development; Constructivism; specific developmental areas
    activity and lesson planning, 281–284, 285, 289, 290
    assessment, 289, 293–297, 298
    and behaviorism compared, 66
    and children with special needs, 238
    goals, 280–281, 352–355
    integrated, 284, 286–290, 372–375
    parent involvement, 81, 289, 297–298
    project approach, 290–292
    schedules, 292–293
DeVries, Rheta, 58, 59, 65, 68, 250, 318, 356, 376, 378
Dewey, John, 40–42, 53, 65, 66, 70, 115
Diet. See Food
Dinwiddie, Sue, 250
Direct instruction, in physical education, 313
Directional awareness, 312
Directions, positive, 92, 143
DiRocco, L., 170
Disabilities
    categories of, 101, 191
    dolls with, 198

Disabled children, 189, 202–204. *See also* Children with special needs; Diversity
attitudes toward, 190–192
classroom environment for, 202, 237–238
development of, 100–103, 188, 238, 322
physical activities for, 322
and playgrounds, 262
technology resources for, 441, 442
Discipline
and guidance contrasted, 136–137
strategies, 145–148
Discipline-based art education, 415
Discovery centers, 225, 374
Divergent problem solving, 313
Diversity, 8, 188–189. *See also* Children with special needs; Gender equity
attitudes toward, 189–193, 206–208
and children's literature, 199–200
encouraging acceptance of, 192–194
experiences for, 81, 201–202
and family differences, 166, 168–169, 189
and games, 114, 198, 260, 321
inappropriate responses to, 194–195
and math and science, 367
and music, 201, 418, 421, 426
and parent involvement, 207–208
tourist approach to, 194–195
toys and materials, 81, 195, 196–200, 206, 235, 278
and visual-aesthetic environment, 200–201
Divorce, 165–166, 344
Dr. Seuss books, 397
Documentation, in Reggio Emilia program, 72–73
Dodge, D., 158, 220, 242, 288
Dolan, K., 184
Dolls, 195, 198, 199, 205
Doman, Glenn, 344, 392
Donated materials, 263
Dopyera, J., 309
Dopyera, M., 309
Do time, in High/Scope curriculum, 61
Doubt, 89
Dramatic play, 39, 120, 124, 390, 394
and emotional development, 343
outdoor, 247, 249, 252, 253, 265–266

Dramatic play areas, playground, 253
Dramatic play centers, 223–224, 374
Draw/paint programs, 445
Dreikurs, R., 146, 332
Drill and practice software, 445
Drums, 426
Dukes, L., 265
Dummer, G., 388
Dustin, D., 170

Early, P., 164
Early childhood associate teachers, 23–24. *See also* Teachers
Early childhood caregivers. *See* Teachers
Early childhood education. *See also* History of early childhood education; Theorists of early childhood
foundations of, 5–8
funding, 14–18
quality, 10
scope of, 8–14
day care programs, 11
infant/toddler programs, 9, 11–12
multiage approach, 12, 13–14
special needs programs, 11–12, 15
Early Childhood Education and Assistance Program (ECEAP), 16
Early Childhood Environment Rating Scale, 219
Early childhood specialists, 24. *See also* Teachers
Early childhood teacher assistants, 23. *See also* Teachers
Early childhood teachers, 24. *See also* Teachers
Early Head Start, 15, 16
Early intervention programs, 11–12, 62
Early picture storybooks, 397
ECEAP. *See* Early Childhood Education and Assistance Program
Ecological model of human development, 368
Edison, Thomas, 410
Edmark Corporation, 439
Education, U.S. Department of, 191
Education, U.S. Office of, 28
Educational meetings, for parents, 179
Educational Resources Information Center (ERIC), 28
Educational specialists, teachers as, 19

Education for All Handicapped Children Act (P.L. 94–142), 11, 190
Edwards, C., 71, 72, 291
Edwards, E., 33, 34, 36, 41, 44, 46, 48, 254, 331
Edwards, J., 442
Edwards, L., 407, 417, 419, 427, 428
Egocentrism, 91, 124, 334, 366
Ehly, S., 170
Eight-year-olds, 100. *See also* Primary school years
Einstein, Albert, 355, 411
Eisenberg, L., 165, 168
Electronic books, 446
Electronic communication, 176
Elementary schools. *See* Primary school years
Eliot, Abigail, 43
Elkind, David, 115, 325, 344, 346, 347, 349, 353
Ellis, M., 116, 118
Ellis, S., 339
Emergent literacy, 391
Emotional abuse, 345
Emotional development, 7, 65, 86, 278, 340–342
curriculum goals, 281
and guidance, 137–138, 151–154, 155
infants and toddlers, 82–83, 88–89, 93, 95
materials and activities for, 342–343
and music, 418
and parents and families, 347–348
and physical development, 305
and play, 127–128
preschoolers, 89, 96, 97, 98, 278, 425
in primary school years, 89, 98, 99, 100
and social development, 155, 331–332, 336
and stress, 344–347
Emotions
dealing with, 137–138, 151–154, 336, 341–342
defined, 340
in families of children with special needs, 182
and physical development, 305
Encouragement, 332
Engel, B., 417
Enrichment education, 68
Environment. *See also* Classroom environment; Playgrounds
constructivist learning, 40

Environment, *continued*
  home, 174
  play, 129–130
  print-rich, 391–393
  respect for, 366
Enz, B., 226, 391, 403
Epstein, A., 74
Epstein, J., 174
Equipment. *See also* Furniture;
    Materials; Technology
  child-sized, 55, 249
  for infant/toddler classroom, 227,
    229, 230
  for motor development, 314
  playground, 248–250, 263–265,
    267–269, 271
    developmental considerations,
      256, 259
    for special needs, 262
  to promote diversity, 196–198
  safety of, 241, 267–269
  selecting, 234–237, 263–265
ERIC. *See* Educational Resources
    Information Center
Eriksen, A., 247
Erikson, Erik, 53, 65, 88–89, 115
Esbensen, S., 247, 252, 270
Essa, E., 160
Ethical sense, and maturationist
    theory, 86
Ethics, 21
Ethnic diversity. *See* Diversity
Ethological theory, 82
Evaluation. *See* Assessment
Even Start, 15
Ewing, J., 39, 91
Excel, pressure to, 344
Exosystem, 368, 369
Expectations, 333
  stereotypic, 278
Experiences, 33, 41
  and art, 414
  for diversity education, 81, 201–202
  in High/Scope curriculum, 61
  language-rich, 389
  sensory, 247, 414
Exploration
  and creative arts, 409–410
  and physical education, 313
Extended families, 165, 189

Facilitators of learning, teachers as, 19
Fact learning, 353–354, 376
Failure
  and play, 115, 439
  positive approach to, 366, 409

Families, 7–8, 171. *See also* Parent
    involvement; Parents
  of children with special needs,
    181–182
  ethical responsibilities to, 21
  mobility of, 169–170
  and physical development, 324–326
  and social and emotional
    development, 347–348
  and social studies, 371
  and stress, 167, 344
  types, 165–169, 189
Family home day care, 11
Fantasy, vs. reality, 92
Fears and dreams, and maturationist
    theory, 86
Federally funded programs, 15, 16
Feelings. *See* Emotions
Feynman, Richard, 411
Fields, M., 138, 152
Field trips, 292, 389, 390, 402
Field work, 292
Fine motor skills, 127, 219, 252, 310,
    314
Finger Frolics, 317
Fish Gobbler, 319
Fitness, physical, 306–307, 316, 323
Five-year-olds, 97–98. *See also*
    Kindergartens; Preschoolers
Flannelboard stories, 389
Flavell, J., 13, 89, 334, 358, 360
Flemming, B., 237, 288, 369, 420
Flexibility, and creativity, 408
Food
  advertising for, 434
  family, 371
  and nutrition, 323, 325
Formal operations stage, 91
Forman, George, 59, 71, 125, 291
For-profit programs, 14
Forsyth, G., 188
Forsyth, P., 188
Foster, S. M., 179
"Four Little Horses" (song), 423
Four-year degree programs, 25
Four-year-olds, 96–97. *See also*
    Preschoolers
Fractor, J., 395
Fraleigh, K., 189
Franz, W., 102, 103, 108, 307
Freud, Sigmund, 53, 117, 305
"Fried Ham" (song), 427
Friendly workplace, 333
Friendship, 98, 100, 335. *See also* Peer
    interactions; Social
    development

Froebel, Friedrich, 36, 37, 42,
    114–115, 158
Fromberg, D., 112
Frost, J., 128, 133, 248, 249, 250, 251,
    256, 267, 268, 269, 272
Fuller, M., 168, 169, 170, 172, 189
Functional play, 119
Functions, integration of, 65–66
Fundamental movement skills, 309,
    311
Funding, 14–18
Funk, J., 436, 437
Furman, R., 151, 152
Furniture, 55, 219, 249. *See also*
    Equipment

Gabbard, C., 312
Galda, L., 403
Gallagher, J., 295
Gallahue, D., 127, 305, 307, 311,
    322
Games, 99
  children's invented, 120
  cooperative, 221, 319, 339
  and diversity education, 114, 198,
    260, 321
  and mathematics, 287
  parent-child, 377
  with rules, 120, 252, 260, 319
  and social development, 338, 339
Gandini, L., 69, 71, 291
Gardening, 365
Gardner, Howard, 85, 104
Garvey, C., 116, 125–126, 133, 388
Gender equity, 190, 199, 204–207
  and math and science, 367
  nonsexist materials, 81, 198, 206,
    278
Geometry, 361
Gesell, Arnold, 42, 43, 44, 85–86, 108
Gesell Institute of Child
    Development, 85
Gesturing, 143
Gestwicki, C., 81, 170, 171, 172, 173,
    177, 178, 185
Getty Center for Education in the
    Arts, 411, 415
Gifted children, 57, 68, 103–106
Ginott, Haim, 18
Ginsburg, H., 372
Glasser, W., 142, 147, 333
Glickman, C., 336
Glowacki, S., 45
Goal-corrected partnership phase, 83
Goals
  and classroom environment, 215

Goals, *continued*
    curriculum, 280–281, 352–355
    of guidance, 137–139
    for school-parent partnership, 164
    of thematic units, 288
Goals 2000: Educate America Act, 164
Goertzel, M., 129, 410
Goertzel, R., 129, 410
Goffin, S., 29
Gordon, Thomas, 145, 147, 154, 155
Gradients of growth, 85–86
Graham, G., 326
Great Depression, 44
Green, E., 392, 394, 396
Greenman, J., 256
Greer, Rosey, 343
Grocery store, pretend, 119
Gross motor skills, 127, 219, 247,
    308–309, 314
Grounds for Play, Inc., 264
Group experience stories, 393
Groups, 63
    guidance of, 156–159
    lesson planning for, 284, 285
    spaces for, 216–217, 232
Growth, physical, 307–308, 324–325
Growth needs, 83, 84
Grunwald, B., 146, 332
Guardian of the gate, teacher as, 132
Guddemi, M., 247, 273
Guidance, 7, 139–140, 259
    for children with special needs,
      159, 189
    defined, 136–137
    discipline strategies, 145–148
    emotional, 137–138, 151–154, 155
    goals of, 137–139
    group, 156–159
    indirect, 140–141
    physical, 142–143
    and relationship building, 141–142
    and routines, 148–151
    of social interactions, 154–156
    verbal strategies, 143–145
Guided discovery, physical education,
    313
Guilt, 89
Guimps, R., 35
Guiros, 426

Hallahan, D., 100, 108
Halliday, M., 403
Hamilton, D., 237, 288, 369, 420, 422
Hand washing, 240
Hardware. *See* Computers
Harms, T., 219

Harris, T., 221
Hartup, W., 331, 335
Harwayne, S., 400
Hatcher, B., 198, 265
Haugland, S., 227, 441, 445, 450
Havriluk, M., 442
Hawley, M. K., 177
Head Start, 15, 16, 47, 171, 184
    and at-risk children, 103
Health, and school environment,
    239–240, 267, 269
Health and Human Services, U.S.
    Department of, 16, 184
Health care, 15, 16, 323
Health education, 322–324
Health impairments, 101
Hearn, K., 325
Heller, R., 432
Hendrick, J., 69, 70, 71, 72, 73, 74, 91
Henniger, M., 129, 175, 176, 196,
    246, 247, 249, 253, 267, 347,
    438, 443
Henri, A., 390
Hernandez, D., 9, 169
Herr, J., 237, 422, 423
Hewes, J., 264, 273
Hicks, J., 237, 288, 369, 420
Hiebert, E., 394
Hierarchy of human needs, 83–84
High school child care programs, 14
High/Scope model, 53, 58–62
    classroom schedule, 62–63
    teacher's role, 63–64
Hildebrand, V., 130, 137, 138, 142, 144,
    148, 155, 159, 160, 189, 281
Hill, D., 204
Hill, F., 59
Hill, Patty Smith, 42, 44
Hill, S., 432, 440
Hirsch, E., 222, 373
Hispanic students and families, 104,
    169, 367
History of early childhood education,
    32–33, 43–48. *See also*
      Theorists of early childhood
    American influences, 40–43
    early European influences, 33–36
    modern European influences, 36–40
Hit the Bull's-Eye, 317
HIV. *See* Human immunodeficiency
    virus
Hodgins, Dan, 92
Hohmann, M., 60, 62, 74
Hokey Pokey, 313
Holidays, 201, 371
Holophrasic speech, 384

Holt-Hale, S., 326
Home, learning at, 174, 376–377,
    401–402. *See also* Families;
      Parent involvement; Parents
Homepage, classroom, 447
Home visits, 177–178
Housekeeping centers, 223, 374
Hughes, F., 124, 205
Hughes, M., 434
Human immunodeficiency virus
    (HIV), 240
Humanistic theory, 83–84
Human needs, hierarchy of, 83–84
Humiliation, 147
Huston, A., 435, 436
Huttenlocher, J., 334
Hygiene, 86, 240, 323–324
Hymes, James, 46
Hypotheses, 365

Identity. *See* Individuality; Self-concept
IEPs. *See* Individualized Education
    Plans
Ignoring
    as discipline strategy, 145, 147
    diversity, 194
"I Know an Old Lady" (song), 425
Ilg, F., 42, 85, 86, 108
I Like . . . (activity), 332
Imagination. *See* Creativity
I Messages, 145–146
Independence, 230, 356, 408
    guidance for, 138–139, 144, 155
Indirect guidance, 140–141
Individual appropriateness, 81
Individual experience stories, 394
Individuality
    and Bank Street model, 65
    in Montessori program, 57
Individualized Education Plans
    (IEPs), 202, 203, 204
Industry, 89
Infant mortality rates, 104
Infants and toddlers, 82–83, 87, 93–95
    books for, 396–397
    classroom environment for,
      227–229, 230, 278
    cognitive development, 90, 93, 94,
      119, 229, 372–373
    and creative arts, 419, 422–423
    language development, 93–94, 95,
      383–384, 386
    playgrounds for, 256, 257
    play of, 93, 95, 119, 121, 256
    programs for, 9, 11–12
    in psychosocial theory, 88–89

Inferiority, 89
Informational books, 397
Inhelder, B., 123
Initiative, 89
Instruments, musical, 426, 427
Integrated curriculum, 14, 284, 286–290
    in Bank Street model, 65–66, 69
    and cognitive development, 372–375
    and diversity education, 196–201
        meaningful experiences, 201–202
Intellectual development. See Cognitive development
Intellectual disabilities, 101
Intellectual performance, overemphasis on, 46–47
Intelligence, multiple, 85, 104
Interactionist approach to language, 383
International Reading Association, 27, 398
Internet, 28, 396, 447, 448, 449
Interpersonal intelligence, 85
Interpersonal relationships, 41, 86, 356. See also Social development
    parent-teacher, 141–142, 172–175
        communication methods, 175–180
    peer interactions, 36, 88, 97, 154–156, 334–336
        in primary school years, 99, 100
    teacher-student, 36, 64, 88, 141–142, 202–203, 333–334
        and punishment, 147
    teacher-teacher, 21, 22, 141–142
Intervention strategies, for socialization process, 334
Intimidation, 147
Intrapersonal intelligence, 85
Iron Mountain Forge, 264
Isenberg, J., 29, 319, 418, 429
Itard, J., 37

Jacobs, P., 128
Jacobson, L., 12
Jalongo, M., 29, 319, 407, 412, 413, 418, 421, 429
Jambor, T., 270, 273, 335, 336
Janitors, teachers as, 19
Jelks, P., 265
Jenkins, Ella, 421
Jobs, presentations about, 183–184, 371
Johnson, 53, 57, 63, 70

Johnson, J., 131
Johnson, Lyndon, 47
Jones, L., 333
Jones, V., 333
Journals, professional, 26, 27
Judgment, suspending, 366
Judy/Instructo, 235
Jumping, 315

Kaagan, S., 415
Kameenui, E., 146
Kamii, Constance, 39, 59, 91, 250, 287, 318, 376
Kaplan Companies, 234, 235
Karnes, M., 260, 262
Kasting, A., 173
Katz, L., 10, 291, 292, 330, 331, 349, 374
Kauffman, J., 100, 108
Kellogg, Rhoda, 412
Kennedy, John F., 47
Key experiences, in High/Scope curriculum, 61
Kicking, 315
Kick the Can, 198
Kindercare, 14
Kindergartens, 12–13, 36, 42, 419. See also Preschoolers
    classroom environment, 229–232
    cognitive materials in, 373–374
    playgrounds, 256, 258–259
Kindness Game, The, 338
King, E., 209
Kirchner, G., 198, 260, 318
Kohlberg, L., 58, 59, 65, 68, 376, 378
Kompan, Inc., 264
Kostelnik, M., 137, 331, 340, 349
Kraus, R., 397
Kreider, H., 170
Kritchevsky, S., 218
Krogh, S., 284, 289, 299
Kuhl, P., 383, 384
Kupetz, B., 392, 394, 396

Laboratory nursery schools, 42, 43–44
Labor Statistics, Bureau of, 45
LAD. See Language acquisition device
Lakeshore Learning Materials, 234, 235
Lally, R., 9
Landau, S., 189
Landscape Structures, Inc., 264
Lane, M., 397
Language
    body, 143, 173, 175
    and classroom environment, 219
    defined, 382–383

and diversity, 201–202, 205
    in High/Scope curriculum, 61
    mathematical, 360
    in sociocultural theory, 38, 87
Language acquisition device (LAD), 383, 385
Language development, 92. See also Literacy
    facilitating, 386–389
    and giftedness, 105
    infants and toddlers, 93–94, 95, 383–384, 386
    linguistic systems, 126, 384–386
    materials, 389–390
    parental role in, 399–401
    and play, 125–127, 388–389
    preschoolers, 95, 96, 97, 384
    in primary school years, 98, 99, 384
    theories of, 38, 87, 383, 385
Language experience approach, 393
Lanham Act, 46
Lapidus, L., 189
Latimer, D. J., 183
Lawler, S. D., 179, 185
Lawrence Productions, Inc., 439
Lawton, M., 434
Learner-centered activities, 40
Learning Company, The, 439
Learning disabilities, 101–102
Learning environment. See Classroom environment
Legislation, 11, 164, 190–191, 442
Leong, D., 295, 299
Lesson planning, 284, 285, 289, 290
Letters, to parents, 176
Levin, D., 346
Lewis, R., 142
Libby, Y., 237, 422, 423
Library, classroom. See Book centers
Liebert, R., 450
Lifelong learning, 355
Lillard, P., 37, 55, 56, 75, 86, 87, 386, 398
Limit setting, 155–156, 259
Linguistic intelligence, 85
Linguistic systems, 126, 384–385
Listening
    active, 143
    to music, 419–420, 421
    and parent-teacher relationships, 173
Literacy, 390–395. See also Language development
    and children's books, 395–397, 398
    and computer software, 445, 446
    defined, 383

Literacy, *continued*
  and giftedness, 105
  parental role in, 399–401
  writing, 397–399, 400, 401–402, 446
    centers for, 226–227, 392
Literature. *See* Books
Little Tikes Company, 264
Locally funded programs, 15–16
Locomotion, basic, 309
Logical consequences, 145, 146
Logical-mathematical intelligence, 85
Logicomathematical relationships,
    59–60
Logo, 362
Lombardi, J., 29
Long-term plans, 281
Looping, 12
Lopez, M., 170
Low birth weight, 104
Low-income children and families,
    15, 16, 47, 165–166, 323. *See
    also* Head Start
  and children-at-risk, 104
  and High/Scope curriculum, 62
  and Montessori program, 55
Ludic sets, 114
Luther, Martin, 33

Machado, J., 395, 400
Macrosystem, 368, 369
Mageau, T., 437
Magical Marching, 316–317
Magnetic boards, 389, 397
Mainstreaming, 190, 202–204
Manipulative areas, playground, 252
Manipulative centers, 220–221, 373
Marching band, 425
Marion, M., 143, 156
Marland, S., 105
Marotz, L., 239, 240, 242, 322, 327
Marston, L., 264, 273
Martin, C., 432
Martinez, M., 395
Maslow, Abraham, 83–84
Mason, B., 114
Matchmaker, teacher as, 132
Materials. *See also* Books; Equipment;
    Toys
  art, 220, 373, 410, 415–416
  in Bank Street model, 68–69
  for block centers, 221–223, 373
  for children with special needs,
    202, 237–238, 441, 442
  community sources of, 182
  computer software, 362, 399, 438,
    439, 443–447

for discovery centers, 225, 374
for dramatic play, 223–224,
    265–266, 343, 374, 390
for emotional development,
    342–343
for housekeeping centers, 223, 374
for infant/toddler classrooms, 227,
    229
for language development,
    389–390
manipulative, 220–221, 373
for mathematics, 357, 358, 445
Montessori, 54, 55–57, 306, 358,
    398
multicultural, 81, 195, 196–198,
    235
music, 224–225, 374, 426
nonsexist, 81, 198, 206, 278
open-ended, 220, 410
playground, 249–250, 263–266
    safety of, 267–268, 269
and play options, 129–130
prepublished, 176
in preschool and kindergarten,
    232, 373–374
rotating, 130, 239
for sand and water play centers,
    226
selecting, 234–237, 263–265
and social development, 337–338
teacher-made, 235–237
and thematic planning, 288
for woodworking centers, 226
writing, 227, 397–399, 446
Math Blaster Plus, 445
Mathematics, 61, 286, 357–362, 367
  activity plan, 283
  and computer software, 445
  and conservation, 90
  and physical development, 306
  and play, 287
Matthews, M., 390
Maturationist theory, 85–86, 383, 385
Mayer, M., 397
Mayer, R., 358
Mayesky, M., 237
McAdoo, L., 74
McAfee, O., 295, 299
McAninch, C., 189
McClellan, D., 330, 331, 349
McClelland, D., 59
McCormick, C., 194, 195
McCracken, J., 346
McMath, J., 278
McMillan, Margaret, 38, 43, 254
McMillan, Rachel, 38, 43

Meal times, 149–150
Measurement, 360–361
Media stress, 344–345
Meetings, parent, 179
Mental/physical unity, in Montessori
    theory, 86, 306
Mental retardation, and Montessori's
    work, 37
Merrill-Palmer Institute, 44
Mesosystem, 368, 369
Messiness, 144
Metacommunications, 126, 388–389
Metallophones, 427
Microsystem, 368, 369
Miller, D., 143, 151, 154, 160
Miller, S., 307, 433
Minnesota Ed. Comp Corp., 439
Mitchell, A., 65, 67, 68, 69, 75, 157,
    242, 287
Mitchell, E., 114
Mitchell, Lucy Sprague, 42, 44
Mobility, family, 169–170
Modeling
  behavior, 333
  computer usage, 449
  language, 386, 387
Models, art, 416–417
Montagu, A., 229
Montessori, Maria, 36–37, 55, 86–87,
    306, 386, 398
Montessori program, 53–58
  materials, 54, 55–57, 306, 358, 398
Moore, K., 284
Moore, S., 335
Moral development, Piaget on, 39
Moran, J., 355
Morphology, 385
Mother Goose, 396
Mothers, working, 166, 167–168
Motivation
  and art, 416
  and Bank Street model, 67
  and children with special needs, 442
Motor characteristics, in
    maturationist theory, 85
Motor skills, 127, 219, 247, 308–312.
    See also Physical development
  importance of, 304–306
  infants and toddlers, 229
  toys and equipment for, 314
Mountain Climbing, 321
Movable playground equipment, 264,
    266–267
Movement. *See also* Active learning;
    Motor skills
  children's inability to control, 92

and group guidance, 158–159
and music, 158, 420
Movies, 128
Mozart, Wolfgang Amadeus, 409, 427
Muk (game), 114
Multiage classrooms, 12, 13–14
Multicultural education. *See also*
Diversity
games, 114, 198, 260, 321
materials, 81, 195, 196–198, 235
music, 201, 418, 421, 426
tourist approach, 194–195
and visual-aesthetic environment,
200–201
Multidisciplinary collaboration, and
special needs, 203–204
Multiple intelligences theory, 85, 104
Multisensory experiences, 123
Munro, J., 29
Murals, 340, 424
Murray, P., 358
Museums, 377
Music, 36, 158, 224–225, 343, 371,
418–422. *See also* Creative arts
activities, 422–423, 425, 427
multicultural, 201, 418, 421, 426
and social development, 338, 340
Musical intelligence, 85
Music centers, 224–225, 374
Mutual support, 172–173
Myhre, S., 223, 224

NAEYC. *See* National Association for
the Education of Young
Children
Nash, A., 189
Nastasi, B., 362, 432, 440, 441
National Academy of Early Childhood
Programs, 45
National Association for Nursery
Education, 42. *See also*
National Association for the
Education of Young Children
National Association for Sport and
Physical Education, 323
National Association for the
Education of Young Children
(NAEYC), 19, 20, 21, 23, 26,
45, 81, 199, 200, 201, 215,
247, 277, 434, 435, 437,
437–438, 447
National Center for Education in
Maternal and Child Health,
327
National Center for Improving
Science, 354

National Center for the Early
Childhood Workforce, 45
National College Athletic Association
(NCAA), 190
National Commission on Children,
165–166
National Council for Teachers of
Mathematics (NCTM), 354,
361
National Council for the Teaching of
Mathematics, 27
National Education Association, 45
National Education Goals Panel, 411
Natural areas, playground, 255
Natural consequences, 145, 146
Naturalism, 35
Naturalistic intelligence, 85
Nature, learning from, 35
NCAA. *See* National College Athletic
Association (NCAA)
NCTM. *See* National Council of
Teachers of Mathematics
Needs, hierarchy of, 83–84
Negative commands, 92, 143
Negative education, 34
Neglect, 345, 346
Neinhaus Montessori USA, 235
Neonatal abstinence syndrome, 103
Networking, for parent involvement,
181
Neuman, S., 397
New, R., 69
Newberger, J., 353
Newbery award, 398
Newcombe, N., 334
Newman, N., 340
News, national, 278
Newsletters, 176
Newspaper, classroom, 394
Nicosia, T., 198, 265
Noise, 144, 215–216
Nonelimination Musical Chairs, 319
Nongraded classrooms. *See* Multiage
classrooms
Nonsexist materials, 81, 198, 206, 278
Nonverbal communication. *See* Body
language
Norms, 81
Notar, E., 346
Notes and notices, to parents, 176
Nourot, P., 124, 125, 132, 133, 334
Novelty, and creativity, 407
Number concepts and facts, 61, 90,
358–359, 445. *See also*
Mathematics
Number Munchers, 445

Nursery schools, laboratory, 42, 43–44
Nutrition, 323, 325, 434

Objectivity, 366
Observation, 35, 106
for assessment, 63, 64, 293–295,
296, 297
and classroom environment, 239
as curriculum tool, 279
and giftedness, 105
and music, 422
of social interactions, 154–155
Ocarinas, 426
Olsen, G., 168, 169, 170, 172, 189
One-year-olds, 94–95. *See also* Infants
and toddlers
On-site day care, 16–17, 46
Open-Air Nursery, 38, 43, 254
"Open education" movement, 70
Open-ended materials, 220, 410
Operation Desert Shield, 372
Opper, S., 372
Optimal arousal, drive for, 118
Orff, Carl, 427
Orff instruments, 427
Organization
and group guidance, 157
in Montessori program, 56
and play, 120
room, 214–219
Originality, and creativity, 408
Orlick, T., 114, 319, 339
Orphanages, 82
Outdoor play. *See also* Playgrounds
and child development, 247,
255–260, 262
importance of, 246–247
organized activities, 318–321
and special needs, 260, 262
types, 251–255
Outdoor prop boxes, 265–266

Paciorek, K., 29
Painting, 424. *See also* Art
Pape, D., 198, 265
Paper, 397–398
Papert, Seymour, 362, 436, 450
Parachute Play, 321
Parallel play, 121
as adult intervention, 131–132
Parent cooperatives, 14–15
Parent involvement, 7–8
Bank Street model, 69
benefits of, 164–165, 170–172
and cognitive development, 367,
371, 375–377

Parent involvement, *continued*
  communication, 69, 106–107,
    173–175, 348
    methods, 175–180
  in developmentally appropriate
    curriculum, 81, 289, 297–298
  in diversity education, 207–208
  Even Start, 15
  factors affecting, 180–181
  Head Start, 16, 171, 184
  and language and literacy
    development, 399–401
  Open-Air Nursery, 38
  and physical development, 324–326
  and playgrounds, 269–271
  Reggio Emilia program, 71, 73
  relationship building, 141–142,
    172–175
  and social and emotional
    development, 347–348
  and technology, 435–436, 437,
    446–447
  types of, 171, 172, 174
Parent meetings, 179
Parents. *See also* Families
  education of, 44, 181, 347–348
  older and younger, 14, 104, 168
  space for, 241
  teachers as substitutes for, 19
  working mothers, 166, 167–168
Parent's Choice Seal of Approval, 421
Parent-teacher conferences, 179–180,
    181
Parker, M., 326
Parten, Mildred, 121
Partnership approach, to parent
    involvement, 181
Pastels, 425
Patterning, 358
Peacemaker, teacher as, 131, 132
Peer interactions, 36, 97, 99, 100,
    334–336. *See also* Social
    development
  guiding, 154–156
  and sociocultural theory, 88
Pelligrini, A., 259, 318, 336, 343
People of Every Stripe, 235
Pepler, D., 123
Pepper, F., 146, 332
Perceptual-motor development, 312,
    314
Perceptual skills, and music, 418
Performances, for parents, 179
Perlmutter, J., 259, 318
Perry Preschool Program, 58, 62
Persian Gulf war, 372

Personal care routines, 219
Personal hygiene, 86, 240, 323–324
Personal spaces, 217
Pestalozzi, Johann, 35–36
Phillips, C., 25
Philosophical outlook, in
    maturationist theory, 86
Phonology, 384–385
Photographs, 370
Physical abuse, 345
Physical areas, playground, 253–254
Physical attractiveness, 308, 309
Physical development, 127, 280,
    313–314, 418
  children with special needs, 322
  and classroom environment, 219,
    229
  components of, 307–312
  and health education, 322–324
  importance of, 304–306
  infants and toddlers, 93, 94, 95, 256
  organized activities, 314–316
    indoor, 316–318
    outdoor, 318–321
  and parents and families, 324–326
  and playgrounds, 247, 252,
    253–254, 256, 259
  preschoolers, 95, 96, 97, 256, 259
  in primary school years, 98–99, 100
Physical fitness, 306–307, 316, 323
Physical growth, 307–308, 324–325
Physical guidance, 142–143
Physical knowledge, 356
Physical/mental unity, in Montessori
    theory, 86, 306
Physical-motor disabilities, 101
Physical/motor play, outdoor, 247,
    248–249, 251, 253–254
Physical sciences, 363
Physical setting. *See* Classroom
    environment; Playgrounds
Physics, 364
Physiological needs, 84
Piaget, Jean, 13, 38–40, 53, 59, 65,
    89–91, 114, 118, 119, 120, 123,
    124, 187, 229, 260, 304, 319,
    334, 354, 356, 358, 360, 372,
    383, 440
Pica, R., 313, 316, 322, 327
Picture books, 397
Pictures, 200, 337, 339
Pin (game), 114
Piñata, La, 321
Pink Tower, 306
P.L. 94–142. *See* Public Law 94–142
P.L. 99–457. *See* Public Law 99–457

P.L. 100–407. *See* Public Law 100–407
P.L. 101–336. *See* Public Law 101–336
Plan-do-review sequence, 60
Planning
  activities and lessons, 281–284,
    285, 289, 290
  classroom environment, 214–219
  and group guidance, 157
  integrated curriculum, 286–290
  parent involvement in, 297–298
  and project approach, 292
Planning time, in High/Scope
    curriculum, 60, 62
Play, 5–7, 13, 36, 39, 325. *See also*
    Dramatic play; Outdoor play;
    Playgrounds
  characteristics of, 113–114,
    438–439
  and cognitive development,
    118–120, 123–124
  and creativity, 115, 129, 410–411,
    438
  defining, 113–116
  deprivation of, 128
  and diversity, 189, 205
  and emotional development,
    127–128
  facilitating, 129–132
  of infants and toddlers, 93, 95,
    119, 121, 256
  and language development,
    125–127, 388–389
  and literacy, 394
  and mathematics, 287
  misperceptions about, 112
  in Montessori program, 55
  and physical development, 127, 247,
    252, 253–254, 256, 313–314
  of preschoolers, 95–96, 97, 98,
    120, 121, 124
  and playgrounds, 256, 259
  in primary school years, 99, 120,
    121–122, 259–260
  resources on, 125
  rough-and-tumble, 318
  and social development, 121–122,
    124–125, 256, 334–336
  and stress, 115, 117–118, 347
  theories, 38, 39, 116–118
  toy selection criteria, 234
Play and pastimes, in maturationist
    theory, 86
Play Designs, 264
Playgrounds, 22, 247–252, 271–272,
    336
  changing, 265–267

and children with special needs, 260, 262
designs, 257, 258, 261
and developmental stages, 255–260
equipment selection, 263–265
health and safety, 267–269, 270
importance of, 246–247
parent and community involvement, 269–271
play areas in, 252–255
Playhouses, 249, 253
Play therapy, 117–118
Playtime Props, 235
Play tutoring, 132
Play units, complexity of, 218
Pleasure principle, 117
Plutchik, R., 340
Poest, C., 306, 309, 323
Point-and-say books, 396
Polaroid photographs, 370
Policies, parent involvement, 180–181
Portfolios, 295–297, 298
Positive directions, 92, 143
Positive reinforcement, 145, 146
Post office, field trips to, 390
Poverty. See Low-income children and families
Pragmatics, 386
Preattachment phase, 83
Predictable books, 397
Preexercise theory of play, 116–117
Preoperational stage, 90–91, 120, 124
Prepublished materials, 176
Preschool, 10–11, 44
    classroom environment, 229–232
    curriculum development in, 278
    and home visits, 177–178
    playgrounds, 256, 258–259
Preschoolers, 87, 95–98, 121, 124
    books for, 278, 397
    cognitive development, 90–91, 95–97, 98, 120, 373–374
    and creative arts, 419, 424–425
    giftedness in, 105
    language development, 95, 96, 97, 384
    and playgrounds, 256, 259
Prescott, E., 218
Pretend communication statements, 126
Primary school years, 13–14, 15, 87, 98–100, 397
    classroom environment, 232, 233

cognitive development in, 91, 98, 99, 100, 120, 260
    and project approach, 374–375
creative arts in, 419, 425–427
curriculum development in, 278–279
language development, 98, 99, 384
playground design, 261
play in, 99, 120, 121–122, 259–260
in psychosocial theory, 89
Print-rich environments, 391–393
Problem solving, 354–355. See also Decision making
    and discipline, 145, 147–148
    divergent, 313
    mathematical, 361–362
    and play, 120, 123–124
    and social interactions, 155, 336
Process
    creative, 408–410, 417
    and play, 113–114, 115, 438
    scientific, 365–366
Professional development, 20, 26–28
Professional preparation, 23–26
Professionals, collaboration among, 203–204
Progressive movement, 40, 65, 66
Project approach, 69, 70, 374–375. See also Reggio Emilia program
Project Follow Through, 47
Prompts, 203
Props, dramatic play, 265–266, 343, 390
Proximal development, zone of, 38, 39, 87–88
Proximodistal development, 308
Psychoanalytic theory of play, 117–118
Psychological development. See Emotional development
Psychomotor skills, and music, 418
Psychosocial theory, 88–89
Public Law 94–142 (Education for All Handicapped Children Act), 11, 190
Public Law 99–457, 11, 190
Public Law 100–407 (Technology-Related Assistance for Individuals with Disabilities Act), 442
Public Law 101–336 (Americans with Disabilities Act), 190
Publishing. See Writing
Punishment, 145, 146–147
Puppets, 389

Quality, 10
Questions, 387
Quick, Freeze!, 317
Quiet centers, 215–216, 221
Quiet times, guidance for, 158

Racial diversity, 168–169, 189–190, 193. See also Diversity
    and math and science, 367
Raffi, 421
Raikes, H., 9, 82
Rain gutters, 250
Rain sticks, 426
Raised gardens, 365
Ramsey, M., 419
Readdick, C., 217
Reading. See also Literacy
    to children, 392, 394–395, 401, 446
    and computers, 445, 446
Realism stage of art development, 414
Reality
    vs. fantasy, 92
    suspension of, 114
Real-world experiences. See Experiences
Recall time, in High/Scope program, 63
Recess, 336
Redefinition, and creativity, 408
Redirection, 143
reflection, 356
Reflexive movement phase, 311
Reggio Emilia program, 53, 69–73, 290, 416
Reinforcement, 145, 146
Remo, Inc., 235
Repetition compulsion, 118
Representation, in High/Scope curriculum, 61
Resources, and classroom organization, 215
Respect, 346, 356
    for the environment, 366
Rest times, 151
Retention, 11
Review time, in High/Scope curriculum, 61
Reynolds, E., 137, 143
Rhyming, 126
Rhythmical language books, 396
Richarz, S., 325
Riley, Richard, 411
Risk, children at, 103, 104
Risk taking, 247, 253, 254, 409, 439

Ritalin, 102, 103
Rivkin, M., 247, 251, 255, 273
Road Runner, 320
Roberts, J., 189
Roblyer, M., 442
Rockwell, R. E., 177, 182, 184
Rogers, Fred, 340
Rogers, L., 59
Roopnarine, J., 53, 57, 63, 70
Rosenblatt, L., 170
Roskos, K., 397
Ross, H., 123
Rote learning, 353–354, 376, 445
Rothenberg, D., 13
Rough-and-tumble play, 318
Rounds, 427
Rousseau, Jean Jacques, 34–35
Routines, 148–151, 219, 227, 229. See
    also Schedules
    and creative arts activities,
        422–423
    and language learning, 386
    and literacy, 393
Rudimentary movement phase, 311
Ruggles Street Nursery, 43
Rules, 39, 335
    classroom, 139, 155–156
    games with, 120, 252, 260, 319
Rush, J., 239, 240, 242, 322, 327
Rybcynski, M., 394

Safety, 227, 234, 239, 240–241, 324
    as human need, 84
    playground, 267–269, 270
Salaries, 44–45
Sandboxes, 249, 254–255, 270
Sand play, therapeutic value of, 343
Sand/water play centers, 226
Sanitation, 240
Saracho, O., 11, 23, 204
Sawyers, J., 355
Scales, B., 132, 133, 334
Scarves, 425
Schedules, 62–63, 292–293, 338. See
    also Routines
Schemas, 89, 118
Schenk, S., 345
Schickedanz, D., 188
Schickedanz, J., 188
Schirrmacher, R., 373, 412, 414, 425,
    429
School-based day care, 11
School life, in maturationist theory, 86
Schweinhart, L., 62, 63, 64, 74
Science, 362–367, 377
Science centers, 225, 374

Scott, J., 394
Scribbling stage, 412
Seagoe, M., 121–122
Seefeldt, C., 17, 416
Seguin, E., 37
Seidel, J., 240
Self, understanding, 368–371
Self-actualization, 84
Self-analysis, of prejudices, 192–193,
    196, 206–207
Self and sex, in maturationist theory,
    86
Self-concept, 67, 128, 172, 305, 344
    of children with special needs,
        322, 442
    dimensions of, 137, 331
    and social development, 331–332
Self-control, guidance for, 138–139
Self-correcting materials, 55, 220
Self-esteem. See Self-concept
Self-regulation, 356
Self-respect, 84
Semantics, 385
Sensitive periods, 86, 386
Sensitivity, and creativity, 408
Sensorimotor stage, 90, 229, 372
Sensory learning, 35, 36, 61
    and art, 414
    materials, 55, 57, 229
    and outdoor play, 247
Separate education, for gifted and
    talented children, 68
Separation anxiety, 82, 83
Seriation, 61, 357–358
Seven-year-olds, 99–100. See also
    Primary school years
Sex
    and self, 86
    and technology, 433–434
Sexism. See Gender equity
Sexual abuse, 345
Shade, D., 227, 432, 445, 448
Shakerees, 426
Shame, 89
Sharing, 92, 97, 338
Shartrand, A., 170
Shaw, J., 367, 378
Shefatya, L., 124, 259
Shellenbarger, S., 16
Shepherd, T. R., 182
Shepherd, W. L., 182
Short-term plans, 281
Silence (game), 114
Silva, D., 434
Silvern, S., 113, 205
Singer, D., 223

Singer, J., 223
Single-parent families, 165–166
Situational variables, and parent-
    teacher relationships, 173
Six-year-olds, 98–99. See also Primary
    school years
Skeels, H., 84
Skepticism, 366
Sketching, 427
Skills, teachers', 21–22
Skinner, B. F., 66, 146, 383
Skurzynski, G., 390
Sleeping Grump (game), 338
Slides, 248–249
Small groups, 156–157
    in High/Scope program, 63
    space for, 216–217, 232
Smilansky, Sara, 118, 119, 120, 124,
    132, 259
Smith, S., 247, 253
Snack times, 149–150
Snider, S., 441
Snowflakes, 427
Sobel, J., 339
Social development, 7, 65, 137,
    280–281, 330–333
    activities, 338–340
    classroom environment and
        materials, 219, 337–338
    and computers, 437, 439–440
    infants and toddlers, 82–83, 88–89,
        93, 95, 121
    and music, 418
    and parents and families,
        347–348
    and peer interactions, 88, 97, 99,
        100, 154–156, 334–336
    and physical development, 305
    and play, 121–122, 124–125, 256,
        334–336
    portfolios, 298
    preschoolers, 89, 96, 97, 98, 121
    in primary school years, 89, 98, 99,
        100
    and stress, 344–347
    and teacher-student relationships,
        88, 333–334
Social-emotional disabilities, 101
Social interactions, learning from, 41,
    91, 356. See also Interpersonal
    relationships; Social
    development
Socialization. See Social development
Social services, and Head Start, 16
Social skills, checklist of, 331. See also
    Social development.

Social studies, 367–368
  understanding others, 371–372
  understanding self, 368–371
Social times, for parents, 179
Social values, teaching of, 41
Sociocultural theory, 87–88
Soderman, A., 137, 331, 349
Software. *See* Computer software
Solitary activities, 121, 217, 251
Songs, 158, 371, 420, 423, 427. *See also* Music
  Froebel on, 36
  and social development, 338
Spanking, 147
Spatial awareness, 312, 315
Spatial intelligence, 85
Spatial relationships, in High/Scope curriculum, 61
Specialized movement phase, 311
Special needs. *See* Children with special needs
Speech and language disabilities, 101
Spelling, 445
Spodek, B., 11, 23, 204
Sports
  competitive, 325–326
  gender equity in, 190
Sprafkin, J., 450
Springate, K., 291
Sprung, B., 364
Sputnik, 46–47
Standing, 55
Starko, A., 407
Stars, 427
State and locally funded programs, 15–16
States, ranked, 167
Stein, L., 137, 331, 349
Steiner, G., 44
Stephens, K., 173
Stipek, D., 170
Stone, Sandra, 6, 125
Storage sheds, 249, 252, 253
Storyboard software, 445
Story books, 397
Stranger anxiety, 82, 83, 93
Straw painting, 424
Stress, 167, 325, 344–347, 353
  and play, 115, 117–118, 347
Striking, 315
Student-teacher relationships. *See* Teacher-student relationships
Sublimation, 305
Substitute output devices, 442
Sulzby, E., 391, 403
Sunburst Communications, 439

Support, mutual, 172–173
Surplus energy theory of play, 116
Suskind, D., 372
Suspending judgment, 366
Sutton-Smith, B., 189
Swaminathan, S., 362, 440
Swick, K., 207
Swings, 248, 264
Swiniarski, L., 197
Symbolism, 91, 94, 124, 440–441
Syntax, 386

Table toys. *See* Manipulative centers
Teacher-made equipment, 235–237, 263–265
Teacher-movable playground equipment, 264, 266–267
Teachers
  and benefits of parent involvement, 170
  and computers, 448–449
  as creative arts facilitators, 413, 415–418
  in High/Scope program, 63–64
  male, 204
  Montessori, 57
  and other professionals, 203–204
  as participants in movement activities, 316
  personal spaces for, 217
  and playground safety, 269
  play interventions by, 131–132
  power of, 18
  in Reggio Emilia program, 71–72
  as resource, 348
  responsibilities of, 19–21
  roles of, 19
  salaries of, 45
  self-analysis by, 192–193, 196, 206–207
  skills of, 21–22
  training of, 23–26
Teacher-student relationships, 36, 64, 88, 141–142
  and children with special needs, 202–203
  and punishment, 147
  and social development, 88, 333–334
Teacher-teacher relationships, 21, 22, 141–142
Teaching, as career choice, 22–23
Teale, W., 391, 395, 403
Technology, 432–433. *See also* Computers; Computer software

  and children with special needs, 441, 442
  television, 92, 128, 344, 346, 433–436
  video games, 128, 436–437
Technology-Related Assistance for Individuals with Disabilities Act (P.L. 100–407), 442
Teen parents, 14, 104, 168
Tegano, D., 355
Telegraphic speech, 384
Telephone calls, parent-teacher, 175
Television, 92, 128, 344, 346, 433–436
Testing solutions, 366
Thematic units
  on cooperation, 339–340
  and multiple intelligences, 85
  planning, 284, 286–290
Theorists of early childhood, 32–36, 42–43, 44, 81–85. *See also* Piaget, Jean
  Dewey, 40–42, 53, 65, 66, 70, 115
  Erikson, 53, 65, 88–89, 115
  Gesell, 42, 43, 44, 85–86, 108
  on language development, 38, 87, 383, 385
  McMillan sisters, 38, 43, 254
  Montessori, 36–37, 55, 86–87, 306, 386, 398
  Vygotsky, 38, 39, 87–88, 383
Theory building, 356
Thomas, Marlo, 340, 343
Thomas, R., 83, 87, 88, 305
Three-way conferences, 180
Three-year-olds, 95–96. *See also* Preschoolers
Throwing, 314
Time
  awareness of, 312
  in High/Scope curriculum, 61
  for play, 128, 130
Time-out, 146–147
Tittnich, E., 118
Toileting, 150
Topic selection, in project approach, 70
Torrance, E. Paul, 407, 408
Touch, 142–143
Touch-and-smell books, 396
Tourist approach, to diversity, 194–195
Toys. *See also* Materials
  advertising for, 434
  for children with special needs, 202
  for diversity education, 196–198, 199

Toys, *continued*
  infant/toddler, 227, 230
  in manipulative centers, 220–221, 373
  for motor development, 314
  preschool and kindergarten, 232
  selection criteria, 234
Tracing materials, 398
Tracy, D., 360
Traffic Jam, 321
Training
  for parents, 44, 181, 347–348
  teacher, 23–26
Transition areas, playground, 252
Transitions, 149, 292
Trawick-Smith, J., 127, 137, 138
Trostle, S., 237
Troy, A., 394
Trust, 88
Tucker, D., 190
Tug of Peace, 319
Turn taking, 97, 124, 335
Two-career families, 167–168, 344
Two-year degree programs, 25
Two-year-olds, 95. *See also* Infants and toddlers
Tying frames, 54
Typewriters, 398–399

Understanding and application, 40
Underwood, J., 325
Ungraded classrooms. *See* Multiage classrooms
Unifix cubes, 358
Unions, 45
Unit blocks, 222, 373

Vandenberg, B., 123
Van Hoorn, J., 124, 125, 132, 133, 334
Van Scoy, I., 207
Vebal thought, in sociocultural theory, 87
Verbal guidance strategies, 143–145
Very Important Person (V.I.P.) of the Week, 332
Very personal symbol and design stage, 412–413
Viadero, D., 11, 418
Video games, 128, 436–437
Videotapes, 177

Violence
  and play, 128
  and technology, 92, 433–434, 437, 438
V.I.P (Very Important Person) of the Week, 332
Visual awareness, 312
Visual communication tools, for parent-teacher communication, 177
Vocabulary, 94, 96, 105, 387, 400
  mathematical, 360
  musical, 421
Voice, and parent-teacher relationships, 173
Volume, conservation of, 90
Voting, 287
Vukelich, C., 127, 227, 391, 403
Vygotsky, Lev, 38, 39, 87–88, 383

Waelder, R., 118
Waiting, 92
Wallis, C., 102
Wanamaker, N., 325
Ward, C., 130
War on Poverty, 47–48
Warren, J., 338
Wash, D., 14
Wasserman, S., 6, 125, 129, 133, 232, 242, 409, 411
Water play, and emotional development, 343
Water play areas, playground, 254–255
Water play centers, 226
Watson, J., 66
Waxman, S., 206
Webbing, 289, 290
Weber, E., 43, 48, 65
Weikart, David, 58, 59, 60, 61, 62, 74
Weiss, H., 170
Wells, H., 332, 349
Wet centers, 226. *See also* Art centers
Whalen, S., 339
Whiren, A., 137, 331, 349
White, Edna Noble, 44
Wilbers, J., 190, 192, 202, 203, 209
Wilkinson, I., 394
William K. Bradford Publishers, 439
Williams, D. L., 180
Williams, J., 306

Winter, S., 237, 256
Wish fulfillment, 117
Witt, D., 306
Wolery, M., 190, 192, 202, 203, 209
Wolfinger, D., 358, 363, 366, 378
Woodruff, M., 395
Woodworking centers, 226
Word choice, and parent-teacher relationships, 173
Wordless books, 397
Word play, 126
Word processing, 399
Work
  in High/Scope program, 61, 63
  individual space for, 56
  in Montessori program, 53–54
  and play contrasted, 115
Working mothers, 166, 167–168
Workplace, friendly, 333
Works Progress Administration (WPA), 44
World Organization for Early Education, 27
World War II, 46
World Wide Web. *See* Internet
Worth, 137, 331
Wortham, S., 48, 248, 251, 295, 298, 299
Worthy Wage Campaign, 45
WPA. *See* Works Progress Administration
Wright, Frank Lloyd, 129, 410
Wright, J., 435, 436, 441, 450
Wright brothers, 410
Writing, 397–399, 400, 401–402, 446. *See also* Literacy centers, 226–227, 392
Written communications, to parents, 176
Written policies, parent involvement, 180–181

Yale Clinic of Child Development, 42
Yale Guidance Nursery, 44
Yawkey, T., 131, 237, 343
Yokota, J., 200
Yongue, B., 309, 314

Zan, B., 356
Zolotow, C., 278
Zone of proximal development, 38, 39, 87–88
Zoology, 364